*Praise for*

# Bowie's Piano M....

'The must-have book in this field.' —Ricky Gervais

'Riveting. Fine prose. What a change from the usual pop/rock/celebrity biographies of modern times.' —Steve Harley (Cockney Rebel)

'Wonderful addition to the Bowie bibliography. A class book for a class act.'
—*Classic Pop*, awards issue 2015 ('Best Book')

'A welcome tribute to a great musician . . . Slapper gives us musical insights.'
—*MOJO*

'Really great and fascinating! A fabulous book.'
—David Bowie guitarist Gerry Leonard

'Quite simply it's a great book: engaging, inspiring, and entertaining; written extremely well and sympathetically about one of the greatest pianists of our times.' —*Blues and Soul*

'A rich, never-before-told account of one of music's oft-unheralded players.'
—*Hot Press*, Ireland's top music magazine ('Best Music Book')

'Clifford Slapper—whose own claim to Bowie fame involves being the piano-playing hand double for Dave's appearance on *Extras*—does an admirable job of picking apart Garson's life and career. Bowie loyalists—and fellow piano men—will lap up Garson's insider insights, as well as keen observations from the likes of Tony Visconti and Trent Reznor.' —*Record Collector*

'It helps that it was written by another amazing piano player, Clifford Slapper. I think it brings a unique angle to the book. Loved it to death. It's fantastic.'
—Glenn Gregory (Heaven 17)

'This is wonderful, Cliff. Thank you for your continued dedication to telling this story in a very honest way.'                                      —Mike Garson

'Bowie fans will obviously adore this thorough and well-researched biography. The fact that Slapper is also a pianist really helps convey the story.'
—*CELLOPHANELAND*, arts review site

'Readable, rigorous, revealing, *Bowie's Piano Man* is musicology of the highest order. It is almost a history of the piano in popular music, such is the range of influences—from avant-garde jazz to Stravinsky and Rachmaninov—that comes within the author's purview. Slapper's insights into the nature of performance itself would make an equally enthralling book. His forensic analysis of the corrosively addictive nature of fame is among the most convincing I've ever read. Brilliant!'                                      —*Tribune*

'A great book and a really interesting read. A must for any music fan.'
—Michael Spencer Jones, photographer for Oasis

'The book is superb—essential reading for Bowie fans, and indeed anyone who loves music. It's a truly fascinating journey.' —Mark Shaw (Then Jerico)

Bowie's Piano Man

# BOWIE'S PIANO MAN

## The Life of **MIKE GARSON**

REVISED AND UPDATED EDITION

Clifford Slapper

Backbeat
Books

An Imprint of Hal Leonard LLC

Backbeat Books
An Imprint of Hal Leonard LLC
7777 West Bluemound Road
Milwaukee, WI 53213

Trade Book Division Editorial Offices
33 Plymouth St., Montclair, NJ 07042

Paperback edition published by Backbeat Books in 2018.

Originally published in hardcover by Fantom Publishing in 2014.

The excerpts from David Bowie's liner notes to the albums *The Buddha of Suburbia* (1993) and *iSelect* (2008) that appear on pages 101, 106, 242, and 269 are reprinted by kind permission of Jones/Tintoretto Entertainment Company, LLC.

Printed in the United States of America

Book design by M Kellner

ISBN 978-1-61713-693-1

Library of Congress Cataloging-in-Publication Data is available upon request.

www.backbeatbooks.com

This book is dedicated to the memory of
David Robert Jones 1947–2016
and
Gary Jay Slapper 1958–2016

# Contents

# Contents

# Preface

THIS BOOK is the first-ever biography of pianist Mike Garson, who was David Bowie's most frequent musician, live and in the studio, from the days of Ziggy Stardust to Bowie's very last shows. It tells the remarkable story of how a young New York jazz pianist had his life transformed overnight by one phone call, in 1972, from Bowie's manager. Garson in turn would have an effect on Bowie's music, too, over the years, and played with him at both his first and last performances in the United States. The pages that follow show how Bowie trusted Garson, and how they developed a special artistic and creative bond.

In addition, the book fully documents Mike Garson's life story and probes the very wide range of other work he has done, spanning classical, jazz, fusion, and experimental genres, composing thousands of pieces himself, and earning a global reputation for his pedagogy, his mentoring, and his mastering of playing (and living) spontaneously, 'in the moment.'

The way this book came about was itself an example of the widespread transformative power Garson has had, inspiring and influencing others. He has helped to shape my own life—twice over. At the age of eleven, I bought my first album, *Aladdin Sane* by David Bowie. From that moment, I was hooked: Bowie would be a towering, enduring influence in my life. However, it was Garson's remarkable piano work on that album that made me determined to become a pianist myself.

I went on to play with many great artists, and in 2006 I worked with David Bowie, playing for his last-ever television appearance in the world. That was a dream job for me, having grown up with his music. A few years later, Mike Garson inspired my path once again, by asking me to write this biography of him, saying that he trusted me, as a fellow pianist who understood him, to do so with integrity and honesty. It has been a labor of love, and has shown me that I want to write. I am currently working on my next book, grateful that the man who inspired me to become a pianist has now also motivated me to become an author.

In January 2016, when Mike Garson heard that David Bowie had died, his profound shock threw him into a long mental process of free-falling, vivid recollection, from which he emerged with a series of deep insights. All of this is contained within this new and expanded edition, which reveals how the loss of his lifelong friend and musical collaborator across a period spanning forty-four years has had a devastating and profound effect on Garson. His memories of his times with David Bowie have been stimulated and made all the more vivid by this loss, and this allowed me to prompt his detailed recollections about all the work he did with Bowie.

I have remained in close contact with Mike Garson, through lengthy and far-reaching conversations every week throughout the year, and continue to be inspired by him. Continuing the theme of Bowie and piano, I have produced the first in a series of albums exploring and celebrating the songs of David Bowie arranged for piano and voice only, on which I play with a range of singers (*Bowie Songs One* by Clifford Slapper & Friends, which was released in 2017). The songs are stripped down to reveal their powerful emotional core. I would love David Bowie to have heard this work, which we started in 2014. He died halfway through the recording sessions. I played the album to his lifelong best friend, the artist George Underwood, whose first words were 'David would have loved this,' which means a great deal to me.

The earlier UK version of *Bowie's Piano Man* was completed in November 2014, consisting of the first fifteen chapters of this volume. This book is based on that, but has six completely new additional chapters, including Mike Garson's personal recollections of 'life on the road with David Bowie' across the nine world tours on which they played together. These new chapters also contain several more interviews that did not appear in the original edition, with friends and collaborators such as Billy Corgan of the Smashing Pumpkins; producer Ken Scott, who worked on six Bowie albums; and saxophonist Donny McCaslin, who led the *Blackstar* band.

There are also numerous revisions, improvements, and additions to the earlier version, including, for example, more detail in the introduction regarding the filming of *Extras*; more detail regarding the New York after-show party incident in chapter 1; and various additional sections in chapter 12 about Garson's work with Billy Corgan.

*Bowie's Piano Man* is not intended to be a conventional biography. It does follow a roughly chronological framework, but is also thematic in structure. My primary aim was to reveal Garson's working methods as a musician, and to show how these relate to his life experiences. It would have been possible to insert some of the additional sections, such as the interviews with Billy Corgan and Ken Scott, at various points in the original text, but I felt that their inclusion in separate new chapters is more in keeping with the thematic approach of the book, as they each reveal further diverse aspects of Garson's life and work. This will also allow those who enjoyed the first edition to locate more easily where most of the new material can be found.

There are numerous biographies of David Bowie available, and this current volume is careful not to repeat the details of his life that can be found elsewhere.

Studying Mike Garson and his work for some years in researching this biography has been an educational, uplifting, and life-affirming experience that has changed my life and that I will never forget. It has also, at times, been extremely entertaining, as Mike's sense of humor is as finely tuned as his sense of rhythm. I feel grateful to have had this opportunity to explore the life and work of such an extraordinarily creative and distinctive individual. The journey has been all the more enriching for his enthusiastic participation in this process, and I am deeply indebted to Mike Garson for the almost unlimited helpful input he has made available to me throughout my work on this book.

Our shared hope is that people might be inspired by the story told in these pages to overcome any obstacles in their quest for authentic expression and creativity, and also that this opens up a wider exploration of how music is created and what it can do.

At one point in what follows, the stylist for the Spiders from Mars, Suzi Ronson, tells me how she had the challenge of getting Mike to glam up with the rest of the boys. There is, however, something very special about Mike Garson, which working on this book has confirmed repeatedly: he has his own internal glitter. He continues to live and create in the moment. When I wished him a happy seventy-first birthday on July 29, 2016, Mike replied, characteristically, 'Thank you, Cliff. It feels like any other day, as every moment is a rebirth.'

Clifford Slapper
November 2017

# Foreword by Mike Garson

I FEEL VERY BLESSED to have been asked by the author to write a foreword to this book. As you may know, many artists are dead by the time their biographies are written. I am fortunate to still be alive and kicking, composing, performing, and enjoying my beautiful family, so I take this as an act of grace.

Clifford Slapper has done extensive research on my musical career and related issues, and has truly been working on this for several years. In addition, he spent countless hours interviewing me, as well as so many other artists with whom I have worked. This book could easily have run to a thousand pages, but he has been excellent at editing the material and sharing the choice words that he felt would make for a good biography.

I am flattered to have this book written, but in certain ways I did not want it released for another ten years, because my career is still developing and building. Nevertheless, there is always the possibility of a second or third volume. From my viewpoint, the main goal for this book should be to inspire future generations of artists.

Certainly, everyone could get something out of this book, but my real hope is for all the new artists coming up to be able to see how I went through my life as a pianist, musician, composer, and performer. The essence of this is that I have led a very clean life, by the grace of God and by my own sense of morals, ethics, and integrity. The bottom line, without meaning to be arrogant, is that I have never used any drugs, I've never been drunk, I've been married forty-eight years, I've been a faithful husband, I have seven beautiful grandkids, I have two beautiful daughters, and I find that I can still do the music and perform.

There seem to be doubts in the world regarding that possibility, so I want to make it known to anyone who reads this book, whatever field they work in, that you can be balanced, you don't have to mess yourself up, you don't have to shorten your life with drugs, you don't have to be crazy to be a great artist. You can be creative, you can be balanced, you can still handle your own business and family affairs. So, that's the main objective from my end.

Obviously, Cliff as a biographer wanted to have the specifics regarding all my years with David Bowie and all of the other artists I've played with, as well as my own music, and of course that's valuable, but that's not where my joy will come from. My joy will come from every letter or email that I get from anyone who says that this book has inspired them to do their thing better, whether it's a new artist coming up or anyone else who this sparks something in.

So I do hope people enjoy it. I feel the book is very well written by Cliff. It is not linear; it moves around, and I like that about it, because it's not just a boring set of facts stating this is where I was born and this is where I played, so it has a lot of joy that way. Let me know what you think.

Mike Garson
November 2017

# Acknowledgments

First and foremost, I want to thank my parents, Doreen and Ivor Slapper, who brought me up with a love of good music. As a young child, our home was filled with the sounds of Harry Nilsson, the Beatles, Georgie Fame, José Feliciano, Stevie Wonder, Dusty Springfield, and Tom Jones, to name but a few—to which they would both sing along energetically, tunefully, and rhythmically. This is what it is all about.

During my work on this new edition, we were hit by the sudden and unexpected death in December 2016 of my brother, Gary. In our shared childhood and adolescence, with my sister Maxine, we developed together a love of modern music, and of David Bowie in particular. The shock of losing him has been immeasurable, and I dedicate this book to his memory, together with that of David Bowie, who also died in 2016.

As a biographer, I could not have wished for a more helpful subject than Michael Garson, who has answered a veritable tide of inquiries promptly and in good humor, night and day, over a period of years. At a certain stage, the eight-hour time difference between London and Los Angeles appeared to lose significance: when you are working, or available, around the clock, it does not matter which clock it is.

A large number of people have been kind enough to help in all sorts of different ways. You will each know what you did, and I wish to thank you all for helping me to steer this project from its origins in the passions of my youth into what I hope is now a useful vehicle through which those enthusiasms can be shared.

For their great encouragement during the research and writing of this book, I would like especially to thank: Funmi Abiola, Adam Buick, Martin Godleman, Laura Mohapi, Nicholas Pegg, and Francesca Spiegel.

Several people kindly read the text at various stages and made imaginative and intelligent suggestions that have improved it: Mark Adams, Adam Buick, Stephen Coleman, Nicholas Pegg, David Perrin, Charles Shaar Murray, Jérôme Soligny, Francesca Spiegel, Paul Trynka, and Louis Vause.

Many thanks to all of the interviewees, who were very generous with their time, recollections, and insights. The great majority of these were interviewed in person, a few via written correspondence: Eric Agnew and SPFC, Zachary Alford, Gail Ann Dorsey, Gary Ansdell, Brooks Arthur, Mark Bakalor, Becker KB, Laura Bedford, Samuel Ben-Horin, Barry Bittman, Barbara Breitbart, Karen Breitbart, Harry Bromley-Davenport, Sterling Campbell, Neil Conti, Billy Corgan, Bruce Donnelly, Christopher Duma, Suzi Fussey Ronson, Reeves Gabrels, Heather Garson Gilbert, Michael Garson, Susan Garson, Gerard Gibbons, Danny Holt, Emilio Kauderer, Oliver Kersbergen, Larry Koonse, Joe LaBarbera, Gerry Leonard, David Liebman, Robin Mayhew, Donny McCaslin, Jim Merod, Hans Morgenstern, Chris O'Leary, Jilann O'Neill, Jussi K. Niemelä, Holly Palmer, Annette Peacock, Mark Plati, Kris Pooley, Trent Reznor, Maggi Ronson, Theo Ryan, Tim Ryan, Ken Scott, Charles Shaar Murray, Jeremy Shapiro, Jennifer Shuper, Peter Shuper, Earl Slick, Jérôme Soligny, Willem Tanke, George Underwood, Brad Vinikow, René van Commenée, Tony Visconti, James Walker, and Tony Zanetta.

I remain permanently grateful to David Bowie, whose genius still burns bright and who was always my distant mentor. Very special thanks also to: Mark Adams, Peter Beren, Mark Bramley, Kevin Cann, Gary Duckworth, Ricky Gervais, Charlie Hanson, Steve Harley, Carrie Kania, Paul Kinder, Simon Napier-Bell, Nicholas Pegg, Tristram Penna, Jérôme Soligny, Francesca Spiegel, George Underwood, Julian Vein, Tony Visconti, Tom Wilcox, and Bill Zysblat, all of whom have helped in such diverse yet vital ways, and shown great generosity of spirit.

I also want especially to thank John Cerullo of Hal Leonard and Bernadette Malavarca at Backbeat Books for bringing *Bowie's Piano Man* to a new, American readership. I am truly grateful for the sensitive, intelligent way in which Backbeat has handled the work throughout its re-creation for this expanded new edition. It could hardly be a more appropriate home for my book, as I well recall seeing the name "Hal Leonard" printed on most of the classical music pieces I learned as a child.

All of the members of the Garson family have been unstinting in their desire to help at every turn, and I hope that in return I have begun to do justice to the compassion, hard work, creativity, and generosity of spirit of the man at their heart.

Finally, I want to thank Mike Garson himself. He embarked on a long and thorough exploration with me of a vast accumulation of work and experiences. As that journey unfolded, thanks to him, I found myself learning vastly more than I had bargained for, about life as well as about his life.

Clifford Slapper
November 2017

# From Wembley to Bell Canyon, the Long Way
## How This Book Came to Be Written

Mike Garson, born in Brooklyn, New York, in 1945, is one of the world's greatest pianists. He is best known for his work with David Bowie from 1972 onward. Bowie had several major long-term accomplices in the creative whirlwind he unleashed on the world since the late 1960s—Mick Ronson, Tony Visconti, Earl Slick, Brian Eno, Carlos Alomar, and others—but in terms of time span (1972 until 2006) and frequency of collaboration, Garson in fact ranks as the one person with whom Bowie chose to work more times, over more years, than anyone else. He can be heard on more Bowie albums than any other musician.

In addition, the range of other artists with whom Garson has worked is also extraordinary, and this is before we even come to consider his own work in jazz and his prolific composing output, including classical pieces now running into the thousands. Some of those other artists he has worked with have included, in no particular order: the Polyphonic Spree, Aviv Geffen, Lulu, Luther Vandross, Sting, Freddie Hubbard, Stan Getz, Stanley Clarke, Elvin Jones, Mel Tormé, Nancy Wilson, Lorde, Smashing Pumpkins, Nine Inch Nails, Seal, Gwen Stefani, Martha Reeves, St. Vincent, Free Flight, Billy Corgan, Jeff Beck, Natalie Imbruglia, Adam Lambert, and the Dillinger Escape Plan.

A number of key turning points in Garson's career came about as a result of apparently random chances or freak coincidences putting opportunities his way. On closer inspection, however, we see that this was also due in large measure to his being receptive and open-minded enough both to spot the chances when they came and to be ready and willing to run with them. This book came about through a similar combination of fortuitous circumstance and open minds.

I had, like thousands of others, emailed Garson years earlier about his stunning piano solo on the title track of David Bowie's 1973 *Aladdin Sane* album. Then, in 2006, I worked as a pianist myself, with Bowie, on *Extras*, Ricky Gervais's HBO/BBC television comedy show, written by Gervais with Stephen Merchant and produced by Charlie Hanson, in which Bowie sang the 'Pug Nosed Face' song to Ricky Gervais's character, Andy Millman.

Bowie was to sing to my piano playing. He sat at a piano and sang to Ricky Gervais's character whilst miming his piano playing to my own playing on a second piano, off-camera. Bowie and I had a day of rehearsal together, and a day of filming, to produce the seamless effect required. It was surreal to 'be the hands' of my musical hero that day. He was a dream to work with: fast, witty, intensely intelligent, supremely professional, and yet modest—and very funny.[1] The show was filmed in June 2006 and was first broadcast in September of that year. It was to become the last television show that David Bowie would ever do, anywhere in the world.

Equally intriguing was my first meeting with Mike Garson in Los Angeles two years later. I contacted Garson again in 2008 and arranged to visit him for some piano lessons. In the course of conversation he told me that a couple of years earlier he had seen an English comedy on cable TV with Bowie in it, apparently playing piano to accompany his own singing. He had spoken to Bowie and joked with him, 'I see you're playing the piano pretty well yourself, now. I guess you won't be needing me anymore!' Garson told me that Bowie had replied, 'No, Mike, that wasn't me, it was some English guy playing.' It was an enjoyable twist for me to be able to interject and tell Garson, 'Well, I was that guy!'

We bonded over this coincidence, as well as the fact that we had now both played for Bowie, and we discovered much common ground whilst sharing stories of our work as pianists and as working musicians generally. It became apparent that Garson is an exceptional man, with a fascinating and inspiring story of his own. I said, 'There are many biographies of David Bowie, but has anyone ever written a biography of you?' I was hoping he might recommend one for me to read, but instead he replied, 'No, but I think you would be the perfect person to write it!'

That our piano sessions had also unfolded into a discussion of history, philosophy, musicology, and specifically Garson's own life history, was not unusual for him. When teaching, his aim is always to inspire his students to 'become whatever they want to become' and to discover what they can in themselves. Through the discipline of his almost meditative approach to the keyboard, wider horizons are opened up. My own initial meetings with him were no exception. We soon agreed that I would write the first-ever biography of this remarkable man, from the viewpoint of a fellow pianist with shared sensibilities and experiences, and with his full and close cooperation. The more I found out about him, the more determined I became to produce a biography that might allow others to discover and find inspiration in his prodigious achievements.

On various visits to Los Angeles from London, I accumulated over twenty-five hours of digital audio recordings of interviews and candid conversations between us, which explored both his life and also some key themes that are central to his values and interests. These recordings cover a fascinating range of subjects and are dense with material—as a New Yorker and a Londoner, we both tend to speak quite quickly compared with, for example, the Californians amongst whom Garson now resides.[2]

From the start, Garson and I found a lot of striking similarities in our experiences and perceptions as working pianists, and we decided to allow the book to evolve as a dialogue between two pianists, revealing his life through the kaleidoscopic lens of these shared passions and concerns. In addition, I then interviewed a number of other people who have worked with him, including musicians like Bowie bassist Gail Ann Dorsey and guitarists Earl Slick, Gerry Leonard, and Reeves Gabrels; his Free Flight collaborator Jim Walker; childhood friend and jazz saxophonist Dave Liebman; Trent Reznor of Nine Inch Nails; and various of his family and friends.

One key recurring theme was the breaking down of boundaries between musical genres. As a teenager, Garson had been determined to conquer the mysteries of jazz using his classical background, since people had said it was not possible. I approached him with a similar challenge, as I was anxious to play jazz too, having come from more of a pop background, and had also been told by jazz musicians that what I played was 'not jazz,' even when I thought it was. On hearing me play, which he described as rock with jazz stylings, he simply questioned the need to prove anything to anyone. He had himself embarked on a long and tangential route away from the simplicity of his first compositions in his early teens, in his determination to master the complexities of jazz, but he came to realize, through that process, that the greatest beauty in songwriting and composing lies in simplicity of structure. He had also been told that he did not have the 'feel' or the timing to play jazz—and yet became a master of the genre.

Today, however, he is more concerned to teach his students to master their own creativity than to navigate the obstacle courses set up by all the little orthodoxies. Garson's career, as will be seen in what follows, has been an object lesson in breaking down these artificial barriers between classical, jazz, and pop, and rejecting the practice of exclusion. As in other areas of life, there are musical genres (particularly in the jazz establishment) that set up esoteric codes for the sake of excluding those who stand outside, non-members of the club, who are assumed to be incapable of understanding its arcane language. But musical creativity does not sit happily alongside the proud protectionism of closed groups or artistic sects and elites.

During our very first meeting, Garson decried the pompous arrogance of performers who are precious about what they do. He contemplated the virtue of creative spontaneity with characteristically amusing directness, in his strong Brooklyn accent, which has survived many years in the warm valleys and hills of California. His impressionistic sketch of prehistory may use broad strokes, but is intended as an admonition to those for whom music is a 'business':

> I hate it. Do you know, the funny thing is, if you think about it, at eleven, twelve at night, they gather around, and a lot of these tribes, there was a prayer to their gods. So, they played the flute, or sang . . . they just did it, it went out into the ether; they didn't try to get a record contract the next day with that hit that they wrote. They never even thought of that paradigm or model, they just thought, 'This is our way of thanking God. This is what we do.' And, now it's like we have to tape things, to hear them over and over . . . but people should know there is still improvised music, and there is the kind of stuff that I do . . . I try to capture it so people can feel that, but I'm moving on to the next piece—I'm already out of the music from last night, out of the music from last week. Certainly, out of the music I did with David in the seventies or in the nineties or 2000, looking for the next thing. If the next thing doesn't come, meaning I don't hear it in my head, maybe I'm moving into another field for a minute, maybe I do some more artwork, computer artwork, or maybe I teach for a few years, or maybe I'm only being a grandfather and a husband and a father. Or, maybe, I do nothing, or maybe I just compose . . . or decompose.

My visit to Los Angeles to conduct these interviews with Garson was the latest in a series of occasional periods there, each of which had been enchanting in different ways. I had first been in L.A. in the late 1980s, and on my first visit to Venice Beach had come across a pianist busking on a real upright piano. I wondered what would happen to the piano when he finished for the day. At the end of his set, he stood up and pushed his piano before him, disappearing into the sunset, the piano set on a wooden raft with wheels.

In 2009, I had got hopelessly lost on my first visit to Garson's home in Bell Canyon, near Calabasas, having got halfway to San Diego (going south out of Los Angeles, rather than north), when the driver finally got his bearings and turned around. But my journey that day was only the final hour or two of a much longer journey that for me had culminated in that meeting.

At the age of six, my parents bought me a toy piano. I was never away from it for long, so the following year they decided to send me for piano lessons. They found a teacher by the implausible name of Miss Beryl Silley, who taught from a run-down split-level apartment in Wembley, north London. My grandmother took me there for a half-hour lesson each week whilst my parents were at work. It was a slightly grim experience. On arrival in the hallway, there was a huge poster of Margaret Thatcher facing the door. By the baby grand piano was a very vocal parrot, and whilst I played Chopin each week, she would surreptitiously nibble shortbread biscuits whilst brewing her tea, ready for after I had left.

Against the background of such an introduction to the world of music, the arrival of *Aladdin Sane* was the 1970s equivalent of joining the first passenger jet into space. As I ran home after school one summer's day in 1973 and anxiously put that RCA orange-labeled 12-inch vinyl LP onto the turntable, a whole new world was about to open. As the needle made contact with the spiral groove rotating at 33 1/3 times per minute, and the familiar analogue scratch whispered out of my parents' Dansette record player (from which we had by then removed the thin, black wooden legs and had it sitting on the floor), the two opening chords of 'Watch That Man,' G and C, were an apt fanfare for the start of my adolescence. Mike Garson's piano playing washed beautifully all over this album of ten songs, and I was lost in it. Lost on the way to Bell Canyon.

I

# Hammersmith, 1973

*'It is pointless to talk about his ability as a pianist. He is exceptional. However, there are very, very few musicians, let alone pianists, who naturally understand the movement and free thinking necessary to hurl themselves into experimental or traditional areas of music, sometimes, ironically, at the same time. Mike does this with such enthusiasm that it makes my heart glad just to be in the same room with him.'*

—David Bowie on Mike Garson[1]

BROOKLYN, NEW YORK, one hot autumn night in 1972. A struggling young jazz musician had just completed another small club gig in his hometown. He returned to his wife and baby in their cramped apartment with just a few dollars' payment for having worked his usual magic up and down the black and white keys of the piano all night.

He was frustrated. The rewards were disproportionate to the effort and creativity he devoted to it. The five dollars in his pocket was not enough to feed three people until the next gig. There was only one way to play a show: he had to throw his all into it. Whilst playing, he did not care about what he was paid because his was a labor of love. But how could he provide for his family this way? So, this time, Mike Garson entered the apartment and announced to his wife, Susan, that he had to find something else to do—something bigger and more lucrative. Of course, he had to continue playing: by now it was second nature to him. But he had to find some way to raise the stakes and the scale of his work. That night they slept fitfully as this grim reality descended on the Garson household.

Cut to the Hammersmith Odeon, one of London's largest music venues, less than a year later. David Bowie is performing his last-ever concert as his alter ego, Ziggy Stardust. The devoted crowd of nearly four thousand fans are wild with excitement. As they wait impatiently for Bowie to come onto the stage, they are introduced to an unscheduled support act. A lone pianist, who will be playing later that night with Bowie and the full band, will appear first. This pianist will not simply keep them entertained with some solo piano, which would be challenging enough, but will play some instrumental piano versions of the very songs Bowie will later be performing in his set. Mike Garson, for it was he, more than rose to the challenge, and was cheered and applauded as he played his instrumental renditions of songs such as 'Life on Mars?' which have since become widely loved classics of modern song.

The story of how Mike Garson made the transition from New York jazz pianist to international touring keyboardist with Bowie and, later, with rock bands such as Nine Inch Nails and Smashing Pumpkins, is an important piece of modern music history. For this is also the story of how musical boundaries are broken down and how new genres emerge from the flux. In this respect, Garson has been an archetype of the trend toward more fluidity in the creative arts, as he developed virtuoso skills in the broadest possible range of fields, from classical and jazz, through avant-garde, to rock and pop, and then continued to cross-fertilize and wander across these genres, led only by his passion for the music itself. His fascinating career, to date already spanning six decades, is a condensed distillation of many key trends of the era.

His triumphant 1973 solo spot onstage for David Bowie in west London came just a few years after Garson had first been called onto a much smaller stage, at Greenwich Village's Pookie's Pub, by Elvin Jones, renowned drummer with John Coltrane, to replace a pianist who had fallen off the stage, drunk. Garson worked hard at his craft throughout his teens and early twenties and after that debut with Elvin Jones had become part of the New York jazz scene. But the work that he has done with Bowie since 1972 began with another extraordinary piece of timing.

In September 1972, Garson was playing in a jazz club on 69th Street and Broadway, in New York. It had been his routine for several years, since his army days, to practice for eight hours each day, often followed by several hours of playing a gig. The night on which our story begins, he found himself in a seriously talented lineup. The sax was played by Dave Liebman, a childhood friend of Garson's who later played for Miles Davis. The bass player was a phenomenal jazz musician called Steve Swallow. The drummer was Pete La Roca, who was superb but later got fed up with gigging, drove a taxi for several years, then became a lawyer. He returned to playing in his seventies, but died in 2012 from lung cancer.

This was not a 'club date' (as it is called in New York—or a 'casual' in Los Angeles), put together for a party or event. This was a true jazz gig. The band contained some of the most virtuoso jazz players around at that time, and yet there was just a handful of paying customers in the room that night. Jazz fans then could be cruel and fickle, failing to support live music beyond the scope of a few big names like Dave Brubeck, Miles Davis, or John Coltrane. Even at 1972 prices, those few dollars would not go far. Garson told his wife that this could not go on; he had had enough of the frustrations of the jazz scene. He said to her that night, 'I think I want to go out and tour with some big rock band, play to larger audiences.'

The following day, in a beautifully felicitous piece of synchronicity, Garson was telephoned with no less than three separate job offers within twenty-four hours. One call was from Woody Herman, who led a famous jazz 'big band' in America at the time. The job would involve touring constantly, playing seven nights a week, virtually living on the bus or staying in cheap motels on the road for little pay. The second offer was from the trumpet player from the Woody Herman band, Bill Chase, who had established his own band. Chase was subsequently killed in an accident on the way to a gig at a county fair, along with several other musicians.

Then there was a call from a certain Tony Defries, with an intriguing offer. It was indeed a rock tour, just as Garson had announced he had wished for, the night before. He had heard of neither manager Tony Defries nor his artist, David Bowie. Bowie was already huge in Britain and on the verge of breaking America, but his name would certainly not have been common currency in the jazz community.

Mike Garson recalls, 'This was going to be a rock gig, and it was going to be easy for me to play, so to speak. But what I didn't realize was that it was a gift, and it was going to bring out my originality and my real style, rather than being limited to just the jazz vocabulary.'

The afternoon that Garson received that life-changing call from Defries, he was teaching a piano lesson at home in Brooklyn, whilst Susan was at work. Defries introduced himself as David Bowie's manager. Garson asked, 'David who?' Defries explained that Bowie was an English rock star who was going to break America, and he asked Garson whether he could be at RCA's studios in Manhattan in twenty minutes. His baby daughter, Jennifer, was by the piano, swinging in a little hammock (which he had written a song about, called 'Jenny's Swing').

> She's floating back and forth; I'm giving the piano lesson; Susan's working— we've always been working people, we didn't come in like the kings and queens of the old money from England, you know what I mean? We were just struggling people, and I said to my piano student, 'Can you babysit my daughter? I have an audition!' I got in the car; I was there in twenty minutes. I left my student to babysit—my wife wanted to kill me, you know. Could have been some sort of pedophile sicko, you know! [*Laughs.*] And he wasn't, but you know, the mother gets scared. So, I run to the studio, I walk in, I see this booth. In those days, it's not like it is now—there was a booth with a window that separated the control room from the studio room.

The first thing he noticed was Mick Ronson's 'wild blond hair' and high socks and boots, Trevor Bolder's 'wild black hair' with silver on the sideburns, and Bowie's red hair, shorter but full; Garson stood there in a T-shirt and plain dungarees, 'and I didn't know where the fuck I was!' The details of what happened next have been told many times in the music press and in biographies of Bowie, but Garson is clear that many of those accounts have been inaccurate, and now offers to give me exclusively his definitive account.

David Bowie, Mick 'Woody' Woodmansey, and Trevor Bolder stayed behind the glass and Mick Ronson joined Garson at the piano, greeting him in his broad Hull accent, saying, 'All right? I'm the guitarist, I arrange some of the tracks, I play some piano. We're coming into the States, we need a piano player.' There was at this point no clue as to how they had found him or what plans they had, and the whole experience was bewildering for Garson. He says now that he was dazed by the whole whirl of it. He is clear that just the night before, after his five-dollar gig, he had specifically said he wanted to go on tour with a rock band, and here he was, hours later, being auditioned for exactly that.

Mick Ronson asked Garson to play by reading from a handwritten chord chart headed 'Changes,' saying, 'This is a song we do, can you read it?' Garson says he looked at the chart: there was 'a C chord, a C-sharp diminished, maybe a D minor, a G, maybe E minor or whatever; there were some lyrics on there, but the intro didn't have words, just chord changes. Ronson held it and was asking, "All right? Can you play this?"' Garson went straight into it, embellishing from those chords. The recorded version had been out for a while, but Garson had definitely not yet heard it at that point. They stood and watched what Garson did with this bare chord structure. After just the first few bars, Ronson abruptly stopped Garson and said, 'You're in! You've got the gig.'

Garson recalls, 'I thought either he's nuts or I'm on an LSD trip, or somebody doesn't know something, or somebody really knows something, and gets it real quick! But, I didn't know which one it was, because I hadn't even got going. But . . . he's a piano player, he knew I could play. And they're all watching from behind the glass.'

His first reaction was to think 'be careful what you ask for' and wonder whether he really did want this gig. He had his baby at home, his wife at work (and coming home soon, possibly in time to find his student babysitting). This would mean being away a lot. A moment later, he was shown an itinerary. The first gig of their tour across America was in Cleveland, Ohio . . . and only a week away. That was it; his whole life shifted. He was hired initially just for eight weeks, but would in fact stay on the tour until it ended in London the following July, having been right across the United States, Britain, and Japan. He was handed a cassette tape with the whole set on it, and had just days to learn these songs and to familiarize himself with the chord progressions through which his life would now change direction dramatically.

At his one full rehearsal, in Cleveland, before joining the tour, Garson had a dramatic introduction to this new world he was entering. At the jazz gigs he had been used to, the piano was usually an upright, or possibly a broken-down baby grand; there would be no monitor speakers; the bass player would have gut strings and no amp. He sat down at a nice grand piano and pointed out to Mick Ronson that the PA speakers were facing the wrong way. Ronson replied, 'No, that's your monitor system, the main speakers are up there!' and pointed up to the high ceiling, which carried some huge speakers. Garson exclaimed, 'Holy fuck, where am I?'

Defries had created a vacuum around Bowie's arrival in the States, whereby only the smallest clues were allowed through about what was coming. There was a genuine air of mystery cultivated around both Bowie and also his band, the Spiders from Mars, in the States. Soon after joining the tour, Garson found himself within the extended entourage and being installed in luxurious accommodations all over the States, in places like the Beverly Hills Hotel, where his wife and child joined him and stayed with him in one of the hotel's bungalows.

Despite his decision to steep himself in jazz over several years in his late teens, Garson still felt that he had not found his own voice. Ironically, it was being thrust into the tighter structure of rock music that allowed him the musical space and opportunity to create his unique style, by fusing elements of classical, jazz, rock, and pop. He attributes this to the tight eighth-note rhythm of most rock music, compared with the swing and syncopation of jazz, in which a series of triplets each have their middle note 'missing' from the rhythm. He characterizes this as the swing of '*ching*, (*chinga*), *ching*' giving way to the rock music idiom of straight '*clap*, *clap*, *clap*, *clap*.' He started to flourish by embellishing creatively from within this tighter framework and straight structure.

It took a while for him to realize his achievement, as he found himself being harshly put down by both classical friends and jazz fiends for his participation in pop. He feels he mistakenly bought into that criticism, and started to believe that what he was doing was of little value compared with the discipline of classical music or the inscrutable complexities of jazz. But by the 1990s, and the second wave of his work with Bowie, the Internet had changed perceptions and communications, with the emergence of email permitting an easy flow of international feedback, and he started to receive a flood of positive comments from fans, including a wave of emails from those who had been inspired in all kinds of ways by his extraordinary playing on Bowie's work of the early 1970s (indeed, one of these emails was from me).

He has received hundreds of messages specifically from people who were inspired to take up music or piano thanks to his inspiration, and especially owing to the wonder they felt as rock fans on hearing his 1973 avant-garde (and slightly Latin) piano solo on Bowie's song 'Aladdin Sane (1913–1938–197?).' These people had not been able to communicate this so easily at the time, in the absence of email. That wave of retrospective approbation in the 1990s was also vindicated by the later Bowie albums on which Garson played, such as *1. Outside—The Nathan Adler Diaries: A Hyper Cycle* (1995), to give it its full title, or *Reality* (2003). On these his piano playing was now adorning songs that were often even more left-field and performance-art-oriented than the glam-rock tracks of the early 1970s.

For children like me, growing up in the London suburbs of the 1970s, going to piano lessons was not seen as something 'cool.' Then this credibly otherworldly music appeared in the form of the *Aladdin Sane* album, featuring layers of elaborate piano over many of the songs, which was the one record that summer that numerous young people were speaking of as the pinnacle of fashion and good taste. With this new perspective, and Garson's sounds to aspire to, playing the piano started to seem rather more appealing as a craft worth cultivating.

Garson says that he had no awareness at the time of any of this. He simply judged what he was being asked to do by the standards of his classical training, and he felt in fact that it was not enough of a challenge. He says that he felt so little stretched at times that he was 'dying': that is, wilting, not blooming. Now, however, he listens back and feels impressed that he could play that well in his twenties. He feels his self-esteem may have been helped at the time if he had been more aware of the enormous popularity of what he was involved with. But surely Bowie must have preferred it this way, that the jazz pianist he had cleverly added to his palette of musical color was himself in his own world and immune to fashions or rock ambitions and vanities. Ironically, in the rock world, Garson was as otherworldly as Bowie was to mainstream society.

He recalls one instance of his alienation from this world into which he had entered. It was an after-show party when the tour reached New York. Garson stepped into a huge hall full of the tour retinue to see the bizarre spectacle of dozens of people simultaneously and openly sniffing lines of cocaine from the tables. He felt awkward, out of place, and dislocated, out of his comfort zone and out of his depth. He was still very new to this world and hardly knew anyone there apart from Bowie himself and the band. Now he was not focusing on his playing or the songs he had to perform, as he had been an hour earlier; he was simply asking himself where he was, and feeling like he was on another planet.

He felt like he wanted to hide, not physically, but rather from himself, to cover his eyes, to flee; he felt so overwhelmingly that somehow he did not belong there. At the same time, he felt no moral judgment at all against what they were doing, simply that it was not for him and he felt totally alien. He was walking around like a zombie, grateful that these massed revelers were too out-of-it even to notice him.

Suddenly, without warning, there was a loud shout of 'Everybody stop!' and the room fell silent and motionless like a freeze-frame, as everyone realized that this was the voice of the rising star who had brought them all there. Garson twitched with the instinctive premonition that this shocking hiatus may have something to do with his sober trespassing on the bacchanalian scene. Bowie indeed pointed at Garson, and continued, 'See that guy there?' Everyone turned as one to gaze at the young jazz pianist from Brooklyn, and hummed their urban and urbane assent: 'Mm-hmm.' 'He's the only fucking guy here who I respect, because he doesn't use any drugs!' Again the group reacted as one, in obedient wonder: 'Wow!' The freeze-frame slowly dissolved back into normal motion and sound, gradually this time, in contrast to the peremptory halt moments earlier, and within thirty seconds they were all snorting cocaine again. Garson tried to remind Bowie of this when they were again together on a tour bus about twenty years later. Bowie had no recollection. But this public disavowal of drugs shows that some part of him had misgivings, even then.[2]

This theme of alienation would recur many times, and it proves constant. Even the cosmic space-alien themes in many of the songs he would perform with Bowie were powerful expressions of the pain of being alienated from others and even more from oneself.

During his first American tour with Bowie, there was a selection of songs on which the piano was not needed, and at that point Garson would slip front-of-house and watch the show from the audience. He soon realized that 'something's going on here. This guy is brilliant . . . He had a charisma, he had a great voice, he looked great and he had a great band . . . even if you didn't like it, you'd have to be an idiot not to see he had something going on . . .' Compared with the classical and jazz repertoire, the material he had to learn for the tour boasted simplicity, although the modulations of certain of the songs, such as 'Life on Mars?,' 'Rock 'n' Roll Suicide,' and, added to the set in May 1973, 'Wild Eyed Boy from Freecloud,' had a good deal of subtlety too. And Garson was now helping to interpret and flesh out these gems of Bowie's, while evolving his own style in a parallel application of self-discipline.

Later, in the recording studio, Bowie would generally strum the chords on a guitar when introducing a new song like 'Lady Grinning Soul' to the band. For that beautifully baroque ballad, which closes the *Aladdin Sane* album, Garson then played the startlingly exquisite piano part in conjunction with, and partly steered by, Mick Ronson's sensitive and typically ecstatic guitar work on it, together creating the delicate dialogue between piano and guitar that closes the album.

Some years later, it finally became apparent to Garson just how he had come to receive the phone call that day from Tony Defries as Bowie's manager. Just a few weeks earlier, he had played on an album, *I'm the One*, by the avant-garde New York singer, songwriter, musician, and performance artist Annette Peacock. The band Garson was in at the time, Brethren, who played rock with blues and folk influences, had been brought in as backing band for the album. When Bowie arrived in the States and was looking for a pianist, it was Peacock who recommended Garson to Bowie.

Bowie and Peacock were recording on the same label. From this connection Defries had started to manage her as well as Bowie, and this was the link that ultimately led to Garson being approached. It seems Bowie may initially have asked Peacock to do the tour with him, either as his pianist or as a separate support act. She certainly did play piano, though not to Garson's standard. Bowie respected Peacock and asked her if she knew a piano player. She told him that the pianist who had just played on her album would be perfect for him. Mick Ronson also knew Peacock. Certainly, Bowie admired her material, and he would have taken her recommendation seriously. He told the story in his own words in 2002. 'It was during our first few days in New York that musician and writer Annette Peacock introduced me to Mike Garson. Always a gentle soul, he fitted into our band remarkably well considering his background was in the more "outside" fringe of jazz. Ronson and I first had him play for us in one of the RCA recording studios. He rattled through an extraordinary reading of "Changes," putting in the kind of flourishes that only Mike can, and we were convinced he was our man.'[3]

Peacock remained a definite influence on Bowie over the years, and Ronson covered two of her songs in his later solo work: 'I'm the One,' with Garson on piano, on his 1974 album *Slaughter on 10th Avenue*; and 'Seven Days,' as the B-side to his 1975 single 'Billy Porter.' The latter had piano played by Ronson himself, but an alternative version, which emerged on the 1997 CD reissue, has an unmistakable Garson performance of blistering blues piano, together with a Hammond B3 organ solo by him too.

Funnily enough, Garson only found out many years later that Peacock had personally recommended him and given Defries his number. For about twenty years, Garson always assumed for some reason that the recording engineer and producer who had worked on the Peacock sessions a few weeks earlier, Bob Ringe, had been the one to recommend him. Ringe went on to become an agent for the William Morris theatrical agency. Every time Garson saw this engineer over the next twenty years, he thanked him profusely for having given him such a huge break, and every time the engineer declined to correct him.

Peacock was a fiercely independent spirit and one of the world's first musicians to make use of a Moog synthesizer. Not only was she instrumental in introducing Garson to Bowie—and thus to a much wider audience—she has also been a key creative force in her own right, helping to overturn expectations with an experimental and truly artistic approach to music and performance over many years. I am pleased to say that, unlike many previous accounts of this moment in rock history, this description of what happened has been referred to Annette Peacock herself, who confirms that this account matches her own recollection, and that 'the arc of the story is fine and it reads well.'

Once Garson had been brought on board and recruited to the band, things moved very quickly. He had to rearrange his whole life within a week or two, with some intense rehearsal and then the first gig in Cleveland, Ohio, just a few days later. Susan joined him at various points on tour, staying with him in Los Angeles, and also later in Florida. They were young, and this was an opportunity to travel. She was also at the show at the legendary Carnegie Hall in New York. There is an old joke about a young visitor arriving in New York for a concert and asking a passerby, 'How do I get to Carnegie Hall?' only to be met with the response, 'Practice, practice, practice!' In Garson's case, his eight hours daily of almost meditative piano practice had already more than prepared him to perform in such an auspicious venue.

Initially, for Garson, this was a good opportunity to do some much larger gigs and earn some money. He was away from the musical settings to which he was most accustomed, but was both willing and able very quickly to adapt. Soon, however, it became apparent that he had become part of something that was going to be huge. In those days, a real piano would be used onstage (though not at all since the 1990s, Garson points out). He had his music on the piano for the first date of the tour in Cleveland. They finished their last encore, and the rest of the band took off down a tunnel backstage and out into the waiting limousine, whilst the stage was being mobbed with crowds of fans in hot pursuit. Garson had been unaware of the need for this routine, learned by the others during their British tour earlier that year, and was left alone onstage, collecting his sheets from the piano, when, as if in slow motion, 'I saw all these people rushing toward the stage and I thought, "I'm going to get mowed over!" So I took off, ran my head off, and managed to get into the limo just as they were closing the door and pulling away!'

For the young jazz musician, this was all a huge cultural shock. In the smoky little jazz bars of New York, rather than being mobbed, the only risk of misadventure on the stage was falling off it like the drunken pianist with Elvin Jones whom Garson had replaced several years earlier. The polite acknowledgment of certain solos and other nuances, which is the customary protocol for a jazz audience, is, by comparison with rock shows, more like the applause at an old English village cricket match.

Garson sees these large-scale rock concerts as 'events' rather than aesthetic or artistic communications. He played with the Smashing Pumpkins in Minneapolis Town Centre for their 1998 free concert as part of a charity tour, in front of over 100,000 people—it was the only city that would let them do this—and could not hear himself or the full band, just the guitars, distorted through the hysteria. And yet he found the experience exciting, 'phenomenal'—as, no doubt, did everyone else there. He ponders the recollection of it. 'So much was just a continuous hiss . . . Hiss-teria!'

In contrast to the Smashing Pumpkins at Minneapolis, jazz concerts are exercises in intimate communication by the participants with each other, as well as with the audience. In some ways, the jazz audience respectfully eavesdrops on a tight and thrilling group dynamic between the players onstage, who create a collaborative and spontaneous improvisation. At a rock show, solos might be acknowledged, but only as part of the acclaim for the show as a whole, as personified by the star at its center. Garson explains that, when playing for a rock star,

> You're supporting another artist. And there's not room for two stars, so to speak, so you know the role to take. I was there to support Bowie. I would love playing and I would always play my best when I had a solo, but it was to enhance the song. I would look forward to that, but even then my role was to support the show. And to give him a chance to rest his throat, and get variety . . . but David Bowie does give people their space; he is very, very gracious onstage. He's wonderful to work for, just wonderful . . . It's his musicality, he's dead serious about his music.

The timing of that call from Defries was felicitous, but it was significant that Garson was receptive to the opportunity when it arose and willing to make the most of it by stepping out of his comfort zone. He says that the best things have happened when he has stepped back, stepped 'away from himself,' stopped trying to control events, and let things happen. The same laid-back approach that makes the most of good fortune and good timing also carries powerful advantages in almost exactly the same way within the performance of jazz music itself.

At the end of 1974, those two intense years of touring the world and recording with David Bowie would end, for the time being, and he would throw himself back into the jazz scene from which he had come, and which he then realized he had missed in spite of the wild excitement and surreal displacement into which he had been propelled. It may have been a brief interlude, his experience of the early 1970s' incandescent and fluorescent glam hysteria, with its rock idioms of world touring and intense recording schedules. But he would never again be limited to the avant-garde jazz world from which he had emerged. He had forged a bridge between jazz and rock across which both he and future generations of musicians could more safely amble.

# 2

# GI Garson

*'Of the whole lot, Mike is the true genius; we are all just toys in his atonal wonderland.'*
—Billy Corgan[1]

THE PREPARATION that enabled Garson to sit at that piano in the Hammersmith Odeon in the summer of 1973 and play those solo instrumentals of Bowie songs for the expectant crowd began long before his audition by Bowie and Mick Ronson the previous autumn.

Garson studied music at Brooklyn College, New York, from 1963. In the first year he loved it, and was getting straight A's. In the second and third years, his grades dropped below C, and at this point during the Vietnam War, any students whose grades fell below C could be drafted into the army. In an effort to rescue the situation, he attended a summer school at Adelphi University on Long Island, where he was awarded three A's. This might have compensated to lift his main grade to a C and saved him from the draft, but Brooklyn College said that they could only interpret Adelphi's three A's as a 'pass,' as the school was not up to Brooklyn's standard. Faced with the risk of being drafted for two years ('in which you could be sent to Vietnam and get killed'), he took the safer option of volunteering for the army band, which entailed serving for three years rather than two, but made it less likely that he would be sent to war—or so he believed—as he would have volunteer status. As he now says, 'I'd rather play music than shoot people, and I had no problem with people in Vietnam on either side—it wasn't my fight, it wasn't my war. I just don't come from that viewpoint. I'd rather have an instrument than a gun.'

He auditioned for the army band and got one hundred on the test, which was mainly on ear training, identifying notes and tones played to him through some headphones. This led to the bizarre spectacle of this young, Jewish jazzman parading with the military band, 'walking down Fifth Avenue in Manhattan playing bells wrapped around me, the glockenspiel, oompah-pah—inspiring!' Being in the band excused him from later military exercises but did not excuse him from basic training, so that he had eight weeks of a grueling regime, with 'a German sergeant who hated

Jews.' They were doing bayonet practice, being encouraged to stab dummies with great violence. This German sergeant saw Garson just touching the dummy very gently with his bayonet, like an artist with a brush, and screamed out to the others, 'Check this out!' Then, shockingly, he said to Garson, 'If you're an example of the Jews, it's no wonder what Hitler did to them!'

The prejudice Garson suffered as the only Jew in his barracks changed one day when he sat down at a rickety old piano in the canteen and played the blues. Almost overnight he became popular, and was looked after by all of the others. Every morning they would have to get up, 'spit-shine' their shoes, take out their frozen rifles, run a mile in sub-zero temperatures, and put their guns together. These guns were covered in ice, and he was scared his fingers would stick to the frozen surface and get damaged, so the others volunteered to do it for him, once they had been won over by his ability to entertain them musically.

To graduate out of basic training after eight weeks, you had to score 300 points across five activities—throwing hand grenades, crawling on your stomach whilst bullets are shooting over your head, running a mile, and so on. He was up to 220 points, and everything hung on his running the mile. And yet, perversely, he went off and got a hamburger and french fries before running. He says now: 'It was like a "fuck you" kind of attitude—it's like, "This is who I am, I'll figure it out." I was always a rebel in the kind of funniest, healthiest way.' What followed is best told in Garson's own words and broad Brooklyn vernacular:

> You had to go around four times—each trip around was about a quarter of
> a mile. Which meant I had to do this run in about five and a half minutes. I
> couldn't even have done it in a car, in that time. [*Laughs*.] So, I started running,
> and get around the first . . . by the time the second one comes around, the
> stomach pains are coming from the greasy, cheap hamburger [*laughs*], french
> fries and the oil, and I'm cramping. Coming to the third time around, I have
> about thirty seconds to finish the third, I'd zoom around again—a car could
> barely do that. You'd have to be going about thirty, forty-five miles an hour, or
> something, to get around the fourth time, so I figured it's over—I'm going to
> have to redo the whole two months' basic training. There were judges on the
> side, and you have numbers on your shirt, and I was '17,' which was my dad's
> favorite number. I come up and I call out to the judge on the left side: '17!'
> Now, I'm supposed to go around again, I have twenty seconds to get around—
> I couldn't do it if I were the fastest runner in the world, because that'll mean
> you're doing a mile in a minute and twenty seconds! I think the record at that

time was Roger Bannister, who was, I think . . . the four-minute mile. So, I called '17!' out to this guy, and then my eye catches another judge on this side, with a piece of paper, writing down how many times you've come around, based on your number. I started running, and I'm running forward—I wish I had a video of this—and I do a little backtracking. Whoooo! Like this! I came around to the right side of the track . . . I ran backward. I ran over to the right side, so this judge doesn't see me—there's a judge on this side too—I just called out to the guy on the left. I did one of these reverses—like when you see a TV go backward. I ran backward about twenty feet, and I came flying forward to the guy on the right, hoping the guy on the left doesn't nail me. And I screamed '17!' . . . got 300 points! The whole barracks stood up and cheered.

The German sergeant, who had been looking forward to picking on Garson for another two months, looked like thunder.

Some of the musicians were duly sent to Vietnam, though at least if they were playing at a parade in Hanoi they might be less likely to be killed than in front-line combat. But Garson got stationed in a fort just over the newly built Verrazano Bridge, which connected his hometown of Brooklyn with Staten Island. He was legitimately able to tell people he was 'stationed overseas,' as it was across the water; and he was able discreetly to return home every night, as long as he was back at the fort by seven in the morning. Garson and some fellow musicians from his fort also established a jazz big band, and played for the generals and the colonels at parties. There were as many as three other very good pianists in the one fort, and all competed to be the player for this jazz band. Garson got the post, but then made a point of creating a role as arranger for one of the others, Tom Salisbury, who ended up with the Pointer Sisters and went on to be a producer in Europe.

It was at this time that Garson stepped up his approach to practicing. Prior to the army, he was practicing for an hour or two per day at most; now, he started a grueling schedule of working on his playing for eight hours every day, and this has continued consistently (albeit including composing and arranging) through to the present day. This regime of practice was initially prompted by mortal fear, since the army's musicians were regularly tested, and any slip in standards, it seemed, might prompt a transfer into ordinary service—with the possibility of overseas postings, combat, and death. In retrospect, he sees that there was not such a safe correlation between musical performance and not being sent into action, but at the time his fear certainly drove him to extraordinary efforts—which persisted long after he left the army and such fears evaporated. His virtuosity is a good example of the adage about genius being '1 percent inspiration, 99 percent perspiration.' At least one study of the phenomenon of musical genius has found that those we regard as possessing it have clocked up thousands of hours of hard work to perfect their art, and that this may well be the most significant factor in getting them to such an enviable position.[2]

As he continued to try to make his skills as a musician indispensable to the army as an insurance against being sent into active service, a random lottery (the 1969 US Draft Lottery) was held, in which musician friends and colleagues were being dispatched globally to Vietnam and other war zones. His friend Danny D'Imperio, a great drummer who ended up playing with Woody Herman and filling in for Buddy Rich after Rich died, was sent to Korea for two years. The musicians in the military continued to be monitored and rigorously graded, allowing Garson to be nominated a 'specialist,' with similar status to a sergeant.

The pressure to excel musically was also motivated by boredom at the position he had been thrust into. He played for the officers' clubs and would be paid an extra fifty or seventy dollars on the side, which was helping him to finance regular piano lessons from some great musicians, too.

He was also keen to come up to the standard of the jazz musicians he found himself with in the army jazz band, and stepped up his game accordingly. Garson had only switched his emphasis from classical toward jazz playing about three years earlier. Some of his fellow musicians there were of a very high standard, having been devoted to jazz since childhood. The bass player was three years older and tended to try to belittle Garson's abilities and standing. They spoke recently, and he was bowled over by Garson's accomplishments. Garson emphasizes how easily confidence can be damaged by the invalidation resulting from negative criticism:

> They say it takes about seventy-five compliments to wash away one of those negative things. And it knocks people out of the arena, every single day, in the arts and the music area, more than anything else, because that's your whole life, and if somebody puts it down, it just stops you dead in your tracks. As artists, we're very vulnerable and very sensitive. And there's always some truth in the criticism, even if it's 1 percent, and we're stupid enough to buy the 1 percent, instead of seeing that this guy's out to get me, and that it's sour grapes. So, there's a whole subject there connected to what happens to musicians—that's one of the reasons they go to drugs.

When he first arrived for basic training at Fort Dix, New Jersey, his long, thick, black hair was summarily shaved as the first step in depersonalization and demoralization: 'They charge you a buck, and they take this razor: *zip, zip, zip!*' Susan came to visit and walked straight past him without recognizing this shaven-headed man. He could only be visited every couple of weeks. And he felt this sudden 'imprisonment' had come about for him basically because he had allowed his grades at college to fall below that cutoff point for the draft. He had been one of the only students at Brooklyn who was actively working as a gigging musician, and composing, and yet he was not as academically inclined or as able to memorize data, parrot-fashion, as were many of the other students. Meanwhile his overriding view of the role of music was that it should exist simply to communicate emotion (or, in the words of E. M. Forster, 'only connect'[3]). In some of his recent jazz concerts for Internet broadcast, the response from the public has been expansive and enthusiastic, with some of the strongest responses being emails praising not his dazzling virtuosity but the simple yet moving emotional ballads he plays, such as his own 'Lullaby for Our Daughters,' or his cover of Irving Berlin's 'Count Your Blessings.'

After leaving the army in 1969, Garson joined the band Brethren (originally managed by Sid Bernstein, who had brought the Beatles to Shea Stadium for their big American debut). Garson replaced the band's first piano player, who was none other than Dr. John. Garson can be heard, for example, playing organ with them on the song 'Everybody in the Congregation,' with elements of gospel, country, and blues. He also wrote 'History Repeats Itself' for their album *Moment of Truth* (1971), and the whole band provided backing for 1972's groundbreaking avant-garde album *I'm the One* by Annette Peacock. All this time, his piano technique was evolving. There is a fascinating piece of footage of Bowie performing 'Space Oddity' as part of his *The 1980 Floor Show* on the American television show *The Midnight Special* in 1973.[4] Garson is barely visible in the darkness to the back and left of the screen, but the introduction is given even greater cosmic effect by his harp-like virtuoso piano flourishes and arpeggios of chords evoking mystery.

When the twenty-seven-year-old Garson joined David Bowie for his tour of the United States in September 1972, he was following an interesting series of short-term pianists who had worked with Bowie prior to that. *Hunky Dory*, the album released the previous December, featured Rick Wakeman, who had also played Mellotron on the 'Space Oddity' song two years earlier. Additionally, jazz pianist and comedian Dudley Moore was invited to play a guest spot on the album but did not respond. For June 1972's album *The Rise and Fall of Ziggy Stardust and the Spiders from Mars*, Mick Ronson played piano.

On the British tour, no fewer than three pianists had been used between April and September 1972. First it had been Nicky Graham, a young British keyboard player who later went on to write and produce for Andy Williams, Bros, Ant and Dec, and Shirley Bassey; then Matthew Fisher, who had played the famous Hammond organ part on Procol Harum's 'A Whiter Shade of Pale,' later the subject of a lawsuit that went as far as the Law Lords; and, for the final part of the British tour, Robin Lumley, cousin of Joanna Lumley, who went on to produce albums by Rod Argent.

Unlike Wakeman, Garson worked for a few months on the road with Bowie before stepping into the studio with him to work on recording *Aladdin Sane*, and this may well have helped to build the musical rapport between them, which can be heard clearly on albums such as *Diamond Dogs* (1974) and, later, *1. Outside* (1995).

Despite the rigors and indignities of army life, this was a key period in Garson's evolution as a musician, during which he refined his jazz abilities and started a more serious schedule of long daily practice. In his case, it was his mortal fear of frontline combat and death that first initiated the extent of that regime. But however it is motivated, it is that kind of application and effort that converts opportunity and potential into real accomplishment.

# 3

# Ziggy's Support Act

*'I had told Bowie about the avant-garde thing. When I was recording the "Aladdin Sane" track for Bowie, it was just two chords, an A and a G chord, and the band was playing very simple English rock 'n' roll. And Bowie said, "Play a solo on this." I had just met him, so I played a blues solo, but then he said, "No, that's not what I want." And then I played a Latin solo. Again, Bowie said, "No, no, that's not what I want." He then continued, "You told me you play that avant-garde music. Play that stuff!" And I said, "Are you sure? Because you might not be working anymore!" . . . So I did the solo that everybody knows today, in one take. And, to this day, I still receive emails about it. Every day. I always tell people that Bowie is the best producer I ever met, because he lets me do my thing.'*

—Mike Garson

GARSON PLAYS ME A RECORDING made by sound engineer Robin Mayhew, from the sound desk, of his performance at Bowie's legendary farewell performance as Ziggy Stardust at Hammersmith Odeon on July 3, 1973. This is a recording not of his playing with Bowie in the main part of the concert but of his almost surreal set that night as a surprise opening act, by personal request of David Bowie himself. This recording would not even have survived, had this not been the very last date of the *Ziggy Stardust* Tour. In those days, each night's show would be recorded on tape over the previous night's recording.

A solo pianist regaling thousands of impatient Bowie fans with four piano instrumental versions of the very songs they were waiting to hear. It took a brave soul to rise to this challenge, and Garson acquitted himself admirably. After some initial uncertainty in the crowd, you can hear their approval start to surge through the auditorium—encouraged, no doubt, by the fact that the master of ceremonies, RCA publicist Barry Bethell (sounding uncannily like the 1980s British comedian Ben Elton), emphasized that this was Bowie's own inspired piece of last-minute scheduling.

Bethell comes on first to advertise merchandise and to announce that on this occasion the number of people who had seen the show had passed the 125,000 mark during its eight weeks across the UK, covering 7,000 miles. A young girl from Hull called Gina Reilly, who had been the 100,000th attendee, in Bridlington, was there at Hammersmith, too. It was already the biggest British music tour ever by one artist at that time.

Bethell then says he has to leave the stage as he gets 'too nostalgic,' joking that 'I'm a star, anyway.' He steps off the stage stressing that there are 'just two minutes till showtime,' at which point we hear the strains of one of the themes from Kubrick's 1971 film of *A Clockwork Orange*, an adaptation of Beethoven's Ninth Symphony. He reappears some minutes later to introduce Garson.

> During the course of rehearsals, Mike Garson, who is the pianist with the Spiders, played an arrangement of his own of four of David Bowie's numbers. Those numbers were 'Space Oddity,' 'Ziggy,' 'John, I'm Only Dancing,' and 'Life on Mars?'—which incidentally is no. 4 today. [*Cheers from crowd.*] David Bowie, ladies and gentlemen, was so knocked out with Mike's arrangements of these numbers, he thought *you* might like to hear them. So, ladies and gentlemen, please welcome, from New York, Mike Garson! [*Cheers again.*]

What follows are dazzling solo instrumental renditions of those four songs. Garson says he was scared to death, and that Bowie told him backstage that he was more frightened that night for Garson than for himself. This was clearly going to be a historic occasion. Mick Jagger, Ringo Starr, Elliot Gould, Barbra Streisand, and many other stars were in attendance that night. He says now that his aim was to play these songs in a way that would show that they deserved to be part of the standards repertoire. In an interview with Charles Shaar Murray in the *NME* a few days later, Garson explained that on the afternoon of the show he had been in the bar with Bowie and played him his jazz version of 'Ziggy Stardust' with the melody obscured, and asked Bowie if he knew what it was. Bowie replied that he didn't know, but that it was a good jazz piece, and to play it again. After a few plays, 'finally he got it and flipped,' asking Garson to open the show with them.[1]

In his short piano set, Garson made some fascinating changes, adding jazz cadences and putting his unique stamp on the songs, to the extent that he suspects even some of the devoted Bowie fans might not have recognized them at first. 'To this day, some people don't even know what I played! You'll know what I played, but I was changing the melodies, adding all kinds of jazz chords . . .'

The sound engineer on the night, Robin Mayhew, vividly recalls the challenges of amplifying real pianos, in the days when digital pianos had not yet reached sufficient quality to become almost universal for rock and pop arenas. 'Piano pickups like the Helpinstill and Countryman were not available back then, so what I did was to mount and secure two microphones in the piano sound box and close the lid. The mics were plugged into a Kustom 100-watt 2x10 ft. speaker amplifier close to Mike, which in turn was mic'd to the PA system. This gave a great onstage sound and bags of gain for the PA mixer channel.'

At Hammersmith, on July 3, 1973, in his solo set, Garson first played 'Space Oddity'—though in B rather than C (though perhaps the recording, originally on an old cassette tape, is running slow and making it sound lower; his version of 'Ziggy Stardust' here also seems to be lowered a semitone, in F-sharp rather than G). He truncates the song at the start by skipping from the intro straight to the bridge. He adds a discordant twist to the two brief stabs on the same chord at the end of each chorus (the two chords that on the original recording are accompanied by hand-claps). He adds some Latin rhythm and frenetic staccato octaves and chords to the middle instrumental section, in an evocative reminder of his solo on the title track of the recently released (April 13, 1973) *Aladdin Sane*, the follow-up album to *Ziggy Stardust*. There follow some subtle jazz progressions that segue into a brief and quite jazz-styled taste of 'Ziggy Stardust,' with at least one imaginative change from the usual chords. With the lyric 'He played it left hand, but made it too far / Became the special man, then we were Ziggy's band,' the group would play D / G / Em / A / C, whereas Garson here played Dsus / G major 7, C7sus2 / Bm7, E7–9 / Am7, Dsus.

He then picks up the pace for a lightning-fast bluesy riff to introduce 'John, I'm Only Dancing,' in which he uses a stridently strong and percussive left hand to cover for the entire rhythm section which would normally create the movement and the feel of the song. In place of Mick Ronson's guitar riff at the end of each chorus on the recorded version (before the drums come in to introduce the next verse), there was an edgy, avant-garde series of open chords laid extravagantly against the insistent pedal note in the bass.

Finally, he lends a more classical treatment to 'Life on Mars?,' with the verse accompanied by softly repeated chords in the left hand reminiscent of Chopin's beau-tiful little Prelude in E Minor. The piece soon builds, however, to an absolutely full crescendo adorned with cascading runs and crashing chords using the entire range of the keyboard. The final chord of Garson's set—which lasted just under eight minutes in total—is met with huge and resounding cheers, even louder than when it was mentioned earlier that 'Life on Mars?' had reached no. 4, for example. The crowd had clearly warmed to him. Garson went back to the dressing room to prepare for his return to the stage shortly afterward as a member of the band. Bowie greeted him backstage with a silent hug, which spoke volumes.

In the days of the great musicals or theatrical shows, it was a common tradition for the orchestra to play a prelude before the show started—an instrumental medley giving a taste of the melodies that would be sung later—and Garson suggests that this was the spirit in which he was asked to do this short spot. In addition, Bowie had carefully planned his shock announcement to kill off Ziggy later that night, with great secrecy and precision, combined with characteristically powerful dramatic imagination. In this context, his invitation to Garson to provide such a prelude to the show that lay ahead appears even more fitting, since this was to be the most theatrical of all his shows to date.

I recounted to Garson a point of comparison with my own experience here. When Jarvis Cocker curated the weeklong Meltdown Festival at London's South Bank in 2007, he booked me to play piano each night as a support act to that day's headline performance. My natural inclination was to furnish just such a prelude or foretaste. As the fans were waiting in excited apprehension of their band taking the main stage night by night at Meltdown that year, they heard instrumental hints from the piano of what was to come. This resulted in the slightly surreal experience of playing songs by Motörhead and Iggy Pop on a grand piano at the Royal Festival Hall to their fans, to which the response was pleasingly enthusiastic.

During the 1972–1973 world tour in support of David Bowie's *The Rise and Fall of Ziggy Stardust and the Spiders from Mars* album, Bowie also recorded and released his follow-up album, *Aladdin Sane*. Garson was asked to play on the new album, and in January 1973 entered Trident Studios in London to record with Bowie for the first time. On the title track of the new album he improvised a piano solo, in one take, that would prove so memorable for so many people over the years that it has become for many an instrumental motif for that period of pop culture. Jazz and avant-garde elements were infused into the more naïve world of pop, and a moment of pure genius imprinted itself firmly on one of the key albums of a generation.

Within seconds of putting the vinyl of the *Aladdin Sane* album onto the turntable in the summer of 1973, it was apparent that this would be a major departure from the feel of *Ziggy Stardust* the year before. It was more rugged, fuller, and even further from the folkier feel of *Hunky Dory* than *Ziggy Stardust* had been. In particular, there was the crisp punctuation of the high backing vocals from Linda Lewis, Juanita 'Honey' Franklin, and Geoff MacCormack, like a glossy overcoat fashioned from 1960s American girl-group harmonies, but with a nod to a more soulful future. And wrenching a sturdy path through all of this was something else quite extraordinary. A brittle, almost angry and demonically percussive piano: first as rock 'n' roll hammered chords on the opening track of 'Watch That Man,' and then reappearing in an altogether different form on the achingly beautiful ballad that came next, the title track.

So much has been written about Mike Garson's playing on this album, and on this song in particular, though there is something about almost all writing about rock or pop music that steers a very thin line between sharing enthusiasm verbally for the music, and appearing pretentious and pompous. Perhaps this is connected with the long tradition of the music press fostering an adolescent house style. However, Bowie's voice on *Aladdin Sane* was simply hypnotic and, as a young pianist, hearing Garson's playing for the first time was halting. It opened up a whole new world of possibility on several levels. The way that he used the piano as a 'tuned percussion' instrument fascinated me, but that was just the start. The EQ on the piano was adjusted by engineer and producer Ken Scott to give predominance to the high frequencies, and the result was brittle, like splinters and shards of glass cascading through the air and settling dangerously on the scenery, giving it a reflective and glinting edge. If this was what could be done with a piano, then my own playing took on a whole new complexion. It was no longer a weekly chore or the mark of a geek, of someone out of touch with the gritty reality of popular culture.

In the first part of the title track, 'Aladdin Sane (1913–1938–197?),' there are sweeping piano runs embellishing the verses, counterposed with high and slightly discordant octaves. The whole sound is delicious: the tuneful bass notes of Trevor Bolder reaching ever higher, the gentle drumming of Woody Woodmansey, Bowie's strumming acoustic guitar and ethereal voice, the plaintive guitar voicings of Mick Ronson and, later, the wailing sax of Ken Fordham. The first sung note of the chorus, 'Who . . .' is a minor ninth, the high A sung against a G minor chord, and this adds to the air of mystery, whilst also perhaps having helped to inspire the piano solo to come.

The chorus introduces some slightly funkier chord rhythms. But then the band seem to stand aside slightly as this other, insistently atavistic voice emerges in the form of an inspired piano solo. At first, this solo voice sounds like the demented and random hitting of the keys by a group of wayward children, but then it takes shape into a tortured work of genius. As Garson's musical soliloquy stutters and its inner narrative unfolds, we start to perceive its intent.

There are paroxysms of temper or unbridled passion, but these moments are threaded together by an inner language that is far from random. The discords are tantalizing, full of meaning, and resolved with aplomb. The strong Latin flavors are woven in with an avant-garde petulance. There is technical know-how and thousands of hours of practice contained in this succession of notes and chords. Yet there is something that transcends that: a wisdom of invention that could only be accessed by somehow bypassing all of the clutter of technical know-how, even whilst using it.

One of the influences feeding into this expression came from New York avant-garde pianist Cecil Taylor, famed for his lengthy and uncompromising performances and described by Garson as 'this wild, crazy virtuoso.' Garson liked a lot of Taylor's work but 'could not take too much of that constant, "outside," avant-garde dissonant banging away, nonstop! I tended to do it more melodically, a little lighter-hearted, and just put an edge on things.' Garson 'hears too much melody in my head' to be happy with such bleakly atonal experimentation. It was precisely this balance in his spontaneous solo that day, poised between resonance and dissonance, grafting melody onto discord, that secured its lasting and compelling appeal. In later years, Garson has accumulated over two thousand emails received from around the world, praising this solo. It clearly caught people's imagination as both a pivotal moment in cultural evolution and as a deeply expressive and inspired piece of musical creation.

Garson's old friend, jazz saxophonist Dave Liebman, once told him that in this solo he could hear the influence of all the many diverse pieces of music they had worked on together in their youth. It brings to mind Shakespeare's phrase, spoken by Polonius about Hamlet, 'Though this be madness, yet there is method in't.' What at first appears to have 'neither rhyme nor reason'[2] gradually reveals an inner structure with its own narrative and intent, in which can indeed be heard the many influences that fed into Garson's psyche, from the old Liberace television shows of the 1950s to his teenage reverence at attending a classical recital by Arthur Rubinstein, via the avant-garde jazz scene of his hometown.

Not only were David Bowie and *Aladdin Sane* seminal in influencing later generations of musicians, Mike Garson's playing in particular also inspired future artists specifically. Gary Kemp, of Spandau Ballet, explains, 'For me, Mike Garson's piano was what lifted that above anything anyone else was doing at that time. It made it exotic, made it decadent.' Steve Harley of Cockney Rebel also comments, 'Musicians like Garson were playing jazz stuff that isn't written on the chord sheet for the song. Garson's playing is eccentric and wild, and beautiful at the same time.'

Having recorded for Bowie's 1973 *Aladdin Sane* and his follow-up album of covers of seminal hits from the 1960s, *Pin Ups*, Garson was also enlisted to work on *Diamond Dogs*, in which Bowie further explored the apocalyptic themes with which he had opened the *Ziggy Stardust* album on 'Five Years.' More specifically, the inspiration here was Orwell's *Nineteen Eighty-Four*, and several of the tracks (essentially the second half of the album) were originally intended for a theatrical production directly based on Orwell's book, which proved impossible as permission would not be granted by the Orwell estate. Despite having played a key role on the album, with songs like 'Sweet Thing,' 'Candidate,' and 'Rock 'n' Roll with Me' being very much piano-led, Garson was not familiar with Orwell's book when I first met him in 2009, which made it easy to decide what I should give him for his birthday that week.

Garson recalls the recording of the *Diamond Dogs* album in 1973 at Olympic Studios in London as having been a great experience. 'It was special because somehow it was really David's project . . . there was no Mick, David was playing the guitar, it's dark, Tony Visconti's part of it [he mixed it], David's utilizing me a lot, he's talking to me about cutting up words like William Burroughs, he's kind of guiding me through certain things, but to tell you the truth he would play me something and the music sort of told me what to do. He's never been one that micromanaged me, which is why I always thought Bowie was my best producer.'

Garson says that he felt the album was deep and honest, and that he 'loved David's guitar playing on it.' The recording went smoothly: he got the train in from Sussex every day for a couple of weeks at most. This was where the Rolling Stones had recorded, and Keith Emerson, too, the latter's recent presence evidenced by a huge Hammond organ with various wires and ropes attached to it ('he would be attached to it and it would go upside down,' Garson says), all of which inspired him. He felt it would be hard to top what he had done on *Aladdin Sane*, so he just did his best on it as a professional recording session. It was only when his attention was drawn to it years later by guitarist Page Hamilton that he started to see that he had done something special on songs like 'Sweet Thing.'

This whole period of the early 1970s was one of intense work for Bowie and all those working with him, as the rapid roller coaster of recording and touring continued. In the two and a half years from autumn 1972 to spring 1975, no fewer than five albums were recorded and released. In addition, there were two major tours, first for *Ziggy Stardust* and then for *Diamond Dogs*. The latter paused in Philadelphia for the recording of *Young Americans* but also gave rise to Bowie's first live album, *David Live*, on which we can hear clearly just what a significant part of Bowie's sound at this time was provided by the distinctive stylings of Garson's piano.

Garson soon developed an affinity with and a deep feel for Bowie's music. Over the years, their working relationship was to flourish, and Garson has a huge respect for the consummate artistry of the English singer whose manager had telephoned him at home in Brooklyn in 1972. 'David Bowie has the ability to absorb art and be it, whether painting, sculpture, lyrics, songwriting, singing, entertaining, acting. He *is* art and he knows how to become it, bigger than life. That's not the kind of artist

I am, but he's got a ridiculous gift that's probably been there all along, like a pool of creativity that, if he jumps in, he just comes out being it. It sits there, it's available to him at any second.'

Three 'bonus tracks' were added to later editions of *David Live*, one of which is a powerful version of 'Time' in which the piano starts quite low in the mix but then, when Garson plays his solo, it sounds as if the whole band drop out and there is a great shift in the rhythm. When Bowie comes back in with the vocal, the timing between him and Garson is striking in its perfection. Putting this to Garson elicits a telling response.

'I'm one of those guys . . . as much as I like to feel comfortable when I'm performing, and know what I'm doing, there's a part of me that is really always searching. For that next rhythm, that next chord, that next tear from the audience member, the next heart-string pulled . . . the next bit of frustration or anger, the next bit of . . . piano playing that was never heard before, the next strange chord—and not for the sake of it, but more for the avoidance of boredom!' he laughs.

When asked whether he means avoiding his boredom more than theirs, he says he thinks so, but adds, 'It is the duty of an artist to keep pushing his own envelope.'

Garson's solo for the version of the 'Aladdin Sane' song on *David Live* is quite different from the original improvisation. Garson says it is more complex and feels that it was played more heavily than when improvised for the original recording. It also seems to have more of a pronounced Latin feel, though this is perhaps due to Pablo Rosario's percussion accompaniment on the live version. He was not entirely happy with this solo. A year earlier, at the original album recording session, he had improvised spontaneously, and it had proved the epitome of his principle of accessing creativity without self-consciousness. For that minute or two he had no distracting awareness of effort, had lost himself in the moment, and therefore tapped into something different, something beyond our everyday limitations and immediate surroundings. That level of inspiration introduces a different musical language and makes everything else seem merely prosaic or formulaic by comparison. Now, however, he was faced with the basically impossible task of repeating or imitating that extraordinary moment—of imitating himself.

He used all his considerable technical ability to do just that, but perhaps not surprisingly did not feel satisfied. He asked Bowie whether he could go into the studio and redo it as an overdub, to which Bowie agreed.

This close collaborative understanding between them has been demonstrated many times over the years. When Trent Reznor wanted Garson to play on the 1999 Nine Inch Nails album *The Fragile*, Garson asked Bowie's advice, and was told,

'Don't play rock, just do your thing.' Clearly, both men are artistically committed to authenticity. Their shared passion for artistic creativity above all else means that for both Mike Garson and David Bowie, 'It is all about the music.'

Garson is not entirely sure which version of his 'Aladdin Sane' solo for *David Live* was used, although the cover of the album does proudly boast, 'These are all live recordings, and there are no overdubs or parts added.' Either way, he was not overly happy with either attempt, as he was inevitably now having to work at this with his head rather than his heart. In addition it was hard to compete with the sound quality of the Bechstein piano at Trident, as engineered by Ken Scott for the studio version of *Aladdin Sane*—the same piano used by everyone from the Beatles to Queen. The piano sound had been compressed by Scott for the album, giving it a punchier effect, and Garson says that Scott 'was extraordinary at mixing and producing, and much credit for the sound of the album goes to him.'

Interestingly, however, the version on *David Live* of 'Space Oddity' features a strikingly original piano part, improvised here by Garson in what amounts to the opposite process. He had not played a piano part on the original recording. At the time *Space Oddity* was recorded he was in the army, playing in a military band, and stationed at Fort Wadsworth, Staten Island. So in this case there was nothing to imitate or reproduce, and as a result his playing on 'Space Oddity' for *David Live* was more fresh and spontaneous.

The *Diamond Dogs* Tour traveled from the East Coast to the West Coast as one band (including the recording of *David Live*) and came back from the West Coast to the East Coast with different personnel, the infusion of more of a soul feel, the previewing of songs from the next album, *Young Americans*—and with Mike Garson at the helm as musical director, for what was now the Soul or Philly Dogs Tour. The new band members included drummer Dennis Davis, guitarist Carlos Alomar, and bassist George Murray. Davis had studied at one point with Elvin Jones, who played such a key role in Garson's story. Garson recalls Davis's drumming on the Soul Tour, saying that 'his feel was unbelievable and his groove unstoppable!'

As backing for the Philly Dogs/Soul Tour, the Garson Band was formed, incorporating several soul singers (including a certain young vocalist named Luther Vandross) to play a support slot throughout the tour, as well as to back Bowie. In addition to Luther Vandross, the forty-minute support set featured Ava Cherry, who would perform Bowie's 'Memory of a Free Festival,' and others. The Garson Band was a great seven-piece *Soul Train*–type band in its own right, with Dave Sanborn on sax. Then Bowie would come onstage and Garson's band would remain on to play for him, too. The backing vocalists included Geoff MacCormack, Ava Cherry, Robin Clark, Anthony Hinton, Diane Sumler, and Luther Vandross.

In each support slot on the tour, Vandross sang his song 'Funky Music,' which was adapted by Bowie as 'Fascination' for the *Young Americans* album. There were also some Garson-penned songs, as well as the jazz number 'Moody's Mood for Love,' which had been made famous in England by the American jazz singer King Pleasure in 1954. Another vocalist with the Garson Band was Bowie's old friend Geoff Mac-Cormack, otherwise known as Warren Peace (punning the Tolstoy novel), who had co-written 'Rock 'n' Roll with Me' with Bowie for the *Diamond Dogs* album.

Some of the audiences, however, were impatient for Bowie to take the stage, and Garson even recalls a raw egg being thrown during their set at the Spectrum in Philadelphia, where there was a white carpet onstage. A similar scenario is recalled by backup vocalist Robin Clark. 'When we toured with David, the Bowie fans were not ready for us. We opened at the Universal Amphitheatre in California. It was the first gig we did. I remember standing on the riser with Luther. A tomato flew right between us. Another time, an apple flew by. They did not want to see us. They were begging for David to come out. When David hit the stage, he garnered us the respect. He had such diehard fans, the same ones he has now. They listened and they got it . . . eventually.'[3]

Why would so-called fans go to concerts having made a point of procuring such ammunition in advance? 'Well, probably in case they didn't like it,' Garson suggests in reply, which sums up all one really needs to know about such people. The egg narrowly missed both Garson and Luther Vandross, and splattered onto the piano and mic. Garson is clear in his analysis of this: 'We started to think, "Uh-oh, we'd better finish the set fast!" They were screaming "Bowie!" even whilst we were playing. The audience wasn't particularly a black audience—Luther was a black guy doing soul music, and people were coming to see Bowie, with his two different eyes and colors.'

Some of the singers who were part of the 1974 Garson Band had come together the previous year in a side project known as the Astronettes, with some writing input from Garson. There are some fascinating rehearsal recordings available online, also made at Olympic Studios in 1973 and featuring vocals from Ava Cherry, Geoff MacCormack, and Jason Guess, with Garson on piano (with some great Latin jazz touches), Herbie Flowers on bass, Aynsley Dunbar on drums, Mark Pritchard on guitar, and finally some backing vocals (and *sotto voce* musical direction) from David Bowie. An album of tracks from the Astronettes sessions was finally released in 1993, though without most of Bowie's input.

The tour ended on December 1, 1974, and the *Young Americans* album was released on March 7, 1975. Bowie went on to star in Nic Roeg's film *The Man Who Fell to Earth* and split from Defries, whilst Garson returned to the relative anonymity of playing jazz for the next several years. There was a short-lived attempt to keep the Spiders from Mars band going as a separate entity in the mid-1970s with a 1976 album release of the same name by Trevor Bolder and Woody Woodmansey, with guitar by Dave Black and vocals from Pete McDonald. Garson was brought in to play piano on some tracks but Ronson did not participate, and that project was not pursued beyond the one album.

Some forty years after his solo piano interpretation of Bowie songs onstage at the 1973 Hammersmith Odeon show as a support act, Garson released an album of Bowie songs reinterpreted by him for solo piano, for which that early performance can be seen as an eerily distant antecedent. That later collection is a subtle and sensitive tribute to the man whom he has accompanied so often during the intervening years, and with whom he shares a true artist's approach to musical creation, in which authenticity and sincerity are twin pillars of all expression.

There were later occasions on which Bowie asked Garson to go on before him and the rest of the band, to play some solo piano in order to warm up the audience or to heighten the theatrical suspense prior to Bowie's own entrance and the start of the show. It is most likely, given Bowie's genius for the fine-tuning of stagecraft, with nothing left to chance and the whole experience choreographed in advance, that such moves were part of his design. From Garson's point of view, however, it appeared spontaneous and dependent upon the whim of whether Bowie felt ready to go onstage yet, and Garson had to use his rich repertoire and canny ear to take to the piano keys quickly and appease an often impatient crowd awaiting Bowie's arrival onstage.

On June 27, 2000, at the BBC Radio Theatre at Broadcasting House in London (filmed and included as a bonus third disc with early copies of the CD package *Bowie at the Beeb*, released on September 26, 2000), he asked Garson to go on first and play some solo piano for a few minutes, and suggested that since they were in London, perhaps he might play Gershwin's 'A Foggy Day (in London Town),' which he accordingly did.

Perhaps the most extraordinary example of this, however, had been a couple of days before at Bowie's return to Glastonbury, on June 25, 2000, for the first time since 1971. Willie Nelson had just come off the main stage, and Bowie and his band (Sterling Campbell, Gail Ann Dorsey, Earl Slick, Mark Plati, Holly Palmer, Emm Gryner, and Mike Garson) were getting ready to start their show. Once again, Bowie asked Garson to go on first and play some solo piano. This time, for the audience of about 100,000, he played a jazz arrangement of 'Greensleeves,' a traditional English folk song dating from 1580, perhaps chosen to reflect the pastoral English setting of the Glastonbury festival at Pilton in Somerset. As Garson played, the band took to the stage one by one, and the atmosphere was electric. It worked perfectly as a device to build the momentum of Bowie's final stroll onto center stage. The huge screen monitors above the stage meanwhile showed some great views of Garson playing the band onto the stage, using the anachronistic and odd combination of old English folk and postwar American jazz to instill a theatricality and air of expectation into this field of a hundred thousand fans, eager to hear their idol's first song. The contrast between the slightly baroque and brittle, syncopated swirl of piano and the far more modernist power of the rock band about to play could not have been better adjusted, as the familiar bass line of Bowie's opening song, 'Wild Is the Wind' (also from an earlier era, originally recorded by Johnny Mathis in 1957) took over smoothly from Garson's nostalgic prelude. It was quite fitting that straight after the third song of the set, the piano-led 'Changes,' Garson was the first band member that night to be specifically name-checked by Bowie.

Mick Ronson (May 26, 1946–April 29, 1993), who with Bowie had auditioned Garson for his initial contract of eight weeks' touring across the States, formed a strong bond with him. Garson says now, 'Oh, we loved each other. Mick was as warm as they come.' Garson had been speaking about moving to Los Angeles to become a full-time session musician, but Ronson warned against this, saying, 'You will become white toast!' meaning that he would become a run-of-the-mill, good, solid piano player, but would lose his magic and his style through having to adapt to the needs of a never-ending sequence of other artists.

'Do your own music!' Ronson urged him, and Garson has valued that advice to this day, doing recording sessions but not all the time, and always being aware of the need to cultivate his own musical expression. He recalls also the boredom of some of that work. He once had to record the piano part for a television movie of the week and had to wait through over a hundred bars of *tacet* on the piano score. At some point during this time, he says, he fell sound asleep. 'Of course, those people never called me back, because it's an insult to them. But the music was so boring that I did them a favor by falling asleep!'

Garson worked closely with Ronson on the Bowie albums *Aladdin Sane* and *Pin Ups*. They both played on Bowie's 1993 *Black Tie White Noise*, though on two different songs. Garson also played, however, on Ronson's first two solo albums, *Slaughter on 10th Avenue* (1974) and *Play Don't Worry* (1975). Ronson was a hugely multitalented musician. In addition to his supremely able and distinctive lead-guitar sound (in 1974 he beat Eric Clapton in the greatest guitarists poll in *Creem* magazine, coming second only to Jimmy Page), he was also a brilliant and largely self-taught string arranger, as well as a producer, vocalist, and pianist. It was Ronson who contributed the beautiful piano playing as well as the guitar on the acclaimed 'Perfect Day' recording by Lou Reed for his 1972 *Transformer* album, which Ronson and Bowie had produced. His wife Suzi Fussey Ronson, daughter Lisa Ronson, and sister Maggi Ronson have all worked hard to keep alive the legacy of this extraordinary force within modern music since his death in 1993.

Ronson played violin as a child and took some piano lessons from Trevor Bolder's grandmother. When he started doing string arrangements for Bowie, he took some theory lessons from his sister Maggi's piano teacher, Mrs. White, but he clearly had an amazing flair for it, and mainly taught himself from reference books and by listening to a lot of music. The beautiful string arrangement on 'Life on Mars?' was the very first he had done. Maggi was just a teenager when her brother introduced her to Garson, and she says now:

> When I first met Mike, I thought, 'If there's anybody who looked like Jesus on earth, it would have been Mike Garson.' He had beautiful eyes and a very kind face, and came over as such a lovely person. I saw him again when he was on Bowie's A Reality Tour in 2003. In 2013 he kindly contributed his beautiful piano playing to 'This Is for You' on my *Sweet Dreamer* album, which was a tribute to my brother Michael. I have always had a lot of love and respect for Mike Garson, the man as well as the musician.

The record we have on those few albums of Garson playing with Ronson shows a powerful rapport in which their ability to converse musically draws the listener inexorably into the music. This is especially apparent on 'Time' and 'Lady Grinning Soul' from David Bowie's *Aladdin Sane* album, but it can also be heard on Ronson's cover of Annette Peacock's 'I'm the One'[4] on *Slaughter on 10th Avenue* and on his beautiful rendition of 'This Is for You' on *Play Don't Worry*, a song that was written by ex-New Seekers member Laurie Heath of the band Milkwood, with whom Ronson had done some work as an arranger. That album also carries Ronson singing Lou Reed's 'White Light/White Heat' with a backing that had been recorded as part of the *Pin Ups* sessions, and includes a Garson piano part bursting with energy and reminiscent of his performance for the version of 'Let's Spend the Night Together' on *Aladdin Sane*. In addition to recording together, from February to April 1974 Garson also went on the UK *Slaughter on 10th Avenue* tour with Ronson, with Trevor Bolder on bass and Ritchie Dharma on drums.

Suzi Fussey Ronson was very helpful and spoke to me about her recollections from that period. Before she was married to Ronson, she was on the American *Ziggy Stardust* Tour as the band's stylist, Bowie's personal hairdresser, and head of wardrobe, and she says that Mike Garson's playing was always stunning, and that he was likeable despite being more reserved than many on the tour. As a married man he shunned the party lifestyle adopted by most of those involved. 'He wasn't remotely "rock 'n' roll." You couldn't imagine him getting his hair spiked or anything like that . . . though he was quite willing to get into the makeup!'

She recalls that Garson's addition to the band was greeted with relief by Ronson, who until then had sometimes doubled up on piano. This allowed him more freedom to focus totally on his performance as guitarist, knowing that the piano parts were in such capable hands. By the time that Garson was recording with Mick Ronson on his solo albums a couple of years later, Suzi and Mick were married. She would see him at their recording sessions and was aware of Garson and Ronson's continuing bond and special musical rapport. 'Mick had the greatest of respect for Mike,' she says, and Garson confirms that this was mutual, speaking of his love for Ronson and calling him 'such a gentle and humble soul.'

The producer of the *Young Americans* album, released in March 1975, was Tony Visconti. The music Visconti has produced reads, for many who grew up through those years, as the soundtrack to our lives. From 1968 to the present day, he has produced classic and definitive recordings by T.Rex, David Bowie, Sparks, Iggy Pop, Thin Lizzy, The Stranglers, Kristeen Young, Kaiser Chiefs, Morrissey, and many others, as well as being celebrated for his string arrangements and his own musicianship on bass guitar. His lexicon of modern music has helped to create and form the sound not just of a generation but now two or three generations. It is against this backdrop that his judgment deserves to be respected and weighted.

Visconti, like Garson, came from Brooklyn. He mixed the *Diamond Dogs* album on which Garson played, and produced three further albums that included Garson's piano: *David Live*, *Young Americans*, and *Reality*. He tells me that his initial impressions of Garson were positive:

> He was very likable. The *Young Americans* sessions were smooth, energetic, and a lot of that was due to Mike's fantastic playing. I found Mike easy to work with on one level, as he is obviously a virtuoso. But his jazz background gave him the authority to declare, 'I never play the same thing twice.' That could be

frustrating, back in the days before Pro-Tools. If David and I referred back to something Mike played an hour earlier, he wouldn't remember unless it was recorded. In the 1970s, that was a problem, if we only had one or two tracks left on the tape for piano. But David could coach Mike really well. I loved watching the two of them together. Mike could play anything David would throw at him, and I think he really enjoyed how David could corral him in slightly to get some of the great iconic moments of Mike on tape! I knew all about his avant-garde style and I loved it, but when he came to Philly to record the *Young Americans* album, I was surprised how funky and soulful he could play. That must be the Brooklyn boy in him. 'It's Gonna Be Me' sounds like Mike was raised in Harlem. That's got to be one of my favorite tracks we worked on together. When I wrote the string parts I picked up some of the phrases he improvised and doubled and harmonized them, so it sounded like it was all prearranged.

Visconti attributes Garson's distinctive quality as a pianist to his sheer depth of musical understanding, as well as his broad experience. Although he only worked with him on those few Bowie albums, he is aware of his other work, and loves his jazz stylings. But, he says, 'if I were to ask him to include Bartók voicings in a session, his fingers would go there in a heartbeat. He seems to understand every music genre as a Zen master. It's all music to Mike.' He believes that Garson's playing has developed and improved over the years. In 2003 they worked together again on the *Reality* album, and Visconti recalls how they created Garson's piano part for 'Bring Me the Disco King':

When I was recording *Reality* with Mike he introduced us to his new technical setup at home, where he has a MIDI grand piano surrounded by six to eight microphones. In New York, he played piano on one song ['Bring Me the Disco King'] on a cheesy Yamaha keyboard, and we did a lot of punch-ins to get a killer performance, and we also recorded the MIDI performances, too. We loved it, even with the limited sound that keyboard could make. But Mike took the MIDI files back to California, and a week later sent us the same performance reproduced on his MIDI grand.[5] It sounded lovely, really round and hi-fi, but by then we had added more instruments and we were too much in love with the cheesy sound . . . next time, Mike! I think he's adapted very well to modern times. He can whip up lots of alternate performances in his home and send the digital files to Mongolia, if need be. He does a lot of remote-recording now. But I would still prefer to be in the same room with him when he records. It's just such a treat to hear him play live.[6]

Like most of those who have worked with him, Visconti was unaware that Garson had never been a drinker or a drug user, unlike so many on the music scene. Garson simply never felt the need, and because he therefore did not feel compromised or deprived by this, he remained cheerful and sociable, even if those around him were indeed drinking. Visconti found him to be 'sociable, but a little reserved. So am I, but in the studio he is very present and sociable . . . upbeat in a studio context, a great team person.' He does recall being loaned by Garson a book on the history of tempered tuning, which he read and returned, and they had 'many conversations about the dark history of tempering on our lunch breaks.' (Tempering involves different systems by which the sounds played by the notes on an instrument such as a piano will be precisely designated. The frequency and therefore pitch of each of the notes on the keyboard is not necessarily arranged in exactly even steps from one note or semitone to another.)

How has Garson's playing contributed to the overall content and impact of those Bowie albums and tours on which he played? There can be few people better qualified to assess this than Tony Visconti, and his description of this is a beautifully expressed testament to the artistic creativity of both Garson and Bowie. He explains how, with the right chemistry, everything comes together with such unpredictably stunning results. His summary also unwittingly demonstrates how his own genius as producer and facilitator was a key part of this equilibrium.

Well, Mike's playing is an undeniable signature sound to many of Bowie's records, along with Mick Ronson's guitar playing. Those two emerged as icons in Bowie's various bands. The *Aladdin Sane* piano parts are exquisitely beautiful. I think fans of Bowie are also fans of Mike: they 'get' him. When they worked together they had a great symbiotic interactive relationship. As a producer, I always jumped in with my suggestions, but when I saw that David and Mike were on a roll of creativity I would just step aside and assist them in any way I could. They worked together really well . . . I think David regards him very highly.

# 4

# Brooklyn, 1945–1969

*'I look into his sincere, green eyes and I ask him to do something, and he nods . . . and then does whatever the fuck he wants.'*

—Tony Visconti

GARSON WAS BORN and grew up in Brooklyn, a borough of the city of New York that has produced a hugely disproportionate number of stars of music and the arts, including Lou Reed, Neil Diamond, Jay-Z, Mel Brooks, Spike Lee, Harry Nilsson, Aaron Copland, Neil Sedaka, Tony Visconti, Barbra Streisand, Larry David, and Larry King (who attended the same school as Garson). The Garsons were a Jewish family, living in one of the most cosmopolitan conurbations in the world. Brooklyn in particular was always a vibrant area with a great mix of different ethnic backgrounds.

His father, Bernard, was a liquor salesman, delivering alcohol to locations in New York, including the Half Note jazz club. One of the regular performers at the Half Note was Lennie Tristano, who became Garson's piano teacher. Tristano was blind and something of a jazz legend. He played with Charlie Parker but was also a prodigious teacher. Tristano was the only jazz musician in New York at that time who gave lessons and really knew how to teach jazz. The other big names on the jazz scene just did not talk about their music in those days, so you could only learn from them by imitation. Tristano was a great player, but he also had a system, a formula, and would set exercises for each student to work on before the next lesson. He also had a very particular playing style that Garson can imitate easily to this day. Hordes of young jazz fans queued to see him. Garson describes how Tristano would teach as many as eighty students across Mondays and Tuesdays, for just ten minutes each, and the young Garson traveled two hours each way from Brooklyn for these lessons.

Garson's father wanted him to be the next Gershwin. Brooklyn was also where George Gershwin grew up; he died a few years before Garson was born. He feels a strong connection with Gershwin, and 'not just because our names both start with G and end with N!' He plays a sensitive tribute, 'A Gershwin Fantasia,' which is available for example on his *Mike Garson's Jazz Hat* album, and is an improvised medley based around Gershwin's themes. Garson believes there was a special inspiration in Brooklyn.

The postwar years saw a decline in the economy of Brooklyn, with heavy manufacturing moving out to cheaper areas, and even the ports slowly becoming less active, since the larger container ships now dominating the shipping trade needed deeper harbors. It was also long before the later periods of gentrification with the various waves of hipster cool and artists' colonies over in districts like Williamsburg. Still, it was lively and ethnically mixed, and despite widespread poverty always had more than its share of vibrant local pride.

Growing up in the 1950s, the family lived in a small apartment on Ocean Parkway in the Flatbush district of Brooklyn, between Prospect Park and Coney Island, on the second floor of a six-story building, with an elevator. Ocean Parkway was built in the 1870s and inspired by the grand boulevards of Paris and Berlin. The Garsons would have been considered as a fairly 'middle-class' family. He has a sister, Barbara, ten years older, who became a model and also gained a psychology doctorate, specializing in biofeedback. She married young, at about eighteen, to Sheldon, who owned a building on Park Avenue in Manhattan. They did very well in real estate and retired to the beautiful town of Sedona, Arizona, with its striking red sandstone cliffs, where Garson has performed a number of times, and his sister and her husband have been very supportive of his career.

From the time he started piano lessons, aged seven, his father would sit in a big comfortable chair a few feet from the piano, listening and offering corrections and suggestions whilst smoking 'big, fat cigars,' of which he would get through 'eighteen per day.' The smoke was so thick that he now recalls that he literally could not see his father across the room, as if there were 'a fog machine.' At the time, he says, this is how people lived and thought nothing of it, but as he now looks back sixty years, it strikes him as bizarre and hilarious that their small Brooklyn living room was dominated permanently by this cloud of strong-smelling smoke. He is, however, grateful for his father's attitude toward his music throughout those early years. Right from the start, he was his biggest supporter and inspiration, never once saying 'you have to teach to make a living,' as others did, but simply 'just go do your music.' He had a natural and instinctive musicality and, though untrained, was able to guide his son's playing toward being 'in the zone' or 'in the pocket,' as Garson puts it, and taught him some quite complex imitations he had worked out of the music he heard on the early westerns. He had learned to play some classical pieces by ear, too, but this 'cowboy film' music was 'the one thing he had composed.'

It is interesting that Garson recognizes his father's improvised creation as a fully

fledged composition, in much the same way that his own compositions are now produced, in contrast to the elitism of the classical establishment, which generally only
labels as composition those pieces that are laboriously scored by hand, note by note.
Garson's father played the melody of his composition in octaves with his left hand,
with chords in the right hand. He imitated this style of playing from the pianists who
had performed in the early movie theaters, providing their live, improvised scores to
silent films. His son can still play, to this day, an example of this 'cowboy' music his
father showed him in the 1950s.

Garson describes his father as a great man who was 'very psychic' and knew that
his son was meant to do music. His mother, Sally, was 'a wonderful lady. She loved
my music and loved me playing.' She had hoped he might pursue a medical career,
but when he switched to music at college she was supportive, and came to many of
his concerts, including at Madison Square Garden with David Bowie. When she
died, she knew he was set and well established in his career.

On the other hand, Garson's father-in-law, Bernard Taylor, continued to see his
music as just a 'hobby' and hoped that he would get a 'real job' right up to when he
reached fifty, even making an attempt to get him back into medical school when he
was already forty-three. He owned a Manhattan trucking company, and was leaned
on by the Mafia for payments in order to survive and trade in that business. This was
a very different world from Garson's, and yet he was keen for Garson to take over
his business—which raises the now slightly bizarre image of Mike Garson supplying
road transport rather than musical expertise.

Bernie Taylor provided the line for an ongoing family joke. They were once all at a
wedding, and the rather mediocre but large band was filling the bandstand. Confusing quality with quantity, he turned to his son-in-law and said, 'Look Michael, now
*that's* a band! They have about twelve people up there! That's what you need, you only
have three . . .' For years afterward, whenever Garson was due to play with a larger
ensemble, he and Susan would joke that he was in luck, as it was going to be such a
'good-sized' band.

There was a piano in his house growing up, as he estimates there would have been
in about 70 percent of Jewish homes in Brooklyn at that time, with maybe one in four
children learning to play. He jokes that if you were a Jewish child in 1950s Brooklyn
who did not like music, 'you were doomed,' as it was so common within that community to have music lessons. Whereas his father played by ear, his mother and sister
played from sheet music. His sister reached quite a high standard, as had his mother.

His father was born in 1906 and went out to California in his twenties to become
an actor. He got some work as an extra but returned to New York and got a job with

Standard Wine and Liquor, selling whiskey to the bars. He was not the last Garson to move to California: in 1978, his son and daughter-in-law themselves moved from Long Island to Los Angeles, where Mike Garson would work with Stanley Clarke and Susan was going to be managing Chick Corea. They have been settled for some years in the remote community of Bell Canyon, in Ventura County. With a population of only two thousand, there is a disproportionate number of celebrated musicians and actors attracted there by its seclusion and security. Bell Canyon is an equestrian community and indeed it is a former horse barn that has been converted into his home studio complex beside his house.

His mother had wanted him to be a doctor—'like all Jewish mothers,' he says—but he failed at biology during his 'pre-med' major as a student, and appealed to the teacher:

> I said to the biology teacher to come to the window—I said, look at the building over there—that's the music building. If you let me out of here and give me a 'D,' I'll never look back, and I'll go and do my music, and you won't have me in your hair. Dissecting this pig, and making 'spare ribs and chopped liver' from this poor fetal pig that I was learning to dissect. Then he laughed, and he said, 'Get outta here'! And he gave me a 'D.' If I'd had an 'F,' I would have had to redo the course . . .

He had started piano lessons at seven. At the time it seemed young, but he now knows from seeing the talent in two of his young grandchildren, Max and Jacob, who in recent years were living with him, that the young brain can absorb so much (Max started playing the drums at the age of two).

Garson recalls one concert at elementary school, aged seven, in which he was to play a piece ('Long, Long Ago' by T. H. Bayly). It had a first section, which would lead into a link for repeating that section, and then the second time around it would go on to an ending. He got stuck in a loop, however, in which he kept playing the link into the repeat, so that he sat there repeating the first section over and over, whilst all the young children in rows sat and stared. Eventually, after ten minutes, two teachers had to walk over, lift up the piano stool with him on it, and move it away from the piano.

In those days, the teacher would visit the home. Most of the children would give up after a while. The Garsons had a telephone in a little closet in the kitchen where they hung their coats. He did not want to practice for any more than about twenty minutes a day, and has vivid memories of his mother threatening to cancel the lessons if he did not practice. But each time he saw her move toward the closet with the telephone in it to do so, he would run back to the piano and start practicing. This went on for five years. I can relate absolutely to this story, as I had exactly the same experience. Not wanting to stop the lessons or the chance to play, which is soon seen as a source of great enjoyment, whilst at the same time finding it tedious and boring to have to practice.

Social environment clearly plays a key role in determining which children around the world are to become the pianists of tomorrow. Garson asks, 'Would I have chosen it, if there was no piano and my sister and my mother didn't play the piano? They were both trained at the piano . . . it was almost like it unfolded, this piano thing.' His mother and sister continued to play a little, but they decided to focus their efforts mainly on training young Michael, who had the 'gift of the ear,' with perfect pitch and also imaginative creativity, whilst his mother and sister were good at reading music and playing classical music elegantly.

His father was utterly devoted to Garson's playing. A few years before he died, he was poorly, he had lost his wife, he was sick and grouchy, 'complaining that he could not get around the corner to get a sandwich,' when his son phoned from California and mentioned that he was playing in Montreal the following night. 'I'll be there!' said his father. And he was.

In the 1980s, Garson played an outdoor concert in Phoenix, Arizona, with Doc Severinsen, the trumpet player who led the band on *The Tonight Show* with Johnny Carson for many years, and was the principal pops conductor for several big American orchestras. His father flew over two thousand miles from Brooklyn for that occasion. He sent a dedication with a bottle of champagne, with tray, glasses, and a handsome tip for the waiter, up to the stage for Doc Severinsen, with a note saying 'That's my son onstage with you!'

Garson now believes that his best teacher was his first, when he was seven: Mr. Scatura. This man was not the best player or the most knowledgeable, but he was 'the warmest Italian man.' Any mistake was punished with a gentle tap with two fingers, but 'it was done with so much love.' In those days, to encourage a rounded position for the hand, teachers would put a little apple under your hand to remind you that it should not be flat. At the end of each lesson he would play Garson a piece by Chopin or Rachmaninoff, which was an inspiration, and the best part of the lesson.

At the age of about ten it seemed right for Garson to move on to a more advanced teacher, but he is sorry now that he could not stay longer with this sweet man whose humor, care, and enthusiasm radiated from his face into the young Garson. He has tended to talk more about the better-qualified teachers who came later, but now he sees that it is really all about the inspiration that, from the right teacher, can come in a split second and last for a lifetime. In that second, your path is plotted, and you are hooked.

Garson moved on to lessons with a neighbor, Leonard Eisner, who came from the Juilliard School. He still carries the painful memory of how Eisner dismissively accused him of having 'delusions of grandeur' because, at twelve years old, rather than play the written notes of Mozart or Chopin, he was improvising over them. This was an early taste of proscriptive negativity from the musical establishment, which is a recurring theme in Garson's life. This teacher was hugely looked up to by the young student, and could easily have couched this in a much more positive light, offering encouragement rather than criticism of this early sign of promise in Garson as composer and improviser. He still recalls how when he 'altered Mozart's Sonata No. 11 in A Major, K. 331, Eisner had a "mental breakdown," and I knew it was all over with him!' Garson moved on to his next teacher, Lee Sevush from Sheepshead Bay, who 'opened up the doors to commercial music and some jazz, some Latin music such as Carmen Cavallaro . . . he prepared me for the Catskills.'[1]

Up until the age of fourteen, Garson had intended to become a rabbi. He scored 100 percent in a Hebrew exam and won a trip to Israel on a scholarship. He played *Rhapsody in Blue* on the ship going over there, and still recalls how seasick he felt, as the piano slid across the floor whilst he played, so rough was the crossing from Marseilles to Tel Aviv. 'I was playing these runs and arpeggios, and the piano would be going in one direction, and I was going in another direction! Everything was swaying. I ended up being sick for days. But I managed to finish the piece . . . though that was at a young age and it was pretty scary. It's good to know that I'm still doing the Gershwin stuff, fifty-five years later.'

At that time he was still playing *Rhapsody in Blue* exactly as it was written, though within a few years he had started to extemporize profusely from such pieces and later created his *Gershwin Fantasia*. He stayed on a kibbutz for a month and studied.

There were a lot of Italians in his school in Brooklyn, and languages taught there also included Spanish and French. Later, at college, he also tried Italian, but did not take to it. He was unusual in continuing his Hebrew studies beyond his Bar Mitzvah at thirteen, and still recalls how devastated his Hebrew teacher, Mrs. Mandelbaum, was when he later told her that he was going to shelve his Hebrew studies in favor of taking up music. The rabbinate's loss was music's gain. Yet he still feels that even if he were a rabbi or a doctor, his identity and his intentions would be the same as those he holds dear as a musician: to help others and to communicate.

Although the popular music of his youth was swing and bebop, and then rock 'n' roll, the music he heard at home was mainly classical. His mother was suspicious of jazz, associating it with New Orleans strip clubs and brothels. He recalls being taken by his father to Coney Island, fishing and getting hot dogs and fries. As a young child he saw the arrival of television in the home, with such shows as *I Love Lucy* and stars like Ed Sullivan, Milton Berle, Dean Martin, Jerry Lewis, Jackie Gleason, and Steve Allen. Allen wrote many thousands of pop and jazz songs, was a good pianist, and also wrote many books. In 1954, he became the first presenter of *The Tonight Show*, which was later associated with Jack Paar, Johnny Carson, and then Jay Leno, followed by Jimmy Fallon.

Jack Paar had a musical director called José Melis, a brilliant Cuban pianist from whom Garson says he took some of his own *schtick*. For example, on the show each night they would ask an audience member for the last four digits of their telephone number, and Melis would then go to the piano, count that number of notes up or down, and make up a song on the spot using those notes. Garson does something similar, asking audiences to choose notes on which he bases the next improvisation, sometimes even letting them help to determine how an improvised piece should end. This has very exciting implications in terms of the group dynamic and the feeling of commonality that builds within an audience, as well as between audience and performer, going right back to our discussion of more ancient forms in which music was a communal, spontaneous ritual or celebration, without division between performer and audience.

One big influence on the young Garson was Roger Williams, who made 'Autumn Leaves' famous in 1956 with his big hit instrumental version, with its great chromatic runs in thirds, which Garson today still imitates in his own live versions of the song, as his tribute to Williams, much to the delight of audiences. They became friends many years later, and it transpired that they had both been taught by Lennie Tristano. Then there was Peter Nero, a conductor who was also a good jazz pianist, with a tinge of pop sensibility; and, of course, André Previn.

Previn has had a huge influence both as pianist and conductor. He has often conducted Garson's good friend and collaborator in the group Free Flight, flautist Jim Walker, for example when Walker played with the Pittsburgh Symphony Orchestra. Another early influence was the one-time PSO Concertmaster Andrés Cárdenes. Previn had also written a jazz book with a song in it called 'Like Young,' which helped to get Garson into jazz when he was about twelve or thirteen.

Together with Dave Brubeck, George Shearing, and Erroll Garner, all of these inputs were key musical influences on Garson in his early teens. He recalls his early years as being very ordinary and peaceful. Despite working in alcohol sales, his father hardly drank himself, though he may have come home a tiny bit tipsy occasionally, if he had been drinking with those he hoped would become clients. The son of a liquor salesman, Garson himself has never been a drinker, perhaps having seen the damaging effects it could have on musicians and others in the bars his father had to visit for his work. It was his father who introduced the young Garson to live jazz by taking him once to the famous Half Note jazz club on Spring and Hudson in New York when he was about sixteen or seventeen, as it was one of the places to which he sold and delivered alcoholic drinks.

That night Lennie Tristano was playing. When he took a break, Garson's father asked if his son could be allowed onto the piano to audition by playing Dave Bru-beck's 'Take Five.' Garson played the melody in E-flat minor and covered the whole bassline with his left hand in the required 5/4 time, without any improvisation at this point. It was difficult enough to adapt the fast top line, which had been played on the original on alto saxophone by Paul Desmond. As Dave Brubeck's drummer, Joe Morello had introduced 5/4 as a popular time signature in jazz in about 1959. In Los Angeles in 2009, I saw Garson play 'Oh, What a Beautiful Morning' in 3/4 with a trio, and when the drummer, Joe LaBarbera, took a solo, Garson switched him into both 5/4 and 7/8 time, to great effect. LaBarbera is able to take this kind of rhythmic complexity to a new level.

At elementary school, Garson did not fare well academically. He did not feel that the teachers adapted their methods to suit the different ways in which different people learn, which in his case was more through listening, observing, and trying to imitate, than by the mechanical process of learning by rote that was still predomi-nant in the 1950s. Not every student learns in the same way. He learned more from watching his piano teacher, Lennie Tristano, playing in the Half Note jazz club than during his lessons with him. Rather than struggling simply to absorb abstract data disconnected from his experience, he did better (like many people) when respond-ing to something that is being done in context, and with meaning. One of the best ways to teach is through a cyclical repetition of practical observation and imitation, which follows a spiral form of gradually building in layers, rather than abstracting information or principles to be learned as something separate. Some jazz players even have a policy of withholding information when teaching, so as not to share too many of their secrets, in an absurd instance of protective elitism within so-called artistic expression.

Educationally, Garson felt increasingly detached and disassociated. Sometimes, at high school, if he felt he was going to fail a test, he would write a funny piece of music for the teacher at the bottom of the paper instead, just a few bars on a musical stave and label it something like 'The Algebraic Cha-Cha' or 'The $H_2O$ Waltz.'

As a boy, he enjoyed playing a little baseball, stoop ball (where they would hit the ball on the steps outside apartment blocks), handball, hardball, chasing games; but he was quite introverted and shy, seeing himself as different from the others. To this day, like many artists, he continues to feel a particular alienation so that, for example, at a party or a reception after a big concert, he feels uncomfortable, a sense of not belonging, at least until he succeeds in locating one person with whom he can get into a good conversation.

In his late teens, he was an impoverished Brooklyn student musician, mixing with other struggling youngsters, their access to the luxuries of Manhattan's entertainments somewhat limited. Of course, they made their own entertainment, and he recalls vividly one such incident. In Greenwich Village in 1962, there was a place called Alberts, which offered an 'all you can eat' steak option priced at $5.95. The teenage Garson was slim but had a big appetite, and he recalls one visit there with some impecunious musician friends. They thought it would be fun and economical to take advantage and have a couple of steaks each, which were served with baked potatoes and vegetables. As the meal progressed, the others dropped out one by one, but Garson finally worked his way happily through no fewer than five steaks before leaving, much to the exasperation of the management, but there was nothing they could do, as he was playing by the rules. He left the waiter a generous tip and walked slowly off, 'pretty full but very satiated.'

His grandparents were all from Russia, though both of his parents were born in New York. His paternal grandmother, Anna, created works of art on copper. His maternal grandmother, also Anna, was extremely loving toward him. Whilst his grandfather took him to the temple (synagogue) every Saturday, his Grandma Horowitz 'was pure love, and every Tuesday between eleven and fourteen years old at noon for lunch I would go to her house, two blocks from my public school "238" and one block from my house, and she would fry up the greatest little fish called smelts.'

He was at home in California when his father died, at eighty-nine, in Brooklyn. At the time that he went into hospital, there was a huge snowstorm, which made it impossible for either Garson or his sister in Arizona to get to New York to visit him. It was at the end of 1995, and Garson had been touring with Bowie. His father had asked him the week before he died which dates he was next due to travel, as if he knew what was happening and wanted to make sure his son would be in the country to attend his funeral. He told him he was due to tour again with Bowie in Finland on January 17, 1996. He passed away a week before that. Garson explains that his father 'did not have to die; he had a stomach ulcer and he would not let the doctors repair it as he felt his quality of life would be limited.' At that point the snowstorm cleared, and Garson and his sister were able to fly in for the funeral. The next day, he was on the flight to Finland to play for Bowie.

Garson's mother had died about twelve years earlier of ovarian cancer. He was due to play with Free Flight at Santa Monica around that time, and his mother called from where she was staying at his sister's house on Long Island, with just a short amount of time left, wanting to see him. He flew out with just a few days to go before the big concert; she waited for him, kissed him, and later that evening she passed away. Both his parents had a strong and practical work ethic, to the extent even of reasoning, as Garson now puts it, 'Michael has to play, no matter who's dying'; he believes that they worked it out in their own spiritual, intuitive way, somehow allowing them perhaps even to time their demise.

He loved them and misses them. He would particularly have loved them to enjoy his seven grandchildren, and also the fact that he has now written such a huge amount of classical music, too, as they were close to that world. They loved to hear him play classical or semi-classical music, especially, for example, the *Warsaw Concerto* by Richard Addinsell, or the theme from *Exodus*, with its strong Jewish connotations. His father said that he would make sure that at his funeral Garson could play on a nine-foot grand piano, and asked that he play 'September Song,' 'Mack the Knife,' and one of Garson's own compositions called 'Admiration.' This was exactly what happened. Garson says of his father, 'I followed his rules.'

He learned as a young adult from many teachers and mentors who were huge in the jazz world themselves, such as Herbie Hancock, and he was even once given a six-hour lesson by Bill Evans. As a teenager, Garson had been determined to master jazz. Less than five years later, he had his chance break with Elvin Jones. Jones was John Coltrane's drummer from 1960 to 1966 (Coltrane died in 1967). He was at Pookie's Pub in Greenwich Village when Jones's pianist literally fell off the stage, drunk. They dragged him out and left him in a stupor on the street, on Spring and Hudson, right across the road from the Half Note jazz club where Garson had played 'Take Five' for Lennie Tristano. The sax player, Steve Grossman, turned to Jones, pointed to Garson, and said, 'That guy can play piano.'

Garson was in a tuxedo, having just played at a wedding. Jones, Garson's favorite drummer of all time, was stoned, but he seemed 'psychic' to Garson, saying, 'Come on up here, Arthur Rubinstein!' Garson wonders now, 'How could he have known that just a few months earlier I had seen the master pianist play Beethoven's Waldstein Sonata, or that I had been speaking every day since of Rubinstein, and of how hearing him play the Third Movement had changed my life?' He ended up playing three consecutive nights with this band and says that it was the greatest apprenticeship he could have wished for, albeit something of a baptism of fire. That week his playing went 'from a three to an eight or nine out of ten, at nineteen or twenty years old.'

It would seem that this tumble by a drunk pianist was not a unique occurrence. Garson tells of the time around 1963 at the Village Vanguard jazz club when he was seated near the stage watching the great Thelonious Monk, of whom he was a huge fan. During a sax solo, Monk, who was drunk, left the piano and was 'dancing in circles on the stage,' which was something he often did during solos. 'He fell into my arms! He felt like he must have weighed nearly three hundred pounds!' In reference to this incident, he has called a new album of Thelonious Monk–inspired music *Monk Fell on Me*.

Garson's break with Elvin Jones was just one of three key moments when he was called on to play in a very unexpected way. Years later, he covered for pianist Michel Petrucciani at the Catalina in Los Angeles (see page 61). Then, of course, between these two times, was that most significant 1972 surprise call from Bowie's manager, Tony Defries, which forms a pivotal point in his career. He certainly sees his own evolution as containing this element of serendipity, finding that whenever he tried to control something or make something happen, it would be more likely to fail or close down, and that the best things always happened 'when I got out of my own way.' His way of navigating through the obstacle course of life as a musician has never relied on the escapism or hedonism of drink or drugs, unlike so many others, but rather on the practice of gratitude and openness, welcoming opportunities but not chasing them.

# 5

# Abstinence Amongst Excess

*'Mike does not drink, but his personality is more than capable of matching the zany, mischievous, or highly energetic states of anyone else who does. He can be high without taking anything; he kind of rises to the same exuberance. His own openness encourages others around him to be themselves . . . Mike Garson has got the biggest heart in the world, he's got to be one of the sweetest, most loving people I've ever met in my life, aside from being an incredible musician who should be on everybody's mind.'*

—Gail Ann Dorsey

IN REFLECTING ON HIS LIFE, Garson describes how he sometimes has a sense of isolation or disconnectedness, especially when having to interact personally with groups, as opposed to either a meaningful one-to-one communication or performing musically to a group of people. The sense of difference or disconnectedness felt by many artists makes them vulnerable to the dangers of addiction. They seek to ease their inner loneliness, at huge long-term cost, with shortcuts to connection or with hedonistic pleasures, as they try to compensate for perceived lacks or losses. The loss of rational discrimination that results from inebriation creates a false sense of connection, as the barriers normally constructed through such discrimination come down. Garson states that although he loves people, he does best either on a one-to-one basis or in the situation of playing a concert, whereas in group interactions or at parties he feels a little lost. It should be added, however, that if such feelings of alienation are particularly common amongst musicians or artists, they are also not uncommon in the population generally, and this is perhaps a reflection of the lack of true community within the present-day social order.

There is a second factor that makes performing musicians more prone to such risky indulgences. The special excitement of a live performance leads many musicians to try artificially to prolong this high after the show is over. Garson has avoided these problems, saying that after a show he prefers to unwind alone in his hotel room, by having a nice meal, watching television or a film, chatting, reviewing the show and making improvements for the next one. He needs time and space alone to refuel his mind and body.

Nobody can be 'up' or intensely creative all of the time. There are scientists, inventors, writers who have intense periods of inspiration and will work for days on end with barely a break. They then sometimes appear to be hibernating in periods of inactivity, but this is sometimes needed, as preparation for the next spurt of creativity. Live performers experience brain-chemical processes with endorphins and adrenaline that are not entirely different from those of athletes, and there are natural euphoric highs inevitably followed by relative troughs. These fluctuations can lead to emotional despondency if there are not other support systems within that person's life, which in Garson's case would perhaps bring us to his love for and from his family, but also to his almost childishly enquiring mind and his unbridled passion for the creative process itself. He takes this far too seriously to risk impairing it with drink or drugs. He has, however, many tales to tell of his experiences of witnessing it all around him.

Whilst playing with the band Brethren at the start of the 1970s, the drummer Rick Marotta would blow pot smoke from his joint into Garson's face, out of irritation at his abstinence as the others smoked it. Garson always remembered the disrespect this conveyed. They were on the road together for a year, opening for Traffic, Santana, and Joe Cocker. Marotta went on to great success as a session player for artists including Aretha Franklin, Roberta Flack, Paul Simon, and John Lennon, and he wrote the theme music for the television show *Everybody Loves Raymond*. Years later, they happened to meet at Capitol Studios in Hollywood. Garson was recording several other pianists recording some of his classical compositions. Marotta was so very complimentary about what he heard, and also about Garson's other accomplishments, that it seemed superfluous to hold any anger over his earlier behavior, which was simply a case of people who indulge wanting others to do the same, because they feel their own weakness thrown into relief by the strength (or lack of dependence) of others.

Garson attributes his ability to be comfortable around others who are drinking or taking drugs partly to long practice. At sixteen he shared digs in the Catskills with a heroin addict. Since then, he has helped people come off drugs and has generally been around it a lot. He says that he has no moral objection to it whatsoever, simply that he does not like to see people he loves die (and he has lost a few) or suffer on a constant 'roundabout of rehab.' At the same time, he has the sense to know when to remove himself from an event, if the level of inebriation is getting too uncomfortable.

During his teens, he saw the great Bill Evans performing at the Village Vanguard, a famous jazz club on Seventh Avenue in Lower Manhattan (which is still there). Garson plucked up the courage to introduce himself as an aspiring pianist who loved

Evans's playing, and asked for a lesson. Evans appreciated Garson's sincerity and had him round for six hours, without even charging. They spoke about Garson's teacher, Lennie Tristano, whom Evans also admired (Tristano's influence can be heard on his 1956 album *New Jazz Conceptions*). The only time Evans left the room during this lesson was to inject heroin into his hand, which on his return showed the needle mark and was inflamed. One of his hands was 'so swollen it looked like two hands' to Garson.

Evans's renowned feel and timing appeared to be enhanced by his drugged state, putting him further still behind the beat. In contrast, toward the end of his life he used cocaine, which made him inclined to rush his playing more. But that injection of more heroin, by removing the pain of his previous withdrawal, was merely allowing his natural talent to reassert itself. Garson dismisses the misguided belief that drugs produce creativity, when in fact that creativity is something that is already in the artist, and can be liberated without risking the spiraling dependency and suffering that drugs bring. It is worth noting, for example, that when great tenor saxophonist Sonny Rollins broke his addiction to heroin, he feared it might affect his playing adversely, but he in fact then went on to far greater success. Many musicians have chased that elusive, mythical moment of bliss or inspiration, only to pay the price when the emotional and psychological problems temporarily avoided and hidden by drugs come back to the surface even more painfully.

In addition to the alienation felt by many artists, and their attempt to avoid the post-show comedown, Garson sees a third factor as being peer pressure, especially within an industry in which heroes and idols are seen likewise to indulge. Even being gregarious within such circles becomes a potential risk factor, as camaraderie so often depends on shared excesses. Garson believes that his passion and intensity about things would make him a chronic addict if he ever dabbled, whereas in fact he has often been the butt of resentment from those whose escapism is marred by his tenacious and teetotal hold on reality.

Unlike those many musical artists who seek fame, Garson has never been even slightly motivated by such concerns. He describes fame as the most destabilizing of all drugs. His motivation is to refine his craft, to tap into his musical inspiration, and to teach others, his past students now running into the thousands. And the role of mentor appears to suit him; he shows a genuine interest in the development of those he is charged with nurturing. He has a willingness and relaxed capacity to impart understanding and ideas, which makes him a natural teacher. For some time he has been mentoring Theo Ryan, the young fretless bassist and son of Tim Ryan, who created M-Audio (see pages 184–186). Garson's guidance to this blossoming young talent has been inspirational to Theo, who has learned from Garson's integration of his music with his whole personality, as well as his living and working 'in the moment,' which paradoxically makes his work timeless. He also describes his mentor's urge to help and to heal, telling me that 'in my time knowing him, he has never changed, by always changing.'

It was only as Garson turned twenty, once he was playing in the army band and seeing the audiences' reactions, that he saw clearly that his path was to be that of a musician. From about the age of twelve he had started to play at his school, Lafayette High School, during a regular show they held called *Sing*, and he was starting to be in demand as an accompanist for local productions of shows such as *My Fair Lady* or *West Side Story*. By the time he was twenty-eight, he estimates that he had played for over a thousand singers. It was in those school productions that he first saw and felt the appreciation of an audience, discovering how, as a player, he would have the power to move people through his performances.

In discussing at length our perceptions and feelings about the experience of public performance, Garson and I continued to tackle the question of why addictions of various kinds seem to be disproportionately prevalent amongst performers. Perhaps the primary addiction of any performer is to the response of the audience. When the applause fades, the gap needs plugging. Vast numbers of people are unduly reliant on the approval of others to make them happy, but live performers have a unique opportunity for guaranteed regular boosts to the ego. Without special care, this can lead them to lose the skills of self-validation.

The moment in which the young performer first notices the effect they can have on an audience is very significant. It appeals to the performer's vanity whilst tapping into the core of any insecurity they may already have, forming a potential pact-with-the-devil kind of implicit contract with 'the audience' as a generalized concept. This global audience—the sum of all the listeners, real and notional, that the musician will ever have—can quickly become a source of comfort to the nascent performer. I am certainly acutely aware of the ways in which public performance has affected my own development. It is hard to say whether a given type of personality wants to perform publicly, or whether public performance forms that personality. Perhaps there is a reciprocal relationship between the two. Garson interestingly recalls of his first youthful taste of audience ovation that 'it felt a little dirty to me.'

Acknowledgment and accolades are a healthy part of the social interaction of any performance. But where appreciation crosses into adulation, or the promise and expectation of it, this 'fix' can quickly become one of the most insidious and subtle drugs of all. The musician's work and creative activity, with their instrument (or voice) as the physical tool or channel, becomes entangled with their need for social validation. This may well prove a key point in the explanation of why other addictions so often follow amongst musicians, as this first process inevitably becomes less able in time to satisfy the need for validation or to plug the gap in that individual's emotional life. It is easy quite quickly to become accustomed to the otherwise bizarre experience of having dozens or hundreds or thousands of people clap and shout for you on a regular basis. Then, if there is a period without such gigs, you can miss this, or feel low, and seek other substitutes for that comfort.

The solution Garson suggests to resolve this paradox is the daily practice of gratitude and humility, meditating on the good fortune simply of being able to bring pleasure to people through music. He has managed to avoid an unhealthy dependence on public adulation (and the substance abuse that often follows from that) by making his interest in audience interaction about what inspiration he can offer them, and not what emotional validation they can offer him. Rather than becoming hooked on the applause, he became fascinated by the opportunity to move and inspire his listeners as an end in itself, with a sense of responsibility more commonly associated with a teacher or mentor than with an entertainer. He still enjoys receiving a standing ovation, but he tries to use that to move forward and strengthen his art.

On the subject of addiction generally, there is a woeful lack of effective research, so this is an area deserving of a lot more attention. It blights millions of lives around the world, and yet all of the most commonly touted ways of understanding and dealing with it have proved so far statistically to be a miserable failure. From this point of view, any fresh insight that arises from considering the special relationship of performance to addiction can only be a welcome step.

A defining feature of addiction is ambivalence. Garson once drove Elvin Jones (his 'favorite drummer ever') uptown from Greenwich Village to pick up some heroin. He got back in the car and, 'even whilst he was actually nodding out,' he was lecturing Garson never to use drugs. The ambivalence of the situation is striking, and the conclusion inescapable: no one engaging in these things really wants to be doing so.

So many rock musicians have stated that, as youngsters, they got into playing music for 'the girls,' the lifestyle, the fame, or something similar. Garson had an intense passion for music from an early age that married the intellectual and the emotional. Having passed through the jazz scene, he joined that first tour with Bowie in 1972 as a young married man with a baby, and he remains devoted to his wife and children over forty years later. Many of the leading musicians of that era have long since renounced drink and drugs, but Garson never seemed to need that escape or hedonism even then. In this respect he again appears as an extraneous presence in the field. He has been something of an outsider at each stage, but has had the confidence to be proud of his individualism. In contrast, despite its pretensions otherwise, the appeal of inebriation or recreational drugs, especially within musical circles, has often been part of an attempted socialization driven by the fear of standing apart.

Was Garson a 'Spider from Mars'? Essentially not, despite playing with the band. His role was different. He came into the band in a different way, he came from a different background, and—perhaps most significantly, given the importance of image at that point—his onstage presentation was not visually part of that tableau. Garson's long-term friend and collaborator in France, Jérôme Soligny, jokes in this context that Garson was 'the only one who looked like he actually did come from Mars!'

Specifically through his work with David Bowie, Mike Garson found himself at the epicenter of an international arts scene in the early 1970s that was only tangentially connected at all to the Brooklyn of his youth or the Manhattan jazz scene of his twenties. After that extraordinary night at Hammersmith in July 1973, there were no more public appearances for a few months, but in the autumn Bowie allowed one more semi-public outing for the Ziggy character, when he returned to one of his favorite venues from his earlier years, London's Marquee Club on Wardour Street, for the filming over two days in October 1973 of a heavily choreographed and quite exotic show, *The 1980 Floor Show*. This was broadcast only on American television, as part of the late night NBC TV show *The Midnight Special*, on November 16, 1973. Garson was there on piano, and this show, which prefigured the *Diamond Dogs* album of the following year with its theme taken from George Orwell's *Nineteen Eighty-Four*, was another fascinating and surreal step for the twenty-eight-year-old jazz pianist and music teacher from Brooklyn, taking him worlds away from the jazz-trio work in small clubs that he had been doing just over a year earlier.

There were guest stars: Marianne Faithfull, Amanda Lear, and the Troggs. The audience comprised a couple of hundred invited guests from the newly formed International David Bowie Fan Club and a colorful smattering of celebrity visitors, including songwriter Lionel Bart, acclaimed producer Tony Visconti and his then wife Mary Hopkin, Dana Gillespie, and Wayne County. Writing in *Melody Maker*, Chris Welch described the scene firsthand: "'The Jean Genie" rocked again and the band developed tremendous power. And although the PA equipment was minimal, there was no doubting the authority of David's singing. "We've written a musical," he announced, "and this is the title song called '1984.' We'll be doing the show in March next year." . . . The star, in high spirits, was remarkably patient. For technical reasons, such classics as "Space Oddity" and "The Jean Genie" had to be performed endlessly, often cut short after a few bars.'[1]

Photographer Mick Rock has said, 'Throughout Bowie was very patient, very up. He filled in the intervals between takes rapping with the audience, teasing, laughing. After each song he would disappear immediately, reappearing dramatically on cue for the next one in a new costume.'[2] Garson, meanwhile, who still felt quite bewildered by all of this, can be heard more than doing justice to the songs with the great precision and feel of his playing. In the rendition of the piano part for 'Time,' in particular, he outperformed even his own superb recorded take for the album version a few months earlier. He describes this live take of the song as having been slightly faster, with a tighter feel.

The *Diamond Dogs* Tour, for which rehearsals began in April 1974, would see more of a growth in Garson's contribution. After Michael Kamen left as musical director, the role fell to Garson during the second leg of touring, in which the elaborate staging of the *Diamond Dogs* show was replaced by the stripped-down Soul Tour, previewing the *Young Americans* material. By this stage, Garson had really started to come into his own. He played a key role in the live interpretation of Bowie's songs, as well as leading the seven-piece soul band that both backed Bowie's performance and filled the support slot nightly during the tour of North America from September to December 1974.

Garson's playing styles, though broad and extremely versatile, may not be thought of as immediately pertinent to the soul period in Bowie's evolution. Yet when we listen to, for example, his gospel arrangement on the song 'It's Gonna Be Me' (an outtake from the 1974 Sigma Sound sessions in Philadelphia for the *Young Americans* album that later appeared on various reissues), his soul and gospel credentials are hardly in doubt. He became more relaxed as the 1974 shows unfolded, and the more tightly arranged ensemble this time placed him more in his element.

Garson was working now with, for example, the jazz saxophonist Dave Sanborn, or the funky guitar of Carlos Alomar, to create a fusion in which he could thrive even more than he had a couple of years earlier. For the album *Young Americans*, mainly recorded in Philadelphia late in 1974, Bowie rehearsed the backing vocalists with exhaustive precision for many of the songs, with Garson always on hand. The exceptionally hard-working atmosphere of those sessions is well captured on some fascinating footage taken at the time.[3]

By 1974, Mike Garson was truly starting to mature into a very rounded and versatile musician, with great powers of expression at his fingertips. He felt more at home and more secure. In addition, he now had more experience of being on the road, and had already become one of Bowie's more established group members. Certainly, his piano playing on the *Aladdin Sane* album was both striking and a key part of the sound, but this was still just an exciting splash of unnerving color brilliantly thrown into the mix by Bowie and executed with sparkling assurance by Garson, as something shockingly alien to the rock genre of the music as a whole. On a song like 'Sweet Thing' from *Diamond Dogs*, on the other hand, the interplay had evolved to the point where Garson's piano parts were no longer a separate interlude or musical visitor from outside but had become integral to the structure itself; this is even more obviously the case on, for example, the piano-led 'Rock 'n' Roll with Me.'

In 1981, Garson was booked to play on a television special called *Get High on Yourself*, with various 1970s stars such as Bob Hope and Paul Newman, to encourage young people to say no to drugs. One of the special guests was legendary boxer Muhammad Ali. There was a slightly surreal sing-along about the dangers of drugs, for which Garson was asked to mime on the piano to something that had been pre-recorded by studio musicians, which he found amusing, since he could have played it a lot better than what he was miming to. When filming ended, the huge frame of Ali approached the piano. He was charming as ever as he asked Garson to 'check this out' as he played a blues scale. Garson recalls that it was with a very hard touch and not very well timed, but he did know the blues scale. He gave Garson a big smile and left.

In navigating his career in music without recourse to addictive traps, Garson's assets have included his own sense of humor and his humanity. Touring with him in the 1990s as part of Bowie's band, drummer Zachary Alford sums this up perfectly:

> Mike is . . . a very funny man. He made me laugh so much on those tours with his love of life and his uniquely Brooklynian view of the world. Despite the generation gap between us, we always felt like 'two peas in a pod,' to use his wife Sue's expression. I guess because he was so young at heart and I was a bit of an old soul, we met somewhere in the middle. He has a lot of faith in humanity and the goodness of human nature, but he's not naïve. He's the kind of person who feels mankind's suffering and wants to do his part to make it better.

# 6

## Supporting Their Eating

*'The most inspiring musician I've ever come across.'*

—Trent Reznor, Nine Inch Nails[1]

FROM THE AGES of fourteen to twenty-two, Garson worked every summer in the Catskill Mountains, 110 miles north of Brooklyn and otherwise known as the Borscht Belt. There were hundreds of hotels and bungalow colonies there, and it was a popular summer holiday resort with Jewish families from throughout the East Coast, with lots of live entertainment. Many of the hotels or chalets were far from salubrious, whilst others were quite elaborate or refined.

Garson progressed through the years from playing at the lower-end venues to playing at the highest. The fees accordingly went from $15 a week to $180 a week by his last year, for a six-night week. There were singers, comedians, dance acts, and sometimes even striptease acts for the bands to accompany. He estimates he must have accompanied five hundred singers during these years alone. The range of the singers went from 'horrible' to people like Mel Tormé, 'who was amazing,' and whom the seventeen-year-old Garson was delighted to accompany. Jackie Mason was just one of hundreds of comedians doing shows there in those years, and Garson played for him two or three times. (Coincidentally, I also played for Jackie Mason, at a run of London shows in the mid-1990s.) This period was a real training ground, and he accumulated experience playing dance music and learning hundreds of standards, whilst also developing his skills in improvising and in sight-reading. They also had jazz jam sessions late at night, where the young musicians learned to refine their art. Friendships were sometimes forged that would last a lifetime.

It was during this time that Garson and his school friend, saxophonist Dave Liebman, formed their first band, the Impromptu Quartet. I spoke to Liebman during his week of performances at New York's Birdland jazz club in August 2014, and he captured that moment. 'We were white middle-class Jewish kids from Brooklyn, which was a densely populated Italian and Jewish neighborhood. Nobody even knew the word "jazz" there in those days . . . we went together to see John Coltrane and

Bill Evans and formed the Quartet, we saw ourselves as some kind of budding young jazz musicians.'

A lot of the young jazz players taught or drove taxis to make ends meet, whilst aiming to play as a side-man to one of the great leaders like Coltrane or Miles Davis in order to make their name. Both Garson and Liebman achieved this by playing gigs with Elvin Jones, drummer to Coltrane, and Liebman later played with Miles Davis. When Garson went for lessons with Lennie Tristano, Liebman followed suit. He recalls how, at band gigs, they would call on Garson to play Gershwin's *Rhapsody in Blue* in full, from memory, to get the audience's attention. 'Mike was always a very studious and serious musician, a very hard worker. Classical and jazz . . . he could do anything . . . Mike can play a variety of styles, very expertly—he can switch between a bebop style and a McCoy Tyner style, and he can play pop, obviously, then he can play Chopin and Bach. He is a complete well-rounded musician, and the truth is, most piano players are the best-trained musicians on the bandstand, because they have to be—because the piano has four to five hundred years of history!'

It was whilst working in the Catskills that Garson met his future wife, Susan. She and her friends were in a bungalow colony just a quarter of a mile from the hotel he was in, the Cherry Hill Hotel. She was from Long Island, though the other girls were from Brooklyn, as was Garson. He was playing *Rhapsody in Blue* and a little old lady, who was watching Susan watching him, pointed and said, 'You're going to marry him.' They started going out together, six years later they got married, and they are still happily married some fifty years later. He points out that 'in a place like Los Angeles, even fifty days of marriage is considered a long time!' It has been very important to him to make the effort required to balance the life of a musician with his commitment to his family, never having to sacrifice either. He credits his wife with facilitating his creativity, calling her the 'missing link' in this story as she 'holds the fort and makes it possible for this to happen.'

I ask Susan how their marriage has flourished for so long, despite the pressures of touring, and she replies, 'Mike is my best friend, and we are always rooting for each other . . . ups and downs don't really matter, as we know we will endure as a team. I think the traveling in some ways (not all!) acted as a bonus for me. When we would reunite, it was always with a shared gratitude for having found this person in my life.'

When the offer came for him to work with Bowie, they were struggling financially, though they were 'young and happy.' The financial relief the tours provided did, however, come at a price, as it meant that she 'would be alone with a brand-new baby.' Both sets of grandparents lived quite nearby and provided huge support, which was a lifeline. Her recollection of the changes her husband's new position brought is vibrant and vivid even now: 'We were not even familiar with who David was at that point. But, we found out soon enough. It was a whirlwind. We had a new baby, and our life as we knew it would never be the same. It was a new adventure, and we had no idea which way it would go.'

The only part of the following years that was extremely difficult for her was their moving away from New York—first to England, later to California—because it meant leaving her family and friends behind. In particular, she lost her support system, and was then alone a lot of the time with two children in a strange place. She says that it took her a long time to recover from this. She 'had to make a choice, and I am glad, in retrospect, that I chose to keep my family together and move. But I missed our family and friends in New York. It took a toll on me.' Garson is deeply apologetic to her over this. If her love for him needed any further confirmation, she adds that her 'only regret, after almost fifty years, is that my marriage will never, ever be long enough for me.'

In the autumn of 1972, Susan and their daughter Jennifer joined the Bowie tour at various locations, including a stay at the Beverly Hills Hotel. 'That was fantastic. It seemed unreal at times. But what fun and luxury we got to experience.' They were staying in one of the hotel's bungalows. Baby Jennifer crawled into the neighboring bungalow, which happened to be occupied by none other than Perry Como, and proffered him in her little hand a cassette tape of her daddy's music.

In later years, Susan worked in the music industry herself, managing jazz stars Chick Corea, Billy Childs, and the band Fattburger, as well as Garson himself. As for Garson's own music, she has seen it steadily improve. She says that he works as hard at it now as he did in his teens when they first met, never resting on his past accomplishments. She sees a maturity emerging in his compositions in recent years, and more warmth. She says that he has also mellowed as a man over the years. Whereas in his younger days he could be more self-absorbed or at least self-involved, he is now more giving to those around him. He has become 'better as a husband, father, and grandfather.' She says that his priorities in life are always family, followed by music and then 'changing lives and healing.'

Garson has many fond and amusing memories from those early gigs. There was a one-off gig in one of the bungalow colonies in the Catskills. These were amongst the lower end of accommodation there, in stark contrast to some of the swankier hotels, such as the Grossingers or the Concord, which he had also enjoyed playing at. A far cry from the bungalows of the Beverly Hills Hotel a few years later, this was 'no better than a mess-hall or dorm' with just an old upright piano, which was out of tune.

Dave Liebman was on sax, Bob Moses on drums, Larry Coryell on guitar, all in their youth then but big jazz names since; and they were mischievous. Garson hated the grind of playing to 'people who were eating, maybe dancing or wandering around, but not really there for the music.' He now characterizes the live music performance at this kind of gig as 'supporting their eating,' rather than playing for people to actually listen to and appreciate the music in itself. Trying to relieve the boredom of the gig, Garson ended up playing with a yo-yo (all the tricks, 'around the world' and so on) with his right hand, whilst continuing to hold down the beat on the piano with his left hand—quite a feat of coordination.

I cannot claim ever to have operated a yo-yo whilst playing, but I do recall sharing Garson's frustration at playing for diners, and I do have one recollection of that kind of my own. I was playing in the 1990s at the Joe Allen restaurant in London and was spotted by the manager, Russell Norman (now a well-known restaurateur himself), trying discreetly to hold a mobile phone to my ear with my left hand whilst continuing to play with my right hand. And this was solo piano, so there was no band to fill in the sound. I had to work extra hard with my right hand so as not to let the diners notice what was happening. Norman was more impressed than put out by this, especially since he noticed that I was talking in French to my French girlfriend at the time. For him, that was the icing on the cake, and he said, 'If you can play, use your phone, and chat in a foreign language all at once, then all I can say is, "Well done!"'

Garson once played at a wedding with his long-term friend, the great drummer Billy Mintz. He hated doing this, sometimes playing six hours straight with just five minutes off each hour, having to carry on playing solo piano even when the rest of the band took a break, but it was a way to earn some money. On this occasion he was playing the bass line on a little Farfisa organ, with Mintz on drums squeezed right beside him. The singer/bandleader always wanted to separate them, as they would mess about. This time, he turned mid-song to see Garson's left hand 'playing' the organ bass line up Mintz's arms and down his legs, whilst Mintz tried not to be distracted and to carry on playing. The singer never booked them again, but it must have made a good comedy routine for anyone who noticed it.

These comic moments from his teens are fond memories. The years since are replete with musical gravitas and accomplishment through which he has earned his place in the fabric of modern culture. He does, however, tell numerous anecdotes of the more bizarre side of his life as a musician through later years, too. There was the time he was asked whether he would play his introduction to 'Lady Grinning Soul' for (what else?) a commercial for eggs. In ten minutes, he earned $1,000, which would normally have taken him twenty long nights of jazz gigs to earn. It often seemed that the perverse priorities of commerce rewarded his least creative or artistic endeavors the most, and vice versa.

On another occasion, in 1981, he was asked to cover a recording session for keyboardist David Foster, who would later go on to produce for Christina Aguilera, the Bee Gees, Mariah Carey, Janet Jackson, Michael Jackson, Prince, and many others. It was for a commercial going out in China to hundreds of millions of people the next day. The producer insisted on every note being separately programmed; they spent nearly twelve hours to produce less than half a minute, but the very next day it was broadcast in China.

May 1974 saw the release of David Bowie's *Diamond Dogs*, with Garson's piano a key feature on several tracks. Many Bowie fans have an especially enthusiastic liking for the album, which combines an eerie take on musical theater with a dark and delicate beauty, particularly on 'Sweet Thing / Candidate / Sweet Thing (Reprise),' with its interplay between Bowie's soaring vocals and Garson's sweeping piano runs.

Garson looks back now on that whole period with a kind of retrospective fascination, enjoying it more now, with hindsight. 'I'm starting to appreciate my life from thirty years ago, thirty years too late! I thought Bowie was great, I thought his bands were great, but to me, it was just like, "I'm playing the best I can for the guy," but I'd be on the stage daydreaming about playing in a jazz club for fifty people!'

He is now appalled at the way he worked through many stadium-scale gigs feeling that he was doing this as a paid job but that he would rather be playing jazz, wishing he was somewhere else. He had a sudden epiphany finally on one occasion in 1995, in which he looked out at the audience and realized how many people he was reaching, how this was musical expression combined with the unique opportunity to communicate. He saw that until then he was 'being this stupid, ridiculous jazz elitist asshole that had something better to do somewhere else. I can't tell you how many gigs that I wasn't a "happy camper" . . . that's showing lack of gratitude!'

He has since worked out that the reason for this frustration was that he did not have as much to do at, for example, a Bowie show, compared with a jazz concert. In a two-hour show he had maybe ten minutes of intensity, whereas with a jazz trio he felt more engaged and stretched for longer periods. 'Bring Me the Disco King' was the longest piano part for him on a live Bowie song, but that did not come until 2003. However, he now sees that being part of the band helping to create one of those two-hour Bowie shows was a collective expression, and therefore the waits of twenty minutes to be called on to solo or play an especially intricate or demanding piano part were also part of the overall performance.

On the question of musicians playing in environments that are not primarily about the music, such as lengthy background gigs in restaurants, clubs, or hotels, Garson has a keen memory for the detail of what he went through for several years, before his profile was raised by the association with Bowie. He estimates he must have played well in excess of a thousand gigs, all badly paid at between $50 and $150. 'They're eating, I'm playing . . . they want you to be a machine.' He felt that 90 percent of what he was doing, musically, he hated. He vowed to turn that around so that he would 'love 90 percent of the gigs and only hate 10 percent.' This is what he did achieve and has enjoyed now for many years.

He made a decision—and, significantly, this was shortly before he got that call from Bowie's manager—that he would no longer play whilst people were eating, that they would have to 'come, pay, see me play . . . even if that sounds a little harsh.' He vowed that as far as audiences were concerned, in bars or clubs, 'they were going to watch me instead of me watching them . . . I was setting the record straight that I'm not there to support their eating, I'm there to perform and raise their aesthetic and spiritual level, with a tinge of entertainment.'

He started to get his first taste of this process whilst playing in the army band in his early twenties. People started to put their knives and forks down, so to speak, and he started to realize the effect he could really have on an audience. We have seen how musicians can be spurred on by enjoying the adulation of the audience, even to the point of addiction to it. Garson, however, is very specific about which aspect of the audience reaction always fired him on the most, and that is the idea of inspiring people.

A further role he is often happy to play is the cathartic one of facilitating the release of emotions that may have been repressed. He has moved many a tear, whether of joy, regret, or loss, through the power of his music on audiences, and he sees this therapeutic function as also being one of his responsibilities as a musician. After the release of such pent-up emotions through the gateway of musical communication, people actually feel physically better, due to chemical processes in the brain being stimulated by the relief of shedding the burden of old emotional processes.[2] The level of seriousness with which he approaches his vocation almost elevates the job of entertainer into a civic duty. He may have given up the idea of becoming a rabbi in his early teens, but he did not give up the idea of playing a pastoral and caring role within the community.

Garson is happy with one major realization of recent years. Despite gaining the adulation of audiences since his youth, he remained for most of his life preoccupied with the process of getting things right, tightening up his performance and attaining technical and even expressive virtuosity, whereas all along the really important thing was the forming of an emotional bond with these audience members. What matters is the beneficial effect on people of this special form of communication, and for him this now transcends the technical. As part of this, he also realizes that his own joy in playing is paramount. It is as if he only now, retrospectively, sees fully what an ecstatic and central part of these past fifty years has been occupied by those spine-tingling moments of live performance where something really happens between player and audience, and everything else is there to facilitate such moments. Even his solitary practice sessions of several hours bring him joy, provided he knows there will also be concerts to play.

Garson recalls times when he has held back from dazzling as much as he knew he could, for fear of outshining others, but now sees this as a kind of false humility:

> You don't want to make others feel bad, so you actually hold back. I think there is also something psychotic and irrational about it, but I could see why I had done it, I've talked to other people who'd done it, and you also said you had an experience like that . . . it's actually committing a sin on yourself, or transgression, because I think people want the best of who you are, and when you're playing at your greatest it's like the Olympics. Someone wins this gold thing: if he's not egocentric, it's everybody's win, and it's a patriotic thing for a whole country or a planet. It shows the best of mankind. Someone who's a Chopin or a Bach or a Bowie or a John Lennon, or Dylan or Mozart or Duke Ellington or Louis Armstrong—I'm not trying to take away from any of those people's genius, but they are a representation of what's best in us, in humankind . . .

By reaching for the highest achievement possible, you lift other people up with you, and it becomes a collective experience. And, in any case, it is only rarely that others would genuinely be hurt by being outshone, so it is a false fear that holds us back.

One specific example of this occurred at a surprise performance by Garson in the early 1990s. He was at Catalina Bar and Grill in Hollywood on August 23, 1991, enjoying a Caesar salad and looking forward to hearing a jazz trio featuring Michel Petrucciani (who had brittle bone disease), whom Garson explains 'would be carried in, he was a diminutive French jazz pianist, very, very short and would even have a special extension to the pedals, and a high seat . . . although, his hands, disproportionately, were full size! He was a great bebop player.' On that occasion, Petrucciani's flight into Los Angeles was delayed, and Garson was spotted and pressed into service mid-salad, asked to step up and entertain the audience until Petrucciani arrived.

Garson knew that, unlike most of his fellow jazz musicians, he tended to seduce audiences with showmanship as well as technical brio. It was perhaps no coincidence that he was once cast as the hands of Liberace in a biopic of that dazzling pianist (a full account of which appears in chapter 8, 'From Lulu to Liberace'). Anxious that this was not his gig, he looked for a way to acquit himself well and yet not make this his show. He says he filtered his performance through an imaginary 'compressor' or limiter, and stopped himself at a certain point when he was going into his 'magic zone.' Petrucciani finally arrived and played the second half of the show, and the reviews were equally good for them both, so that Garson achieved his aim. However, he now feels strongly that the zenith of excellence in art should constantly be challenged and stretched, under all circumstances. There is no ceiling. You must challenge yourself at all times, for your sake as well as that of the audience:

> Because people should experience the fact that you can play at your greatest and this can make them inspired to think there's something in them that is that great too, be it as a journalist, a poet, a singer, composer, any other role or job, at the maximum ability you have. Your comparison should not be another musician, but it should be yourself . . . nobody could play better Oscar Peterson than Oscar Peterson, and no one can write better Chopin than Chopin, and no one can write better Mozart than Mozart, and no one can be a better Bowie, no matter how many imitators there are, than Bowie . . . So, you may as well be the best you can be, because certainly you can only be second or third or fourth best to anyone who's your idol. But you can use them for inspiration.

The night before our first discussions, in the summer of 2009, Garson had played a jazz trio concert in Los Angeles with Joe LaBarbera, who was Bill Evans's last drummer. Garson observes that every jazz pianist would love to play with LaBarbera, as he can play softly with brushes, or step up and be exciting, and develops an almost telepathic rapport with other musicians. He speaks with reverential respect for this 'conversation' between the fellow interpreters in a trio: 'There's something magical about three, and the whole is certainly greater than the sum of its parts.' It does not remain a 'straight-ahead' jazz trio throughout, however, as Garson often experiments with the addition of a synthesizer on top of his grand piano, improvising on it, for example, during an extended jam of Miles Davis's 'All Blues':

> There's a certain abandonment that I have when I play it. I sort of throw away all my touch and technique and become a different player because, you know,

I'm using the three wheels on the synthesizer as well as the little strip to modulate tone, and we have these three wheels which each do different things, sometimes I don't even know what they're going to do . . . but I like the freedom that it allows me. It's almost like, 'Throw it all away!' take off your clothes, and just like, 'Go for it!' It was fun for me, and I get a good response from the audience when I play the synths actually.

Once inspiration strikes, he feels himself to be an avenue through which the music can flow, and at such times is resistant to over-direction from producers or directors. His friend, the award-winning Argentinian film composer Emilio Kauderer, refers to this phenomenon as 'the cable company.' Garson is humble in this sense about his own individual role, referring to such a flow as 'a synonym for consciousness or universal energy or God . . . so, the "cable company" sends these notes down, let's say—it's coming down the stream, coming down the pipe. Now, someone comes over to me as the flow's coming and says, "Can you do this, make that chord an F-sharp, can you play it slow, can you play it like Trent Reznor, can you sound like Oscar Peterson here?" They cut the flow from the "cable," they're interrupting the message!'

Garson often uses this 'cable company' metaphor to refer to the process of connecting to the ineffable flow of musical inspiration. Jay Landesman (1919–2011) coined a similar phrase for his efforts to advance cultural expression in St Louis in the Southern States in the 1950s and beyond: the Cultural Conduit. Landesman and I produced a series of live music nights together in London in 2006 under that title, and he called his biographical memoir *Tales of a Cultural Conduit*.[3]

The inspiration of Garson's 'cable company' is his way of joining the stream of cultural creativity. Kauderer first went to Garson for a jazz piano lesson. It turned, typically, into a six-hour meeting, which, he says, 'marked the future of my career in an invaluable way.' He found Garson to be 'an inspirational force.' In much the same way, my own first visit to Bell Canyon for a lesson from Garson led to my writing this book, which was the second time he had inspired a new direction for me (the first being my own career as a pianist, for which the seeds were sown by hearing him play in 1973).

These days, when playing with his jazz trios, the warm smile of satisfaction spreads from time to time over Garson's face, and not just when he is himself playing—it happens equally when one of the others is soloing and he hears that same flow inhabiting one of his bass players or drummers, since for him there is no separation between the individuals involved, once this process of group creativity begins.

In contrast, when he is over-directed against the flow of what feels instinctively right, his playing suffers badly.

In the early 1990s, he was hired by a very well-known producer. On this occasion Garson was literally instructed to 'do a solo like those on *Aladdin Sane*.' This was inappropriate for the type of song—it did not make sense at all—and he felt like he was 'dying inside' as his 'cable company' flow was not only interrupted, 'it exploded!' Failing to understand the moment in time that was represented by those original recordings of 1973–1974, such production values are anathema to true creativity. By saying 'just stick one of those on here!' as if they were repapering the walls of a house, or perversely splashing some older paint onto a new building, such producers show a disregard for their own creative process in the present, as well as for the earlier process that they are attempting to pillage.

Garson continued to play this studio session, however, and is once again amusing in describing the outcome:

> So, like an idiot—I'm trying to be a nice guy, and I'm playing these styles over this ballad. Each track was more obnoxious than the other—I hated my playing, because it was so wrong, but I was being paid as a studio musician. This goes on for two hours . . . we didn't get any of it, so we sit down, I sit down at the piano, and the producer's talking to me—every bar he stopped me and told me what to play. Every bar—it had about ninety bars, so we stopped about ninety times, every two or three seconds. 'Play this little triad here, play less there.' This is a nightmare, right? We ended up with a track. I was ready to throw up and never play the piano again. [*Laughs*.] We ended up with this piano part; it sounded okay. I might have even played it myself in the first place if they had shut up, and not said a word! And I, out of the side of my mouth said, 'You know, that sounds like Nicky Hopkins.' You know what the producer said? 'Oh! That's the guy I meant to hire! He played with the Rolling Stones? . . . You played with Bowie? I had your names confused!' . . . And I had, during the session, found Nicky's way of playing, because Nicky, when he was alive, was a student of mine.

Hopkins had wanted to find out more about jazz, and wanted to get into composing for film, so came to Garson—who, in turn, loved Hopkins's style of pop playing on great songs like 'Angie' by the Rolling Stones, for example. He says he could never have played perfect pop like Hopkins himself as that was not him, but he ended up that day doing 'second-rate Nicky' under such duress, and they were happy with it.

Sadly, Garson never got the chance to tell Nicky Hopkins this story, as Hopkins died soon after, in 1994. Coincidentally, during work on this book I played piano on a song for a Marc Almond EP ('Love Is Not on Trial' on *Tasmanian Tiger*, Cherry Red Records, 2014), which was also worked on by Tony Visconti, who kindly wrote, 'I really loved your piano. Reminded me of Nicky Hopkins and Leon Russell.'

Garson recalls a week around the same time rehearsing in Tunbridge Wells with Jeff Beck for some concerts with Stanley Clarke at which Beck guested, at the North Sea Jazz Festival. There is footage viewable online of this, in which Garson can be seen lending his support on keyboards, in a very different genre once again from either the 1972–1974 work with Bowie or his jazz-trio work. This was real jazz-fusion, and although he says that in retrospect it is not for him the most strongly felt style, being more about technical performance than soul or passion, nevertheless you can see and hear that he was accessing his own reserves of creativity. Beck had also made a guest appearance and traded solos with Ronson on the last *Ziggy Stardust* show at Hammersmith, playing on 'The Jean Genie'/'Love Me Do' and Chuck Berry's 'Around and Around,' so this was not the first time Garson had played with him.

This adaptability is needed for the many sessions Garson performs now, which are often organized at long distance. Whilst I am there, he receives a request from a rock band to play (yet again) 'some *Aladdin Sane*–style piano' on one of their tracks. His description of part of this process gives an insight into his working methods and attention to detail.

> I put on their track, set up the computer and I push 'RECORD'—this was about three hours ago—first take. I saw their chord chart but it was wrongly written out, so I ignored it and played by ear. Now, tonight or tomorrow, after editing, cleaning it up, making sure the time is lined—because I just went 'off the cuff,' so I got it in one take, but it means now it needs refinement—then the re-recording of it. I recorded it on a sample piano. Now, I will record on a real piano. I have the MIDI data so the piano will play itself. I have a whole process to get it to sound right.

Garson's recording studio, which adjoins his home in California, has a slight natural reverb due to its hard surfaces and high ceiling. He uses a Disklavier player-piano for playback, whereby he can watch what he has played and recorded as if it were physically being played again, as the Disklavier keys actually move up and down to perform the playback. The special beauty of this setup is that once he is happy with the MIDI recording, which he has worked on digitally, the final recording is made using a nine-foot grand piano, which is a 'real' piano as well as a Disklavier, so that the final audio sound file boasts the unique resonance of real hammers hitting real strings.

He estimates that he has recorded parts in this way for over two hundred artists over the past five years, including many who are already dedicated fans of the work he did with Bowie or with others, and often openly request something in the style or spirit of particular tracks on which he has played in the past. He does, however, always make a point of trying to give these clients something new of himself, rather than simply to regenerate the stylings or solos of earlier years. He often seems to understand better than they do what they really want. They may not always see this until the work is done, but he has found that by being himself and trusting his own instincts in interpreting their instructions, they are rarely disappointed.

The most important element of Garson's approach to his music—and even to life—is not to 'get in your own way.' For him, it is all about flow. As soon as he is thinking about the process he is in—even though he will still very likely deliver a great performance, or one that is more than competent—his heart will not be in it, and he will not be producing his best work. What we aspire to as creative artists is to avoid that self-consciousness, that introspection, which becomes an obstacle to true creativity. This is a paradox, because we also benefit in life in general from an awareness of ourselves and the situation we are in. Perhaps the moment of creativity and inspiration is the moment in which that otherwise healthy self-awareness takes a step back. This letting go of ego, whilst remaining present and aware, is key to Garson's outlook. One of his compositions is called 'Getting Out of Your Own Way.'

A sometimes-vacant expression whilst playing can be a reflection of just such a moment, of getting 'lost in the music.' Everyone has experienced this phenomenon in their daily lives. When you are engaged in something that totally absorbs you, time passes in an instant, because the activity takes you over. What was work or obligation then comes to transcend the petty transactions of time, commerce, or duty. By apparently disengaging the brain, or at least the cognitive part, 'looking out of the window,' fully relaxing and yet continuing to perform, it is amazing how much musical memory can be accessed—even of songs that you did not think you knew at all. It is as if, by relaxing, by disengaging the part of the brain that actually tries to recall details, this information floats back into use naturally. For Garson, this disengagement from active thinking is a spiritual matter, and of great importance to him as a musician.

What is the nature of that additional element in emotional musical expression that lies beyond rhythm, melody, and harmony? By using subtle mathematical combinations of sounds, with their myriad permutations of pitch, timbre, duration, tempo, and beat, we generate an emotional meaning—a feeling that is greater than the sum of these parts. Garson believes that one of the first steps toward learning to play at a higher level is to have the humility to 'unlearn' and 'unknow' everything that is getting in the way of that true inspiration. This is the point at which a deeper learning begins.

If we think of music as simply another form of communication with its own linguistic tools, we can acknowledge that, just as it would be misguided and offensive to suggest that someone with a limited vocabulary or one different from our own might therefore have nothing of value to say to us, so in the same way it is foolish for musical snobs of any genre to discount the creativity of those who use a different idiom or linguistic code. Some musicians may lack certain techniques, and yet their 'intention'—their purpose, heart, and passion—is just as valid.

Garson grew up in the 1950s, when it was respected to be a virtuoso, and his determination made him one, too. It was the tail end of the period of classical piano virtuosos that had peaked around the early-to-mid twentieth century, with masters of the keyboard like Vladimir Horowitz (1903–1989), Josef Hofmann (1876–1957), or Arthur Rubinstein (1887–1982), all of whom, as Garson says in his Brooklyn vernacular (a highly expressive linguistic code), 'just tore up the piano!' with their dazzling skills.

Today, it is possible to bypass some of the special skills previously required even to create and present original music. Change in recent years has been more and more rapid in this direction. The cost of a professional standard recording setup (even the need for a studio has been reduced, hence the arrival of this term) has been slashed again and again in recent years, thanks to rapidly advancing technology. Now, for a few thousand pounds or dollars, or even a few hundred, people can make and record music at home to a standard that, whilst not by any means as exacting as would be achieved in a fully financed industry project, nevertheless is presentable. This is having a huge effect on people's relationship with the creative process, as well as their understanding of music as a whole.

That tradition of cultivating pianistic virtuosity, typified by Horowitz or Rubinstein in the mid-twentieth century, is in decline now, at least in the West. 'It has been picked up by many Asian pianists,' Garson observes. 'There's a lot of phenomenal machine-like pianists these days, though only a very small percentage have the magic. They adopted the overview of Western music; they missed some of the essence, but there's amazing discipline, and now some are actually getting the feel too.'[4]

But moments of true inspiration within musical performance are precious and rare. In any hour of live music, in any collection of songs on a recording, what percentage really will leave a person with that spine-tingling reaction of wonder? In one of his jazz concerts lasting two hours, Garson estimates that on most occasions only about fifteen minutes at most reach that memorable peak. He recalls when he was seventeen years old, having heard Rubinstein play the Waldstein Sonata and been so affected by it that he could not stop speaking about it. Yet even then it was the Third Movement that grabbed him; he barely remembered the rest of the program. In that Third Movement something special happened for him, even with Rubinstein's tiny slips or blemishes, which Garson noticed and enjoyed, because this was part of its special expression. Years later, Rubinstein's son heard Garson play and said, 'You know, you play really well. You remind me a little bit of my dad,' which was the ultimate accolade for Garson, who says he was 'struck dead.'

Garson recommends Rubinstein's two-volume memoirs,[5] mentioning that Rubinstein was a bit of a playboy in his early years, 'so he really wasn't taking care of business.' In corroboration of this, Rubinstein has been quoted as saying (pre-dating top footballer George Best's famous statement many years later that 'I spent 90 percent of my money on women and drink. The rest I wasted'), 'It is said of me that when I was young I divided my time impartially among wine, women, and song. I deny this categorically. Ninety percent of my interests were women.'[6]

So all of the technical preparation—what Garson refers to as the 'hard work of chops, and scales'—is only a means to the end of moving the audience emotionally and 'communicating love.' When that happens, he says, 'I've done my job.'

Garson recalls one moving experience from the mid-1990s that has often motivated him since. Since the age of about twelve, he had always loved playing that 'war horse' of classical repertoire, Rachmaninoff's Prelude in C-sharp Minor. On this occasion, he heard a particularly perfect and moving performance of a Rachmaninoff concerto, so expertly played and conducted that, unusually, it left him feeling inadequate and dissatisfied with his own work and accomplishments. He felt 'small' as he reflected on the 'little notes' he plays in rock and jazz; that much of it meant nothing compared with the complexity and genius he was listening to. He says he felt in that moment more depressed than at any other time, because he was allowing himself 'the biggest mistake which any artist can ever make, which is comparison.' He spent a couple of hours contemplating giving up playing. But then he happened to pass by his Disklavier, which he kept permanently in record mode to capture any inspired improvisations. In the next thirteen minutes he played and thus composed instantaneously his own Sonata Number 3 in G Minor. It is undeniably a masterpiece of modern classical composition on every level, quite breathtakingly so. This turned things around for him, as it occurred to him that this level of instantaneous composition would be something Rachmaninoff himself may not have been able to do. It reminded him of his own powers, that everyone has their own strengths and weaknesses, and that we must each keep doing what we do best, working on ourselves without comparison to others' achievements.

In a lighter-hearted parallel recollection to that epiphany, he tells another Rachmaninoff-related story. He was employed in the 1980s and 1990s by Yamaha to record hundreds of the floppy disks they sold for use with their Disklavier. These would generate a re-creation of his performance in which the keys and pedals would move up and down and real hammers would hit the real strings, as a fully detailed virtual 'memory' of what had been played. They also converted some 1930s recordings that had been discovered, which had been played by Rachmaninoff himself on the player-piano predecessor of the Disklavier. As a practical joke, he set one of these performances by the great Russian composer and pianist to run, and hid behind the door. Susan, who was not aware of this new technology he was using, heard her husband's grand piano being played beautifully and entered the room only to find the keys moving up and down and nobody in sight. She was speechless, as it seemed the ghost of Sergei Rachmaninoff had come to modern California to play for them. They laughed long and hard when Garson stepped out.

# 7

# Breaking Down Barriers

*'What can Mikey do? He can go from classical jazz and then sit down and play raucous barrelhouse piano like a real guy—he's not faking it! That's a rare bird. I don't really know anyone on this planet that I've sat in a room with, or even listened to for that matter, who can do what he does, the way that he does it.'*

—Earl Slick

GARSON IS WELL KNOWN for the diversity of the styles in which he performs. Once he is in any kind of live concert or recording, he works 'in the moment' and he does his best to deliver the best he can within that genre of music. The hardest point for him is the changeover from one genre to another. It is those transitions that he says he finds the most challenging. On one occasion he had been commissioned to rewrite and arrange some of the works of Duke Ellington for a string quartet and opera singer, as well as a jazz sextet and jazz singer, at the Kennedy Center in Washington, D.C. Two days later, he was performing rock music with Trent Reznor and Nine Inch Nails at the Wiltern in Los Angeles. Once in either situation he was fine, but the switch whilst traveling (literally and metaphorically) between them was horrendous. This is no doubt because the policy of living in the moment, whilst providing the best system for authentic performance within each situation, does not provide for the journey between them, which in this sense is not a real moment. The story also illustrates, however, just how diverse his work is.

Bowie once described Garson as the best rock pianist in the world, 'because he doesn't play rock.' This statement was followed within months by Garson's inclusion in *Melody Maker*'s list of the top pop pianists of the world, alongside Elton John and Stevie Wonder. This paradox still defines Garson's music. He works across the artificial musical boundaries around which others tiptoe. He happily confesses to a lack of familiarity with rock music and even the Bowie repertoire, telling me, 'You know the Bowie stuff better than me; it's not the music that resonates with me—I mean, he has some songs that changed my life, in terms of how great they are. But I live in the world of classical jazz, and I think that's what he loved about me.'

Garson recalls Bowie's advice to him, when he was working with Nine Inch Nails, not to 'play rock' but to do his own thing:

> I listened to that and respected it, because I'm really not a rock pianist. I'd say you're a rock pianist, with jazz flavorings, but I think you, literally, live in that world and come from that world. I came from a classical tradition—very classical—for many years with Juilliard teachers and everything, and then jazz was a puzzle for me that I wanted to de-codify and demystify, and I did it because people said 'you can't play jazz' and I wanted to prove them wrong, and show that it can be figured out. Everybody said 'you can't study it—if you can't feel it, forget it,' because I didn't feel it, I had bad rhythm, and I didn't know the vocabulary . . . so, I found all these great teachers, had a great ear, had perfect pitch, I took the solos down, I notated . . .

This raises important questions about the nature of jazz. If Garson was able to 'de-codify' the genre using his musical intelligence and classical training to reach the accomplishment and acclaim that he has in the world of jazz, this must make us question the arcane mystery that so many jazz players claim for their craft. It also suggests that, to some degree, feeling can be learned or acquired.

Most of Garson's life has been dedicated to pursuing his musical path without allowing artificial obstacles to impede him. And amongst the most significant obstacles have been the boundaries that are set up between various musical genres. Garson is extremely versatile and adaptable in his playing. He 'lives between the cracks' and does not fit neatly into any of the categories of music, whether jazz, pop, or classical. He could be a great pianist in any one of those specific genres, along with rock or fusion, but says he would hate such limitation. As long as he can simply play what he feels in any moment, he is content.

It is interesting that when the composer Gunther Schuller coined the term 'Third Stream' in 1957 to designate music, often improvised, that was neither jazz nor classical but a new genre halfway between them, he found that the most strenuous objections came from jazz musicians who saw this as an 'assault on their traditions,' even though the classical world has a far longer heritage to protect.[1]

This building of closed orthodoxies, with egotism and one-upmanship in place of the freedom and collective openness of true creativity, has been a sorry feature of many areas of human endeavor. In religion and political systems, as well as in music, codes are set up in order to exclude those without access to their mysteries. This in turn stems from insecurity within people, seeking solace in belonging to a superior inner circle. Garson observes that 'ultimately, they have to mature from that—it's a spiritual evolution where you have to grow out of that.'

It is an important fact that throughout the majority of human history and pre-history, in hunter-gatherer societies, there was no permanent delineation between performer and audience. Singing and dancing were simply a collective activity in which everyone took part. It is possible that individual performances were judged or appraised as such, but all sang or danced. It is only in the past few hundred years (very recently, in terms of the lifespan of *Homo sapiens*) that we have created this artificial wall, dividing performer from audience.

In playing on such a variety of recordings, it has been necessary for Garson to be something of a chameleon, and he is happy with the moniker. He knows how to absorb the style of the musicians around him in order to contribute to that sound, whilst at the same time retaining that part of his own style that is unique and distinctive to him. If you listen, for example, to his playing on 1975's *Young Americans* album by David Bowie, it is far simpler and less elaborate than the rococo embellishments of songs like 'Lady Grinning Soul' and less harshly percussive than songs like 'Watch That Man,' both from *Aladdin Sane*, released two years before. He had to allow space for his playing to be shaped by the new direction in which Bowie was moving. On the *Young Americans* album, the ornamentation with which Garson had adorned *Aladdin Sane* fell to Dave Sanborn's distinctive saxophone, leaving Garson to sit sensitively and gently in the groove, adding rhythmic depth with soul and subtlety.

After Bowie's retirement of Ziggy Stardust in July 1973, Garson had gone to record the *Pin Ups* album with him at the Château d'Hérouville in France. Elton John had recorded there—it had provided the title of his *Honky Chateau* album of 1972. Mick Ronson and Trevor Bolder were still on board, for the last time, on this album, though Woody Woodmansey was replaced on drums by Aynsley Dunbar.

The piano performances on *Aladdin Sane* had set the bar high for Garson. The style of the next album was very different, though, as it was Bowie's affectionate homage to the songs he grew up with and loved in 1960s London. This time, Garson's jazz sensibility is reined in, in favor of his gritty and brittle rock style, combining percussive and splintered piano cascades with serried rows of hard chords containing sparse, harsh internal intervals such as fourths and fifths.

One *Pin Ups* song on which Garson's piano especially stands out is Syd Barrett's 'See Emily Play.' The song was given a new take on its psychedelic origins through heavy use of the same distinctive piano style that marked the title track of the previous album. It ends with an instrumental *mêlée* led by Garson's piano. This long play-out starts with Garson quoting Strauss's 'Also Sprach Zarathustra,' which had been used by Stanley Kubrick as the opening music for his 1968 film *2001: A Space Odyssey*—a film that in turn had given Bowie the title for his 1969 song 'Space Oddity.' The alarming storm of conflicting voices proceeds through an agitated dialogue between piano and violin, and ends with a beautiful string quartet (arranged by Mick Ronson) of J. S. Bach's Partita No. 3 in E.

During the *Ziggy Stardust* Tour of 1972–1973, Garson had moved with Susan and his daughter Jennifer to England, as that was where the rest of the band were based. They shared a house in Sussex with Mick 'Woody' Woodmansey and his wife, June. Trevor and Ann Bolder also lived nearby. In 1974, when Susan became pregnant with Heather, and Bowie embarked on his US *Diamond Dogs* Tour, they moved back to Long Island, New York, and then in 1978 on to California, where they have remained since.

Garson has a collection of recordings showing his playing styles at various times in his life, from his teens in the Catskills, through his army band days in his late teens and early twenties, into his early band work with Brethren and various jazz collaborations. There are recordings on an acetate of him playing a version of 'Quiet Village' by Martin Denny, and 'It Ain't Necessarily So' by Gershwin, from *Porgy and Bess*, when he was only about fourteen. These are in the safe keeping of his lifelong friend, saxophonist Dave Liebman. His musical style was slowly evolving in his teens, with less craft or depth than he was to acquire later and yet, like the photo we stumble across or the younger speaking voice we hear on an old tape of someone, it carries all the same essential elements. The essence of the person is there to be heard in these recordings.

The two childhood friends followed quite different paths over the years, and it is possible to discern an enduring competitive edge to their friendship. Liebman always remained something of a jazz purist, and for him jazz music is in part an intellectual challenge: 'We all strove to get better, because this music is a difficult music, and you've got to learn it.' Garson recalls that when he began touring with Bowie, Liebman taunted him for 'selling out' rather than remaining true to their shared jazz roots. Liebman went on to play with Miles Davis and remained rather elitist regarding Garson's role in the rock world. Conversely, these new rock or pop colleagues of his saw him as harder to relate to, as he was a 'jazzer.' So Garson knows better than most just what a negative impact can come from these boundaries around genres.

Liebman came with his daughter to see Garson playing with Bowie on the *Reality* Tour in 2003, when they played Pennsylvania, near Liebman's home in the Pocono Mountains. She subsequently persuaded her father to have a good listen to 1973's

*Aladdin Sane* album, and Liebman wrote to Garson praising it, commenting that he enjoyed recognizing, in the title track's solo, fragments of various pieces from their youth that Garson had referenced such as 'Tequila,' some Gershwin, and others.

The doubts that had earlier been voiced by Liebman about the validity of crossing from jazz to pop and back have been a recurrent theme of contention in Garson's life, so I made a point of discussing this in detail with the acclaimed saxophonist and jazz expert eleven years on from his visit to the *Reality* Tour, with interesting results. What emerges is the self-perception of jazz as a kernel of intellectual integrity, whereas Garson has found that the soulful feeling inherent in expressive music is at least as compelling in other genres.

Liebman starts by explaining that when he and Garson were in their impressionable teens in the 1960s, people might listen to Bartók, Coltrane, and Jimi Hendrix all in the same day. Theirs was the first truly eclectic generation because it was becoming possible to hear every genre of music from all around the world more easily. In addition, no young person living through the explosion of rock 'n' roll in the 1950s and 1960s could remain immune to its social impact. Liebman says that this led young musicians like Garson and him 'to be eclectic with pride, and to say, "We do switch styles, and you know what? That's part of our name and game, and it's okay!"' On the other hand, he qualifies this by saying that the goal is still to master something, and that if you 'spread yourself too thin' then such mastery is less possible, because 'you're giving away a little bit of your heart and soul.'

Garson has indeed spanned various genres, but he has limited his field of expression to his highly distinctive style of improvised piano, and in that sense he has remained highly specialized. He acknowledges that, were he to limit himself further still and exercise this craft purely in the jazz genre, it may be true that he would advance further his expertise in jazz, but he finds the thought of that limitation a very boring prospect. He rejects the notion that one musical form is intrinsically superior to others. Some music is more aesthetically pleasing or spiritually deep, but that can come from any genre. Jazz was never truly in his social background, and he wanted to find his own honest forms in which to work.

The excitement he felt when he heard Coltrane was significant, but he wanted to find his own way to express that essence rather than to stick necessarily with the jazz idiom within which Coltrane happened to work. There is a musical essence to be tapped into which does not reside in the techniques of jazz, but rather in the feeling that Coltrane expressed through that language. Garson's take on this captures the essence of his approach, with all of its spontaneity and sincerity: 'I need to hear what I hear, when I hear it, and play it as I feel it.'

Liebman claims that there is a difference between musical fields that is 'aesthetic, spiritual, emotional' rather than just technical, and he contrasts the commercialism and accessibility of pop music, 'which speaks directly to the normal person—you do not have to be an expert to understand it,' with the idea of jazz as something that it is only possible to appreciate with effort and special knowledge: 'You *must* get some kind of aural education to understand most jazz, you got to get educated. Pop music is about numbers and it enters into the big business. We know about that world, it's a different intention, and when you're with people like that you can't help but be affected by it.'

It is precisely this insistence on special knowledge, the lack of interest in speaking directly to the 'normal person,' and the importance of remaining untainted by other genres and even people, that has earned the jazz establishment its reputation as elitist and excluding. Liebman concedes, however, that working with Bowie, 'That's the top of the line, you don't get any further ahead than that in experimental rock,' and that 'if anybody could do it, Mike is certainly capable of switching styles and being very credible . . . he's always searching, he's constantly growing.'

Liebman enjoys receiving the original compositions that Garson sends him from time to time even now: 'We have our musical language together.' Despite their differences in outlook, Liebman clearly retains a high regard for Garson's distinct path and groundbreaking accomplishments. Garson in turn tells me that he has 'immense respect for Liebman's dedication to cultivating the jazz heritage and finding new territory.'

A different angle on this question of moving between genres comes from jazz drummer Joe LaBarbera, who was Bill Evans's last drummer, and who also later played for Tony Bennett. He has played with Garson many times, from the 1990s up to Garson's *Symphonic Suite for Healing* in 2014, and sees this cross-fertilization in very positive terms, as bringing something additional to each field, rather than diluting anything. 'I have to assume that the benefits derived in his jazz playing from the other sources work in the same way when he is approaching classical or pop. I have heard Mike spontaneously improvise pieces at the piano that sound fully composed . . . Mike is the real thing as a jazz performer. He rarely repeats himself and is always looking for new ways to express himself. When you add these qualities to a complete understanding of the rich tradition of jazz you get a very rewarding experience.'

At twelve, Garson played Chopin's 'Revolutionary' Etude in C Minor (Op. 10, No. 12) for a celebrated New York classical music critic who was deeply unpleasant and slammed him for over-pedaling. Even now, he recalls the invective unleashed by this critic as being like 'the plague that no one wants to experience,' and says that this set back his confidence considerably. Likewise, in jazz he was often told that he would not be able to interpret what was then seen as largely a black idiom, since he was 'a Jewish guy from Brooklyn.' Then, when he was called up by Defries to play with Bowie, he knew nothing about pop or rock music, but he was able to use his classical and jazz cadences to effect something new there.

In the late 1970s, having relocated to Los Angeles, he worked with bassist Stanley Clarke in the jazz fusion style and felt slightly closer to home, since fusion was itself already a mix of jazz, funk, and rock, to which he added some classical touches; ultimately, however, he found fusion a dissatisfying genre of music that tended toward superficiality, speed, and virtuosity more than toward any deep feeling. Its main redeeming quality was as an exercise whereby you could 'get your chops together.'

In the 1980s, Garson went on to work with bebop star trumpeter Freddie Hubbard, a superb musician and a giant of the jazz scene, who played with Sonny Rollins, Quincy Jones, McCoy Tyner, Ornette Coleman, John Coltrane, Wayne Shorter, and Herbie Hancock. His behavior, even onstage, could be erratic and unpredictable, to say the least. In a jazz club near Venice Beach they played a great set including 'Up Jumped Spring,' on which Garson performed a long improvised solo with avant-garde and classical elements. Hubbard had some 'heavy associates,' and they were walking ahead with him after the show, with Garson walking behind. Hubbard suddenly looked behind and said to Garson, 'What the fuck was that shit you just played?' Garson replied, 'Well, Freddie, you know, it's jazz, and it's just what I heard in my ear, my inner ear . . .' They all gave him a dirty look and moved on, but then suddenly Hubbard turned around again and said, 'Let's record that shit!'

Three months later, they were playing in Alaska, and on Hubbard's 'Red Clay' (an adaptation of Bobby Hebb's 1966 hit song 'Sunny') Garson played a rock-style rhythmic interlude that got the audience clapping along. Once again, Hubbard confronted him afterward. This time, however, after Garson told him it's just what he heard in the music at the time, Hubbard thought for a moment, and declared, 'Let's take that shit to Vegas!' Hubbard plays a beautiful flugelhorn solo on a song of Garson's called 'Together Again,' which is on an album by Stanley Clarke called *I Wanna Play for You* (1979).

Back in their days at the Catskills, Liebman would introduce Garson to the stage as an entertaining imitator: 'Now Mike will play like Dave Brubeck!' Or, later, Erroll Garner. He was not rewarded for sounding original but for sounding like others. Things have remained that way, and he points out that pianists are still rewarded for sounding like certain well-known performers, whether Peter Nero, Roger Williams,

George Shearing, André Previn, Dr. John, Vladimir Horowitz, or Arthur Rubinstein. In his early twenties, Garson would practice for hours on end and record himself playing. He found the results resembled Herbie Hancock, Chick Corea, Keith Jarrett, McCoy Tyner, Bud Powell, or Wynton Kelly, but felt sick with frustration as he asked himself where his own identity might fit: 'Where is Mike Garson?'

There was one positive aspect to being spurned by the various purists. By being buffeted around between specific genres, rather than being safely accepted by any one of them, he has remained a more independent and free spirit. Somehow out of all this there finally emerged a strong and original identity, which he had yearned to find in those early days of imitating all the greats. More specifically, it was the call from Bowie, and Garson's subsequent sudden transplantation from the jazz world into the rock world, that helped him to locate his own unique style. Prior to 1972, he was exploring all the myriad styles of jazz and sounding primarily like a bebop player. Then, the wrenching of his evolving jazz style out of its natural context and its being transplanted into the field of rock or pop created a jarring juxtaposition. This helped to liberate his style from the constraints imposed or self-imposed on those who set up home in one of the more rigid sectors of musical production. 'Because I was working in the jazz vocabulary and, at that time, I was learning to imitate all those guys, and I forgot there was . . . where's the . . . *"Will the real Mike Garson please come to the stage?"* He saved my spiritual and musical life, Bowie.'

Even when he started to find this distinctive voice in the 1970s with Bowie, 'I didn't even know I found it . . . because I was still brainwashed by the jazz world.' In recent years, he has also been approached by university music departments keen to appoint him as a visiting lecturer, only to be turned down once they fully understand the extent of his involvement in the rock world.

When composing in the 1980s, he tried at different times to draw on Bach, Chopin, or something from jazz. It was a question of tuning in to these influences and 'channeling' them. It is through this process that he became more spiritual in his beliefs, as he started to strive to connect with whatever they themselves had 'tuned in to':

> That's the message that came to me, that was where it was a little cryptic, that day. It's like a little voice, but it didn't seem like a voice in my head like when you're in the mental house—it felt like more of an angelic kind of a communication, where I needed a little help from a bigger 'I,' or whatever. It felt a spiritual moment, as if it was that part of my brain they hadn't discovered—you know what I mean? I would probably have to call it the true *self*, as opposed to the individual ego . . . all of a sudden, my music went to the next level.

At the point when Garson found himself returning to relative anonymity and home life in the late 1970s, he realized that he had been missing jazz, with its more relaxed and intimate attitude toward time signature and timing, so very different from the frenetic scope of a world rock tour. When the *Ziggy Stardust* Tour had passed through Tennessee for the Memphis date of the tour, some jazz friends had been playing a club gig in a Holiday Inn hotel, so Garson slipped into the club to see if he might sit in and play with them. He says they were laughing at him, as he had 'lost it' at that point, as a result of being away from jazz for so long.

He was ready to start reintegrating all of the strands that had been feeding into his playing. His strong classical foundation would stand him in good stead in helping him to become ultimately comfortable with virtually any idiom: country, rock, bebop, avant-garde, fusion, blues, though always with his own distinctive style. He says that there is a 'rubber band' elasticity to his timing, so that he works around the steady beat, which is nevertheless still always there. He describes this as not always having to be 'in the pocket.' Having first mastered the art of playing perfectly in time, he started to add a floating element around that framework, as well as more complex syncopations. This is a further development from the *rubato* ('robbed' time), which is a feature in Chopin. With jazz, we are often slightly behind the beat.

Surprisingly, Garson says that he did not get his timing really straightened out until his twenties or even his thirties. 'I learned poorly, rhythmically, from the beginning, and I didn't understand rhythm and time. I understood harmony and melody before I understood time . . . it allowed me to become a good teacher, because I didn't have these abilities, so I couldn't just say to my students, "You just feel it and you do it, otherwise get out of here." I had terrible timing, and fixed it, so that means I could work with somebody and fix theirs.'

Garson was told that he lacked the elusive 'feel' of jazz, the ability to 'swing' behind the beat effectively. As a form of rebellion against this jazz orthodoxy, he determined, in his teens and twenties, to use his classical discipline and love of music to conquer this challenge. How ironic then that, in the decades since, he experienced numerous examples of being dismissed by the classical establishment for being a jazz person, as well as being scorned by some popsters for his avant-garde jazz or classical background. As he says:

> Welcome to Planet Earth! Doesn't this also happen in actual exclusive clubs that you go to in New York? Doesn't that happen in every religion on the planet? Doesn't it happen in the classical world? I worked for the opera world for a while—forget about that! They're like the 'opera police' or worse than

all of them put together. They don't even let some singers sing until their late thirties or forties—they won't even put them in the good operas because they feel it might ruin their voice. There is some risk of that, but it is taken way out of proportion.

Even in the country/blues/jazz/folk-rock group he joined, Brethren, there were intimations that he was not 'feeling the groove' the same way they were.[2] Such judgments have more to do with building group securities for the initiated by invalidating others than with the exciting and collaborative project of exploring creativity. Some people have tried to use biological determinism to claim that such competitiveness is inevitable, but there is plenty of evidence showing how the human brain is capable of great cooperation and collective creativity. Every performance by every orchestra bears testimony to this.

The great variety of human expression across the globe encompasses a myriad of different styles of music and beat. However deeply tied these may be to various groups or cultural strands of evolution, they can also all be learned. Whether or not there is any genetic component causing certain groups to feel more affinity with certain musical rhythms or styles, Garson is clear that this is an area that can be learned and developed, and has demonstrated this by successfully challenging himself over many years to enhance his own sense of timing. He has also taken this a step further by teaching it to others, and many of them have far surpassed what they had thought themselves capable of.

The main factors here are environmental, social, and cultural. Different types of musical understanding and feel can be learned or absorbed if we are steeped in them enough. The individual who grows up schooled in the rigors of classical music is less likely to be able to dance, sing, or play with swinging rhythm than someone who was surrounded from birth by syncopated beats or soulful melody. When Bowie created his sound for the *Young Americans* album, it was a distinctive amalgam because, although his voice remained unreconstructed, it was now embedded in the sound and feel of the soul tradition. Garson is positive about this: 'If you like something, you can get it—anything—if you're willing to work at it. You might find you have your gifts here, and those people have their gifts there, maybe they meet in between . . . Bowie was listening to Aretha Franklin for the *Young Americans* tour; whilst we were driving around in a limo, he had the earphones on, going through America . . . and then he sang soulfully. He's not Marvin Gaye, he's not Ray Charles—but you could tell he had absorbed that music, and was great at it.'

Garson then also had to adapt to the situation. His playing on Bowie's Soul Tour in 1974 with the Garson Band, and on the *Young Americans* album, was soulful, bluesy, and simpler by far than it had been on *Aladdin Sane*, because that is what the new genre required. Whilst he was working on this, he found his fingers would not even go off in a jazz direction if he wanted them to, as he had reconditioned his mind to play in a different way for this project.

Staying with the theme of adaptability, Garson has toured with Lulu, and her voice has a great black soul timbre and feel to it, regardless of her being Scottish and white, which is another demonstration that you can, if you choose, absorb the essence of whatever cultural and musical forms you find yourself amongst. By listening, imitating, and incessant practicing, Garson has also proved the possibility of mastering almost any other genre of musical expression.

Mike Garson was born in 1945. In 1973, he recorded with Bowie for the *Aladdin Sane* album. In 2017, he still receives communications almost daily on this: sometimes about tracks like 'Time' or 'Lady Grinning Soul'; sometimes about his extraordinary playing on the subsequent Bowie album, *Diamond Dogs*; but the vast majority, and he has accumulated thousands of them, focus on one solo. Garson has created thousands of pieces of music and played on hundreds of albums for many different artists, some of which we explore elsewhere in this book, and yet huge numbers of people still want simply to compliment and discuss his playing on that one album by Bowie, and one track in particular (the title track)—and even more specifically the solo on that track. Even a live version of the 'Aladdin Sane (1913–1938–197?)' track (on the *David Live* album), with a very similar—Garson says possibly more complex—solo, still does not attract comment in the same way. Garson deals with this potentially frustrating situation both philosophically and patiently, by reflecting, 'You have to say, at that moment, it's bigger than me and everybody else connected with the project. And it's crazy, it's crazy.'

He maintains an admirable poise in fielding patiently the endless questions he faces about this, even when they misguidedly concern parts of Bowie's work that Garson did not happen to play on. This attitude is founded on his recognition that Bowie's decision to bring him on board in 1972, and at various times since, did indeed transform his profile and life. For that he remains steadily and genuinely grateful, whilst at the same time pointing out that the musical credit for his contribution rests with himself, in that Bowie knew why he wanted Garson's input. Bowie's genius for selecting, combining, and absorbing artistic influences has never been doubted, and Garson's own unaffected and inspirational brilliance has proved a key ingredient in much of Bowie's output.

Garson believes that Bowie's music will outlive him by possibly as much as a hundred and fifty years, whereas the Beatles may be remembered ultimately more for their social influence than their music. We struggle to think of many other names from the popular music of recent decades whose music is likely to be remembered so far ahead. Songwriters like Bacharach and David, or Stevie Wonder, perhaps? But there is undeniably something unique about the range of influences, musical and otherwise, that have rippled out from Bowie's groundbreaking artistry over the past forty-five years or so; and Garson's combination of wild and avant-garde unpredictability with soulful and mellifluous musicality was a significant part of Bowie's accumulation of work. Given David Bowie's prolific ability to absorb influences on himself as well as to influence others, the success of his art can be seen as a measure of his extraordinary ability to filter cultural inputs and convert them into something new, which in turn becomes seminal itself. He was like a highly conductive substance.

Garson recalls occasions when he was there as various other stars and acclaimed artists came to meet David Bowie, and he was always struck by the awe in which they all held him. For example, Elizabeth Taylor, during the *Young Americans* period: 'Her beauty was breathtaking, she just sat there and she loved his music.' Paul and Linda McCartney visited the rehearsals in London in 1973 and stayed for a couple of hours. Blondie, Billy Corgan, Trent Reznor, Russell Crowe, Dave Grohl, and many others all clearly regarded Bowie with huge respect. Garson says that these stars would be standing and chatting, looking at him, 'and they can't say what they want to say, which is, "Oh my God, you are the greatest innovator in rock 'n' roll ever!"' Even Lou Reed, 'who in some ways was senior to Bowie and had inspired him in the early days,' showed that respect as 'David overtook him with his extraordinary brilliance.'

Bowie never lost this childlike fascination for the culture around him and those who shaped it, whether Anthony Newley, Bertolt Brecht, Jacques Brel, or George Orwell. In terms of Garson's own panoply of available musical styles, they always had a good working relationship, in which Bowie was the consummate producer and director:

With Bowie I knew exactly how far I could go with my jazz and my classical, my harmonies, my pop, and my avant-garde. I knew what he didn't like and what he liked, so I played within that window and I narrowed it down. He didn't like to hear bebop and jazz lines, but he liked classical things, he liked avant-garde sounds, and he liked to hear interesting chords and harmonies, and he liked 'less is more' at times, just simple little motifs; other times he liked some of my wilder stuff. But he didn't want to hear familiar jazz or any-thing like that—that was all done in the 1950s, so why do that? So, I knew his 'window.'

Garson is indeed sensitive to the people he works with, which has made him very much in demand as a session player. He is able to bring elements out of his own musi-cal personality to match their styles and their needs, and is very good at feeling where the spaces are that might be filled—and where they are not. But he does this without losing his integrity or his own sense of identity, because he is 'able to be them as much as I'm able to be me. Others find it a threat to be someone else, insisting, "This is what I do, this is my territory and I won't ever cross the line," but I love people and I want to interact with them so, you know, why would I start talking Polish when they're speaking English?'

This is a refreshingly well-formed and humane approach to collaboration, in which the individual ego is strengthened rather than threatened by joining with others.

In 1975, Garson had a call at home in Brooklyn from the producer of *The Rocky Horror Show*, asking him to play piano for the Broadway production starring Tim Curry. At the first rehearsal he sight-read the whole show, and they were delighted. On the second day, he started to improvise on the score. They were still pleased, and interested to hear him putting his stamp on it, but there was a ripple of concern in the room that this was not *The Rocky Horror Show*. By the third day, he says, he really went to town with the improvisation, so that 'it was a Mike Garson score, I was turning it all around and inside out.' There was no fourth day. Once again, he was discovering how alien it was for him to play the same notes each time, whether on Broadway or on a pop stage.

In 1976, Garson was told that Stevie Wonder was looking for a keyboard player, and despite some misgivings about whether this would be right for him or allow him to express himself in the authentic way he had been able to in working with Bowie, he did go to the audition, and ended up spending a week in the studio with him in New York. 'From the moment Stevie Wonder stepped out of his limo and into the studio with his headphones on,' he recalls, 'he was just flowing with the music, he *was* music, he *is* music! Drummers were coming in: if they couldn't get it he would sit down at the drums himself and show them; it was just scary, music comes out of every bone in his body.'

More than ten keyboard players passed through. The job went to a young late-comer to the sessions who was a huge Stevie Wonder aficionado and had recorded instrumental versions of all his hits. Garson could see immediately that this was his gig. This was Greg Phillanganes, who later went on to play for Aretha Franklin, George Benson, Eric Clapton, and Michael Jackson, amongst others. However, Garson stayed on and jammed jazz with Wonder, who loved Garson's jazz interpretation of 'You Are the Sunshine of My Life.'

Prefab Sprout drummer Neil Conti, who played with Bowie at Live Aid in 1985 and contributed to the same year's recordings of 'Absolute Beginners' and 'Dancing in the Street,' has some telling reflections on working alongside Garson. In 1999, Conti briefly replaced Bowie's then regular drummer, Sterling Campbell, for an appearance on Chris Evans's *TFI Friday* on Channel 4 television. He recalls Garson's reluctance to rehearse a song repeatedly in the same arrangement, as his spirit of invention and improvisation was always active. 'He'll never play the same song twice! Even when you're at rehearsal, and you play it twice in succession, he'll suddenly go completely off-track, and start playing a kind of Latin piano part over a rock song . . . it's fantastic, because he's so talented he always manages to find a way to make it fit, and to keep throwing ideas out!'

Garson loves to experiment, and the band came to expect that each performance of the piano part for a particular song might differ slightly from the last, which Conti found both likeable and amusing. He describes Garson as 'relaxed, friendly, and yet intense, musically—and, from the technical point of view, astonishing.' What sets Garson aside is that in addition to having the technique to master and fuse classical, jazz, and rock styles, he has the flourish to be expressive through these vocabularies. 'There are some musicians who have a lot of technique, but don't really know what to do with it, and that's what's so great about him, the way he . . . he's got a lot of humor in his playing,' says Conti. 'That's so important in music. There's not many . . . there's a lot of musicians who have got great technique, but they're very serious. And, Mike realizes the value of humor, he throws in things when you're playing live, keeps everyone on their toes, and keeps it fresh. And that's great!'

Conti further recalls how Garson gave him a copy of one of his albums of improvised classical music and told him 'this hilarious story of how he had once played it to a professor of classical music by whom he had been taught, who said, "Oh, that's great! Who wrote it?" And on hearing that Garson had improvised it himself suddenly changed his mind and dismissed it as worthless!'

This terrible snobbery threatens to fossilize and marginalize the classical and jazz establishments. Garson's love of making music regardless of labels or categories 'shows when he plays—he's got a lot of feeling when he plays,' says Conti, who compares him in this respect with Weather Report keyboardist Joe Zawinul (who also played with Miles Davis). When asked whether jazz was the highest form of musicianship, Zawinul once responded that it is not, but that being able to compose while you play is the highest level of musicianship. Garson also epitomizes this free combination of performance and creation, summed up well by Conti: 'It's not to do with what style of music you're playing, it's to do with being able to almost step outside of what you're doing, and hear the whole thing and, actually, come up with melodies and ideas, instead of being stuck in your technique.'

Although quiet during rehearsals and calm onstage, Garson would open up and become quite sociable after the gigs. During the performance itself, it was always his musicality that took over. According to Conti, 'When he really gets going on the piano, he's capable of lifting a whole band . . . an endless stream of ideas . . . a throwback to a different era where every night was different, they just played what they felt. That's what I love,' whereas increasingly the tendency now is for all variables to be ironed out, and for live shows to be programmed and standardized to within an inch of their lives.

This complete spontaneity of expression is part of an outlook that fosters creativity without boundaries. It signposts the future freedom with which new generations of performers and creative producers may increasingly cross-fertilize between disparate fields of music and art. Any truly great musician does not balk at classifications. After years as a jazz master, Herbie Hancock went on to record a Ravel concerto and has collected the scores of the complete Beethoven symphonies and *Tristan and Isolda*, saying that he felt like a kid in a candy store. He is another great instance of a truly creative musician moving comfortably around and through the artificial barriers of musical genres.

Jim Merod is professor of American literature at Soka University of America in Orange County, but is also a renowned jazz recording engineer who has recorded Tommy Flanagan, Sarah Vaughan, Ella Fitzgerald, and Stan Getz. He has an encyclopedic knowledge of jazz and has worked with Garson many times. In the liner notes to Garson's 2012 album *Wild Out West*, he says that he saw Garson as having arrived 'within the circle of genuinely masterful jazz pianists' including Bill Evans, Art Tatum, and Thelonious Monk. A couple of years later, he tells me that, in his experience, only André Previn and Herbie Hancock match Garson's range of artistic expression across jazz and classical idioms. He says that there is undue social pressure toward specialization within one genre—whereas, in fact, 'too much grounding in a particular genre . . . can limit a musician's access to other modes of expression.'

Like drummer Joe LaBarbera (see page 76), he clearly sees working across genres as musically enriching, rather than diluting. He mentions Garson's 'artistic ubiquity' and believes that whereas he has been especially acclaimed by the rock world in earlier years, his status as 'maestro' in jazz is just beginning to be acknowledged.

# 8

# From Lulu to Liberace

*'I was surrounded for so many years by so many cults—not only religious churches but the jazz cult and the classical cult, all these snobby, intellectual, brilliant, scientific people; consequently, it's only been in the last ten or twenty years that I've been able to peel these things, and it always fascinates me that every day I find a lie connected with some bizarre belief system that came across as total truth, and turned out to be just bullshit.'*

—Mike Garson on belief systems

IT WAS IN FRANCE in 1973 that Lulu recorded David Bowie's 'The Man Who Sold the World,' taking it to no. 3 in the music sales charts in England on February 16, 1974. It was recorded as part of the *Pin Ups* sessions, with the same lineup, and Garson contributing some gentle electric piano. The song was later also covered by Nirvana and many others, including live performances of it by Nine Inch Nails, with whom Garson would also play. His electric piano is not very prominent on Lulu's version, but it can be heard on close listening. Bowie and Ronson produced it for her, with Bowie contributing sax and backing vocals. Garson was a fan of Lulu and her British television show (*It's Lulu*, 1970–1973) and the two of them became good friends.

She did a UK tour soon after. She had lined up a good pianist previously but now wanted to work with Garson, and he proceeded to tour with her, also taking on the role of musical director. The pianist he replaced complained to the Musicians' Union, and since at that time United States citizens were supposed to live in the UK for one year before being entitled to work there, Garson was forced to step down from the tour. He says that he does not blame the other pianist, even adding that perhaps Lulu should not have replaced him in the first place, as it was his gig.

Garson recalls with pleasure his work with the great Scottish singer, saying that she was great fun to accompany live onstage. He especially enjoyed her cover of Tom Jones's 'It's Not Unusual,' and her rendition of the theme song from the Sidney Poitier film *To Sir with Love*, as well as her celebrated first hit, 'Shout.' Lulu and Garson would meet once again in 2000 when she came to David Bowie's London concert at the BBC that year, released as part of the *Bowie at the Beeb* CD compilation.

After that first intense and exciting period of working with Bowie from September 1972 to December 1974 had drawn to a close, Garson got a gig playing for a Chinese artist in Belfast, a 'very average' singer, at the time when the conflict there was at its peak. In what sounds like the beginning of a joke, he says the band had a Jew, a Chinese woman, a Catholic, and a Protestant—he was 'afraid everyone was going to kill each other!' He hated playing with this covers band, but once again he had to do this in order to survive. Even now, he would take on whatever work comes up and whatever work he needs to do in order to support his family, and he is extremely dedicated to looking after them.

Garson's first daughter, Jennifer Shuper, born in 1971, remembers falling asleep to the sound of her father practicing, composing, and teaching throughout her childhood. Although his home studio was his haven, she and her sister were always welcome, and he often played them pieces he had written. She loves music, and sings. Jennifer took piano lessons from her father and has collaborated with him on writing lyrics. She works now as a college professor, teaching Spanish at Pasadena City College. She regards her father as 'a spiritual healer for whom music is just one way that he channels his extraordinary abilities.' She reveals a side of him which perhaps modesty kept out of my interviews with him, explaining how he has acted as a counselor to many people, describing him as 'the best listener and advisor you could imagine.' She adds, 'He is a master of making everyone with whom he connects feel special and feel understood.' A few years ago, her marriage hit a rough patch and he sat her and her husband down in his studio and proceeded successfully to help them repair the situation, acting 'as mediator, therapist, spiritual guide, and mender of hearts,' something for which she is eternally grateful. Her husband, Peter Shuper, also points out how Papa Mike, as they and their children affectionately call him, has inspired respect through his emotional insight and lack of partiality. They have two daughters, Maya and Hannah, and a son, Jeremy, who sent me this moving comment on his grandfather: 'He's one of the busiest guys I know, and he always makes individual time with me regardless of what his day consists of . . . I would come to him for something before my closest friends . . . he's an incredible person and the best grandfather a young teenager could really ask for.'

Garson's younger daughter, Heather Garson Gilbert, was born in 1974. She is also a teacher, and says that growing up in a musical family 'was amazing—there were always musicians coming in and out of the home, lots of rehearsals, tons of noise and creativity.' She says that they had a great childhood and used their father's '"healing" techniques and wisdom to become responsible adults.' Regardless of the pressures of touring, he always made his family an absolute priority. When she went into labor prematurely with her son, Max, her father was mid-concert at the NAMM show (the world's largest trade-only event for the music products industry, held annually in Anaheim, California), but left immediately to be by her side, waiting for Max to be born before he went back. Heather also took piano lessons from her father and dabbled with cello and violin, but says that perhaps it has 'skipped a generation,' as both Max and her older son, Jacob, are already very keen musicians. Max has played drums since he was two, and has often jammed with his grandfather. They performed onstage together as part of Garson's *Symphonic Suite for Healing* orchestral world premiere in March 2014. Heather explains that Jacob has autism and has been greatly helped by his grandfather, who has been able to 'bring him out of his shell and help "heal" him. Since Jacob was a baby he always loved listening to music, especially my dad's. It used to relax him so much that he would bury himself in my dad's arms and melt into him.'

Now, a few years on, Jacob has started to bond further with his grandfather through a love of the piano. He has started to show an extraordinary ability, even at thirteen, to master all kinds of complex modal scales, and will sometimes telephone his grandfather to discuss something like the Dorian or the Aeolian mode, which are beyond the comprehension of many professional musicians. Heather says, 'I am so thrilled Jacob has found music; it is a great way to express himself.' Both of Garson's daughters name 'Lullaby for My Daughters' and 'Song for Susan' as amongst their favorites. At any performance of these, both daughters and their mother are guaranteed to be in tears. This is a family with a really inspiring degree of love and care for one another, and Garson's music seems inextricably woven into its emotional fabric.

In 1988, Garson was cast to play the piano as Liberace in an ABC 'Movie of the Week' biopic.[1] It was a demanding role, requiring Garson to reproduce the dazzling pyrotechnic style for which Liberace was famous in both his classical and more popular repertoire. This was long before Steven Soderbergh's 2013 HBO film *Behind the Candelabra*, which for performance scenes was able to use twenty-first-century CGI special effects to simply 'graft' the head of lead actor Michael Douglas seamlessly onto the body of pianist Philip Fortenberry. In 1988, the methods required were more laborious. Garson's hands and arms were filmed for those scenes in which Liberace was playing, as a sort of 'body double,' and these were then alternated with headshots of Andrew Robinson, the actor who played Liberace. (Robinson, who was cast partly for his facial resemblance to Liberace, had previously played the killer in the first *Dirty Harry* film, opposite Clint Eastwood, and went on later to play Elim Garak in *Star Trek: Deep Space Nine* on television in the 1990s.)

Garson explains how Liberace was an honest entertainer—a showman pianist with an amazing classical gift. He shellacked the piano hammers to create a brighter tone, so that his piano was almost bell-like in its sound. This was all part of his persona. Garson had to live with Liberace's music for months and recorded the parts at a recording studio in Burbank on a beautiful nine-foot Baldwin grand piano similar to those used by Liberace.

Liberace had a pointedly flamboyant style, playing with his hands going up into the air, which was all part of his overall projection. He was, in fact, a very successful communicator, because he really connected with his audience and reached out to people. When Garson was a child, Liberace had a television show based in New York that was on every day, and the young Garson was an avid viewer—this was one of his first influences. He recalls hearing Liberace on screen, playing Debussy's 'Clair de Lune,' and then, years later, had to play it himself in Liberace's style for this film. They brought in as musical director the man who used to conduct Liberace for television, so Garson was directed by the same man all those years later. 'He had conducted thousands of shows, he never missed one! When Liberace got sick once or twice, this guy played the whole show; and yet I was still hired to be the pianist for this TV movie.' The musical director might have been able to perform these pieces for the soundtrack, but he would not have had as much as Garson did of the musical flair required to actually play as Liberace.

Garson recorded the piano parts for the Liberace film in just three days, but he stayed on set for months as he was working closely with the actor, Andrew Robinson. In some shots Garson's hands would be seen, and in others it would be Robinson's. Garson made most of his income from the film by clocking up all that extra time on set, often going into overtime through the evening. He was called on to teach Robinson to play (the latter turned out to be quite a fan of Thelonious Monk, and he and Garson became good friends), so that his posture and movement when at the piano would be realistically convincing. This was sometimes challenging, since Robinson's arpeggios 'went the wrong way!'

They had to disengage the action of the piano on set so that it could be played by the actor (and, for close-up shots, by Garson) without making any sound. In a number of scenes they filmed Garson's hands playing this silenced piano, which felt awkward, as he was miming to his own performance, but without the keys he hit making any sound. There is one scene in which we accidentally see his face in a long shot at the piano, rather than the actor's. He attributes this, with amusement, to the television movie's budget having been rather different from that of a feature film. They had, however, acquired the use of Liberace's actual clothes and rings, and he was told he had to lose eighteen pounds of weight in two weeks (which he did through a diet of fruits, juices, and a lot of water) in order to get the job, so that his arms and hands could take those rings and clothes for the shots of him playing.

As he sat late every night on the set, happy to accumulate considerable extra earnings, the director urged him on to play higher or harder up the keys. He hammered on this silent piano to give the impression of his playing, for example, Chopin's 'Fantaisie-Impromptu'—which he had in fact recorded at Burbank, months earlier, in the style of Liberace. But some nights he found himself playing more like Horowitz. At that point, he recounts that he had the sense that Liberace, who had died just eighteen months earlier, was coaching him from beyond the grave. Garson is emphatic that this presence was as real and vivid to him as our interview or any other meeting:

> The director is directing me to play like Liberace, so he's saying, 'Do this!' So, I'm doing this, and he's saying, 'It's not up high enough!' and, I'm bleeding, and the rings are on there, and I'm hitting the piano that doesn't play back . . . it's midnight, and I hear in my head—I swear to you—Liberace appears, with those hands up in the air the way he played, and in his voice, it was hilarious . . . he coached me from the 'other side'! And I start doing it, and my body had chills through it, and he said, 'That's right!' And I used that spirit when I played the piece.

As for the experience of wearing Liberace's own hairpiece and jewelry, Garson recalls:

> They gave me some rings prior to filming, and said, 'Try these now, see how they feel, because you'll be recorded with them.' They put his wig on my head—looks pretty good—I got a kick out of it, you know? I had hair then, but they still put his wig on, and it had a particular vibe, and I go into Hollywood showing all my friends the rings! On set, they told me they were just costume rings, so as not to worry me. I just walked off set with them on. But it turned out they were his real rings! My phone started ringing at two in the morning—off the hook—'Where are you?'—I had millions of dollars of rings on my hands, walking through Hollywood, showing all my friends!

Another amusing anecdote from this time comes from Brad Vinikow, a musician and technological consultant who first met Garson in the 1980s when he went to introduce the then groundbreaking new MIDI Grand Piano to him on behalf of

Yamaha, and who remains a close friend and collaborator today. At the time, he was due to visit Garson in Bell Canyon with a video crew from Yamaha to film the two of them for a training film on Yamaha equipment. When the door opened, he recalls, 'It was not actually Mike there to greet us, but Mike dressed as Liberace: complete with wig, huge rings on his fingers, and outrageous clothes that only Liberace could wear.'

Vinikow also sheds useful light on Garson's approach to technology, commenting that from the start, the question he asked about the new instruments shown to him was not 'How does this work?' but 'What new creative vistas will this open for me?' as his mind 'instantly whirled with possibilities as I demonstrated and explained the instrument.' Another time they worked together to record every national anthem in the world for a multimedia encyclopedia by Microsoft. This protracted process was stressful at times, especially with some of the 'less than musically satisfying' anthems, but just when they thought they had finished, they had to start again on the anthems of the newly formed Eastern-bloc countries, following the breakup of the Soviet Union. Vinikow speaks with great affection and admiration of Garson, who on their first meeting had a 'shock of silver-grey hair, which exploded in as many directions as his endless musical ideas,' which has led him to amicably address Garson ever since as 'Professor.'

Garson continues to hold Liberace and his music in high regard and cites his autobiography as a good read. Liberace's musical director, on hearing Garson's rendition of Debussy's 'Clair de Lune' in the style of Liberace, was amazed that it recalled exactly the way that Liberace used to play it. Garson attributes this less to his months of work for the film than to his having absorbed Liberace's style when listening as a child. It should also be noted that Liberace played his part, too, in breaking down the musical boundaries between classical and pop music, by creating popular adaptations of well-known classical pieces.

Another project that began for Garson in the 1980s and flourished into the new millennium was Free Flight, a jazz flute quartet with a classical repertoire, which has made a huge contribution toward the softening of the boundaries between those forms. Founder Jim Walker has played principal flute for the Los Angeles and New York Philharmonics as well as the Pittsburgh Symphony, and is widely respected as a recording artist in both classical and jazz, as well as being a prolific teacher. He explains how, in 1982, original Free Flight pianist Milcho Leviev had left the band, so he was looking for a talented jazz improviser who also had a classical background. He heard Garson playing with his trio at Two Dollar Bills in Hollywood. Walker was originally from Kentucky but has long been based in California. They had an hour-long meeting at which Walker recalls sounding off passionately about things he had 'been unhappy with in the previous situation,' which they laugh about today. (Walker says, in true Californian style, that he 'had not really had any therapy at that point,' and that he vented and downloaded it all on Garson.) He appreciated that Garson was 'a great listener.'

Walker explains that some of the best crossover or hybrid pianists in the world are based in Los Angeles, so that they can do a lot of different things in the commercial field. By now, Garson too was living in California, as was Walker, and he had about ten or twelve such pianists available to consider. It became clear, however, that there were very few who could also bring the creative elements that Garson could bring. He had 'an unbelievable abundance of jazz vocabulary knowledge. There is not any-one who knows the language of bebop and post-bebop harmonies anywhere close to what Mike knows.'

Garson once again proved able very quickly to assess the needs of the situation, and was willing to meet the demands of both long rehearsals and considerable travel that the band also demanded. He also brought some of his own compositions with him into the band's repertoire, and it quickly became a vehicle for his own ongoing exploration of the meeting of jazz and classical music idioms and his uninhibited combining of these forms. A couple of the first additions to their repertoire that Gar-son suggested were the First Movement of Beethoven's 'Waldstein' Sonata, and also the Toccata from Prokofiev's Seventh Piano Sonata. Those monumental piano works are very difficult on the piano, but to arrange them to incorporate a flute quartet was an incredible challenge. Walker describes the Prokofiev arrangement as 'one of the highlights of my musical life, that we were able to make that work, and it's an incred-ible version. I once played our recording of that to Alexander Toradze, a fantastic Russian classical pianist, who knows the piece very well, and he said, "Oh, Prokofiev absolutely would've loved it this way—it takes it to the next level!"'

Both of these arrangements can be heard on the 1984 Free Flight album *Beyond the Clouds*, which also carries four original compositions by Garson. When Garson joined in 1982, the group had been going for a couple of years and had already had some success, including a recording contract with Palo Alto Records and appear-ances on *The Tonight Show* with Johnny Carson. On one occasion, Carson was so impressed that he invited them back the very next night. They also performed a concerto with the Los Angeles Philharmonic. Their unique combination of classi-cal virtuosity, folk spirit, and jazz cadences made a big impact. Through the 1990s, Garson continued to play for Free Flight despite periods of touring or recording with

Bowie and others, but by the early 2000s the pressure and uncertainty of his availability pushed Walker to have to find at least a partial replacement, which came in the form of pianist Bryan Pezzone. Since 2004, there have been occasional outings, with either Garson or Pezzone filling in on piano according to availability. Walker and Garson also sometimes perform concerts as a duo.

Garson himself describes Free Flight as

> truly an amalgamation of classical and jazz. We were ahead of our time; many bands are doing things like that now but not as good . . . mind you, we played Hollywood Bowl, the Lincoln Center, Johnny Carson two or three times, a lot of great art centers throughout the States, master classes . . . though in terms of recording, each of our albums never sold more than about thirty thousand. But it was a great band, which kept me practicing at that time and forced me to push my levels—things I couldn't do now, because I'm just hearing what I'm hearing when I'm hearing it, so it's a little different now.

What makes Garson's participation in Free Flight of special interest, given the themes that emerge from a consideration of the range of his work, is that here was a project in which he could be creative without feeling any constraint of working within one genre or another. Here it was possible, indeed their very aim, to use the idioms or musical language of the classical, jazz, and folk worlds, all within the same recording or concert. They took pleasure in including, within the same concert, quiet ballads, rock-driven high-energy pieces, synthesizers with electric flute, piano with acoustic flute, bowed bass. As Walker puts it, 'To be able to do that was . . . almost amusing to us. It was like, "Oh, my God, look what we're able to do!" So cool and, I think, for all the guys in the band especially, in that fifteen-year period, it was a great outlet for us to be able to do, in one two-hour concert, so many different things, and each of us got our own feature along the way.'

This impossibility of categorizing the Free Flight sound was a nightmare for concert promoters, booking agents, and even record stores, much to the band's amusement. At one concert they challenged the audience to suggest a name for the new amalgam they were creating, and one woman shouted out, 'That's easy—this is "Real Music"!' They have recorded over ten different albums, though one of Walker's favorites is that on which Garson first heavily featured, 1984's *Beyond the Clouds*. What they have found is that jazz lovers come away with a new understanding and liking of classical music, and classical fans learn an appreciation of jazz. Within the band there have also been such journeys. Walker himself grew up as a classically trained flautist who listened to jazz but did not even start to improvise until his late thirties. He still defers to the improvisational genius of someone like Garson but feels he has succeeded in crossing an important boundary himself with the energy and dedication he gives to this project, and has learned a confidence in his playing that rules out inhibition or insecurity.

He explains the subtle difference in playing jazz flute as opposed to classical, how it uses a more diffused sound, less clean, more easygoing. It is, however, a continuum, and there is nothing to prevent some of that technique being deployed within a classical context. He just plays more cleanly than many jazz flautists who come from a jazz saxophone background and like to double flute, citing his role model as 'Cannonball' Adderley, 'who was about as clean and pure as any improviser I've ever heard of on a wind instrument, as opposed, you know, to Coltrane or Charlie Parker, who were brilliant and played all the notes, but "Cannonball" was like some sort of computerized machine. He never hit a suspicious note—it was ridiculous!'

In the same way, a jazz pianist uses a different touch in eliciting sound from the instrument than does a classical pianist, usually a harder edge. Again, though, that is a question of degree and there are jazz pianists like Bill Evans with the ability to deploy a wonderfully soft touch. Instead Walker emphasizes improvisation as the key difference, since in classical work there is no improvisation other than at the interpretative level, through which a melody may be conveyed differently at different performances. Only in jazz might the actual notes differ between performances. In exploring the different skill sets and techniques used to play jazz and classical, however, it becomes clear that they are a continuum. When Walker switches between playing jazz and classical, he simply draws on different parts of his abilities and alters the emphasis. This recognition that the skills required for classical and jazz work are not so different opens the door for others to become more free to experiment with crossing these boundaries.

The meeting of classical and jazz has a long thread of its own and can be heard vividly, for example, on Nina Simone's solo on 'Love Me or Leave Me,' which is based on J. S. Bach's Inventions. Leonard Bernstein had a sensibility toward jazz, and Previn, as mentioned, also crossed these boundaries, as indeed did Gershwin. What marks these people out is not some special genius as much as the desire and willingness to cross into other territories with a sense of adventure rather than fear.

In Walker's last year with the Pittsburgh Symphony Orchestra in 1976, André Previn became the conductor. As a child, he had enjoyed Previn's jazz recordings, and on one occasion he asked him if he missed playing jazz (this was before Previn got back into doing jazz again). Previn replied, 'You know, I just miss the improvisational spontaneity that you have when you're playing with a small group.' You can hardly extemporize around the music, or reproduce that intimate process of spontaneous creation, in a symphony orchestra of a hundred musicians.

Like Garson, Walker also reflects on the fact that he was determined—in his case, to win an orchestral job, as well as to be able to play jazz, and worked hard, for many hundreds or indeed thousands of hours to reach these goals. Any acclaimed player of 'genius' or extraordinary ability tells the same story of 'one part inspiration, ninety-nine parts perspiration.'[2] Walker also cites the case of Charlie Parker, who it is said was not so competent when he was first heard of, but then 'went into the tank for a year' and became a quite different player. (Parker went on record as saying that he practiced up to fifteen hours a day during one period of three or four years.) Sonny Rollins also disappeared from public view for a self-imposed sabbatical year, during which he practiced daily on Williamsburg Bridge.[3]

On the question of composition through improvisation, Walker wholeheartedly endorses Garson's contention that this is a process worthy of respect and with major precedents in the classical world, despite its lack of acceptance within most classical circles today. He describes some of Garson's improvised compositions as 'absolutely remarkable, really beyond belief. I never will forget what he played for me when he was studying the work of Olivier Messiaen and created a piece based on that study, and I was blown away by it; he did the same thing with a homage to Ligeti, it's unbelievable!' These and others can be heard on Garson's 2003 album *Homage to My Heroes*.

Within the remit of paying homage to a given style, Garson fully deploys his improvisational skills to create a piece spontaneously in real time, with minimal editing afterward, and Walker believes this is threatening to many of the traditionally trained composers and critics alike. He contends, for example, that Franz Liszt would have given anything to have had the technology to preserve his improvisations as efficiently as we are now able to, with recording software that makes a full digital record and score of whatever is played. Walker believes that with these tools, J. S. Bach would have composed five times as many of his wonderful compositions. There are also differences in aptitude, however, and he estimates that many composers may not have the degree of improvisational technique available to Garson, just as Garson may lack some of 'the patience to sit down with pen and pencil, without a piano, and write a piece of music—it's just not his vehicle, and he doesn't need it to be.'[4]

Garson observes that the great majority of composers in the modern period themselves played primarily piano or harpsichord rather than other instruments. Similarly, pianists in a modern context appear more likely to be improvisers. Is this a reflection of the structure of the piano itself, its orchestral range of possibilities in one entity, the polyphony it offers by having all the pitches set out to be struck directly by either or both hands, without the need to shorten a string or alter a sound chamber with one hand? Garson theorizes that the training of young pianists to access notes in the way that only the piano offers somehow develops their brains in that inventive direction.

In twenty-two years of performances by Free Flight, they did not fail a single time to receive a standing ovation. Their shared goal was always to communicate with the audience and to 'allow the audience in on our party,' complete with the guarantee of 'some great fireworks . . . because you never know where Mike is going! I mean, we can have our tents very well laid out and organized but there's always the place where it's open, and you just have to hang on for dear life, hoping that you catch him!'

Free Flight are still taking occasional bookings where budgets are adequate, and Garson and Walker have spoken about the idea of relaunching as 'Free Flight 2' in the coming years, building something new on the foundations of the best of what they used to do. Meanwhile, Walker is being kept very busy with a lot of orchestral work and playing for film scores, as well as solo work and teaching. He finds that budgetary support for music has been crumbling in California, as elsewhere, with a few notable exceptions, due to the financial crisis as well as 'the American preference for sport, gaming, and films, above live music events.' Finally, Walker describes Garson as 'one of the most incredible human beings that I've ever encountered . . . one of the deepest searchers or seekers, both philosophically and musically' and adds that 'as a performing colleague, he is a powerhouse.'

Garson is indeed a seeker, and he has always been devoted to trying to understand the deeper truths of life. He was brought up in the Jewish faith and took his studies in it seriously. He retains his belief in God, and this inspires his musical creativity. He despairs of the way that organized religion has corrupted the simple core values of true spirituality. He never denounced Judaism but began a long quest that saw him at different times over the past fifty years studying theosophy, pursuing macrobiotics for three years as a way of life, becoming involved in Scientology through the 1970s, following Helen Shucman's *A Course in Miracles*, and finding insight in the works of Jiddu Krishnamurti and then Dr. David R. Hawkins. In the case of his music, he had found that he was able to arrive at his own musical voice only by thoroughly studying and practicing all of the established techniques, schools, and genres of music for many years, before 'unlearning' and transcending them. In exactly the same way, he has found that he needed thoroughly to explore the many forms of spiritual enlightenment before evolving, through his own personal epiphanies, into a higher state of awareness himself. It has become increasingly clear to him that 'the answer lies within.'

At the time of his first tours with David Bowie from 1972 to 1974, Garson tried to persuade fellow band members and crew of the merits of Scientology. 'If I had the life experiences I have now, I think the one modification I would have made at that time might be to have kept my philosophical and religious viewpoints to myself,' he says. 'Perhaps more like "live and let live," rather than imposing my ideas on others. Through the years that attitude softened and morphed into a more humble viewpoint.'

Garson's childhood friend Dave Liebman says that Garson's inquiring mind began in childhood with his study of Hebrew and his plan to become a rabbi. Jewish households like theirs put a special emphasis on education. Liebman says that the mantra was always, 'You're going to be educated and then you're going to do something for the world.' A college education was far from the norm in the 1960s, but there was a determination amongst many Jewish parents to see their children study, whatever it took. He describes Garson as 'the kind of guy who does not stand still; he wants to push the envelope, and he has done that for years,' and says that his tireless exploration of spiritual philosophies 'was him being Mike, just looking, trying to search and find out more.'

Garson takes personal responsibility for the decisions he made, both to get involved with any of the philosophies he encountered and later to move on, saying that in all cases it was the right thing for him to do at the time, not blaming others for his choices, and he remains positive about what he learned. In 1973, British music journalist Charles Shaar Murray interviewed Garson and Chick Corea together for *New Musical Express*. When I asked him about his impressions of Garson, Murray said that although Garson did indeed try to interest him in Scientology, he felt that he was clearly honest in his conviction that this might be beneficial to Murray. When he declined to take any interest, he says that Garson was as pleasant and friendly as he had been before. He adds that he has always found Garson to be 'a wonderful musician and the proverbial diamond geezer.'

Garson believes that he learned from each of the philosophies or movements with which he has been involved, that he was able to absorb the good or useful lessons that he could from them. He simply moved on when he found that something was no longer working for him. (For a more detailed look at Garson's involvement with Scientology, 1970–1982, see pages 252–254.)

The 1980s were a period of relative isolation that he describes now as 'somewhat lonely,' but that he used to move his music onto a new level. It was in the late 1980s, for example, that he first began to develop his distinctive approach to classical composition through improvisation. He also returned in earnest to his jazz work during that time, and was performing with Free Flight and others. In addition, he started to practice the piano even more each day, and did more composing to further evolve his artistry.

This also became a period in which he dedicated himself to the contemplation and practice of his own spiritual beliefs. 'In some ways it's as simple as just being yourself, acting with integrity and kindness and following one's own passion.' He says that he holds to the true meaning of education from its Latin root of *educare*, which is to 'draw out from within.' Only a minority of educators approach it this way, despite this being clearly indicated in the term itself. He is also emphatic about the distinction between religion and spirituality. He feels sadness at 'what's happening to both religion and education on the planet. I'm disappointed but still have infinite faith that things can be improved with the universal solvents of love and music. God is within us, as well as everywhere. A good definition might be "all that is," both manifest and non-manifest. I'm talking about thoughts and feelings that I have experienced, and I am certain it's connected with everything I've done, my music and my family—and I am eternally in a state of gratitude and humility for it.'

He gives the example of how this book came about through an unexpected bond between two people, which for him has something to do with synchronicity, serendipity, and spirituality. 'There are these things that are "in between the notes" that are happening in this book, and will happen between the lines.'

Garson's perspective is remarkably humanistic. Drummer Zachary Alford recalls one of their lengthy philosophical discussions in which he was telling Garson that he lamented the fact that we cannot all be 'truly as one,' that he could not be in everyone else's head at the same time. He says that Garson did not agree that this is not possible, arguing that we are indeed all deeply interconnected. 'I'm not sure he convinced me of it, but he was not ready to give up on the concept as a lost cause.'

With passing years he finds himself increasingly averse to fixed systems of belief of any kind, which prevent free thought and imprison the mind. He shows a growing humility with age as his questioning nature becomes more pronounced. 'I was surrounded for so many years by so many cults—not only religious churches but the jazz cult and the classical cult, all these snobby, intellectual, brilliant, scientific people; consequently, it's only been in the last ten years that I've been able to peel these things, and it always fascinates me that every day I find a lie connected with some bizarre belief system that came across as total truth, and turned out to be just bullshit.'

One of the secrets of his strong survival instinct, of his ability to enjoy a long and happy marriage in a field in which that is especially rare, and of his steady creative progress as a musician despite all of the obstacles, is his striking honesty both to others and to himself at all times. Having explored many spiritual philosophies, he says that his favorite quotation in the end comes from the Bible: 'Love is patient, love is kind. It does not envy, it does not boast, it is not proud. It does not dishonor others, it is not self-seeking, it is not easily angered, it keeps no record of wrongs. Love does not delight in evil but rejoices with the truth. It always protects, always trusts, always hopes, always perseveres. Love never fails.'[5]

All through the 1980s, Garson continued to work on multiple musical projects including his improvisational classical compositions, which eventually accumulated into the thousands. There was no indication that he would necessarily ever work again with David Bowie. However, the time came when he once again got the call that would bring him back for a second, much longer period of working with Bowie.

# 9

# Inside *Outside* and the 1990s

*'I personally think Mike gives one of his best-ever performances on this piece and it thrills on every listening, confirming to me at least that he is still one of the most extraordinary pianists playing today.'*

—David Bowie on 'South Horizon,' from *The Buddha of Suburbia*[1]

AFTER A LONG HIATUS, Garson and Bowie were reunited in the 1990s, as Garson was brought in to play on such projects as *Black Tie White Noise* (1993), *The Buddha of Suburbia* (1993), *1. Outside* (1995), and *Earthling* (1997), as well as *Reality* (2003). During the same period, he started to tour and record with Billy Corgan and the Smashing Pumpkins, playing on their *Adore* tour and their concerts in 2000, thought at the time to be their last, then going on to record with Trent Reznor and Nine Inch Nails for *The Fragile* (1999) and playing live with them, too.

With Corgan, he co-wrote the score for the 1999 film *Stigmata*, including the Natalie Imbruglia song 'Identify.' He can also be heard on Seal's *Human Being* and on a hidden track at the end of No Doubt's *Return of Saturn* album of 2000, an exquisite instrumental version of the song 'Too Late.'

In 1991, Garson was approached by the French singer, songwriter, and music writer Jérôme Soligny and asked if he would be willing to play on a film soundtrack that Soligny was composing for Arnaud Sélignac's *Gawin*. This simple invitation would lead to a friendship and collaboration that continues to this day.

Soligny had started writing songs for French singing star Étienne Daho in the 1980s, and had been signed by Emmanuel de Buretel to a publishing deal with Virgin Music France. He knew and loved Garson's work from the earlier Bowie albums, and although at this point it was a full sixteen years since Garson's last work with Bowie, the cascading notes of beautiful piano that tumbled from the tracks of *Diamond Dogs* and the others had never been off Soligny's turntable for long. He had also sought out some Free Flight tapes and heard how versatile Garson could be. In addition, in his capacity as a music writer he had also written a book about Bowie in his native French.[2]

It was difficult to track down Garson, who had immersed himself back into the jazz/fusion scene in California during the 1980s. It seems incredible now, but in 1991 email was not in general use, and there was certainly no social networking. He and Virgin Music France found Garson via the Musicians' Union in Los Angeles and sent him a letter—by what we would now call 'snail mail.' In this letter, Soligny introduced himself as a French composer who would be honored if Garson might find the time to work with him on a film score. With typical modesty, Garson sent back a fax, saying that he thought Soligny must have the 'wrong guy'; he had a neighbor living by him in California, also a musician, who did work with people in France quite often, so it must be him they were looking for. Soligny telephoned this time and convinced Garson that it was indeed his playing he was so impressed by and wanted to use.

That trip in 1991 was Garson's first to the Paris area since recording for *Pin Ups* in 1973 at the legendary Château d'Hérouville. Soligny recalls Garson's formidably tall and broad frame squeezed into the passenger seat of the little car in which he went to pick him up from his hotel. His elbow was protruding from the side window, and he seemed a little nervous of the French traffic in these narrow cobbled lanes, worlds apart from the wide freeways of California. He reassured Soligny, however, that it was okay, as he remembered this from his trip of 1973, and had been scared then, too.

Garson was modest but not falsely so, and appreciative of Soligny's hospitality, with the unaffected humility and gratitude of one who is rebuilding himself. At their recording sessions, he took pleasure in playing a lot of takes and then discovering what had made it to the final mix, sometimes surprised by how good his own playing sounded and modestly acknowledging, 'That's not bad!' Later that year, Soligny completed an album with BMG, his first and last with a major label, and this time Garson joined him to record in Brussels. From that time their friendship flourished.

Between those two projects, Soligny was sent by Virgin Music France to take part in a Los Angeles gathering of songwriters. During the conference downtime, whilst other participants continued to mingle at the Sunset Marquis, he took the opportunity to spend some time with Garson, who had been living in the Los Angeles area for some years by then. Soligny felt at the time that Garson came across as someone who was working on himself, taking stock of his direction in life, in a way that he has since experienced himself, since he is now roughly the age that Garson was when they first met. 'That's the good thing with age,' he says, 'that obviously you're not young any more, but you're young in another way—you discover things in yourself which you never saw before . . . I think he also was discovering things in himself that he didn't see before, and he was in a situation where he said, maybe I'm like a new me, and I've got this music that's pouring out of my very skin, and people love it, and I should do something good with it.'

The BMG recording sessions went well, and Soligny noted Garson's willingness to again provide numerous optional takes and also his apparent lack of concern for the lyrics, finding meaning far more in the notes than in the words, and not professing to be able to understand a lot of the verbal content of the lyricists with whom he has worked.

The fascinating thing about Garson's perceptions of others is that he describes so many others as quirky, because he is comfortable enough in his own skin to feel that he resides in his own normality, his own steady boat from which he observes the waves around him. Yet ironically, many others looking at that vessel can themselves see a craft of charming eccentricity that, whilst seaworthy, nevertheless has some quite alien and exquisite embellishments.

Soligny describes Garson as blissfully unaware of many of the narratives around him. He was never fully cognizant with the Ziggy Stardust character, its creation or demise. When Bowie 'killed off' Ziggy, it would have meant little to him, as he had hardly been aware of the presence of such a character in the first place. Soligny adds, 'He's been playing his way through all this, tickling ebony and ivory . . . that's why he jokes that you and I know more about his music than he does!'

Soligny found that it pays to record all that Garson does from the very first take onward, as 'he starts to play and create as soon as he first discovers the song.' Their latest work together at the time of writing is for Soligny's album *The Win Column*, which also features string arrangements by Tony Visconti. There is a remarkable song called 'She's Ocean' for which Garson created a long piano part that forms a spellbinding coda at the end of the song, and that sets a high future benchmark for any such musical metaphor, since his arpeggiated stylings are more than evocative of the undulating and crashing waves of the sea.

As a prolific writer for the major French music magazine *Rock & Folk*, Soligny first interviewed David Bowie in 1991, with the arrival of Bowie's band, Tin Machine, in Paris. After the interview, Soligny ventured to mention that Mike Garson 'sends his best wishes.' Bowie was understandably perplexed by this. It turned out that he and Reeves Gabrels had been speaking about Garson just the day before. Until this point they had not even been aware of Soligny's own work as a musician. Bowie asked about how Garson was, and how he had been in the studio. Soligny confirmed that his performance was superb, as always.

This additional reminder about Garson, with its implied prompt about his availability, may possibly have played some part in helping to bring about the invitation

Garson received soon afterward to contribute to Bowie's next album, *Black Tie White Noise*, after such a long hiatus in his work with Bowie. Certainly, Soligny says that this was essentially his hope and intention in mentioning Garson to Bowie at this first interview and meeting with him, and Garson gives credit to Soligny for that. (For more detail on Garson's return to working with Bowie, see page 256.)

In a 1997 *Q* magazine article, David Bowie mentioned that in the 1970s Scientology had caused one or two problems, and that what finalized his decision to have Garson back in the band was hearing that he was no longer a Scientologist.[3] In fact, Garson had left Scientology as early as 1982. Film and music writer Hans Morgenstern, who has published an extensive and excellent series of interviews with Garson on his *Independent Ethos* blog, makes a subtle but important distinction about this, that 'one should not confuse these facts as *factors* in the collaboration of Bowie and Garson as musicians.'[4] Bowie's reasons for wanting to use Garson in the early 1990s were, as ever, musical and artistic, and any other issue would have been secondary to that—a case of ensuring that there were no obstacles or impediments to that creative choice. This is clear from the rest of the *Q* magazine interview, in which Bowie went on to describe Garson as having an extraordinary gift, explaining that he specifically wanted his distinctive, eccentric stylings in the early 1990s on both 'Looking for Lester' (on 1993's *Black Tie White Noise*) and 'Bring Me the Disco King' (first recorded for that album, then again for *Earthling* in 1997, but not released until it was recorded yet again for 2003's *Reality*). Bowie says he knew that Garson could easily drop his musical jewels into these tracks. The feature went on to note that Garson was enjoying working again with his old boss, and had been seen at soundchecks performing virtuoso classical pieces quite casually, without even looking at the keys.[5]

It had been about eighteen years since they last met, and in that time David Bowie had himself released nearly a dozen different albums and evolved through a bewildering array of shifting styles. Their shared commitment to artistic integrity and musical experimentation meant, however, that once they were back in the studio, it was business as usual. The session was at the Hit Factory in New York. Garson says it was great to see Bowie again, and that Bowie told Garson that he had not changed much. To Garson, Bowie 'always looked great,' and within minutes it was back to work:

> He introduced me to Nile Rodgers, who was sort of a fan of my playing, and we got along great, and the next thing I know we're recording, and I loved it . . . I loved playing 'Bring Me the Disco King' (though the version we did then was not used and the song not released until 2003). It was just fun to be back in

the studio and playing. We've always had that kind of relationship between us where there's really no sense of passing time, and I guess music is maybe the only form that allows for that phenomenon.

*Black Tie White Noise* was a return for Bowie to solo work after Tin Machine, and Garson played a great solo toward the end of 'Looking for Lester,' a track that Bowie co-wrote with Nile Rodgers and that also featured the trumpet of Bowie's namesake, Lester Bowie (1941–1999). Mick Ronson also got the call and played on 'I Feel Free,' although he was already ill and sadly he died soon afterward, just after this album appeared.

Garson was then also asked by Bowie to play on *The Buddha of Suburbia*, an album loosely based around his soundtrack for the television drama adapted from Hanif Kureishi's first novel, and so the early 1990s saw the beginning of Garson's second, longer period of work with Bowie. In contrast to his good friend Soligny's solicitous concern, Garson himself had never doubted that if and when the time was right, Bowie would contact him again, whether it had been one year or twenty years since the last call, and in 1992 he cheerfully adopted his place again upon the piano stool he had last occupied for David Bowie in 1974. Garson expressly recognizes that Bowie has always been a consummate creative director, as well as a uniquely inspired and driven artist. Hence the *dramatis personae* he builds at each point is itself a work of art and meets the needs of that moment. He compares this sensibility of Bowie's to that of Miles Davis in jazz. He also often stresses Bowie's ability to 'pull' great performances out of him in the studio. For his part in the process, he suggests that his special ability in this context is to play the piano 'as Bowie might if he were the pianist,' to be 'kind of inside his head.' He finds an irony in the fact that, despite being so different from one another in so many ways, he and Bowie do have a very strong connection artistically. 'While we were totally different individuals, we still creatively were on the same page, even though we never talked about it. I may come across like more straight-ahead, the normal nine-to-five guy, but when you look at the reality . . . we both like to be spontaneous and trust what comes out of us.'

Garson was becoming something of an elder statesman amongst the lineup for the Bowie albums of the 1990s and early 2000s, capable where necessary of mentoring younger, though immensely capable, recruits such as Gail Ann Dorsey. Garson also showed he possessed the humility and generosity of spirit necessary to take his place again as part of a wider group, and to be directed when required; not just by Bowie himself, but on the *Reality* Tour of 2003 and 2004 by the newly appointed musical director, guitarist Gerry Leonard.

It is perhaps Garson's fundamental versatility that helps to explain the durability of his working relationship with Bowie, as well as the extensive trajectory of his musical career in general.[6] Other musicians who played with Bowie in the early 1970s would simply not have fitted with some of the genres and styles later adopted by him. Garson's technical wizardry and essential musicality have proved able to operate in a very wide range of musical languages.

For *The Buddha of Suburbia*, Bowie had created the soundtrack for the television drama series but was also developing the material further for an album of the same name (from which only the title track corresponds to the music he wrote for use in the series). He called Garson at short notice, saying that he had the album almost ready but wanted Garson to play on two of the tracks; he was on his way to join Garson in Los Angeles, and would have just three hours, by which time it had to be completed. In the absence of any charts or time to prepare, Garson simply added piano arrangements spontaneously, drawing on the improvisational ability that is his trademark, and the results are astounding on these two tracks, the instrumental 'South Horizon' and 'Bleed Like a Craze, Dad.' The piano parts Garson laid on in this extremely tight timespan were left very high in the mix, and as a result they serve as a great master class for any musician in the art of creating piano parts sensitively and responsively, to be added to a given piece of music.

Unusually, David Bowie himself penned sleeve notes for the album, which throw fascinating light on some of the experimental techniques employed—as well as providing yet another positive review of our subject's contribution. 'On my favourite piece, South Horizon, all elements, from the lead instrumentation to texture, were played both forwards and backwards. The resulting extracts were then intercut arbitrarily giving Mike Garson a splendidly eccentric backdrop upon which to improvise. I personally think Mike gives one of his best-ever performances on this piece and it thrills on every listening, confirming to me at least that he is still one of the most extraordinary pianists playing today.'[7]

Bowie goes on to denounce the 'redundant narrative form,' confirming his spurning of linearity in his work. This manifesto lays a fertile ground for the musical improvisation that was at the heart of Garson's playing, and would be developed further in the recording of *1. Outside*. Bowie continues, 'My own personal ambition is to create a music form that captures a mixture of sadness and grandeur on the one hand, expectancy and the organisation of chaos on the other.'[8]

Chris O'Leary provides a very rich discussion and cultural context for all of Bowie's works on his strikingly well written and researched website, *Pushing Ahead of the Dame*.[9] He makes an interesting contrast between Garson's playing on *The Buddha of*

*Suburbia* and his better-known work on *Aladdin Sane*. In doing so, he also manages the difficult task of writing about the latter in a way that does not merely echo the huge and often clichéd supply of commentaries that have already been written about *Aladdin Sane* and Garson's work on it. 'Garson, on his "Aladdin" solo, sounded like someone who had managed to soak up every speck of music that he'd ever heard, and who was able to reproduce it at will, like God's player piano,' he writes. 'His work on "Horizon" is nothing as outrageous: it's more concise, more conciliatory, still crafty. Knowing he could play anything, he often chooses here to keep silent, or just give a hint of some greater pattern.'[10]

Garson says that on this project he felt at home because of what he recognized as the jazz-influenced elements of the music. 'It was such a comfort zone for me to hear that music because it was kind of jazz, ride beats coming from the drums, jazz trumpet, you know . . . but I thought, "I can't just do any lick and stick to my comfort zone, that's not what Bowie has ever wanted from me, if I just did that it would be musical cheating!"'

He decided instead to create a less easy response by 'listening to the spaces' between his notes. By focusing on these gaps between the sounds we create, we realize that they are equally a part of the music, and that a space between two staccato notes rising from D to A, for example, is a very different space from that between the repeatedly slow murmur or throb of a low B-flat. These interstices between the musical sounds we create are what could, for example, either generate a pulse via the *ostinato* recurrence of a pedal note, or alternatively provide the melancholy of a halting or hesitant melody line. It is precisely the laying down of those gaps, like the cement between the flagstones along a path, that carries the intent of musical expression. With intent comes the suggestion that you have a destination that you are heading for, and this is what makes it exciting for the listener.

During this period, tracks on which Garson played started to be featured on film soundtracks. For example, 'The Hearts Filthy Lesson' from *1. Outside* can be heard on the final credits of *Seven* starring Brad Pitt (1995), and was also featured in the 1997 television movie *House of Frankenstein*. Bowie and Eno engendered this piece from improvised material at Mountain Studios in Montreux, Switzerland, during the 1994 sessions for the album: they landed on an F-sharp minor groove, Garson established a hook (with some E major inversions over the F-sharp minor), and they jammed for an hour over that until the song emerged. In 1997, the soundtrack for the David Lynch film *Lost Highway* was partially produced by Trent Reznor and made particular use of Garson's playing on 'I'm Deranged' from *1. Outside*.

Although Garson did not play on Bowie's 1999 album *'hours . . . ,'* he was on the subsequent tour. Already accustomed to the challenge of finding subtle, suitable piano parts for the live performance of songs that had none on record, such as 'Little Wonder' from *Earthling*, he devised an especially striking piano line for 'Something in the Air' at that time. When that song was used for the opening sequence of the film *American Psycho*, Bowie sent it to Garson in California for him to record an additional piano part on it within one day, for the version to be used in the film. The result was spectacular, though Garson points out that producer Mark Plati had to use a MIDI piano sound rather than Garson's preferred real grand piano because, at that time, even at the turn of the century, it was still not yet possible to send the large files that we take for granted as sendable now.

From its conception, Bowie's 1995 album *1. Outside* was more an experimental work of art than an ordinary album. Before work began on the 1994 sessions in Switzerland, David Bowie and Brian Eno visited the Maria Gugging Psychiatric Clinic just outside Vienna and spoke to some of the patients there about their renowned art. This was the *art brut* ('raw' art) referred to by French painter and sculptor Jean Dubuffet, who was influenced by Hans Prinzhorn's 1922 book *Artistry of the Mentally Ill*, and which would later be referred to within the broader idea of outsider art.[11] Bowie and Eno's project was to generate a modern avant-garde opera, originally called *Leon*, through a range of improvisational methods. The album that was released is merely a fragment of the material that was created as a result. Musicians were brought in as artistic resources, making on this occasion even more real the metaphor of Bowie selecting his band as a palette with which to produce art. The album was completed with some additional recording in New York early in 1995.[12]

For the improvisational sessions that generated most of the material for the album, Brian Eno introduced a fascinating though eccentric method of injecting more interest into the interaction between the musicians. Each participant was given a simple prompt card (a more elaborate version of the 'Oblique Strategies' cards produced by Brian Eno and Peter Schmidt, which are still available on eBay today), giving them a role or identity to play out fully throughout the day. The cards were on their seats, face down, before they arrived, so that each person would only see their own instruction.

It is an interesting fact that the recollections they have all shared since then of what instructions they were given seem to differ markedly from what, according to Eno, was actually on their cards. Writer Chris O'Leary suggests this may be due to 'the capriciousness of memory as well as the potential that Eno and the players altered the "storylines" during their recording.'[13] Eno's directions are imaginative, detailed, and expertly futuristic, with something of an Afro-centric angle in several. Here is one example:

> It's 2008. You are a musician in one of the new 'Neo-Science' bands, playing in an underground club in the Afro-Chinese ghetto in Osaka, not far from the University. The whole audience is high on 'dreamwater,' an auditory hallucinogen so powerful that it can be transmitted by sweat condensation alone. You are also feeling its effects, finding yourself fascinated by intricate single-note rhythm patterns, shard-like Rosetta-stone sonic hieroglyphs. You are in no particular key—making random bursts of data which you beam into the performance . . .[14]

Part of the idea of this was to clear people's creativity by encouraging them to step out of themselves. The musicians were also given new names for the sessions. Mike Garson was called 'G. Noisemark,' Reeves Gabrels became 'Elvas Ge'Beer,' and Erdal Kizilcay was 'Azile Clark-l-day.' Garson says the results were 'hilarious, as well as quite liberating.' He respected Eno's intentions, although he felt that in his own case it was less necessary, since he had long worked specifically on the art of 'not getting in your own way,' as he calls it. Even a cursory listen to the striking outcome in *1. Outside*'s introduction of a narrative sequence (a possible four further albums were mooted but not produced), with its nerve-wrackingly brittle aural soundscape, confirms that Eno's directed style of producing succeeded in drawing excellent results out of the ensemble, even though it seems one or two of the musicians may have had misgivings about some of Eno's directions at the time. Meanwhile, David Bowie had set up an easel and was creating charcoal sketches of the musicians too, which only served to enhance the recording session as a piece of performance art in itself. His portrait of Garson was deeply expressive and really captured something about him. A further experimental feature used at the time by Eno was to play familiar songs through headphones to them, such as 'Dancing in the Street' by Martha and the Vandellas, whilst asking them to play along with the spirit of the song but without any of its external features. (By chance, in 1971 Garson had been pianist and musical director for a Martha Reeves and the Vandellas concert at Madison Square Garden.) All of these methods were used to prevent the group improvisation from falling into the twelve-bar blues jamming that is so often synonymous with that term.

Bowie also returned to a technologically updated version of the Burroughs 'cut-up' method first used on *Diamond Dogs* to generate random lyrics out of his own writing, in the hope of revealing subconscious thoughts, for *1.Outside*, by using a program for his Mac that could randomize word order. (For the *Earthling* sessions in 1996, he took this a step further by creating his own 'Verbasizer' device for processing verbal raw material.) Garson reveals, however, that despite using this method on *1. Outside*, Bowie did still refine the words that came back out of the computer, and Garson says that he respected Bowie for retaining this 'human' touch. Garson points out that both Bowie and Eno subscribed, like him, to some form of Dadaist theory whereby there are subconscious and also apparently chance elements of human meaning, which nevertheless hold significance despite (or perhaps because of) their ostensibly random nature.

As for the role-playing games, it has been documented that Erdal Kizilcay, as a long-term Bowie collaborator, resented the antics of Eno as being pointless and unnecessary, without musical foundation, whereas both Reeves Gabrels and Garson found it fascinating. When interviewed about his choice of musicians at this time, Bowie commented that they all represented different points in the work he had done by then, and that they 'are the ones who are the most open to experimentation. With Mike Garson, for example, we could just say, "Mike, just be yourself," and it's so nutty that there was no need to set parameters.'[15]

Garson was very much in his element as an avowed improviser himself, and he recalls feeling able to take the lead in laying down many of the experimental musical frameworks within which Gabrels and the others would unleash their own expression. For David Bowie, the *1. Outside* sessions saw him also reveling in the opportunity to give full rein to the artistic experimentation that had always been his starting point even as he made his first creative endeavors in the 1960s. In a 1994 journal entry written during the *1. Outside* sessions and shown in the touring 'David Bowie Is' exhibition from 2013, he wrote that he was enjoying the improvisation, with its lack of specific reference points, from which jewels emerged. He also wrote of an idea he had the previous year, whilst recording *The Buddha of Suburbia*, that he might create a fourth 'Berlin' album by rearranging the ingredients of the other three.

This period in Bowie's work was extremely fertile, and Garson was able to flourish in such an experimental environment. Brian Eno's fascinating diary of 1995, which was published as *A Year with Swollen Appendices* in 1996, even refers to the whole *1. Outside* album as 'Garsonic':

> Listened to D.B. disk (after swimming and park and lunch). Strong, muddy, prolix, gritty, Garsonic, modern (self-consciously, ironically so). Every rhythm section superb (even mine). Some acceptable complexity merging into not-so-acceptable muddle; several really beautiful songs ('Motel,' 'Oxford Town,'

'Strangers,' others). The only thing missing: space—the nerve to be very simple. But an indisputably 'outside' record. I wish it was shorter. I wish nearly all records were shorter. Spoke to Damien Hirst. He will give some pics to PFW [Pagan Fun Wear—a fashion event for War Child]. He mentioned rolling in the gutter and barking with Gilbert and George, as though it was just another ordinary evening out.[16]

By the time of *1. Outside*, Bowie was starting to show his paintings around the world, and this album was conceived as a multimedia work of art. Garson was ideally suited to this with his jazz background, his passion for improvisation, and his amenable and open-minded personality. Other musicians involved brought other qualities to this, such as Erdal Kizilcay with his multi-instrumental virtuosity or Brian Eno with his extraordinary intelligence and instinctive ability to subvert, to work outside of any expected framework.

'Mike Garson is a cathedral of music.' With these words, Jérôme Soligny, who knows him better than most, sums up perfectly what has made Garson's role distinctive. He describes Garson's command of musicology as being key, with his ability to reference Frank Zappa as readily as Rachmaninoff, with both detail and integrity.

The combination of this knowledge and technique with the more intuitive and emotional expression in Garson's playing and composing is what gives it a special power. There are many who excel in one or other of these two complementary dimensions of musical creativity, but few who excel in both, without allowing either to overpower the other.

Most of the time he succeeds in keeping a fine balance between expertise and simplicity. It is the rarity of the exceptions to this that make them easy to enumerate. Just one example comes up, mentioned by drummer Neil Conti, who recalls playing alongside Garson for one of Bowie's television appearances, the Channel 4 show *TFI Friday* in 1999. They played some additional songs in the television studio that were not broadcast, including 'China Girl,' on which Conti says Garson 'nearly fluffed the intro, because he was trying to do something clever, again with some Latin theme . . . I think he was in the wrong key . . . David looked very amused . . . but at the same time he didn't look surprised . . . he's realized that Mike is what he is, and you get the best out of him if you just let him get on with it!'

Young drummer Sterling Campbell lived in the same apartment block in New York as Dennis Davis, who played drums for Bowie on 1974's Soul Tour. One day in May 1978, Campbell bumped into Davis in the lobby and was invited to go with

Davis to a Bowie gig he was doing at Madison Square Garden. He was fourteen at the time, and this was the start of his friendship with Davis and his fascination for the music of Bowie. He loved the combination of ambient music with funk and rock that Bowie was creating at that time, and that would prove so hugely influential from the 1980s onward. Fifteen years later, he was playing with Bowie himself, having played with Nile Rodgers, Duran Duran, and the B-52's.

I interviewed Campbell about the many tours and recording sessions on which he subsequently worked with Garson. He recalls Garson taking easily to the role-play and other experimental aspects of the *1. Outside* sessions, adding that he was expansive, open-minded, and spiritual. In the years that followed, the two of them would often spend the time after a show getting into deep philosophical and spiritual discussions. He is amused to recall that, even when their bedrooms were virtually adjacent on a hotel corridor on the *Reality* Tour, they would spend hours chatting on the telephone.

He was fascinated by the fact that Garson had been around in the 1970s, had seen such a lot, and had always been clear-headed, so was able to recall things properly, from the 1960s New York jazz scene through the days of Ziggy Stardust. He wonders whether Garson's disinterest in drink or drugs may even have prevented him from getting gigs with certain bands at times, since people who are using heavily do not like someone 'straight' around to reflect that back to them. In any case, from the late 1990s on, Campbell says, people in this circle had grown up and 'the only drinking would be a glass of wine with dinner—in contrast to the 1970s, whose decadence has perhaps been matched only by that of the 1920s.'

He describes Garson as a very gentle and caring family man, with a strong moral compass. He has seen how he has been able to respond to Bowie's desire to bring some jazz-influenced complexity fleetingly into a song, then to have it fade away again, and compares this with Pink Floyd's Richard Wright using one beautiful jazz chord from Miles Davis's 1959 album *Kind of Blue* when writing 'Breathe' for *Dark Side of the Moon*. Garson is highly skilled at controlling the amount of complexity or jazz influence he allows through his 'valve' in meeting the requirements of Bowie's music.

Sterling Campbell observes that Bowie grew up against a background of Coltrane and Miles Davis being at their peak, along with James Brown, Bacharach, and so many other influences, which he is a master of weaving into the fabric of his music, presenting it all through a pop sensibility. In this sense it is not so surprising that he was joined in the 1970s by a pianist from the jazz avant-garde. Moreover, jazz musicians have often moved into popular forms. Most of the musicians in Motown

and early pop did come from a jazz background and moved into pop out of neces-
sity. Campbell condemns the snobbish attitudes and one-upmanship that sometimes
creep into this situation.

Above all, what he recalls of the tours with Bowie in the 1990s and early 2000s is
the humor. When he and Garson played 'Battle for Britain (The Letter),' he says they
were often almost laughing at the incongruity of their situation, playing this 'wacky
duet' yet again together. Paradoxically, he says, they cared deeply about the music.
They had worked it out and prepared it minutely, and that is the point at which the
laughter emerges—perhaps as a release of nervous energy. On one level, they were
not taking themselves too seriously, at the same time as taking the music entirely
seriously. Likewise, whilst recording *1. Outside* they were always 'having fun, having
a laugh.'

The greatest music has always had this humor, especially in a British context, and
Campbell cites the infamous clowning of Keith Moon whilst drumming brilliantly
onstage with the Who, and indeed the Beatles, with their taking of song titles like 'A
Hard Day's Night' from Ringo's diatribes rather than some profound 'shoe-gazing'
seriousness. That sense of comedy is a necessary companion to the tough side, the
hard work, and the years of effort that someone like Bowie went through before he
got to where he did.

In particular, Campbell recalls a running joke over Garson's piano solo on 'Life
on Mars?' Throughout the late 1990s and early 2000s, Bowie would do an arrangement that was just piano and voice until the last chorus, at which point the band
would come in. There would be a piano solo after the first chorus, in place of the
string-section bridge on the original. Garson would veer so far away from the key
and the theme that it seemed impossible that he would be able to resolve and pull
it back in time for the second verse. Each time he would veer further, and the band
would be thinking, 'How on earth is *this* going to resolve in time?' They almost had
a sweepstake. 'We were all looking at each other and thinking, no way is he going to
get back. . . . Sometimes there was only a bar left and he still had not started doing
the descent yet!' and yet he always did it; from the very edge, he would 'find this
chord to resolve it. It was one of the most amazing things to watch. He did a different
solo every night. I was nervous at times!'

On one occasion, Garson was standing at his keyboards in a long black velour coat
at an outdoor show at the Greek Theatre, Los Angeles, in 2004, playing the intricate
'Battle for Britain (The Letter)' duet with Campbell. Campbell had learned the drum
pattern in minute detail from the original recording on the *Earthling* album, on
which Zachary Alford had played drums, and Garson had likewise transcribed his

own solo from that album, as they had agreed to recapture the recording perfectly. A breeze started blowing his coat against the screen of his MusicPad computer, however, resulting in the pages being rapidly turned. This caused much mirth amongst the band as Garson became flustered by this, but then gave up and created a new solo. Nature had intervened, and the inventive muse had to respond.

Campbell also loved watching how one of Garson's runs could encompass 'four hundred years of music,' from baroque to modern classical to Coltrane. He says that Garson was coming across as a 'mad scientist.' He would look over and Garson would catch his eye and smile, and 'it was funny! There was a real sense of humor to it. I used to love that.'

This humor and mischievousness is not just a key part of Garson's personality—it can also be heard in many of his improvisations and solos, which often end with a signature playful little exclamation from the very top and/or bottom of the keyboard. This calling card was first noted at the very end of the 'Aladdin Sane (1913–1938–197?)' track, but is in fact an integral expression of the humor and humanity he brings to his music.

After recording on *1. Outside*, Sterling Campbell was unable to do the *Outside* Tour because of scheduling conflicts and his place was taken by Zachary Alford, who also played on the *Earthling* album and tour a couple of years later. Alford, who had been playing for Bruce Springsteen prior to that, soon formed a bond with Garson on tour too. Although he had not really played jazz, he had met many jazz musicians at Berklee, and 'I knew how standoffish some of them could be. Mike wasn't like that. He was very encouraging and smiled when he played. But the first time he really blew my head off was our first *Saturday Night Live* performance. We played "The Hearts Filthy Lesson," and when he came to the piano solo he just killed it. There was blood on the walls. I was like, "Damn, this guy's an animal!" From then on I knew it was on. We were taking no prisoners. It was really exciting!'

On the *Earthling* sessions, he recalls Bowie wanting something quite specific from Garson's organ solo for 'Seven Years in Tibet,' and so he took him through it in detail and Garson followed this direction, whereas he gave him more free rein on 'Battle for Britain (The Letter)'—other than the suggestion of Stravinsky as inspiration—so that 'Mike got to put his personal signature on it as only he could.'

I asked Alford whether he felt that Garson's jazz background meant that he had to adapt when in a rock context, and his reply was revealing. 'Well, Mike didn't have to adapt. He was creating a new vocabulary . . . he is exceptionally gifted at playing all styles. He's not a jack-of-all-trades but more a master of all trades. So if you want stride, you get stride. You want boogie-woogie, you get boogie-woogie. Mike is a musician's musician. He's an artist. What drives him is pushing the limits of his own musical abilities and the harmonic possibilities of music and how that can enrich people's lives spiritually and emotionally.'

Also working alongside Garson with David Bowie for the recording of 1995's *1. Outside* and 1997's *Earthling* and subsequent tours through the second half of the 1990s was guitarist Reeves Gabrels, whose fondness for Garson and his music had begun twenty years earlier. As a teenager, he used to put Bowie's *David Live* on his parents' stereo system and try to play his guitar along with Bowie's then guitarist, Earl Slick. He noticed that sometimes if he played a wrong note it would match the note that the pianist was playing—which was Mike Garson's dissonant improvising around the guitar line. He started asking himself, if it is wrong for the guitar to be playing that note then why was it okay for the piano to be playing it? 'It set me on a whole slightly more twisted path,' he tells me now, indicating that Garson had influenced his playing long before they met. 'In many ways, Mike taught me that you could play "outside" . . . I tried to figure out how he got away with it, and why I liked it.'

As a young session musician, Gabrels took some lessons from jazz guitarist John Scofield, and went to study at the Berklee School of Music in Boston. He bought a copy of Garson's 1980 solo album *Avant Garson* as he loved the music of Gershwin, which Garson reinterpreted on this album (on a track entitled 'Avant Garson'), and had enjoyed his playing on Mick Ronson's solo albums, too. 'I kept getting these tastes of much more interesting chords than the guitar players were playing.' When they finally met, he told Garson, 'You're like my uncle!' On tour in the 1990s, the rest of the band would refer to 'the Garson faucet' because of the way the music just pours out of him like water from a tap. 'You just turn him on and what was going to come out was pure Garson. You just had to turn it off when the water was hot enough!' Just as you cannot get the same water twice out of a tap, so you are unlikely to get the same notes in the same order twice from Garson.

Their first meeting was in March 1994, at the recording sessions for *1. Outside* in Switzerland. Gabrels had flown in a few days earlier, but Garson was still jetlagged as they began on one of their first improvising sessions together. His eyes were starting to close whilst he played and Gabrels suggested he might have to return to his hotel and sleep it off. Garson said he would 'go on autopilot—as long as you guys stick with the same key I'll keep playing,' and, sure enough, his eyes fully closed and he appeared to be playing excellently in his sleep. Gabrels caught the eye of Erdal Kizilcay on bass and whispered, 'Let's move up a semitone!' They did and, sure enough, Garson woke up abruptly and adjusted his playing accordingly.

Working in the 1990s before the development of notator programs for scoring, Garson would send recordings of possible piano parts to his copyist at the time, David Arana, back in Los Angeles to be manually transcribed so that he could read the music for the final recording. Gabrels recalls working on 'Bring Me the Disco King' during the *Earthling* sessions (in the end it was held over and finally appeared on *Reality* in a much stripped-down version). Garson played as many as five alternative versions of a piano part for the song. As a joke, Gabrels and Plati discreetly layered all five versions simultaneously in one single track and sent it to LA. When the resulting transcription finally came back, it looked like 'The Black Page' by Frank Zappa—a mass of notes. They handed it back to Garson and said, 'This is the part we need you to play.' That bizarre score, faithfully produced by Arana, was displayed on the studio wall for a while.

Garson played a Kurzweil keyboard onstage at that time, leading the band to nickname him Colonel Kurtzweil after the Colonel Kurtz character played by Marlon Brando in the film *Apocalypse Now*. Reeves Gabrels recalls that Garson could sometimes look intimidating: 'Some people used to be scared of him, but when you get up close he's a sweetheart. His upper body strength is phenomenal, from playing piano. If you want someone to crack your back for you, he's your man!'

Gabrels explains some of the differences in how *1. Outside* and *Earthling* were produced. The former was based on lengthy periods of improvisations by the musicians, whereas for *Earthling* the songs were more prepared, at least in their initial conception as basic structures, even if they were then embellished over. Also, technology was advancing so quickly that for *Earthling* they were able for the first time fully to edit digitally, which had not been possible two years earlier. As musical director on live tours and television shows with Bowie during much of 1996 and 1997, Gabrels says that he and Mark Plati worked on a lot of the sequenced parts in a way that maximized the sonic possibilities: 'We made sure everything had a very strong center spine so that there was always some sort of pad playing the chord changes, and my reason for doing that was because I wanted Mike and I to be able to always have something to push against . . . something to hold it together between us and Gail Ann Dorsey, who was like a rock. You'd always be able to hear the harmony around David's voice, no matter where Mike and I went.'

This approach worked because David Bowie trusted the creative instincts of the highly skilled musicians he had assembled and allowed them to sometimes 'go on an adventure,' as Gabrels puts it—within certain limits. If something was played a new way once, it could be enjoyed as spontaneous expression. If it were played that same way a second time, then it would have to be questioned as either a recurring mistake or a rearrangement that had not been decided on. Gabrels's regard for Garson as an innovator was clearly reciprocated. When asked by *Q* magazine in 1997 whether Bowie's music was very different to play compared with in 1974, Garson said that whilst retaining its rock essence, Bowie's music on *1. Outside* and *Earthling* now had more complexity and was more nuanced in its depth. He also praised Gabrels's musicianship, saying that he approached his playing as if he were reinventing the guitar.[17]

The onstage mischievousness of Gabrels and Garson was not always limited to wild improvisational creativity. Gabrels had noted Garson's liking for always having his notes and scores in front of him on the piano. On the final night of a tour he walked across mid-song, climbed Garson's keyboard riser, lifted the music book and took it back with him, to drop it on top of his guitar speaker cabinets, as another practical joke. But no sooner had he arrived there than, looking over his shoulder, he saw the imposing figure of his pianist friend walking toward him promptly to retrieve the book and carry it back, to resume normal service.

This comradeship between Gabrels and Garson, based on a shared subversive disregard for form or expectation, is part of a long-standing mutual respect. In October 1996, at Neil Young's Bridge School benefit concert, David Bowie played an acoustic set with just Gail Ann Dorsey on bass and Reeves Gabrels on guitar. Gabrels spontaneously re-created the 'Aladdin Sane' solo on a guitar synth (with an acoustic transducer), which gave it a piano sound, with striking virtuosity. He refers to this now as a proud tribute to the pianist who inspired him all those years earlier.

On another occasion, on tour with Bowie in Europe, they 'swapped parts' whilst playing 'Aladdin Sane'—Gabrels using his synth guitar to imitate the piano, whilst Garson accessed a guitar sound from his keyboard and played the guitar part for the song. Garson comments, with dry humor, 'The only thing I can tell you, my "guitar solo" was better than his "piano solo"!'

Since 2012, Gabrels has been a member of the Cure, alongside other projects. There is also the possibility of some improvisational live performances with Mike Garson in Los Angeles in future, with the promise of further joint subversion of expectations: 'Mike and I—and I guess it's Mike's influence, too, to some degree—we're hearing more than the limits of the harmony of the genres, and sometimes it's hard to behave yourself!'

# 10

# Reality, 2003

*'David Bowie has the ability to absorb art and be it, whether painting, sculpture, lyrics, songwriting, singing, entertaining, acting. He is art and he knows how to become it, bigger than life. That's not the kind of artist I am, but he's got a ridiculous gift that's probably been there all along, like a pool of creativity that, if he jumps in, he just comes out being it. It sits there, it's available to him at any second.'*

—Mike Garson

ONE FELLOW MUSICIAN who has worked closely with Garson, both via their joint collaborations with Bowie and also on a separate project of his own, is Irish guitarist Gerry Leonard. A genial and witty presence as well as a modest carrier of great musical talents, Leonard has spoken to me in detail of his work with Garson.

Leonard first played with Bowie in 2000, providing overdubs for the ultimately unreleased album *Toy*. Garson had already recorded his contributions to the same sessions, so the pair did not actually meet until two years later, at rehearsals for Bowie's live 2002 performance of the *Low* and *Heathen* albums at New York's Roseland Ballroom, and then at London's Meltdown festival in the summer of 2002, which Bowie curated.

At this point, Leonard was the newest member of the band and was therefore preoccupied with finding his feet and getting used to being part of this very high-quality and high profile-project. In one rehearsal break he introduced himself to Garson and complimented him on his legendary piano solo for the *Aladdin Sane* title track. Garson appreciated the fact that Leonard was aware of this role of his on the earlier albums, and they started to click. They both have a strong and sometimes mischievous sense of humor, and Garson has a great capacity for recounting interesting anecdotes in a highly entertaining way, which was not lost on Leonard. He recalls Garson's illustration of the vicissitudes of a musician's life: playing two nights at Madison Square Garden and being able to request a white grand piano one night and a black grand piano the next, then three nights later, back at home, being asked by his wife to take out the garbage.

The following year, as musical director on the long world tour entitled A Reality Tour, Leonard was responsible for the band's faithful re-creation of a wide range of Bowie's songs, whilst at the same time wanting, for example, to allow Garson's unique musical voice to be able to step forward at the right time and in the right way. Once a rapport was established, Garson was amenable to such direction, even where it might sometimes mean limiting himself to a one-note synth line, if that was what a song required.

Leonard was aware that Bowie's earlier songs had been tinkered with at times over the years in terms of the arrangements, even though 'the essential breadth of work that was there was so well sculpted' that he wanted simply 'to pare it back and let the songs breathe again.' Leonard was playing guitar in unison with that of Earl Slick much of the time in order to achieve a clean, bold sound. He made it part of his job to ensure that there would be places where Garson could 'play the way that he plays,' and that there would be room in the music for that to happen, whilst maintaining the simple integrity of these great songs. This is evident on the *Reality* Tour live recordings, both in Garson's solos and his playing around the other instruments and Bowie's voice, to complement them without intruding on them.

Leonard initially felt, however, that he would need to rein in Garson's prodigious inventiveness and told him, 'Mike, you can't just improvise over David Bowie songs!' and that sometimes something extremely simple was all that would be needed. On the Roseland/Meltdown project, they re-created live the albums *Low* and *Heathen*, and Garson's skills were marshaled to that end. Then, when the earlier songs were presented as part of the *Reality* Tour, a lot of effort was put into finding the original keyboard sounds, with Mellotron or Jupiter patches being nailed down and old tapes scoured by producer Mark Plati and the programmers. As the tour unfolded, Garson was gradually given more expressive leeway to add his trademark twists and embellishments within the piano parts.

Leonard exhibited great skills in managing the artistic side of the production. He methodically ascertained for each individual band member 'how they liked to do things, how they liked to be treated, communicated with, and receive their information.' When it had come to Garson, he had been keenly aware of the latter's long years of service with Bowie. He had waited a couple of weeks and then called him, specifically to talk through how things might work. This, characteristically, became a lively and enjoyable three-hour philosophical discussion. Garson ended that call by reassuring Leonard, 'You know, Gerry, in the past I've always fucked with MDs. But for you, anything!' We see elsewhere how reluctant he could be to follow direction on those occasions when it seemed ill-informed or pointless, but given the respect he developed for Leonard and the way he had revealed his thinking, Garson became extremely amenable on this occasion.

One example of Garson's genius being allowed to shine out in concert can be seen in 'Battle for Britain (The Letter),' with its complex dialogue between Sterling Campbell's highly syncopated drums and Garson's distinctively dislocated cadences in a skirmish toward the end of the song. Garson was 'happy to know that he had a place in the orchestra that the band was,' according to Leonard. He adapted effortlessly to the new material, and showed the ability to supply the powerful quality of backup that Bowie demands live onstage. In Leonard's words, Garson's 'energy is a good match for David's.'

He continued to be amazed by Garson's skills in both improvising and sight-reading music: 'He could read . . . flypaper! I got him to play different songs with different hands just to see if he could do it—and he could!' To make this impression on the MD was all the more remarkable given that many of the other musicians involved were also highly extraordinary themselves. Leonard describes drummer Sterling Campbell as 'a great musicologist,' bassist Gail Ann Dorsey likewise as having huge musical instinct, while guitarist Earl Slick 'tore up the charts' and played it anyway.

The great atmosphere amongst the band and crew on the *Reality* Tour is quite evident from the backstage footage that was shot throughout the tour, intended to have been an extra on the DVD, though in the end not included. One practical joke stands out in particular. The way that Leonard recounts the story provides a fascinating insight into the camaraderie and spirit of fun that prevailed. Garson had a piano with little speakers set up backstage on which he would practice (as he always has) daily. On one occasion there was a dark curtain by the piano, behind which Leonard hid, having first arranged with Earl Slick to engage Garson in conversation about running through a song together. Whilst Slick and Garson were playing, Leonard from behind the curtain invisibly took away first one, then the other speaker. 'We were a little slap-happy,' he recalls. 'Slicky was going to say, "Hey, Mikey, let's go over that new song?" Whilst he was playing and not looking, the speakers would disappear . . . but Mike just kept playing, even though this mysterious mayhem was going on around him! There's a lot about Mike in that.'

The funny thing was, despite realizing that something weird was happening, rather than stop and question how it could be that the speakers had 'disappeared,' he simply carried on playing. This illuminates his open-minded view of mystery and the supernatural: he wore a slightly intrigued expression but seemed perfectly happy to press on with the music, presumably on the assumption that this was just some unexplained bizarre phenomenon. In addition, there was an element of his commensurate professionalism in ensuring that 'the show must go on.'

The band members on that tour really gelled, whilst at the same time feeling that they each had a musical space in which to breathe. Bowie was very positive about it, and he set them the task of learning a large number of songs from which the nightly sets might be chosen: a list of options that reached at least sixty-four songs at one stage, to Leonard's recollection. This included a 'killer' version of 'Win,' close to the original but with an even greater feel, which was only ever rehearsed but never played onstage. Regarding Garson's own work in the recording studio for Bowie on the *Reality* album, Leonard confirms that he is always both very quick and very amenable.

Earl Slick is a great rock guitarist who, like Garson, comes from Brooklyn. He is of Italian origin, and he speaks with the down-to-earth honest style for which that borough is famous. He is the only person, aside from David Bowie himself, with whom Garson played Bowie tours in both the 1970s and the 2000s. He also played on John Lennon and Yoko Ono's *Double Fantasy* and more recently has toured with the New York Dolls. I had a long conversation with him about his experiences of working with Garson, and he was very helpful and candid about his recollections, opening with the statement that 'Me and Michael are the Bowie dinosaurs!'

He first met Garson when Michael Kamen brought him (together with David Sanborn) into Bowie's band for the *Diamond Dogs* Tour in 1974. Slick was just twenty-one when he began the tour, and was tasked with reinterpreting the guitar parts that Bowie had played himself on the album. He had not been very familiar with Bowie's songs until then, with one exception: '*Aladdin Sane* blew my fucking mind when I bought it. In hindsight a lot of it had to do with this weird mix of rock 'n' roll and this insane piano player. That piano got my attention . . . I loved acoustic piano, but I'd never heard anything like that before.' He continues to be impressed by Garson's authenticity in any genre:

> Michael can do any fucking thing, and he can do it convincingly. If I try to do certain genres of music, I'm fucked, that's why I'm not a session player; but Mike, what he can do is he can go from classical jazz and then he can sit down and play raucous barrelhouse piano like a real guy, he's not faking it—that's a rare bird. I worked extensively with Nicky Hopkins back in the day. What Nicky did is what Nicky did, and he did it better than anybody, but Mike, it's way broader. Of any piano player I've ever played with, Mike has definitely got

the broadest range. His blues playing would be just as fucking convincing as his jazz.

In 1974, Bowie's fame in the United States was huge. As Slick puts it, *Diamond Dogs* was 'when he just really exploded' in the States. 'Being in Bowie's band was like a notch right behind being in the Beatles.' After touring together through most of the second half of 1974, they would not both be on the road with Bowie at the same time again for some years. Garson played on Earl Slick's *Lost and Found* album of material recorded in 1975, which was later retrieved and released in 2000. They would not have the chance to play together again until the period 2000–2004, when once again they were both playing for Bowie, live and in the studio, as well as on many television shows.

This time around, they quickly became much closer friends than they had been in the 1970s. Slick had given up drink and drugs in the intervening years, and he feels that he was able to relate better to Garson as a result. In addition, he and Garson were now bonded by the shared experiences and memories of having played together for Bowie in the 1970s: 'We had a connection that the rest of the band didn't have.' They both played on 2003's *Reality* album, though by then the older approach of having the whole band in the studio together had been updated, with many of the parts being recorded separately.

There is great respect as well as rapport between these two musicians, and Garson also speaks with affection of his old bandmate: 'Slicky is the real deal, and a real character. He tells it like it is, a man of integrity. You know where you stand with him. He also happens to be an amazing rock guitarist.' He jokes that Slick is like one of the more likeable characters from *The Sopranos* or *Goodfellas*. Nicholas Pegg, author of *The Complete David Bowie*, sent me this recollection: 'Generous performer that he is, David Bowie has always made a point of introducing his band members one by one during a gig—and on at least one occasion, I've seen Mike Garson spontaneously breaking into a piano rendition of the famous theme from *The Godfather* to accompany Earl Slick's introduction—much to the delight of the band and the audience! You can really sense the affection between those two great players. It comes off the stage in waves.'

For the long *Reality* Tour, the stage design placed Slick to the left of the stage (from the audience's point of view) with Garson just behind him on a riser, which allowed for a lot of eye contact and communication between them, for example when Garson's wild inspiration would strike. 'Every time he would do something *insane*, which he always fucking did, I would just turn around and smile and go, "What the fuck, where did that come from?"!' But Garson would always return to the underlying structure somehow just in time: 'Mikey could do the most insane shit on the planet, and then all of a sudden, he's right back to it. Never misses a beat.'

For 'Bring Me the Disco King,' Slick was not playing, so would watch Garson from the side of the stage. 'I used to love watching him do that . . . and always with a different twist, every night.' He says that he had a musical affinity with Garson because he is also less inclined to stick rigidly to parts than some guitarists. 'We take the essence and we work around it,' he says. 'That's why we're there—in one way we are there as an anchor, but in another way as loose cannons! Obviously we stuck to the framework, but there would be certain parts in songs where you didn't know what he was going to do for sure, and sometimes he didn't know what I was going to do. I would throw something out and look at Mike, and there would be a big smile on his face—and vice versa!'

Slick believes that the band for the *Reality* Tour was the most perfectly configured of any band lineup throughout the years he has worked with Bowie, both musically and in terms of personality. There was no competitiveness or ego issues. They played well, they were treated well, and they had fun. He applies this to Garson in particular, adding that they were always friends onstage and friends offstage. That remains the case to this day. He says Garson is one of a very short list of people with whom he feels he will always stay in touch, and can rely on to be 'consistent, honest, and straight up. And as for Mike's musical ability, Christ almighty, unless you're fucking deaf, it speaks for itself!'

I mention to Earl Slick that several people have said that Garson is a spiritual person, and ask whether he would concur. He has a refreshingly different take on the word, which he feels is often misused:

Religion and spiritual have nothing to fucking do with each other. The way I look at spiritual people is that they have their feet anchored in reality, which Michael does. Mikey is one of the most straight-up, realistic people I ever met in my life, and to me, that would be the spiritual part. I call spiritual, *honesty*. Honest about yourself, how you act, how you treat people. Most people live with their fucking heads up their arse, they lie, cheat, and steal, and then they go to church. Fuck that. To me, a spiritual guy is a guy that wouldn't mistreat anybody or do anything to somebody which they wouldn't do to themselves, and that's Mikey. He's not ever been malicious, he doesn't hurt people, he does the right thing and he's a straight-up guy. Now, that's what I would consider spiritualism!

Slick goes on to point out that Garson is very sensitive. 'Michael, unlike me, can get his feelings hurt.' If others are dishonest or disrespectful with him, or otherwise mistreat him, he really feels it. This, in turn, makes Slick all the more furious over the handful of times he has seen people act that way despite knowing how badly Garson would feel it. 'Besides being one of the most fucking amazing musicians I've ever played with in my life, he is just one of the nicest fucking giving, caring guys I've ever met in my life. And he can be one funny guy as well, he's got a great sense of humor; one thing me and Mikey did a whole lot of when we were out on the road was really laugh, you know, and that's good medicine.'

Ten years were to pass before David Bowie's next album after *Reality*, 2013's *The Next Day*, on which Leonard also played and indeed co-wrote two songs. In an impressively efficient publicity coup, the new album was kept entirely under wraps during its production, and was revealed to exist to the world only on January 8 with the unexpected release of the single 'Where Are We Now?' and the announcement that the album would follow two months later. Gerry Leonard suggests that Garson's lack of involvement on the album may well be attributable to these extraordinary circumstances: it was recorded in New York under a veil of total secrecy that was assisted by keeping the personnel local (Garson being based in California). In addition, most of the album is in a rock vein with no piano, the only exceptions being the first single released, 'Where Are We Now?' and 'You Feel So Lonely You Could Die,' on both of which piano was provided by New York jazz pianist Henry Hey, who had been previously working with *The Next Day* producer Tony Visconti, and the synth and keyboard parts elsewhere were picked up by Bowie himself.

In contrast, in 2006, when Bowie made a rare appearance at an AIDS benefit concert in New York and performed with Alicia Keys, it was only Garson who got the call. He has always been happy with this understanding that Bowie would call him if and when that was the ingredient he needed for a given project, and not otherwise.

On the question of what Garson was like to tour with, Leonard explains how they were often on the bus together and shared various interests, including the quest for good food on the road, enjoying great conversations about music or spirituality over a meal. On days off, Leonard would sometimes schedule a gig with his own project, Spooky Ghost, and Garson was happy to play at some of these shows as a guest on one or two tracks, in particular 'The Palace,' which lent itself to some great piano improvisation solos. The ambient explorations of Leonard's guitar make a beautiful contrast with the scattered, rhythmic, and brittle pyrotechnics of Garson's piano.

Bassist Gail Ann Dorsey had never met Garson until she was asked by David Bowie in 1995 if she would join his band. She was aware of his having played some 'crazy piano stuff' on early Bowie but had never been a Bowie aficionado, having been 'more into Queen and softer rock.' In the band that then started rehearsing for the *Outside* Tour in the summer of 1995, there were two relative Bowie veterans, Garson and Carlos Alomar, and then, to a lesser extent, Reeves Gabrels, who had played with Bowie in Tin Machine a few years earlier. She felt privileged to be there, and had no idea then that she would go on to play with Bowie for many years to come.

Dorsey was soon brought up to speed by Garson with numerous fascinating tales of the early Ziggy Stardust days. At the time she had a girlfriend, Sara Lee, also a great bass player, who played for Gang of Four, the B-52's, and others. Dorsey later discovered that Sara Lee had called Garson and asked him to look after her, as she was so afraid and nervous in this very high-profile and exacting new job. Garson still says how touched he was by how caring and lovely this message from Sara Lee had been. So he took her under his wing, and Dorsey still feels that connection to him even today. She says that both Garson and Alomar were there by her side to boost her confidence and help her through the first couple of years, which though thrilling were a tough challenge: 'I was hoisted into this whole new world of music that I could never have imagined!'

Drummer Zachary Alford and Garson forged a friendship on tour around their love of good food. Dorsey has a lot of footage she took of them at the time and says that she wanted them to have a television show called the Gourmet Brothers, as they were inseparable and 'ate their way around the world for two years,' spending all of their *per diems* on fine food and delicacies which they would discuss and compare notes on. To this day Garson loves cooking, too, and uses that as a way to relax after a long or intense session of composing or other work.

Zachary Alford also fondly recalls this mission to explore the cuisine of the world whilst on tour. He says that he and Garson would always ask the hotel concierge for the best restaurant in town, then compete to see who could order most exotically or extravagantly. Finally, they would then adopt the stance of food critics and pronounce their appraisals to one another of every aspect of the meal. 'This is all before . . . the whole TV Food Network craze hit . . . We were dealing with classically trained chefs in restaurants that had been around for years. For us it was our education, which we were almost as dedicated to as the music we were playing!'

Dorsey had very little music training; she does not read music and, incredibly for such an extraordinarily accomplished musician, continues to play largely by ear. She pays tribute to Garson's great teaching skills, since during the time of David Bowie's *'hours . . .'* Tour in 1999 she wanted to know more about the music she was playing and had found a piano teacher in her home neighborhood of Woodstock in upstate New York. He had her buying various books, whereas she had in fact asked him to go from basics as if she had been five years old and had never seen a piano before. 'Apparently, they give a five-year-old a book! I guess they do . . . I couldn't get it, and even though I'm a musician, to me it was like . . . I don't understand this, I can't relate these notes to the keys and do all the stuff.'

Like so many misguided piano teachers, he was putting paper and notation before the interaction between player and instrument. Garson asked how her piano lessons were going and asked her to show him something she had learned, using the little two-octave Casio electric piano she had with her on the road. They put it across their laps, and she tried in vain to think of something she could show him. He then said he would call out the names of some notes for her to play. When she took more than a moment to find a note, he interjected, 'Too late!' and explained that she 'had not learned anything,' in that the first priority should have been at least to visually recognize those notes and go naturally to them. This was her first lesson with Garson, 'and from that day on, I took some lessons with him and bagged the teacher!' She still achieves her amazing performances without recourse to formal notation, but says she was shown a new approach to learning by Garson.

Dorsey sees him with his grandchildren, and she also worked with him a few years back on an online teaching project, trying to help young students start from scratch, through which she saw how open and easy he was with children and students, too. 'There's no time projected, he's just there with you wherever you are and whatever's happening,' she recalls. 'He can just get on any level and relate to someone right away, and that's rare . . . It goes back to him having that big and loving heart, really open, to let people be who they need to be. If the world were more like that we'd be in much better shape!'

Garson believes that *1. Outside* will come to be recognized in time as being as groundbreaking as *Aladdin Sane* was twenty-two years earlier. In many ways it was the Bowie project most suited to Garson's whole *modus operandi* as it was conceived by Bowie as an improvised creation, which Garson says was first put to him by Bowie as, 'I'm going to do this improvised album, and pull in a lot of my favorite resources'—including Reeves Gabrels, Eno, and Garson himself.

Gail Ann Dorsey suggests that Garson's addition to the lineup both in 1972 and again in the 1990s not only added a jazz aesthetic to Bowie's palette but brought an additional expressive spirit into the mix, too:

Nothing David does is just about the technical . . . all his compositions and the way they've been recorded, the arrangements of things on early records and even on live shows . . . it's all very, very musical. I didn't realize that until I started to play them as a musician . . . when you start to dissect them you realize how musical and incredible they are. So Mike, I'm sure . . . he's the perfect person to fit that bill for David, because he's not the traditional jazz guy but he had the elements that were necessary, I think.

The styles that emerged on that 1995 album had brought out a very different pianist than the gospel or soul voicings Bowie had elicited from Garson for 1975's *Young Americans*, for example. Garson picks out tracks like 'The Hearts Filthy Lesson' or 'The Voyeur of Utter Destruction (As Beauty)' as being especially experimental, and 'The Motel' is without doubt one of the ultimate showcases of Garson's elegant fusing of his diverse stylistic threads.

On 'Seven Years in Tibet' from *Earthling* (1997, co-produced by Mark Plati), Garson plays an organ solo (using a Farfisa sound generated from his Kurzweil) that he recalls Bowie telling him was one of the best things he had heard him do since *Aladdin Sane*; although totally different in style, it was equally special. Also on *Earthling*, Garson himself regards 'Battle for Britain (The Letter)' and 'Dead Man Walking' as being of interest pianistically. The former features a frenetic piano interlude that builds from about 2:50 with some absolutely classic Garson expression, with progressive layering and embellishment.

In the case of 'Dead Man Walking,' Garson says it was 'the first time I ever played jazz on a Bowie album—straight jazz. Then I ended with this funny little Latin thing. It's hilarious! David doesn't normally like when I play straight jazz in his music, and I did it at the end of that song, I was just playing like it was a "burning" bebop gig. But, against that kind of feeling beat. And, it was natural—I never thought they'd keep it, because there's a long fade-out, but it was really great!'

Likewise, songs like 'The Loneliest Guy' on Bowie's 2003 album *Reality* see Garson's contribution evolving in many ways beyond its role on *Aladdin Sane*, despite the earlier work still receiving more attention.

Another song from the later Bowie albums of which Garson is deservedly proud is *Reality*'s 'Bring Me the Disco King.' This song had first been sketched out by Bowie as early as the 1970s, and had then been recorded for both 1993's *Black Tie White Noise* and 1997's *Earthling*, but was still not used on either. It only finally made it onto *Reality* with a dramatic makeover in which the earlier version was reduced to half the tempo (having started life as something of a satirical stab at the 120 bpm[1] of

1970s disco). When it was finally unveiled in 2003, it had been stripped bare, leaving just a regal piano accompaniment by Garson and a four-bar loop of Matt Chamberlain's excellent shuffle drumming (recorded during the *Heathen* sessions) to create the poignant sense of retrospection that now revealed itself within the song.

Bowie's patience in not using the song until it felt right, on the third album and the third attempt, elicits the exclamation from Garson, 'Talk about integrity of an artist!' He vividly describes the scene as he was asked to play across this drum loop with Bowie on the mic. He was playing on a Yamaha synth that he had given Bowie as a gift (he believes it may have been something like an SY99). Bowie encouraged him to use a chordal progression to build the song rather than any individual notes. For most of the final two minutes he solos using mainly chords. He says he took elements of Brubeck, Shearing, and Evans from the 1950s and 1960s and added some of his own sensibility. He felt the desire to give to Bowie something different than what he had delivered for *Aladdin Sane* or *1. Outside* or *Pin Ups*, and ended up going back to jazz chords. He says that Bowie loved some of the jazz he grew up with too, like Charles Mingus or Stan Kenton. Until now, on his own recordings for Bowie, the piano had only ever been at most 'jazzy,' with a twist (with the exception of the coda discussed above from 1997's 'Dead Man Walking'). But now, Garson found himself on this one occasion pulling in this resource, and the risk paid off, as Bowie loved it.

Garson was not sure whether other instrumentation would be added, but in the end the minimalist treatment was retained, even in terms of the Yamaha electronic piano sound they had been working with in rough:

Well, here's the thing. David—talk about integrity—we recorded the MIDI file into Logic, because that's what Tony Visconti uses. The piano was out of tune in Philip Glass's Greenwich Village studio,[2] so David said, 'Why don't you just play it on this? Then take the files and transfer it into your MIDI grand piano at home?' I get home, record it, spend three days with my engineer, and a fortune just to get it gorgeous and right, by playing the synth recording through my nine-foot Disklavier player-piano and recording that with mics. Sent it to David. Guess what? He decided to leave it as the original sound, because he liked the vibe of that Yamaha synthesizer, that I happened to give him as a present a year earlier, and I was freaked out! I actually called him and said something like, 'David, how come you're not using this great piano one but that little toy?' He said, 'Because I like it.' You know, you've got to love it and you've got to respect him for that, because he knows what he wants. He knew the integrity of the magic of that moment, intention-wise, is going on the acetate or on the CD. And that's being captured more honestly and sincerely than me reproducing and, maybe, having it more refined on a beautiful piano. And Tony is a great enough engineer that he still made it sound like a piano.[3]

Backing vocalist Holly Palmer recalls how Bowie's shows at the turn of the century would often start with an acoustic version of 'Life on Mars?' with just a spot on Bowie, and Garson playing the piano introduction, and how this would transform the space by creating a strongly focused atmosphere and a bond with the audience.

Palmer's first encounters with Garson coincided with having to learn the backing vocals for what she describes as 'song after incredible song that we were rehearsing.' She had released her own album, but this was the first time she had done backing vocals for another artist. Having grown up with his 1980s hits, some of the earlier material was new to her, and she became more and more taken with it. Correspondingly, to realize that Garson had been playing with Bowie in the early 1970s began then to evoke some awe in the sheer weight of experience that his presence brought, knowing that he had been part of that history. She says that she found the whole experience very educational and inspiring.

When introducing the band in 1999 on the French-Canadian television show *Musique Plus*, David Bowie jokingly introduced Garson as 'Erik Satie on keyboards,' before correcting himself. This appears to have been a very happy period within the Bowie band, with much good humor all round.

Mark Plati first worked with Bowie in 1996, initially as a studio engineer, but soon graduating into production of both live and recorded work. He also joined the band, playing bass and guitar on the *'hours...,' Heathen*, and *Reality* albums, in addition to various keyboards and programming duties. Plati and Garson worked alongside one another on the *Earthling* album, the unreleased *Toy* album, and also *Live and Well*, a live album made available exclusively through the David Bowie website, www.davidbowie.com. They played together at the Madison Square Garden show on January 9, 1997, to mark Bowie's fiftieth birthday, and again later that year on the *Earthling* Tour. In the latter part of 1999, Plati became musical director for Bowie's touring band, which meant working with Garson again on the *'hours...'* Tour (1999), the 2000 Glastonbury mini-tour (which included headlining the Glastonbury Festival, as well as the BBC Radio Theatre performance), and the *Heathen* Tour in 2002. There were also many television performances during this period.

Plati reveals his first impressions of Garson:

I first met Mike on one of the first tracking sessions for *Earthling* at Looking Glass Studios in New York . . . I recall Mike being set up in the Looking Glass control room with his Kurzweil piano, which had been specially flown in for him, along with Reeves Gabrels and Gail Ann Dorsey. Zach Alford's drums were set up in the live room. We would then overdub like this, though usually one at a time, so we could concentrate on individual parts. I had already been working with Reeves for a time, so I was almost used to that level of musicality and sheer musical genius—he stole that thunder in a sense, and by the time Mike arrived I kind of expected everyone recording with Bowie to be a walking, talking musical phenomenon. Mike certainly didn't disappoint in that regard—if anything he upped the ante, as his particular sensibility was more classical than Reeves while at the same time he was a monster improviser. Between Mike and Reeves it was like musical jousting, almost a contest—who could pull the most outrageous trick out of the musical hat, yet make it work. It was always exhilarating!

Like Gerry Leonard and others, Plati singles out Garson's solo in 'Battle for Britain (The Letter)' from *Earthling*, which he calls 'just perfect,' and recalls that it was inspired by Stravinsky. In fact, David Bowie specifically asked Garson to listen to Stravinsky's 'Octet' in preparing that solo. Garson had studied Stravinsky in his youth but had not heard the piece for some time. There was a Tower Records store just down from Looking Glass Studios at the time, and Bowie suggested Garson pop down and pick up a copy. His usual method is to listen and absorb such prompts and then to 'do his own thing,' though with that input in mind. On this occasion, he says, he found it an especially stimulating cue. He also recalls Bowie asking him to include part of a Vaughan Williams symphony as an introduction to one of the songs whilst touring during the 1990s, and remarks on Bowie's eclectic taste and wide frame of reference: they were both keen, for example, on the music of Stan Kenton. (A Vaughan Williams symphony was also included in June 2013 as part of the soundtrack to a film shown within Jeremy Deller's 'English Magic' exhibition in the British Pavilion at the 55th Venice Biennale, which featured images from Bowie's 1972–1973 tour.)

Plati says that Garson was a support for him on his first tour with Bowie, which was also his first experience of being musical director; he was missing his family and Garson could relate to that. Also, like Holly Palmer, he has a special memory of the shows on the '*hours . . .*' Tour and elsewhere in which they started with an acoustic version of 'Life on Mars?' performed only by Bowie and Garson. Garson would take to the stage first, to play the familiar piano introduction, to great cheers and applause, after which Bowie would make his entrance, to even greater cheers and applause. Plati recalls being at the side of the stage 'bidding adieu' to Garson as he would walk out, essentially to open the show, and then hearing that wave of enthusiasm from the crowd as they recognized the opening bars.

For Glastonbury, Earl Slick had rejoined the band and was playing with Garson for the first time since the 1970s. Plati was positioned between them onstage, and was struck that he was positioned now 'right in the middle of the *Diamond Dogs* Tour. Those guys were just doing their thing, and it was like no time had passed for them.' Plati, like several others, also reminisces about the love of good food that Garson exhibited, recalling a visit to Milan during which Garson took him and Sterling Campbell to a small restaurant hidden away on a side street, a wonderful little family place, which Garson had remembered from a previous tour. There was also a large group meal in Paris when, asked what he wanted for dessert, 'Mike simply swiped his finger down the list and ordered the entire dessert menu for us all!'

Plati's enduring impression of Garson was of someone who was always searching to top his previous efforts, that it was a constant musical adventure to see what he would pull out of the bag next. Some musicians reach a point of stability that they are happy to inhabit and work within indefinitely, and there is nothing wrong with that, if it works for them. But it was fascinating to see someone of this caliber still constantly questioning, reaching out, and experimenting.

# II

# Music in the Moment

*'He's a master piano player . . . he was the first person who probably introduced my young
mind to the concept of atonality. Bowie's music at the time in the '70s was the first music I
ever heard that I thought, "This is different, where did this come from?"'*

—Billy Corgan, Smashing Pumpkins[1]

FOR SOME YEARS, Garson's pianos have been tuned by Samuel Ben-Horin, an exceptional man who tuned for the Italian opera house La Scala for many years, and then
also for several top jazz musicians. Oscar Peterson even called him onto the stage to
thank him at the end of a concert. Through his proximity to such musicians he has
heard a vast amount of the very best in musical creativity, and he offered me some
telling insights into the distinctive qualities of Garson's playing: 'I am very much
impressed by Michael, as his ability to create is limitless in my view. He has no limits
at all, he is so free in his invention. His creativity is so high. He does not wait for
inspiration, he hears it, it's under his fingers. He goes everywhere: one moment it can
be Scriabin, the next moment something that no one has ever heard . . . it is inspired
and absolutely limitless!'

As a young classical composer, Garson had started out using pencil on manuscript paper, but felt the results were mediocre, whereas through improvisation he
could soar. Today, he mainly uses the Disklavier, which is Yamaha's modern version
of the old player-piano, in order to create classical pieces via improvisation, and has
established this as a specific new form called 'Now' music. This is basically a more
spontaneous and rapid form of classical composition, and as a way of creating new
pieces of music it is no less valid or creative than handwritten scoring. With modern
scoring software these creations are easily converted to printed sheets that others can
then study, learn, practice, or disseminate, as well as perform. In many ways this is a
natural step forward in musical evolution, brought about by rapidly advancing technology and what it can facilitate.

This is just a small part of the wider history of cultural and artistic evolution in
which technical innovation has gone hand in hand with changes in the forms of

output appropriate to that technology. Critics and purists protest that improvisation is not the same as composition, but Garson responds that improvisation is just a very fast form of composition, and he seeks in his improvisations the balance that one finds in classical music.

There is plenty of evidence that some of the most respected composers of the classical era also used improvisation. We may not be able to listen to recordings of Chopin or Liszt improvising, or see scores printed out digitally from their spontaneous performances, but the scores they wrote out by hand did begin their life in some cases more on the keys than on the page. Improvisations, in the absence of any method of instant transcription, would be performed repeatedly until they started to congeal into a more consistent composition (and until their creator could memorize them well enough for them to have a specific identity). Those pieces that met with most favor when performed would be given special attention, to the point at which they solidified into the 'classics' we celebrate today. In this sense the art of improvisation is actually more in keeping with the best traditions of musical composition than is a mechanical devotion to the schematic construction of plans for a piece, in advance of its execution, or a genuflection to manuscript, paper, and pencil.

The most eminent scholar of the role of improvisation in classical music was Ernst Ferand, whose publication in 1938 of *Die Improvisation in der Musik* documented the use of improvisation in various periods of European history and was seminal, though largely ignored by a music establishment that had long forgotten the spontaneous methods of many of the great composers. Ferand, a Hungarian musicologist, further developed this theme and in 1961 edited and wrote the Preface to a book entitled *Improvisation in Nine Centuries of Western Music: An Anthology*. In a review published the following year, it was elegantly stated:

> The final act of composition—the act of setting down a new piece in written symbols—can easily make music motionless, sterile and null, especially if the composer looks on the performer as no more than a rather expensive and unwieldy gramophone whose sole duty is the unerring reproduction of the composer's wishes. If composition can freeze, then improvisation must thaw. For nearly a thousand years Western composers—which is to say notationers—have repeatedly tried to write down their sound-patterns in exact and unalterable symbols, only to find the warm breath of the performer just as repeatedly melting the finished design.[2]

It is important to note with regard to this observation that in several prominent cases the composer and the performer were effectively one and the same person, and as such a process of notation through experimentation was taking place within the creative life of that individual. This would apply in particular to eighteenth- and nineteenth-century composers such as Mozart, Beethoven, Shubert, Chopin, Schumann, and Liszt. With the advent of recording technology in the twentieth century, we start to obtain fascinating insights into the interpretation and develop- ment of their own pieces by Rachmaninoff, Stravinsky, Shostakovich, or Scriabin, all of whom can be heard performing their own creations.

In 1974, Bruno Nettl contributed 'Thoughts on Improvisation: A Comparative Approach' to *The Musical Quarterly*.[3] This also confirms the validation of improvisa- tion as a long-established method of composing, and is strongly reinforced by Dutch music professor Willem Tanke.[4] In recent years, many scholars such as Dana Gooley at Brown University or Lynn M. Hooker at Indiana University have continued to focus on the importance of this thread in the creative process. Hooker writes, 'Liszt also used his musical skills to endear himself to his audience: part of his recital arse- nal was improvisation on tunes favored by or suggested by his audience, and during his 1839–1840 and 1846 tours of Hungary he used popular Hungarian repertoire in such improvisations. Some of these improvisations became the *Magyar dallok* and the *Rhapsodies hongroises*.'[5]

When choosing to improvise within a specified form, Garson enjoys the con- straint of that structure, creating a sense of 'infinite discipline with infinite freedom.' And the listener, too, seems to feel something satisfying about this combination of 'wildness' with structure. He says that someone like John Coltrane can do amazing things over just one chord—melodic improvisation is even more of a challenge when there is only minimal guiding harmonic structure to work within.

He explains that his 'Now' music compositions often start from the challenge of improvising from zero but then progress into adding layers of harmonic progression that interrelate with the melody line. Just as the construction of a building requires foundations and underpinning to go deep into the ground, so the crafting of an improvised composition, whilst using spontaneity, can still benefit from a layer of harmonic progression on which to build. Then, against some simple chord changes, it becomes possible to build tension by straying further and further from the most expected melody, like the stretching of a rubber band, only to return finally to a resolution that is as dramatically satisfying as the preceding diversions may have been discordant. Such resolutions can be found of course throughout classical rep- ertoire as well as jazz. Garson sees a thread of invention, and indeed improvisation, running from 'Bach's composing in a baroque style followed seventy years later by

Mozart's operating in a classical form and Chopin later still developing a romantic voice . . . two hundred years later, Philip Glass doing it with minimal music and repetition . . . and I say we know Bach and Chopin improvised. We have no records of it because there were no tape recorders or player-pianos.'

There is a revealing contrast between Garson's many improvisational compositions and those he made earlier using more conventional techniques (of pencil and manuscript rather than software for scoring more spontaneous creations). He says that these days he feels there is little difference in the outcome whether he writes something out longhand or whether he plays it in, as he knows what he wants to express either way, but twenty-five years ago, when he was more inclined to stick to traditional methods, his written pieces were less spontaneous and more 'heavy,' which is something he is glad to have moved away from. At that time he was 'trying to write sophisticated classical music that would be accepted by my peers.' In 1980, he played a piece to Chick Corea that he had written out by hand; Corea loved it for its form and structure, but Garson felt it was too intellectualized. He wanted to find a way to surpass his own musical vocabularies and eventually started to do this by evolving his technique of improvising to the point where it was capable of creating bona fide pieces with spontaneous structure.

Three elements determined the emergence of his 'Now' music. The first was purely physical. In his teens, as a dedicated pianist rather than composer, practicing several hours a day (as well as doing some weightlifting), he developed severe wrist problems. He was told at one point that he would have to limit his practice to a couple of hours per day, unless he were to have surgery, which he was too fearful to pursue. At times he neglected to take this advice and ended up having to resort to ice packs and anti-inflammatories to reduce the swelling. This motivated him toward composing; some of his improvised creations were extremely difficult to play and would have necessitated many hours of practice, which he was not in a position to do at that stage so he began to pass them on to other classical pianists to work on. In addition to the wrist pain, he was also becoming increasingly committed to the idea of creating something and then moving on each time. It became an integral part of his working method not to dwell but to create and then move forward to the next output, in order to ride the wave of his own creative flow.

Through later years he found that from playing hard and long he would sometimes suffer from soreness, not in the tips but on the sides of his fingers, and acquired the habit of putting Band-Aids around his fingers before performing. This has sometimes attracted more interest from shallow reviewers than his playing. He also comments that he should have had an endorsement deal as he has got through thousands of these, and the brand he prefers is not cheap. Sometimes he even has two or three around the thumb and the little finger. He comments with just a slight trace of humor that people may ask whether this might lead to him playing any wrong notes, adding, 'Well, occasionally, these minor second intervals get hit when they shouldn't . . . but, you know, that only adds charm to my style which is a little dissonant anyway!'

He also says that he is probably not hitting the keys perfectly, otherwise the sides of the fingers would not be so affected, but people develop their own way of playing, and if it works it is best left alone. Whilst it is not 'standard,' he says, neither is anything else he has done in relation to the piano. Yet he retains what he refers to as an obsession with the piano. Unlike others, he was never really interested in experimenting with other instruments, orchestrating, or arranging. Instead he has dedicated himself single-mindedly to making this instrument the tool of his creations, in conjunction with the simple notion he says he was first taught by Lennie Tristano, that true jazz is playing what you hear in any moment.

He says that second to this physical origin of 'Now' music was the mental aspect. 'Mentally, they came about—I tell people as a joke—because I don't remember anything! I have to improvise these things, so I'd better get each one when it's new. As you get older there's some truth to that.'

The third element he refers to as the spiritual:

> If you've practiced your whole life, it's quite a gift and an honor if you can then sit down with all those languages of music . . . and use all that, express how you feel in the moment, using laws of music, rhythm, melody, and harmony . . . When you're in a relationship with another person you can always say, I feel tired today, I feel sick, I feel in love with you, I feel disgusted with you . . . you're expressing how you feel and then the conversation might go from there. But with music, people have a gig, they have to prepare these things. Someone wants this, someone wants that, so you don't always have that opportunity. So I'm trying to create that opportunity by saying, 'Okay, this is what I'm feeling this minute.'

In 2004, Garson was on the panel of judges for the Yamaha Young Performing Artist Award and selected the brilliant young composer-pianist Becker KB as that year's winner in the piano category. They did not meet at that point, but Becker explored the full range of Garson's work (including his work with Bowie and other artists outside of classical music) in the following years, finding a great affinity with Garson's whole approach to music. In 2011 he contacted Garson, and they have remained in close contact since, with Becker recording a number of Garson's compositions, and an album of these is planned for the near future. From their first meeting, Becker tells me, it was apparent that Garson was a 'man of substance' who combined 'great knowledge and experience' with humility and generosity, who was a natural teacher as well as constantly inquiring and seeking to learn as well as teach.

Those first impressions have been confirmed with time. He jokes that, given the genuinely guru-like wisdom he felt was being imparted by his mentor, it seemed apt that on first visiting him he discovered that the home from which Garson was sending such valued advice is situated 'at the top of a mountain'—or at least halfway up. In the intervening years, Becker's own accomplishments have also been exceptional, and he has generously provided much further insight into Garson's music, and especially the way in which his 'Now' music works. Becker has the highly developed technical virtuosity as well as the emotional understanding and versatility to do justice to Garson's compositions. Several of these recordings can be heard online and have been very well received, especially his interpretation of Garson's *Ballade in G-Sharp Minor*, which has proved of particular fascination to other concert pianists.[6]

On hearing in 2011 Becker's own compositions made during the previous seven years, Garson said something that has powerfully inspired Becker in his work ever since. He noted that Becker was in the first stage of his development as a composer, suggesting, 'Something tells me I can push you to and through the next stage because I've not only been there but I understand your creativity and how to go deeper with you . . . you have done your homework and now are ready to throw it all away.' It is Garson's view that the essential groundwork of technical and musicological hard graft must be undertaken, as something of a baptism of fire in self-discipline, but that this knowledge must then be superseded or put aside in order to attain fresh creativity.

Inspired by this, Becker then went on to compose his Piano Sonata 1 and *Enticements and Eternity*, both of which have since won numerous awards. Becker describes some common features between his own works and those of Garson (and credits Garson's influence here, too, though Becker already exhibited some of these elements himself), such as 'intensity of gesture, harmonic adventurousness,' jazz-like lines 'ripping across the keyboard,' a sense of the wild, and improvisational methods used to compose pieces that end up fully notated. Alongside his classical work, Becker also fronts and writes for a highly credible rock music project, KB and the Frozen Heat.[7] He is delighted that Garson has also at times been inspired to create something new in response to receiving a new piece by Becker 'even occasionally referencing my titles in his new work. The synergy also occurs when he hears a performance of mine of some other repertoire and subsequently feels led to write a new piece. He and I are always looking for new sources of creative fire.'

Having now evolved into a prominent interpreter and performer of Garson's compositions, Becker has a keen insight into the concept of 'Now' music. He explains how the idea here is to focus on newness, to capture the feeling of the moment, but to do so with a powerful arsenal of musical tools, resulting in something that is well constructed and challenging on every level, something that can then be transcribed, studied, and performed. Becker is a highly accomplished, award-winning classical pianist, and he describes these pieces, once transcribed, as 'concert pieces of complexity and coherence with much attractive and memorable content, satisfying and stimulating to play and hear. To compose music like this through pure improvisation is insanely difficult.' His appreciation is in stark contrast to the response from some critics from the classical establishment who have condescendingly dismissed Garson's compositions because of his disrespect for conventional boundaries or methods. For example, a review by Timothy Mangan, classical music critic for the *Orange County Register*, on March 2, 2014, of the performance the night before of Garson's *Symphonic Suite for Healing*: 'This was not classical music (despite some claims).'

It is important to distinguish between the relaxed improvisation for its own pleasure that many may engage in, and the focused discipline of this form of composition via improvised classical-sensibility or 'concert' music. Garson has long worked to develop the ability to make judgments in real time that other composers have the luxury of long contemplation over, such as the most desirable length of a section or of the piece as a whole, how far to take a motif, how much development an idea is worthy of, and so on. Through all this there is also a fine balance between intellectual, technical precision and the emotional expression that drives the music. Becker observes:

> Mike's piano music comes from an unadulterated pianist's approach. Since it is conceived via playing, it follows this would be the case . . . one can sense Mike's technical breadth and specific feel for the piano in touch and sonority through the music . . . I know for myself how 'physical' composing can be: my hands like to find and do certain things and this no doubt shows through for Mike as well. While much of Mike's work is highly challenging to learn and play . . . it is extremely playable in the hands even with its virtuosic demands, much like Chopin or Liszt.

Becker has studied, analyzed, performed, interpreted, and memorized many of these creations note by note. He finds, as a highly accomplished pianist, that playing them is both as challenging and as rewarding as playing many of the masterpieces written in more traditional ways by Chopin or Rachmaninoff. This speaks volumes for the success of Garson's project, since around 1990, to harness improvisation as a tool of composition. The elements of jazz and classical styles within his influences and sensibilities are interwoven throughout. Becker singles out Garson's *Ballade in G-sharp Minor* as his favorite. Garson also says that he had been keen to have someone other than himself perform it since creating it in 1998. Of the *Nowtudes*, Becker comments that the *C-sharp Minor* stands out for its passion and intrigue, whereas the *A Minor* and *D Major* have 'surreal' textures. In Garson's *Elegy*, he hears traces of both Bill Evans and Messiaen. One of his favorites is Garson's *Dvorak Largo Variations*, whilst one of Garson's own favorites is the *F-sharp Major Nowtude*, which he has arranged for other instruments. The *Prelude in G-flat* is described by Becker as 'gorgeous, touching, from the heart.' It was orchestrated and retitled *Grace* as a movement for the *Symphonic Suite for Healing*. These are just a selection from the thousands of sonatas, nocturnes, preludes, suites, ballades, homages, and other pieces that Garson has created.

In a series of recorded conversations from 2005 between Garson and his long-term friend and orchestrator/copyist, Bruce Donnelly, we really get to the heart of his working methods and approach to music and to life in general. Donnelly is a highly respected composer in his own right and has orchestrated on several major Hollywood films, as well as playing piano with the San Diego Symphony and Chamber Orchestra.

As an amusing starting point, Garson recalls a presentation he and Jim Walker had done for Yamaha in which the company insisted every word be scripted and checked. Walker had complied whilst Garson had refused. When Garson was MC'ing one of their festivals for young classical pianists, however, and the same rule applied, he submitted a script for approval and then 'when I went up for the final show I changed it around. They haven't called me since then! But I felt more honest about the action!' He contrasts his improvisational approach to performance with the more disciplined temperament of those great artists, whether classical masters like Rubinstein and Horowitz or top singers on Broadway, who are able to perform exactly the same notes night after night, albeit with slight variations of interpretation.

Garson explains how such repetition is not within his nature:

I met a guy who gave a lecture on digestion a few weeks ago. This guy was the funniest guy I've ever seen—he made the subject the most interesting I've heard (it's the most boring subject) and he told me, the following day—he's a chiropractor—I went to visit him, he said this is the six hundredth time he'd done the same lecture. Word for word, the jokes and everything! And, I can't play the same lousy piece once. I almost got in a fistfight with Billy Corgan of the Smashing Pumpkins! We were doing the music for the movie *Stigmata*, and there was a scene that I saw, going by on a roof, and I sat down at the piano and played. He said, 'That's great!' and I knew I'd nailed it. Then he said, 'Try it again.' I tried it again, and it was different. He got very upset—he said, 'Can't you play the same notes?' So, I played it again, trying to remember the same notes. He said, 'Well, they're the same notes, but the phrasing is different.' So, he kept . . . he thought I was messing with him. Corgan said he could repeat a guitar solo, and by the seventeenth time it would be really amazing. But if you don't get it out of me on the second or third time, it's downhill. I might go home and practice it a thousand times, but if you don't get it from me at the start, then . . . I've spent the last twenty years trying to cultivate the ability to play in the moment, because that's what my music has been, with jazz and with classical.

Lennie Tristano, with whom Garson studied, had that spirit; he 'didn't want you repeating your licks,' whereas perhaps 80 percent of the phenomenal performance of Oscar Peterson could be from the classical tradition in terms of its programmed structure rather than spontaneity. Garson has created thousands of classical pieces that he now barely knows, as he has handed them to classical pianists to perform. He may return to the discipline of classical performance at some point but made a decision a long time ago to concentrate on pushing back the boundaries and possibilities of improvisation as a way of letting music live 'in the moment.' If he returns to writing with pencil and paper, he doubts he could compose better than Bartók, Stravinsky, or Chopin, but did they develop their improvisational skills as much as he has? Probably not, as he has devoted nearly half a century to this form of composition, whilst continuing to respect and admire those who work differently. He mentions Larry David's HBO comedy series *Curb Your Enthusiasm*, which is mainly unscripted, as well as the flourishing traditions of 'improv' comedy and even film dramas without scripts.

This was the essence of his term 'Now' music, which he coined in 1995 but which has since become an increasingly commonplace idea. He avoided the term 'improvised music' at that time in order to break its association with jazz and to expand the method back into classical forms, which is where in any case it first began. There is a compelling honesty about capturing how you feel at any one moment, regardless of the vocabulary being used. Only a certain percentage of performances—and indeed of improvisations, too—falls into the 'magic area' or special zone of ultimate inspiration and beauty. Such successes, Garson says, tend to occur 'when I'm getting out of the way of myself,' and losing all self-consciousness. The same variability of quality may have applied to the classical composers, as the discovery of some unpublished works by Chopin may be said to have shown, since they seem to lack some of the genius of those that we know best, suggesting that only the best were prominent enough to endure.

Garson's spiritual beliefs are directly tied in with his musicianship. He sees true musical inspiration as involving a connection to something much larger than himself. He may have worked hard to perfect the technical expression of this, but he is keenly aware of the significance of that special added ingredient that, he says, must make the difference between two artists who have worked equally hard or reached the same degree of technical competence and yet differ in their creation of something truly special. Getting out of the way of yourself is a process almost impossible to teach or learn, as by discussing or trying this you then inevitably bring the mind and the self in. 'Somehow we separate out and create individualities for whatever reason,' he says, 'but when we get into a special moment we connect back to that source.' He cannot credit his musical inspiration purely to his own ego, training, or individual personality, however much of himself there may indeed be in this process. Yet he also desists from the false humility of denying his role as, after all, the 'whole' to which he sees himself connecting also encompasses himself alongside everything else.

Nor does he see shortcuts to accessing that. Keith Jarrett can be seen sitting still sometimes for a minute or two before starting one of his improvisations, presumably a form of prayer or meditation to get 'centered,' but for Garson there is no guarantee there, either:

> I just sit down and play it. It's like I either get it or I don't . . . there's no real scarcity: I could sit down and do it again a minute later, or a day later, so, you don't want to get hung up on the moment of the time. I've rested for twelve hours, and I've eaten perfect, and I play a lousy show one time. I've missed planes. I was filthy, no shower, dirty when I was onstage. One of the best concerts of my life. You can't plan these. The only thing you can plan that'll work is the hard work you do your whole life, to be able to get to where you even deserve

the privilege to have this conversation. In 1972 I turned down both Freddie Hubbard and Joe Henderson, as I thought I wasn't ready for the gig; friends of mine did it, and then on hearing the albums years later . . . I was playing as good or better . . . I was scared to go out and do it because of what we as artists do to ourselves.

The plus side of such perfectionism is that 'it keeps you going—and you get great.' The downside is that 'you never go out and play!' Garson respects 'a lot of the rock artists who grab a guitar and, within a year, they learn three or four chords, and they're writing songs, and they're communicating.' As time goes on, he finds he keeps rediscovering simplicity in music. The reason something works may have complex harmonic, mathematical, or psychological reasons behind it, but often it is the simplest progressions that carry the most compelling beauty. He has also found that the older and better he gets, the more he realizes how relatively little he knows. From thinking he 'knew it all' in his twenties or thirties, he now sometimes feels that he only has a tiny fraction of the musical knowledge or understanding available.

What happens in his mind at the moment of improvisation? Does he think about how long a solo might run? When at his best, he says, he is thinking nothing. We are taught to think of time as linear but it can just as well be conceived of as circular or stacked vertically, but ultimately there is only the moment. There have been times when he has found himself thinking about a mistake from two bars earlier and if so the chance of the finest creativity is lost. During the learning process there have been times when what he hears himself playing has led to what he plays next, but such a process can be too intellectual and only when that is transcended can the best creativity occur.

Beethoven used his genius to develop an initial 'improvised' inspiration, a theme or phrase or movement, into a finely crafted masterpiece possibly carved out over months. Garson's 'Now' music takes this special moment and celebrates it spontaneously. He says that whilst his material may not be at that level he has nevertheless had moments where he truly feels that degree of magic in the initial instant, but that the long process of memorizing and crafting from that is not where his gift lies. He is joyful instead to work with the art of improvising, with its succession of spontaneous present moments.

There is consolation and encouragement for many a frustrated young musician in the way that he describes his own struggle to achieve musicality in his earlier days. He is happy to deal with the question of how he was able to progress. 'I've been asked these questions at master classes for twenty or thirty years. And I'm never tired of the questions. I'm tired of questions like, you know, "What's it like playing with David Bowie?" and "When did you shave your head?" I'm not totally tired of them, but I'm pretty tired of them. But, these kind of questions, each person you're talking to deserves the answer geared to them.'

For several years he kept asking himself when his playing would really start sounding like music. He perfected 'I Got Rhythm,' but it sounded stiff. He asked the bass player and drummer in his trio to 'walk' the beat in time whilst he improvised around it; they would laugh. He turned the time around; he would lose his place. He wrote out an eight-bar solo for the piece but would rush it and they would be laughing again. He would try it in another key, and copy a solo by Wynton Kelly or Bill Evans, but it was still not swinging, and it sounded stiff. Then one day, after several years of this frustration, it finally came together, and he started to find his own musical voice. He believes this was just the accumulative effect of his efforts reaching breaking point. But he remembers those days in his early twenties as very painful:

> I thought it was hopeless at one point. I was totally crazed one day—I remember sitting in my house saying: Who am I? What do I want to play? What is my contribution? . . . I would sit there, I would try playing like Herbie Hancock, Art Tatum, Bud Powell, Sonny Clark, or Phineas Newborn. Because I had the ability to play like all those people or, at least, the superficial aspects of it. I'd play it, and then I'd listen back and say, 'I hate that!' Worse than that, I'd try to play like me, and there was no 'me,' because it was a mixture of them.

He felt humiliated by not having the jazz feel and therefore put himself through the 'torture chamber' of ten or fifteen years of virtually nonstop, self-imposed training of technique until he finally found himself able to crack that code, which has left him with even more expressive tools than before. However, he sees the main obstacle to classical pianists stepping into improvisation as being their own lack of self-belief. They believe that they are unable to step into that freedom, and therefore they are. Even Horowitz did not believe he could create something new, so respectful was he of the achievements of Chopin, Schumann, or Rachmaninoff. Yet the help he gave the latter on one of his sonatas and even his own arrangements of 'Stars and Stripes' indicate that he could have been a great composer.

Self-confidence is always key, and Garson says he has often taught students who proved not suited to being pianists, so he has been content to build their confidence in other ways, to help them find their true vocation even outside of music, and set them on that path.[8] He advises against the harsh self-criticism and mutual criticism so common amongst musicians. People picture their old music teachers 'standing there ready to slap you if you don't get it right,' and even he still sometimes recalls things that were said to him fifty years earlier that prevented him from doing things and taking chances.

One example he gives of his own inner critic in action will ring painfully true with great numbers of serious musicians:

When I was playing in Radio City with David Bowie, I heard two notes that I played wrong. Now, nobody has told me they heard those two notes, but I know where they were—they were in the arpeggio at the end when I was playing across the keyboard. He had asked me to transpose the piece right before we did the song, so I was in an unfamiliar key, and I heard these mistakes, and it really messed me up. But, when I listened to it on television I barely could hear it. And nobody mentioned it to me, and I asked David if he heard it, and others; but it messed with me, is what I'm trying to say. Now, that's not the sign of a rational, sane person. And yet, that's how I grew up, so I try to take the plus of that, which is, it pushed my envelope, I didn't get complacent. But, as for the downside of it, well . . . you just have to talk to my wife for a few hours, you know!

# 12

## Nine Inch Pumpkins

*'My latest thing I'm hot to do is collaborate with some other people. Probably at the top of my list this second is Mike Garson from Bowie's band . . . I don't understand how that sound's coming out of his instrument . . .'*

—Trent Reznor, Nine Inch Nails

GARSON HAS A GODSON christened Sebastian Bach, who is now in his thirties. He used to stay with the Garsons as a young teen in the 1990s, and he went through the normal passions of early adolescence. At eleven, it was Michael Jordan and basketball, but at twelve or thirteen he became an aficionado of Billy Corgan and the Smashing Pumpkins. Garson told him that he was more of a jazz and classical musician but that he had played a lot with David Bowie, to which his godson replied, 'That's nothing, you have to hear Billy Corgan!' with all the certainty of youth.

In December 1995, Garson traveled to Paris, France, for one of Bowie's appearances on the Canal+ television series *Nulle part ailleurs*, filmed at Taratata Studio, on which various major bands were featured. On this occasion, the Smashing Pumpkins were included, so Garson came out of his dressing room to listen. Sure enough, he saw what his godson had meant. They were extremely striking, with an amazing drummer and the vocalist 'just screaming so loudly this wild song "The World Is a Vampire," with such a big and powerful sound!' A little later, Bowie's bodyguard came to get Garson from his dressing room, saying that Bowie was discussing with Corgan about the idea of God, and wanted Garson to be a part of the conversation. In this way Garson met Corgan. Footage exists of this show, and when Corgan and Bowie are interviewed together, Bowie indeed mentions how they had been discussing, before coming on to perform, the existence of God. The context, Bowie goes on to explain, was that he was pleased at the time to see a lot of new artists returning to the eternal questions of why are we here, where are we going, and where do we come from, and that a renaissance in the quality of popular music would be predicated on such a return to the fundamental issues, in contrast to the relative superficiality and frivolity of popular culture in the 1980s. He says there may have been exceptions to this lack of quality in the 1980s but he struggles to find any, 'including myself!' He attributes this gradual return of eternal questions to *fin de siècle* anxieties, amplified by millennial angst.

On January 9, 1997, Garson was playing at Bowie's fiftieth birthday concert at Madison Square Garden, and Billy Corgan was featured as one of many special guests that night, so this would have been the first time that he and Garson had played together onstage. Early in 1998, Garson was touring with his jazz group, Free Flight, and heard that Billy Corgan was auditioning piano or keyboard players, as his previous keyboard player, Jonathan Melvoin, had died of an overdose. Garson knew Nancy Berry at Virgin Records, so he called her and asked about this. She asked Corgan and came back with the message that if Garson wanted to join him and the Smashing Pumpkins, there was no audition necessary.[1]

The *Adore* tour for which he then joined Corgan was, Garson says, a change of direction for the band. Drummer Jimmy Chamberlin, who had been with Melvoin when he overdosed, was no longer part of the band, and had been replaced by a hugely powerful rhythm section featuring drummer Kenny Aronoff and percussionists Dan Morris and Stephen Hodges. James Iha was still on board, however, as was bassist D'arcy Wretzky.

Garson says he found Corgan to be a great singer, musician, songwriter, and person to work with, and thoroughly enjoyed touring with him. A lot of the live dates were recorded by Corgan on DAT tape and may be released at some point. On December 12, 1998, Garson and Corgan played an acoustic set together at the Shrine Auditorium in Los Angeles, as part of a show also featuring Depeche Mode, Garbage, and others. Film of this strikingly stripped-down duet reveals some truly powerful moments, with Garson's piano complementing Corgan's visceral and raw delivery with a great combination of passion and delicacy.

Garson created a long piano solo over a series of motifs written by Corgan called 'Le Deux Machina,' which can be heard only on the bootleg cassette tape *Friends and Enemies of Modern Music*, a collection of various demos and live tracks from that period that is not to be confused with the album *Machina II/Friends and Enemies of Modern Music*. The latter album contains a much shorter version of the same theme, played on a synth, which was created by Corgan first, who then asked Garson to take this as a starting point to expand into the piano version heard on the bootleg. This piano solo by Garson also appears, chopped into segments, in the middle section of 'Glass and the Ghost Children' on the *Machina/The Machines of God* album. He also played on this latter album's 'With Every Light.'

This piano track, which lasts nearly six minutes, had never been heard by Garson since he recorded it in 2000, but when I play it to him now he recalls that Corgan wanted him to record it on an old upright piano, as he loved the sound of this particular piano. This was a 1910 upright from Toronto with a naturally out-of-tune, broken, old sound that today sits in Billy Corgan's living room in Chicago. (The piano used on 'Annie-Dog' on the *Adore* album, by contrast, was a beautiful 1940s Bösendorfer, which Garson later played on himself for a live session at a local Chicago radio station.) Garson did not like the sound of it at all and found the old piano a nightmare to play, but he respected Corgan's wishes, as it was his song, and they were pleased with the results. Listening back now to his own work on it, Garson finds the piece 'a little heady, but certainly interesting. It's a complicated kind of a harmonic piece that he wrote, with that progression, and certainly more enjoyable than the synth version!'

Garson and Corgan went on to collaborate on the soundtrack for the film *Stigmata*, released in August 1999, which also included a Bowie song, as well as 'Identify' by Natalie Imbruglia, which was co-written by Garson and Corgan and produced by Nigel Godrich. The *Stigmata* soundtrack album contains ten tracks performed by 'Billy Corgan and Mike Garson,' six of which are credited as co-writes by the two of them, though Corgan tells me that he had a struggle over rights as the film company insisted on retaining ownership of the original music commissioned from him for the film. In these pieces of music there are some deeply moving and often dark moments befitting the demonic theme of the film. Corgan was interested in twelve-tone scaling at the time. The song 'Identify' had been intended for Shirley Manson of Garbage, but her management turned it down without consulting her, so it passed to Natalie Imbruglia.

Garson also played on the Smashing Pumpkins' *VH1 Storytellers* television broadcast, recorded on August 24, 2000. Later that year, he rejoined the band on their *Machina* tour, and was with them in Chicago on December 2, 2000, for the emotional last show before the band broke up for the first time. There were a host of special guests brought on with whom Garson also played that night. They had chosen to play in the same small venue that they had started in as a band twelve years earlier in Chicago, the Metro. Garson was in incredible form. At the end of the night, while the audience were showing their appreciation, Corgan whispered into Garson's ear, in a heartfelt way, 'I couldn't have done it without you,' which, Garson says, was the warmest moment, adding with a chuckle, 'and that's the last time I saw him, I think.'[2] He did, however, work again with James Iha, playing on the track 'Appetite' for Iha's second solo album, *Look to the Sky*, released in 2012.

On his way to Chicago to rehearse for the Smashing Pumpkins' *Adore* tour, Garson got a call from Trent Reznor, who asked him to play on three tracks for the new Nine Inch Nails album, *The Fragile*, which was then in production. Corgan let Garson miss three days of rehearsals in Chicago in order to fly to New Orleans to record with Reznor. Garson is modest about having been in such demand, reflecting that, like any musician, he just felt he should make the most of a busy period in his career.

It is a mark of the respect that Garson has earned from his fellow musicians that, when he heard in 2014 that I was writing a biography of Garson, Reznor took the time to call me at home in London whilst on his way to soundcheck with Nine Inch Nails for a show in Virginia, to recount in detail his experiences of working with Garson from 1995 onward.

In 1995, Nine Inch Nails were rehearsing with David Bowie and his band for their joint tour of North America, which began on September 14, 1995. Reznor was already flattered to have been invited to tour with Bowie, and he felt slightly intimidated, which was reinforced when he got to rehearsals and saw 'this imposing figure behind a keyboard' looking over. The rehearsal studio was full of 'this unbelievable piano-playing . . . but you couldn't see his hands, he was looking straight ahead . . . I remember thinking, "Where the hell is this coming from?" Incredibly complex and beautiful music, which . . . he was improvising.'

That tour was artistically experimental on many levels. At the end of NIN's set, Bowie would come onstage and sing with them. Then his band came out, and the bands played together for a song or two, after which NIN left the stage. Reznor stayed on with Bowie's band for a song, then finally left the stage, whilst Bowie and his band continued. Sometimes, Bowie and Reznor duetted on Reznor's song 'Hurt.' Bowie had made it clear that this tour would not be a showcase for past hits but a continuation of the artistic experimentation of the *1. Outside* album. The night was 'two and a half hours of musical evolution,' recalls Reznor, who, like Bowie, handpicks his musicians to challenge and inspire the audience, and carefully curates stage shows rather than just performing at them. On July 11, 2012, a *Rolling Stone* magazine readers' poll put NIN on this tour among 'The 10 Best Opening Acts in Rock History,' even though both artists here had equal billing.

Of Garson, Reznor now says, 'Being in the same room as him every day for soundcheck, it's hard not to get drawn into his world, because it's amazing.' He had heard him play on the Bowie albums but did not know what to expect on a personal level. He found him 'approachable, nice, warm . . . thoughtful and cerebral.' It amused him when Garson told him that in the seventies he had 'toured,' in the eighties he had 'practiced'—as if each decade were merely an afternoon.

Perhaps this reflects Garson's very long-view perspective on his own evolution as a pianist, as well as that of society. For his part, Garson had been recommended just earlier that year to listen out for Nine Inch Nails by a young opera singer he was working with, fourteen-year-old Jessica Tivens, just as his young godson Sebastian Bach had put him on to the Smashing Pumpkins. He was still not generally an aficionado of rock music. Garson gives his own parallel description of that first encounter with the NIN sound, during the rehearsals for their joint tour. 'We would nod to each other in the hall when we passed through in soundchecks and rehearsals, and there was a warmth between us. Then I hear these guys playing and I thought, these guys are out there. And the music was so loud, and literally screaming at the audience, songs like "Starfuckers, Inc." and "Closer," things just like flying out, and guitars flying onstage, wild words . . . Again, I knew they were great, it just wasn't my cup of tea, but I couldn't refute the brilliance there.'

After the tour, Garson was reading a magazine and saw Reznor quoted as saying that one of the people he would most like to work with was Garson, while also mentioning that they had played a little together during soundchecks, and that he had been amazed by the phenomenal results Garson could produce with his instrument.

A further couple of years passed before Garson got the call to play on *The Fragile*, and he appreciates that 'these guys make a mental note and when the time is right they call you . . . there was something about him as a visionary and Bowie as a visionary, there was a big connection; David respected Trent a lot and vice versa.'

This latest turn in Garson's career was again completely unexpected. None of the classical, jazz, or even pop or rock that he had moved between in earlier years had made an invitation to play for Nine Inch Nails seem a logical or likely step, but as passionate and distinctive creative artists, neither Reznor nor Garson was willing to let such artificial boundaries or demarcations between genres or styles matter one iota. Reznor recognized something in Garson that he could add to his band's music, which he says he did not even see himself until it was proposed.

Interviewed once again in *Keyboard* magazine after having worked with Garson on *The Fragile*, Reznor updated his report: 'Mike has been a huge inspiration to me; he's such a monster player, he never disappoints.' On the prevalence of real piano sounds on the album, he added, 'Especially in what's already this harsh, alien environment of distorted guitars and violent drums, there's something beautiful and honest about an unadorned piano anchoring it all.'

Reznor explains to me that from *The Downward Spiral* (1994) onward, he has always tried to bring in musicians to play on each album who will approach the music from a different perspective from his. In the case of *The Fragile* (1999), he thought Garson might lend an interesting dimension to the music and invited him to do whatever he felt inspired to, and not to be limited by what was there. This clearly paid off.

On September 10, 2009, Garson guested on several songs at a very emotional gig at the Wiltern in Los Angeles at which Reznor retired NIN from any future live work (though in fact they did resume touring from 2013). The show lasted more than three hours and featured almost forty songs and various guests, including Dave Navarro, the Dillinger Escape Plan, and others. It ended dramatically with each of Reznor's bandmates leaving the stage with a wave, one by one, finally leaving him at the keyboard singing under a single spotlight:

'You know none of this is real,
You will find a better place in this twilight.'

In the summer of 2014, Reznor was completing work with Atticus Ross on scoring David Fincher's film *Gone Girl* and needed some piano for a scene. It needed to evolve out of a synth sound cue that was already in place. After just a short briefing, Garson instinctively knew what was needed and quickly sent Reznor four variations, all done in real time. When he heard them, Reznor 'got goose bumps; it was a thousand times better than how in my head I thought it might sound.' Fincher, who had also directed *Seven*, which used 'The Hearts Filthy Lesson' in its closing credits, was equally delighted—it had 'just the right aesthetic, the heart' that he wanted.

Reznor tells me that he has always found Garson to be of even temperament, attentive, and sharp at taking direction. If he has sometimes had to point out that something is too avant-garde or in the modern jazz idiom for his music, he finds that Garson can swiftly be guided how far to reel it in, to the shape or space needed. Generally, however, he just leaves Garson to do his own thing.

Yet again, like so many others, Reznor identifies Garson's distinguishing feature as the combination of virtuoso technique with an ability to be spontaneously expressive—in other words, with emotional literacy. Reznor had himself in his youth been encouraged to train as a concert pianist, but he had decided that such a life was not for him. He saw how the devotion to technique over many years left some virtuosos relatively devoid of spirit or spontaneous emotive fire. He followed the path instead of becoming a composer, multi-instrumentalist, and producer, and expressing himself through a variety of channels. In Garson, however, he sees someone who did specialize in one instrument and who applied himself single-mindedly to the discipline of mastering it, yet without having lost his multidimensional, expressive personality.

Boyhood in Brooklyn, 1949. *Garson Family Archive*

With sister Barbara, 1950. *Garson Family Archive*

Mike Garson's parents, Sally and Bernard Garson, 1951. *Garson Family Archive*

Fishing with Dad near Coney Island, 1953. They would leave by boat from Sheepshead Bay in Brooklyn or from Montauk at the very end of Long Island. *Garson Family Archive*

The Impromptu Quartet at Prospect Park, 1961. *From left:* Mike Garson, Dave Liebman, Gary Zehner, Robert Katz. *Garson Family Archive*

With Susan: childhood sweethearts in the Catskills, 1962. *Garson Family Archive*

Elvin Jones, Garson's favorite drummer. *Garson Family Archive*

In the army band, stationed at Fort Wadsworth, Staten Island, 1966. *Garson Family Archive*

Mike and Susan Garson on their wedding day, March 24, 1968. *Garson Family Archive*

At the piano with baby daughter Jennifer, 1971. *Garson Family Archive*

Brethren, 1972. *From left*: Rick Marotta, Mike Garson, Stu Woods, Tommy Cosgrove. *Garson Family Archive*

Hotel allocation list for the St. Regis Hotel, Detroit, during the *Ziggy Stardust* Tour with David Bowie, October 8, 1972. *Robin Mayhew*

On tour with David Bowie, 1973. *From left*: Ann, baby Sarah, and Trevor Bolder; Geoff MacCormack; June and Woody Woodmansey (crouching); three others; Mike Garson, Mick Ronson. *Garson Family Archive*

David Bowie and Mike Garson, listening back to *Diamond Dogs* at Olympic Studios, London, February 1974. *Kate Simon*

The *Diamond Dogs* Tour at the Universal Amphitheatre, Los Angeles, September 8, 1974. *From left*: Earl Slick, David Bowie, Dave Rausch, Mike Garson. © *Gerard Gibbons*

michael garson • musical director - keyboards/ emir ksasan • bass/ pablo rosario • percussion/ carlos alomar • rhythm guitar/ dennis davis • drums/ david sanborn • alto saxophone/ earl slick • lead guitar

garson band

Detail from the program for the David Bowie Soul Tour, Radio City Music Hall, New York, October 1974. *From left*: Carlos Alomar, Dennis Davis, Mike Garson, Emir Ksasan, Pablo Rosario, David Sanborn, Earl Slick. *Garson Family Archive*

Recording session for *Young Americans*, 1974. *From left*: Mike Garson, Bruce Springsteen (seated), Tony Visconti (seated), one other, David Bowie. *Ed Sciaky*

Performing live with the Incredible String Band, 1974. *Garson Family Archive*

At a party to celebrate finishing recording *Young Americans*, Sigma Sound Studios, Philadelphia, November 1974. *From left*: Mike Garson, David Bowie, Luther Vandross. *Dagmar*

Contact sheet from a shoot during the
recording of Young Americans, 1974.
© Iconic Images / Terry O'Neill

Detail from a contact
sheet from a shoot
during the recording
of Young Americans,
1974, with David Bowie
drinking from a carton
of milk, which, with bell
peppers and cocaine,
constituted his entire
diet at this time. © Iconic
Images / Terry O'Neill

With stars of jazz, funk, and fusion, backstage after playing with Stanley Clarke, 1980. *Standing, from left*: Mike Garson, one other, Rodney Franklin, Herbie Hancock, Chick Corea, Stanley Clarke, George Duke, Jeffrey Osborne. *Seated*: Paco De Lucia, one other. *Garson Family Archive*

Portrait of Mike Garson by David Bowie, created during recording sessions for the *1. Outside* album at Mountain Studios, Montreux, Switzerland, 1995. *Garson Family Archive*

With Reeves Gabrels: a "Casablanca" moment. *Garson Family Archive*

With Billy Corgan during the Adore Tour with Smashing Pumpkins, 1998. *Garson Family Archive*

With David Bowie at the soundcheck for BBC TV's Parkinson, September 2000. © *totalblamblam@davidbowie.com*

David Bowie and Mike Garson at the filming of *Parkinson*, September 2000.
© *totalblamblam@davidbowie.com*

Reznor told me that singing his 1994 song 'Hurt' live with David Bowie and Mike Garson on piano on tour in 1995, together with hearing in 2002 that Johnny Cash wanted to cover it, have been two of the proudest moments of his career so far.

I asked Trent Reznor to sum up his perceptions of Garson overall. 'Mike reminds me of what's possible,' he says. 'He plays and speaks from the heart and is able to maintain humanity and compassion. You can feel it behind the notes that he plays and in his approach to music. He's generous, inspiring, accommodating. I feel like when I'm around him I step my game up. He really has it together. I think I work pretty hard but when I see him I see the results of focus, and what seems to be a real commitment to excellence, and I find that very impressive.'

On November 7, 1997, Garson was in Buenos Aires, Argentina, again touring with David Bowie, this time on the *Earthling* Tour, with Reeves Gabrels on guitar, Gail Ann Dorsey on bass, and Zachary Alford on drums. It was the last date of the tour, and the support band was No Doubt. He had not known them previously, but he had been watching them onstage, and he was impressed. Gwen Stefani would be 'climbing up scaffolding onstage, singing and spitting into the audience, the drummer would be playing naked, the audience always loved it, and they were just characters.' No Doubt keyboard player/trombonist Gabrial McNair and Garson became friends; Garson even gave McNair a piano lesson.

Two years later, No Doubt were recording 'Too Late,' a track for their *Return of Saturn* album, with string orchestration by Paul Buckmaster, who had worked as an arranger on David Bowie's song 'Space Oddity' in 1969, as well as on many of Elton John's albums. They were finding the arrangement too crowded, so they decided to hold it back, and a much more rock-style version, with vocals, appears on the album. But they still had the beautiful orchestration of the other version, and decided to put it on the end of the album as a bonus track, with Garson on piano. It was produced by Glen Ballard, who wrote 'Man in the Mirror' for Michael Jackson, and appears as a hidden track about five minutes after the end of the album. Garson describes it as 'just movie theme stuff, but gorgeous,' and says that he had a wonderful time working with Stefani and the band. Stefani was sobbing as she stood in the studio and heard the piano version for the first time, as she felt it brought an aspect of her music to life in a special way that she had not heard before, and this cemented an enduring bond of friendship between her and Garson.

In 2005, Gwen Stefani was playing a solo show in Las Vegas as part of her Harajuku Girls tour. She arranged with Garson that she might bring him up onstage to join them to play on 'Long Way to Go.' He was in the front row with his family.

Zachary Alford was on drums, Gail Ann Dorsey on bass. Stefani's keyboard player and musical director, Kris Pooley, had sent Garson the song just three days before. There were seven thousand people in the audience. There was an M-Audio keyboard set up onstage with a piano sample using Reason software. It was 'as if some of the young crowd in the audience were not used to hearing even the sound of a piano,' recalls Garson. He played an extended introduction and a long piano solo at the end, and felt he was really able to 'stretch out quite a bit,' adding that it was 'a total joy' for him. He comments that Stefani is one of the few successful artists who has retained her humanity, dignity, sweetness, and humility through all of the fame.

Kris Pooley was good enough to let me hear a recording of this performance, and it was absolutely stunning. Reunited with his Bowie bandmates, Garson and the others really let rip. It had been decided to allow the ending to play itself out freely, which meant suspending the time-code elements of the program, with lighting, video, and backing held whilst the live performance ended. 'Everyone had to be on board, because time code was going to stop, they had to jump out of their automatic program changes, so we had to let everyone know, "Let's not have the lights go off!"' explains Pooley. As he stood aside to watch, he was amazed at what Garson did. 'It was a purely punk-rock moment, in the context . . . it took a really sharp left turn!' This was a pop concert in Vegas, after all, and there was something strangely subversive about Garson's performance. His jazz licks were faster than ever that day and took on a new color, here being played against a strong and funky pop beat unlike anything he had played with previously. The performance ends dramatically, and we can hear guitarist Warren Fitzgerald exclaim at the end, 'Wow! God damn!' and start clapping.

Pooley, who has also toured with Katy Perry, Kesha, Morrissey, Siouxsie Sioux, and Smashing Pumpkins, is a long-standing friend of Garson's and has a lot of insight into his life and work. They first met soon after Pooley had moved to Los Angeles in 2001, and he recalls that Garson was extremely kind and generous, finding work for him and being supportive of him, clearly keen to help a young pianist who was also jazz trained and was trying to make a go of it. By then, Garson had already recorded with Gwen Stefani and, coincidentally, Pooley would go on later to become her musical director.

Their first meeting came when Pooley was assisting Garson and David Arana with producing Yamaha Disklavier disks on which Garson would play over famous pop or jazz recordings, from Céline Dion to John Coltrane to Counting Crows, so that people in their homes could see as well as hear what he had played, together with the original CD, on this modern player-piano. Some of them were albums that he had played on originally himself, so he would be inventing a second piano part and playing it with his own first part. Some of the keyboards in the range at that time were not fast enough in their action to keep up with Garson's 'lightning left-hand speed,' and Pooley had to adjust the MIDI information to make it more easily playable by the automatic action. In other cases, his subtlety and finesse in playing really quiet notes inside clusters of chords did not have sufficient velocity for the Disklavier keys to be activated. It would have spoiled the effect simply to increase the volume of these notes, so they had to clean up the MIDI data in more subtle ways.

In explaining this, Pooley incidentally expresses a wonderfully accurate summary of some key features in Garson's playing, such as his using classical or avant-garde stylings in the right hand mixed with frenetic, boogie-woogie- or blues-influenced rolled notes and clusters in the left hand; a lot of modal stuff; block voicings; and all of this laid over deceptively simple chord progressions. He throws pop music into stark relief by playing modes over it in a way that is unique to him. This is why certain artists want him on their material, Pooley emphasizes: 'They want the big question mark, which stretches your ear over what otherwise would be fairly standard harmonic patterns which they are using.' Pooley trained extensively in jazz, to the point where he no longer liked it so much, but he is especially interested when he hears Garson using his jazz skills in other contexts, or performing his own classically oriented works of original composition through improvisation. They have remained in contact through the years, and Pooley still admires Garson's distinctive style.

# 13

# Teaching People to Find Their Voices

*'Once I dissected the pig and made spare ribs and chopped liver, I knew I was meant to be in the music department!'*

—Mike Garson, on giving up studying medicine

GARSON HAS ALWAYS ENJOYED the process of teaching as part of his repertoire of communication, and he has been happy to pass on his skills, at whatever level, ever since he was first asked at the age of seventeen by a young girl from his school to show her how to play like him, to which he said, 'Right, give me three dollars and I'll start teaching!' He takes the view that the student 'cannot do anything wrong,' and that it is up to him to get them to achieve what their dream is, which can be anything they ask for. He recalls one woman, working as a secretary in an office, who had no desire to work as a musician but simply wanted to learn 'all of the old-school blues licks in C—not even jazz blues but old-time blues, like Meade Lux Lewis or Doctor John.' He did this with her for a whole year, at the end of which she shook his hand, said thank you, and left.

I never saw her again. Looks like she lived happily ever after. Then, one girl came, about ten years later—she says, 'I just want to play New Age music, and I only know a few chords, and I don't like jazz. I don't want to read, I don't want to play classical, I don't want to play scales, I don't want to play Bach, I don't want to open a page of music, I just want to play for you what I sit and do at home. I sit at my piano, and I play five or six hours a day over an A minor and G chord, and I just keep playing.' She says, 'I just love doing it.' So I said, 'Okay.' I'd sit on the couch, and she'd start playing. I'm listening to her for a half-hour, forty minutes. Finally, I fall asleep. I wake up an hour later; she's still playing. I said, 'I apologize, is that okay?' She said, 'Oh, no problem, go back to sleep . . . I'm learning, I'm good.' And, we did this for a few years. She made a record—she loved what she did. She became pretty good at New Age piano playing. And, three years later, I get an email—she's working on her first symphony. She went to study orchestration with somebody; she learned how to score; she learned how to read music. She did it when she wanted to do it, but when she was with me, she just wanted to do that other thing.

Given the goal of New Age music to be relaxing, perhaps Garson's falling asleep was the best compliment he could pay her. He does not mind what or how someone wants to learn, provided they have a commitment to, and passion for, their own goals. Many of his former students went on to become highly successful in different ways. Vonda Shepherd, who was the featured singer/songwriter in the television series *Ally McBeal*, had been a student of his when she was only fourteen.

He has had some unfortunate assignments, however, such as one student who could barely play at all and yet would pepper the lessons with inquiries about David Bowie, and to some extent about Garson himself. Garson's wife Susan had this student pegged as a stalker who was using the lessons to get access to Garson, though he took longer to suspect this. He recounts this anecdote, like so many others he tells, with the most hilarious deadpan delivery:

I started to get the idea, this is just an obsessed fan, he's got another agenda, he's just willing to pay for the lesson to really talk with me . . . but, I kind of went into denial—this couldn't be, you know? I should've known when I saw him hiding behind the bushes when I opened the door one day, and saw him sneaking around! Anyway, this went on for a few lessons, he brings his keyboard to the lesson, and the keyboard had a sequencer and, as you know, a sequencer's like a modern-day tape recorder. He says, 'Can you play for me on this so I could study it at home? What you played on the *Aladdin Sane* album for David Bowie? . . . I can go home and study it, and slow it down.' I thought it was a pretty creative idea on his part. So, I played this very advanced solo, thinking to myself, 'How's he going to play this? He can't play a C scale. But this is what he's asking for, I'll give it to him.' I get a call about a month later, and the guy is in tears. I said, 'What's the matter?' You know, I was very concerned. He says, 'Well, I have to confess to you, I took this recording which you made, and I brought it to this young rock band that had just signed with a big label, who's looking for a keyboard player, and I played him this thing, and told him it was me playing . . . And they said, "Come to the studio next Monday, we'll have a big nine-foot piano for you to play on our album."' So, he goes to their studio, and he sits down, and he starts, like, barely playing the C scale. And they're hysterical, laughing, the rock band, they thought he was putting them on. So they said, 'Okay, let's record now!' And he starts going [*hums*], and they realized this guy was a fake. They wanted to kill him because they had booked studio time and everything. Now this guy was delusional and out of his mind. I said, 'What were you thinking? Now I can't teach you anymore, you know, I can't help you, you're not here with the right motive, you did a dishonest thing.' Furthermore, the band had said, when they first heard the recording, 'Hey, you sound a little like Mike Garson! You know, we think you'd be good in this band!' Of course, it was me playing, so it should sound like me. Wasn't as great as I play on record for David Bowie, because I was playing on this little keyboard, and trying to give him a rough idea, but still it was good enough to get into this band, and for them to want to hire him on sight!

Another time a man had accidentally heard Garson play in a club, as he was starting in accountancy and had walked into the wrong doorway, the club being next to the accountants' office. He said he liked the idea of being a pianist instead and was impatient to be converted to that by Garson, who had to explain that this was something that would take several hours a day for many years. He soon capitulated, confirming that he had already spent the past four years in school preparing to be an accountant and was not prepared to put that sort of time into the piano, as he was doing graduate studies now in accountancy. Such whims are common and easily redirected, and Garson simply pointed him back into the correct door, quite literally.

He taught a former military man in his seventies. He had been a colonel in the marines with secret intelligence information during World War II. They would joke about this, and Garson would tease him to reveal the nature of the operations he was involved in but he would never divulge anything, except that he had loved playing the piano earlier in life and now it meant a lot to him to return to that simple pleasure. He had as a younger man played old standards like 'Up a Lazy River' and wanted to get back to that in his old age. He said, 'I'm preparing for the next life!' Garson spent two years trying to teach this man not to add a fifth beat to one of the bars when playing in four time. Then one day it occurred to him, 'He was not going to play with a bassist and drummer, and he was not going to Carnegie Hall, so why not leave the guy alone? So I started to say, "Good for you, Matt, you go for it." He died a few years later, but this meant a lot to him.'

Another excellent principle of teaching espoused by Garson is to recognize and praise what is great in what a student is doing as much as identifying their weaknesses, aiming for a fine but essential balance between building on what they have, to give them validation and confidence, and dealing with the flaws. This may sound obvious, but it is extraordinary how much music teaching has traditionally failed to take this balanced approach. Garson credits his lively and off-the-page approach to teaching to what he has learned from playing in the world of rock music, where the methods of learning and communicating new songs are diametrically opposed to the way in which he had originally been trained. Many people find they learn better by hearing or imitating than by reading symbols on a page. He still has books on his shelves about 'how to write a fugue' and to this day 'cannot get past the tenth page.'

Garson's own composition and harmony teacher was Robert Starer. For a final assignment he was meant to compose in a baroque style with no parallel fifths or octaves. Mischievously, he intentionally wrote every melody note with a parallel fifth or octave, but Starer said that he could not give him an 'F' as his doing it so wrongly proved he must have known how to do it correctly, so he said, 'I'll give you a "D," and get outta here!'

In three lessons from Herbie Hancock, Garson felt that wonderful sense of the transmission of something. Hancock spoke of his love for Ravel, Miles Davis, and Oscar Peterson, just played a few things, and showed him a particular diminished scale. Hancock heard Garson ten years later and said he could not believe how far he had progressed, as Garson was soloing some bass lines with his left hand, which Hancock said he would not have been able to do in the same way.

Amongst the many teachers Garson himself was trained by, there was Hall Overton, who had done the arrangements for Thelonious Monk's big-band albums of 1959 and 1963. He was teaching at Juilliard but had a great jazz understanding and had made his own transcriptions, taken by ear, of Monk tunes that at the time had not been published. There was also an exceptional young teacher named Larry Schubert, who was the best at breaking things down and really explaining the structures of jazz. There was also his visit to Bill Evans for one long lesson, as described earlier.[1]

All of these lessons came between the ages of about seven and twenty-seven, whereas from the age of twenty-eight until the present time, Garson set himself the challenge of 'unlearning' it all and restudying everything on his own terms. Those early years had seen him giving full vent to an almost compulsive discipline and exhaustively methodical approach.

I dissected solos . . . I used to slow down the tape recorder to exactly half the speed, so that it was one octave lower, and I would notate it note-for-note; the left-hand chords, and the right-hand lines, and I would practice it with the tape recorder, then I'd bring it up to speed. Sometimes I'd take a four-bar phrase I liked out of it and learn it in twelve keys, and then take one line of the four-bar phrase and alter it. Make five versions of my own, and pick my favorite version of those. Then play that in twelve keys, and then I'd do that with another four-bar phrase, and then I might also have thirty-two bars, and write it out, and I'd have one whole solo which I'd learn, take that solo and learn it in twelve keys, and then go on to another song, you know? There was a period of six months, I think I only played 'Stella by Starlight' every day.

He finds it hard to prescribe how best to acquire jazz skills now as each person has individual needs, though to acquire a swing feel and jazz vocabulary he suggests starting with Dixieland, through to bebop and on to avant-garde. He sees a lot of European jazz musicians and teachers starting to move things forward in new ways in recent years, where previously they had merely imitated American trends. There has also been a refreshing revival of interest in Ellington, Armstrong, and so on led by modern exponents such as Wynton Marsalis. However, he notes a tendency to fossilize jazz now as a new classic form, whereby people are playing 'written' solos or merely imitating the bebop of Charlie Parker or Miles Davis.

He still does not see himself as primarily in the jazz tradition. He grew up listening to Chopin, Mozart, and Beethoven, and learning to play Rachmaninoff's Prelude in C-sharp Minor or Liszt's Hungarian Rhapsody No. 2. By borrowing the improvisational model from jazz and applying it to classical music, Garson is being more true to himself than if he were just to play straight jazz, as this combination epitomizes his roots and gives expression to a wider cross-section of his personality.

He has followed quite a circuitous route in many ways. At seventeen, he was playing with Dave Liebman and Randy Brecker at the Town Hall in New York, and they were playing his compositions, but then people started to convey the idea that he should be sounding like Miles Davis, McCoy Tyner, Coltrane, Sonny Clark, or Phineas Newborn, and so it took him years to study all of that before coming back to find his own voice again. Now, when students come to him, he assesses each one differently to determine what they most need, and this assessment is a cornerstone of his teaching method. His studio sits only twenty feet from his house, and yet after working there sometimes for sixteen hours and losing track of time he barely makes it back to the house and on occasion sleeps in the studio. He feels it has become a beautiful space in which to create, now redolent with the music of all those who have passed through its walls or had their compositions worked on there.

Garson's sound now is very distinctive. The greatest compliment I have received as a pianist was being told on certain occasions that my playing sounded like his. And I take great comfort from his success in the face of all of the negative and proscriptive attitudes that he has come up against throughout his professional life, many of which sound only too familiar to me as a fellow pianist. His theorizing or philosophizing about music and creativity acquires credibility through his ongoing hard work, practicing relentlessly to refine his technique. His work ethic has become his guide for filling in what he calls the 'missing instruction manual' and finding ways, for example, to help overcome the fear that so many musicians experience when they go onstage. They are not pre-warned about that, he says, and many end up resorting to drugs to deal with the nervousness. He returns frequently with an almost missionary zeal to the idea that we need to spread the idea of connecting to something bigger and deeper through an exploration of artistic creation:

> I believe people want to hear this sort of communication. Not everybody wants to hear just about the sex and the porno, and the bodies, and the food and the diets, and the heart attacks, and the cholesterol. I think we've had enough of that. You know, we've had enough of those conversations. I think everybody is innately connected to God, and is God, and everybody, innately, wants to talk their version of this. It could be connected with computers or software, or connected to finances or business, or medicine, or piano playing, or viola playing . . .

The tools of this approach are spontaneity and openness: letting a conversation or a lesson be guided by whatever questions are posed at the time, rather than bringing a prescribed set of answers to the table.

He plays me a recording of a master class in which he gave some truly extraordinary examples of improvisation on the song 'How About You.' The original melodies and harmonies are only just hung onto, borne in mind at times like no more than a fleeting ghostly presence. The music strays further and further from the original, embellishing and disguising its origins. Yet the essential melody and harmony of the original song remain 'inside' the music as he plays it. This approach is in some ways less accessible, but it repays dividends, because 'if you're willing to go into the layers of Coltrane, or Bach, you're going to hear something each time that is so deep.' Unfortunately, however, people do not have patience; they have a short attention span, or, at least, they *believe* they have. Garson prefers to see this as a social problem: 'It's the *group* consciousness which can't concentrate for more than five minutes and follow a focus.' He sees it as the role of creative artists to project whatever pieces of beauty and harmony they have in them, which can help to counteract, with disproportionate power, the swathes of negativity emanating from elsewhere in society.

Calling for a greater respect to be accorded to the creative arts as helping to shape society itself, Garson says specifically that 'a person doesn't have to be poor and starving to have something valid to offer . . . the artist should be the first person to be taken care of, because they're projecting what the future society is supposed to be,' and goes on to expand his understanding of 'artists' to include scientists, doctors, and anyone else who makes or does something useful and takes that to a level that transcends mere technique.

Most sincere and diligent creative artists, including musical composers or improvisers, are contributing joy to the world, as opposed to conflict, damage, or environmental pollution. In his passion for the positive social significance of art and creativity, Garson's views are not far from those of William Morris, who in nineteenth-century England saw the impulse to create things of beauty suffocated by the economic constraint of antisocial priorities.

On the responsibilities of creative artists, Garson's ideas also echo at times those of Kandinsky, who in the wake of the industrial revolution and witnessing the beginnings of the commoditized and alienated society to come, attempted to uphold art as a spiritual antidote to consumerist values. In his view, 'The artist has a triple responsibility to the non-artists: (1) He must repay the talent which he has; (2) His deeds, feelings, and thoughts, as those of every man, create a spiritual atmosphere which is either pure or poisonous; (3) These deeds and thoughts are materials for his creations, which themselves exercise influence on the spiritual atmosphere.'[2]

In terms of teaching methods, Garson sometimes encourages an almost meditative focus on one song, for example asking his students whether they might be willing to practice a given piece for two hours every day for thirty days, to a metronome, without stopping, no matter how many mistakes are made, and without losing the timing. He explains this by pointing out that 'one song is every song' and notes that Thelonious Monk used this kind of intense method with his own songs.

Above all, Garson continually returns to the idea of music as therapy. To create music spontaneously through improvisation is, for him, far more than a profession or even a vocation. Increasingly he is interested in welcoming others into this practice as a contrast to and defense against the negative forces in the world: destruction, war, torture, poverty. He observes the relative happiness amongst those who are creating something, making something, from nothing, whether in music, film, visual arts, or written word.

In the early 1980s, Garson played at the Cannes film festival along with Stan Getz, Paul Horn, Joe Farrell, and others. He felt that Getz's pianist was somehow performing better than him, and on inquiry found that he had played for over two hundred almost consecutive nights on the road prior to that, in jazz gigs. This prompted him to put a band together and do likewise. With that steady application of work, the mastery of the craft allows the individual to emerge from their shell. It is discipline that opens it up and allows the artist to emerge as themselves.

Garson recognizes that, despite never having trained as a teacher, he took to it naturally from the first lesson he taught at the age of seventeen. Other than the ability to compose melodies well, this is the only aspect of his work that he feels he has not needed to train at all for. He is passionate about the importance of music being taught universally across the world to young children, and he derides the way that 'fast food,' shortcut culture has devalued genuine musical exploration and the idea of training hard to acquire skills. He gives the example of having asked one of his grandsons when he was six whether he was ready to do some more piano together and getting the reply, 'Oh no, that's okay, we already did that last year!'

One musician who has close experience of collaborating with Mike Garson is the Dutch organist and music professor at Rotterdam Conservatory (now part of Codarts) Willem Tanke, who studied organ and improvisation in Utrecht with Jan Welmers. He is an acclaimed performer and composer who, like Garson, has always tested the boundaries of improvisation as a method of creating music. They met in 2006, when Garson was invited by René van Commenée (having played for his 'Mr. Averell' project) to give a master class in Rotterdam. Garson and Tanke had a shared passion for the organ works of Messiaen, all of which Tanke had recorded as organist.

Tanke was pleasantly surprised to find that, despite his fame, Garson listened closely and questioned him methodically on Messiaen rather than sounding forth himself. With van Commenée, they ended up repairing to Tanke's home to explore further their common interests. Garson and Tanke bonded, and one year later they did a television appearance together, as well as making a four-handed organ recording, starting to experiment with joint improvisations, and appearing together at two concerts in a cathedral in Rotterdam. They also have eighteen fully mastered tracks together for possible future release, which were made by Tanke sending his parts from Holland to the States, where Garson would overdub his own. These were all for two pianos. They have also discussed the possibility of combining organ and piano in a further joint improvisation.

They traveled to a small village in the north of Holland and played one of the most remarkable organs in the world, an eighteenth-century instrument with an extraordinary quality of sound. In addition to all this, they also opened a long-term and ongoing discourse in which they are exploring what new forms might lie beyond the once experimental but now possibly exhausted frontiers of 'free jazz,' and are looking to move away from the twentieth-century preoccupation with categorical boundaries between 'classical,' 'jazz,' 'pop,' and so on.

In discussion with Tanke, I ask about his working methods with Garson, and his precise and sensitively thoughtful responses generate a fascinating exploration of the way in which creative artists and even humanity in general absorb and process our experiences as input and then—occasionally—are able somehow to give birth to something genuinely new, going beyond the mere reshaping of earlier influences and inputs. Tanke suggests that to improvise without revealing any historical or cultural antecedents is virtually impossible:

> It's all there always, the whole input that you have, and of course you cannot deny that. But sometimes you have to say to yourself that you 'intend' to deny it, to come one step further, to liberate yourself in a way, and then it might happen. I think maybe of all the stuff we play, 98 percent is in a way premeditated, practiced, memorized, but then on some special occasions something new might come out of that, and that 1 or 2 percent, maybe even less, that is the real freedom and improvisation, and that can be a starting point for your next session. I don't believe too much in a naïve view of improvisation that you can be spontaneous all the time and develop new things . . . you are supported by the input that you have your whole life. But there is also a little room for new things, and if you focus on that, if you are keen to be there in that space, then you can come there. But of course it needs a lot of practice.

Tanke dissents from that idea of free improvisation, popular in the 1960s, that anyone can innovate randomly without special effort. However inspired or spiritual one might be, that does not supply a shortcut to achieving great things; in general, exciting growth and innovation in virtually any field comes after sustained efforts to absorb and process the best of what has gone before. We all stand on the shoulders of our predecessors, and the delights of musical improvisation are no exception to this. As regards how those influences show in our creations, perhaps we might initially aim for *reflection* rather than imitation, as a stepping-stone toward our goal of transforming rather than recycling such strands.

Tanke emphasizes that both Bach and Mozart were known as very able improvisers. One of Bach's contemporaries even described him as a better improviser than composer, and it is thought that each of his written pieces were in a sense one final version of something he had been improvising around, which then became crystallized as a fixed masterpiece. As expressions of improvisation, however, each of these now well-known, precise sequences could easily have taken another shape from the same starting point of inspiration. Likewise with both Chopin and Liszt, especially given their use of the *partimento* instructional system, which involved building complex but prefigured structures and patterns into pieces. This was common, especially in the eighteenth century, and facilitated both improvisation and the creation of original compositions with unprecedented swiftness as well as elegance. It was not until the nineteenth century that composers had some idea that they might enjoy posthumous fame, so these earlier composers were not inclined to leave detailed notes on their methods. However, it can be seen that improvisation and composition have long been interwoven processes. This interplay rather than opposition between these facets of musical creation is still key, and is acknowledged in his own work by Garson. Improvisation, composition, and performance are recognized by him, as they were in earlier periods, as three parts of the same continuum.

Tanke also strongly endorses the work of Nettl, as referred to in chapter 11.[3] Another commentator recommended by Tanke on these issues is Marcel Cobussen, who teaches Music Philosophy and Sound Studies at Leiden University in the Netherlands, and whose research explores the relationship between improvisation and non-linear systems. Some believe that Mozart, in particular, had sufficient genius and speed to be able effectively to write his compositions directly whilst improvising. He did not choose to have sketches or preliminary notes to work from (other than in the last two years of his life). Now, with programs like Logic and Sibelius or Finale, we are able to narrow further still the distinctions between improvisation and composition. First comes an idea, and some performance to try this; then a look back at this and some modifications before settling on a more finished form. At different stages in the process, the musician switches the emphasis from a more spontaneous part of creating to a more schematic, solidifying part of the process, using mouse, cursor, and keyboard (or pencil and manuscript paper) to move some notes around from what was performed. They then click 'SAVE' (or finish off the handwritten score).

Were the greatest recipes in the classic cookbooks first scribbled down on paper at a desk in a moment of inspiration, perfected in the mind, and then handed down to the chefs to cook? Of course not: they were evolved through experimentation in kitchens and at dining tables, and there is no reason to see other forms of practical creativity differently. It is only the classical establishment's fetishizing of the pencil and the paper score in composition that clouds this fact.

In the oral tradition, composers benefited from highly trained memories, which made it possible to repeat on successive days the same melodies and harmonic structures in their performances. Today's improvisers may rely instead on being able to play their sequence of notes into a computerized notator such as Finale to generate a score or a digital recording, but the general principle is the same. If anything, the computer can be seen as enhancing this process as it allows an even more intuitive and organic evolution of a composition, through more rapid alternating stages of improvisation and adjustment.

Artists who are happy to make sculptures in ice or in sand that they know will soon melt or be washed away by the tide—and there are many examples of such transitory art around the world—show us something about the joy of creation even when (and, for some, especially when) it leaves no trace. It is the ultimate power of a message that has the boldness not to need its own permanency. There is a strong link there to the idea behind Garson's coinage for his own music as being called 'Now' music.

His friend, the Argentinian film composer Emilio Kauderer, who has won a Latin Grammy, an Emmy nomination, and many other awards, describes for me the features he discerns in Garson's 'Now' music, and goes on to assess the capacities of such a creative method as 'well-defined style, balanced harmonic structure, and extreme dynamics . . . Many of us composers take weeks to get through the few bars that Mike can deliver instantaneously. To see him create feels like watching a connection to a highly spiritual inspiration. I used to joke about him being connected to the "cable company."'[4]

Finally, Tanke summarizes his view of his friend and collaborator Garson as being undoubtedly 'an extremely gifted genius.' He says that although that term has become sometimes devalued, he believes that it is truly appropriate for someone with Garson's scope of vision, feel, inspiration, and passion wedded to such extreme agility, versatility, and technical mastery. His love of Liszt, Chopin, and Bach influences him as much as his immersion in jazz. Most people know him primarily for his great work with Bowie, and yet before he even met Bowie he was already an established jazz pianist, and he knows and can improvise on virtually any jazz standard that has ever existed, too. He really does live the philosophy of his 'Now' music by being truly spontaneous. Tanke says that they had spoken a few days previously, and then, inspired by their chat, Garson had sent him a new finished piece, finely constructed and played, just a couple of hours later. In all of this, Garson is motivated by the idea that it is coming not from him but from something bigger.

Tanke characterizes both Garson's and his own musical preference, if there were no other pressures or demands in life, such as the need to support family and earn a living, as being to dive into the 'experimental and improvisational' world entirely. He hesitates to use the term 'avant-garde,' as it carries the connotations of late-twentieth-century trends that are already in the past, and above all theirs is a project of freedom beyond even that label. He says that Garson's genius lies in being able to meld all of the genres in an instant, and in one piece. Once that stage is reached, the categories cease to exist in any real way, as they are all transcended. 'Free jazz' can itself be seen as a social product of the liberation politics and new cultural attitudes of the 1950s and 1960s. In that sense it is not free of its own time and place either, and thus holds limitations.

The need to try to shock through music has passed, as we enter an age in which the ability to shock has reached vanishing point. Garson is genuinely happy within conventional or mainstream jazz or rock, too, as he has the capacity to entertain himself within it. For Tanke, though, the music he and Garson make, in which there is no limiting form other than the honest emotion of creativity and integrity, is the most valuable work of all. It is no longer even a case of knocking down boundaries for the sake of it, but rather simply a case of expression.

# 14

# 'Music Has Charms to Sooth a Savage Breast . . .'

*'My grandson Jacob, who is ten years old and has autism, inspired this. I must have done fifty versions of this piece over three months until I found the correct series of notes and intentions that describe Jacob and the millions of children with this condition. Jacob holds his head high and creates his own beautiful world. Jacob is totally non-judgmental and brings unconditional love and joy to anyone who is blessed enough to be around him. About five years ago, when his autism was much more severe, I would put him on my lap at the piano and play Mozart for him. He would melt into the music and totally relax. Another example of how music heals.'*

—From program notes by Mike Garson for the March 2014 world premiere of his *Symphonic Suite for Healing*: '11. Oneness with All/Gratitude'

THERE ARE NEW PROJECTS being added to Garson's schedule every week, all of them musically rich and expressive. It is against this current background of varied and intense creative activity that the past couple of years have seen the beginnings of an undertaking he now believes will occupy the next big chapter of his working life. In 2013, he was commissioned by Newport Beach–based brain surgeon Dr. Christopher Duma to compose and produce a 'therapeutic' symphony, which premiered on March 1, 2014, in Costa Mesa, California, for a forty-four-piece orchestra with piano, keyboards, a fifty-five-voice children's choir, a jazz ensemble, vocalists, and dancers. The concert was partly intended to raise funds for a charity created by Dr. Duma, the Foundation for Neurosciences, Stroke, and Recovery, which provides physiotherapy, psychotherapy, and a whole range of other support to patients. The concert was attended by a capacity audience of 3,000 at Segerstrom Hall, part of the Segerstrom Center for the Arts (formerly the Orange County Performing Arts Center).[1]

The *Symphonic Suite for Healing* was one of the pinnacles of Garson's career to date. He describes it as 'unquestionably the best concert in my life, from beginning to end. I played with a twelve-piece jazz group including a string quartet in the first half, doing Gershwin, some newly written additions to my Paganini *Variations*, also

"Space Oddity," and some Brubeck. In the second half it was the whole of my original *Symphonic Suite for Healing*, all twelve pieces, which were chosen from thirty by the patients of brain surgeon Dr. Duma.'

The performance of 'Blue Rondo à la Turk' by Dave Brubeck was made all the more poignant by the fact that Brubeck had died in 2012, aged ninety-one, and had been a lifelong musical influence and love of Garson's, right back to when his father took him to the Half Note jazz club and he played 'Take Five' to audition for Lennie Tristano in 1961.

The idea of allowing patients to determine what the symphony should finally consist of was a first in a production of this kind, and just one of several important and groundbreaking aspects of this event. One hundred patients had been asked which of the compositions made them feel better (or worse) before the final selection was presented. Dr. Duma, who is also involved in research on new treatments for brain cancer, Parkinson's disease, and Alzheimer's, gave his Parkinson's patients a dexterity test to assess their functioning both with and without the various pieces of music, and the results showed specific improvements in some cases. The film and audio recordings of the event will be made available to patients, and in addition to raising funds for new research into the possible role of music in helping people with neurological conditions, the aim was also to raise awareness of the medically healing potential of music in general.

Garson had always been keenly aware of the healing power of his own and other music, though his interest intensified in 2011, when he heard how music therapy had helped Arizona politician Gabrielle Giffords recover the power of speech after a gunshot wound to the head. In Western culture, the idea of music as a healing force is seen as early as the biblical account of how the tormented King Saul 'was refreshed, and was well, and the evil spirit departed from him' after being serenaded by David on the harp.

In ancient Greece, the use of sound to heal was considered a sacred science. The lyre was used to treat illnesses such as gout and sciatica, as well as trauma and mental upset, and the Greek god of medicine, Apollo, was also the god of music. There are similar examples in most cultures. Specific uses of music within medical practice in the modern period are seen from about the eighteenth century, though the broad professional practice of music therapy dates from the twentieth century. The rapid changes in music technology in recent years have opened up new possibilities, with, for example, the Music and Memory project[2] bringing personalized digital music collections to many elderly people, who have shown great improvements in animation and happiness through such stimulation.

Garson once took his grandson Max to buy drum brushes at the Los Angeles branch of the Sam Ash music store, which he himself used to visit as a child in Brooklyn. Whilst he was there, a young goth girl with rings in her nose and what seemed like an engagement ring came in looking very distraught. The salesmen hovered around her 'for two reasons: first she was an attractive girl; second they wanted to sell her a piano.' She was very upset; she said that she had had a very bad day. Garson thought that perhaps her boyfriend had left her, and she simply asked whether she could sit and play for a while. Max was watching closely. She played very softly, so as not to disturb anyone, as if she were writing a song, around three very tentative chords. After fifteen minutes, she stood up and kind of danced or skipped over to some other part of the store, seeming to have been 'healed' by her own music. And yet she had come in with the body language of someone who was very stressed.

There are few creative endeavors that can have such a dramatic effect in self-calming or soothing a 'troubled soul.' Garson's father always used to tell him that 'music soothes the savage beast.' This common saying derives from the English poet and playwright William Congreve, whose play of 1697, *The Mourning Bride*, opens with the lines, 'Music has charms to soothe a savage breast / To soften rocks, or bend a knotted oak.' In popular usage, 'breast' has been replaced by 'beast.'

Having come into adulthood in the early 1960s, Garson still bears the stamp of having been a sixties 'love child.' He hates violence and malice and responds to it by playing. This strikes a chord for me, as my own childhood tantrums or upsets were invariably coped with by running to the piano and letting loose with some stormy improvisation—which is what Garson says Max does when upset, getting rid of a lot of anger by playing his drums.

Garson's music has not always been perceived as relaxing or therapeutic. He recalls meeting David Bowie's son, Duncan Jones (now an acclaimed film director), backstage at a Bowie show in the 1990s, and being told by him that when he was eight or nine years old, Jones had been terrified of Garson's 'Aladdin Sane' solo, which gave him nightmares. Now, forty-five years after recording that solo, he has been working to create music that seeks to soothe rather than scare. He jokes that 'this is my amends project' for having been so scary in the past.

Certainly there is much evidence now of music having a demonstrably curative effect. For example, many research findings gathered and endorsed by the independent Cochrane Collaboration in the UK (which compiles a meta-review of research into the results of medical practices, which can then be used for the commissioning of services) have been positive. Protocols such as the NICE standards for clinical excellence have also shown favorable outcomes. MRI scans have been used to show the beneficial responses of the brain to certain music. Research is still at quite an early stage on the neurological mechanisms by which all of this functions, as is our understanding of which musical features have what effects and why. The tension followed by resolution that music can manufacture, however, may well prove to be a natural relaxant and analgesic through the release of naturally occurring brain chemicals such as dopamine and opioids.

One of the very best reviews of recent work in this field is 'The Neurochemistry of Music' by Mona Lisa Chanda and Daniel J. Levitin,[3] which concludes that music 'may reduce stress, protect against disease, and manage pain.' There has also recently been a growth in work and research within the emerging field of Music, Health, and Wellbeing, and this is well documented by Raymond MacDonald, who co-edited a book of that title[4] in 2012 and is professor of music psychology and improvisation at Glasgow Caledonian University. Other research cited by Joshua Grill, professor of neurology at UCLA, has shown that some stroke patients that have suffered damage to the part of the brain used for language, though unable to speak, can still sing.

Garson's *Symphonic Suite for Healing* reflects equally the classical and jazz strands in his music, epitomizing his eclectic art. Dr. Duma, also originally from New York, studied classical piano for nine years and plays in a rock band called Vital Signs, as well as playing with surf band the Chantays, who had a huge hit in 1963 with 'Pipeline,' since covered by artists ranging from Pat Metheny to Johnny Thunders. As a former member of the board of directors of the Philharmonic Society of Orange County, he consulted the organization's president and artistic director, Dean Corey, who it turned out was familiar with Garson's music, and the 2014 concert was produced together with the Philharmonic Society.

Dr. Duma spoke to me from one of several California hospitals at which he works, and explained some of his findings. The type of music that an Alzheimer's patient would brighten up to, he says, is very different from that which would help a Parkinson's patient. 'We had a trial with one hundred patients, and some of those with cognitive issues [such as Alzheimer's] on hearing some of Mike's music actually took their headphones off and threw them down—it was too complex, atonal, and contrapuntal for them, whereas if you played them an old Benny Goodman tune from the forties they just brightened up, loved it, and smiled the rest of the day. In contrast, one Parkinson's patient specifically requested an Argentinian tango from Mike, and then she was able to dance!'

Whereas the Alzheimer's patients responded to music that evoked their deep recollections, bypassing their lack of short-term memory, the Parkinson's patients needed a rhythmic beat, however complex. Dr. Duma is keen to explore further, for example, the relationship between emotion and movement in such patients. Parkinson's affects the basal ganglia, a part of the brain that helps to ensure smooth movement, but when patients become more relaxed, the symptoms often ease.

He has also patented a radical development that involves using the in-ear monitors used onstage by musicians to hear the parts of the music needed for their own performance, but for the medical purpose of 'delivering' regular periods of pain-relieving and therapeutic music. He is developing this with Jerry Harvey of JH Audio, which has already pioneered the necessary hardware. When a three-time or four-time piece of music is gently played into the ear of a Parkinson's patient several times each day, Dr. Duma believes that this subliminal relaxant may possibly restore motor control sufficiently to allow more normal movement. It could likewise reduce hypertension in those with high blood pressure.

Composers and concert pianists traveled across the country to be present at the *Symphonic Suite* concert, and the response was resoundingly enthusiastic. The patients' final selection of twelve parts for the *Symphony* starts with a fanfare and closes with an equally optimistic affirmation via the mellow 'Lullaby for Our Daughters' and a contemplative piece, 'Gratitude,' in honor of Garson's grandchild Jacob, whose autism has been noticeably improved by Garson's playing for him.

The lineup for the jazz band in the first half included his long-term friend and colleague from Free Flight, flautist Jim Walker, as well as legendary jazz drummer Joe LaBarbera, opera singer Jessica Tivens, and many other stars in their various fields, including conductor Lori Loftus, orchestrator Bruce Donnelly, and jazz vocalist Nnenna Freelon, who has toured with Ray Charles and George Benson and been nominated for six Grammy Awards. With more than one hundred people onstage, the event successfully put the whole close relationship between music composition and therapeutic communication soundly on the map. Another of Garson's grandchildren, Max—already a competent drummer at eight years old—joined him onstage at the end to play the congas.

Jazz guitarist Larry Koonse has been a featured soloist with the Los Angeles Philharmonic, as well as working with John Dankworth and Cleo Laine, Mel Tormé, Billy Childs, and Bob Sheppard. He performed that night, too, and said afterward, 'Before collaborating with Mike Garson on the *Symphonic Suite* I had never met any single musician that could weave classical, pop, and jazz musics in such a seamless way and possess the level of virtuosity to perform the music with such mind-blowing creativity and power. Mike is that rare kind of genius that can think outside of the box and has no fear in realizing his creation.'

Another person who came on board was Dr. Barry Bittman, CEO and president of the Yamaha Music and Wellness Institute and also a senior neurologist whose research is pioneering the development of 'whole person' approaches to health, and helping to further establish the connection between musical creation and human well-being. In addition to his many other activities, Bittman is a keen pianist— though he feels that traditional music education thwarted his creativity. On first meeting Garson, he told him, 'You're the first virtuoso musician I've ever met who has a truly balanced life!' Garson assured him there are others.

Bittman flew in to assist Garson with the production in the final days before this world premiere performance of the *Symphonic Suite*. Bittman and Garson have found a great affinity with one another's work and vision, and have even formed a duo called the Physician and the Musician, performing shows for audiences of doctors and patients. Bittman begins with a presentation about current research into the ways in which music can be used in a medical setting, then the audience is asked to share emotions, which are conveyed by Garson on the piano. They have also played for large groups of patients, and there have been some very poignant moments. Garson explains:

> We have this *shtick*, a bit like two Jewish comedians onstage, in a funny kind of way: we play off each other and I improvise things; I always do a little Gershwin, I do my four-note improv . . . in Lexington, Kentucky, I played in a hospital music theater and it was filmed and broadcast into the rooms of patients who could not get to the theater. When I asked for my four notes from the audience in the theater I got some crazy, dissonant choices so I played this absolutely crazy atonal piece from that, which made 'Aladdin Sane' seem tame! I suddenly got worried how the patients in their bedrooms would take it, and feared my healing might backfire and that we would lose a few of them!

Bittman emphasizes that, 'in ancient times, the physician and musician were one and the same.' He also says that he has 'had the joy to work with Mike Garson over many years' and finds, as a doctor and a researcher, that Garson's profound creativity, together with his essential humanity and caring involvement with those who play music with him, has helped to generate music that 'resonates with our DNA.' He argues that Garson's performances can have a transformative effect on audiences. He has been engaged in a wealth of cutting-edge research into the possible effects of music at the deep biological level, and explains, 'The science of creative musical expression is in its infancy, yet in the last decade alone we have been able to demonstrate psycho-social changes, biological changes, and DNA changes. I believe that music truly resonates with us on a cellular level, that we are each hard-wired for music.' Crucially, the data shows that merely relaxing in some other way does not have as pronounced an effect as engaging in a specifically musical experience.

The emphasis of Garson's work with Duma on the 2014 *Symphonic Suite for Healing* and beyond is the composition and performance of music that might contribute to the healing and comfort of a wide range of patients. The longer-term aim is for composed music to be delivered to patients as a supplement to, or even replacement for, certain medication. Garson and Duma would like to see suitable pieces by various composers supplied into hospitals worldwide, as well as the establishment of music rooms in community centers and in all hospitals, just as they all have chapels today. The creation of music has always been seen as more than simply superficial entertainment. 'I think this is where my next twenty, thirty years will be dedicated,' Garson comments, adding that there is increasing awareness of the possibility of healing with music: 'We've been doing it our whole life by playing music, we just didn't use that word . . . I think we're tapping into something which in twenty years will be commonplace.'

Having explored with Garson so many of the mixed experiences in other avenues of his musical career to date prior to his *Symphonic Suite for Healing*, it is quite moving to witness a creative artist who has finally arrived at an endeavor that comes closer than ever to expressing his own essence. It allowed him a degree of control and collaboration and the free flow of his own creativity, whilst at the same time offering the chance of reaching out to help other people. 'It's maybe the first concert in my life I could say, from beginning to end, I was totally present there and loved every minute of it, even though you wouldn't call it a perfect concert in terms of technical expertise, as there were so many moving pieces to deal with, but the spirit of it kind of nailed it.'

Duma and Garson are already planning further concerts and presentations. I explained to Duma that I had been involved myself in some related work in London for the previous two years. Since 1992, at the Royal Free Hospital, there has been an excellent complementary therapy service run by Keith Hunt as a voluntary massage service for cancer and a variety of other patients. In 2012, he was awarded an MBE in recognition of his dedication to this unit, which now provides more than 25,000 treatments each year, and these have been found to ease pain, nausea, and poor sleep patterns, as well as reducing anxiety and promoting relaxation. In consultation with Hunt, I have composed a series of suitable pieces of music for use during these therapies to increase the effectiveness of the treatment by supporting both therapist and patient, and have released a first album of this music on a collection called *Massage Music*, which has been very well received by therapists and patients worldwide. Duma was enthused by this English counterpart to the work with which he and Garson have been involved, saying that this is exactly the sort of thing that they want to work on next.

Another associate of Garson's with a keen interest in music as a healing force is Dr. Gerard Gibbons, who is something of a renaissance man himself, working variously as a filmmaker, photographer, author, musician, eye doctor, and brand strategist. He first heard Mike Garson's playing at Long Beach Arena in California on the *Ziggy Stardust* Tour on March 10, 1973. This concert saw Bowie's live debut performance of 'Aladdin Sane (1913–1938–197?)' and 'Time' from the *Aladdin Sane* album, which was released the following month.

The sound of Garson's piano permeating the arena from the shadows at the back of the stage had a profound effect on Gibbons, who was then still in high school. Many years later, they met at an intimate classical concert by Garson in 2014, close to where Gibbons lives, and became firm friends. In recent years, Gibbons has been working with Garson as an *aide-de-camp*, tour photographer, and consultant in 'strategic professional development.'

He speaks eloquently of the extraordinary fusion of talents and inspiration in all of Bowie and Garson's work together. 'Mike would always articulate the music in a way which was intertwined with David's expressiveness. He was Bowie's best collaborator, the jewel in his crown. He enhanced and elevated Bowie's genius, and Bowie likewise brought out the best in Mike.'

Gibbons says that the unusual trajectory and diversity of his own career were encouraged by his early exposure to Bowie and Garson, with their improvisational approach to music. He has long been committed to exploring the power of both music and storytelling as tools for improving both mental and physical health. He says he admires the fact that Garson's virtuosity came through relentless perseverance and hard work over many thousands of hours: 'Mike is authentic, genuine, and open to what the present moment reveals. He listens, he builds rapport. He's the real deal.'

Nordoff-Robbins is a British-based music charity widely respected as a center for the practice of music therapy and the education and training of music therapists.[5] Its director of education, Gary Ansdell, explained to me how the long history of this area of endeavor has produced different approaches in different parts of the world, with a huge range of both practice and research. Therapies are broadly either 'receptive' (listening) or 'active' (making music). Most of Nordoff-Robbins's work has been in the latter, as it also eliminates social isolation. If someone is severely withdrawn, Ansdell explains, 'You can coax them into both listening and playing music. We use improvisation all the time, so it's kind of sculpting the music that's appropriate for making a musical conversation with someone, or even just to recall them back into the human world of relationship and community through making music with them.'

Ansdell has worked as a music therapist for twenty-five years and has countless experiences of the many ways in which this has worked.[6] He places an emphasis on the social and cultural engagement that various forms of music can bring to a vast array of suffering individuals, whether they have medical conditions, learning difficulties, severe injuries from accidents, or suffer from depression and isolation. He sees musical therapy as being above all about building a relationship between people, rather than being simply something passive or technical.

Mike Garson decided in 2014 that the main work of the next part of his life would be to develop much further his contribution to the use of music for healing. What happened in January 2016 changed this plan, with much of his schedule now being dedicated to performing and celebrating the music of David Bowie, but he still intends to allocate half of his time in future to developing music for healing.[7]

He takes an interest especially in the idea of integration and acceptance for children, including those on the autistic spectrum, and plans to have a diverse group of children performing together onstage for his next orchestral work. He passionately opposes the negative ways in which some children are sometimes perceived, emphasizing that 'we're *all* on a spectrum,' with strengths and weaknesses in different areas. In his program notes for the premiere of the *Symphonic Suite*, he states:

> The inextricable link between music and healing has survived the test of time . . . healing is truly about putting back into our lives what is missing, and can occur even in the absence of disease. Music enables healing to begin. It's a fact that in ancient times the physician and musician were one and the same. Yet now, thousands of years later, the scientific basis for music as a healing strategy is finally becoming understood . . . The true intention of this music is to bring joy, to inspire, and to remind us of who we are and who we are really meant to be.

# 15

# From Ventura to Fitzrovia, a Pilgrimage Complete

*'Mike Garson is a cathedral of music.'*
—Jérôme Soligny, editorial consultant, *Rock & Folk* magazine, France

As a teenager, I painted the walls of my bedroom in silver-grey, with bright red on the paneling. I only realized years later that the unusual color scheme had been inspired, subconsciously, by the cover of David Bowie's *Aladdin Sane* album. My fascination with those songs helped to shape my formative years and much that has happened since. In this I was similar to many thousands, if not millions, of others worldwide who were inspired by that album.

This book began with a couple of days spent working with Bowie, followed by a pilgrimage of sorts, a visit to Ventura County and the home of the pianist whose fingers had rippled over those keys nearly forty years earlier on that album. Telling his story in these pages has been a cathartic experience, as well as a joyful opportunity to celebrate the vast influence that has emanated from this music.

In the early 2000s, Bowie gave several live and broadcast performances of the song 'Life on Mars?' in which his voice was accompanied only by Garson's piano. First there was 2000's Yahoo Awards at Studio 54 in New York, at which Bowie won the 'Online Pioneer of the Year' award and his BowieNet site was named 'Best Artist's Site,' and where they also did a spectacular version of 'Wild Is the Wind,' with Garson's piano orchestral in its sweep. Then there was the BBC television show *Parkinson* on September 21, 2002, for which Michael Parkinson interviewed first Tom Hanks and then David Bowie. Bowie performed 'Everyone Says "Hi"' with a full band and was then interviewed, after which he sang 'Life on Mars?' accompanied only by Garson on piano. By this time Bowie had taken to performing it in the much lower key of C, rather than the original key of F. Mid-song, Garson plays a very beautiful, gentle variation on the original instrumental section, starting with an augmented fourth note moving to the fifth, which is a frequent feature of his music, as it was for Gershwin. After the recording of the show, Tom Hanks came up to Garson and simply said with a big smile, 'The master of the eighty-eight!' (referring to the number of notes on a piano), shook his hand, and moved on. The show ended with a big band, led by Laurie Holloway, playing Billy May's arrangement of 'Skyliner,' originally recorded by the Charlie Barnet Band. Garson stood by the side of the stage and listened in fascination, whilst reflecting that he would be just as much at home playing that music as he had been that evening playing the two songs with Bowie.

On September 8, 2005, at Radio City Music Hall in New York, the same song was performed, in the same way, at the Condé Nast Fashion Rocks show in aid of victims of Hurricane Katrina. This was an emotional occasion, as it was Bowie's first performance since facing serious health issues the year before. His and Garson's only opportunity to rehearse together was in the venue that afternoon. The key was dropped further still, this time to B. Yet it all came together, and it was an emotional rendition, full of feeling and evoking a tender vulnerability.

On November 9, 2006, Garson again played with Bowie, this time at the 'Black Ball' for the HIV charity Keep a Child Alive. Unlike on the other occasions referred to above, this show at New York's Hammerstein Ballroom did not include 'Life on Mars?' but Garson did play for Bowie on 'Fantastic Voyage,' 'Wild Is the Wind,' and (as a duet with Alicia Keys) 'Changes.' This show was with a band, but Garson's piano was heavily featured, and he was graciously introduced by Bowie, with 'Wild Is the Wind' performed by Bowie and Garson alone. It was Bowie's final public performance. In 2007, Bowie curated New York's High Line Festival, and Garson played twice. One performance was with his trio at the Blue Note in Greenwich Village, the other with the jazz violinist Chris Howes, opening for 'word jazz' pioneer Ken Nordine at the Kitchen.

To understand Mike Garson's general and ongoing creative impetus, it is necessary to recognize him as something of a renaissance man. For example, he has always enjoyed teaching as well as performing. He now regards 99 percent of the thousands of lessons he has given over the years as having been a success, whereas perhaps only 20 percent of his few thousand concerts were great, in his eyes. In the role of teacher he feels he can be more selfless, but onstage 'the ego moves in a little bit.' He works strenuously to increase that percentage 'to at least 90 percent—in recent years it has been around 75.' The pressure from audiences wanting to be impressed produces the temptation to oblige by showing off what you can do, rather than simply to create joy through the music. Pyrotechnics are one thing, but he derives more pleasure ultimately from playing, for example, a simple ballad of his own, such as 'Lullaby for Our Daughters.'

Most of the people interviewed for this book have been unreserved in their praise for

Garson, and as such it has been difficult to explore any criticisms, even in the interests of balance. I invited him to comment on what he would himself regard as his own weaknesses, and he seized the opportunity to identify those issues he continues to work on.

He went through a period in earlier years, he says, of being overbearing in his attempts to persuade others to take an interest in his spiritual beliefs, but he now takes a more questioning approach.

He says that he is a slow learner, though when he grasps something, and if it has meaning, he can run with it for a lifetime. Hall Overton, one of Garson's greatest teachers, taught him so much, so well about harmony and chords that even though it took several months for him to really get it, it then became something he still uses, all these years later, in all of his work and across all genres. He wants people to know that he worked long and hard through a slow process to achieve the level of performance he enjoys, in the hope that this will inspire others to do likewise, rather than passively assuming that he was born to some natural talent that they could not possibly access.

He also feels his ability to forgive is not as great as he would wish, and that by hanging on to things he is damaging himself more than anyone else. 'You can be angry or have discussions about something,' he says, 'but just to sit with it for years and let it stew is a little unhealthy.' He adds that he sometimes has a short fuse and a tendency toward intolerance. If you feel you have mastered something, there is a danger of assuming you are 'above the law' and judging others as inferior. This is a trap he believes he got into at times in the past but has largely overcome now.

He points out that it is also easy for kindness, compassion, and love to drop out of the equation if you ever forget why you are doing creative work, by getting too caught up in all of the technical concerns, meeting deadlines, monitoring standards, and so on. You need a system of constant internal gratitude. He has worked hard for his achievements, but he still feels thankful for the opportunities, the abilities, and the potential that is his and that in this sense has been a gift. Continuing with this rigorous inventory of introspection, he also observes that he can become quite obsessive in focusing too narrowly on something that he is absorbed with. This can produce great accomplishments but can also lead to the neglect of a wider and more open-minded viewpoint.

We listen to his *Mike Garson's Jazz Hat* album, with Dizzy Gillespie's 'A Night in Tunisia' taken at breakneck speed and yet losing none of its passion. Like much of his material, it was produced by 'Prof' Johnson, a great technical innovator who experimented with the early possibilities of digital recording. He would use old valve amplifiers without cases, for example, as he wanted everything exposed to the air, and in some cases he 'avoided putting tracks on a CD plate, taking the piano recording straight to the mastering lab by bouncing it off Mount Wilson, fifty miles from L.A.'

Garson's work has encompassed a very wide variety of genres and concepts. In 2008, he was approached to work on some of the tracks for a compilation of Jewish music and comedy, *The Jewish Songbook: The Heart and Humor of a People*, produced by the greatly talented Brooks Arthur. This included a very moving rendition by saxophonist Dave Koz of the old Jewish song 'Raisins and Almonds' (which my own mother sang to me as a childhood lullaby). One of the only songs in the collection that is not comedic, it features some unmistakable playing by Garson. He comments that the song's depths had not previously been adequately captured on any recording, since 'earlier versions tended to be crummy, cheap, old arrangements by Jewish accordion players.' One of the other tracks Garson plays on is a hilarious performance by Jason Alexander (George Costanza in *Seinfeld*) of 'Shake Hands with Your Uncle Max' by the legendary 1960s comedian Allan Sherman.

The *Jewish Songbook* album's producer, Brooks Arthur, has known Mike Garson since the 1970s and worked with him on many occasions. Garson had composed music for Adam Sandler's comedy album *What the Hell Happened to Me?* (1996), which was produced by Arthur, and more recently appeared as a pianist in Sandler's 2017 Netflix film *Sandy Wexler*. They are also going to work together on a new jazz version of 'At Seventeen': Arthur actually engineered and produced the Grammy-winning original recording by Janis Ian in 1975. Garson and Arthur also worked together on a series of successful albums such as *Sax at the Movies* in 1993.

Brooks Arthur is one of the most gifted and exceptional producers in Hollywood, and has worked with Van Morrison, Neil Diamond, the Grateful Dead, Bruce Springsteen (whose *Born to Run* album was recorded at Arthur's 914 Sound Studios in Blauvelt, New York), and Carole King, as well as producing comedy albums by Robin Williams, Jackie Mason, and Adam Sandler. When I interviewed him, he said that he remains convinced of Garson's distinct contribution: 'Mike Garson adds a certain harmonic structure that's unparalleled. It's like having six fingers on each hand.'

They were at the same high school in Brooklyn, and were aware of each other in the late 1960s, but Arthur recalls that their first proper meeting was in 1975, when Garson had been 'adding his jazz cadences, his "Garsonisms," as I call them, to a rock 'n' roll canvas.' He says that although Bowie was a genius in his songwriting,

Garson 'added something to make it more cinemascopic.' Likewise, with the Smashing Pumpkins and all of the other many varied acts he was invited to play for, 'he always bumped it up a notch.'

Arthur is a charmingly modest man despite his own huge achievements. His own dream was always to be a crooner, and in fact he has a beautiful voice, which Garson describes as being 'very soothing, like the Perry Como or Eddie Fisher of our times.' The two of them recorded an album for just piano and voice in 1998 called *Songs Are Like Prayers*. Whilst not having had major commercial success, Arthur says that this album still gives him great pride and pleasure, describing the pared-down arrangements as 'the naked truth,' allowing greater focus on the lyrical content.

Whilst working with Bruce Springsteen, Arthur was aware of Garson's extraordinary talent and wonders now how Springsteen's future output might have been enriched if he had introduced the two for one or two recordings—though of course Garson was busy at that time with his work for Bowie. He mentions that Adam Sandler is a big fan of Garson's work with Bowie and is proud of his friendship with Garson. He also pinpoints Garson's loyalty to his friends and colleagues. I ask him how he sees Garson's contribution to the production process:

> Mike's free-form, spontaneous, and intelligent approach makes every take fresh and different. This may not always make it easy for the producer, but when you go through his takes, you find that each time he brings more to it. Each take has its own kind of genius. He always comes up with what Carole King or Gerry Goffin might call 'some kind of wonderful.' He's painting a new picture into the frame, without wanting any of his colors to get in the way of the artist he's working with . . . painting a blue or a yellow—which sometimes may turn green and sometimes not, but still the blue and the yellow are always there.

Continuing the artistic theme, Arthur speaks of Garson's recreational photo art as reflecting his pianistic style, as being like 'visual jazz, rather than audio jazz.' He concludes:

> There's a lot of unfairness in life, and even more unfairness in music and art. Unfortunately sometimes somebody has to pass before they are honored or recognized. I have experienced just how he works through his accompanying my singing in pursuit of my dream to be a great crooner and I can see that Mike Garson is a master of virtuosity, and has had a brilliant career to date,

but the public would be even more rewarded if he were to be a household name, recognized as an artist in his own right, rather than as a sideman. But, oh, what a piano man!

In 2009, Garson produced an album, *Fast Jump*, by the young classical and avant-garde pianist Danny Holt, after chance meetings had twice brought them together: first when Garson was judging a piano competition and chose this young prodigy as a winner; then, some months later, when Garson was lecturing at the California Institute of the Arts (CalArts).

When we learned of the suicide, on August 11, 2014, of the comedian and actor Robin Williams, Garson was particularly affected by the news, as Williams had been a lifelong favorite of his, and hours later he sent me a beautiful sonata he had written fifteen years previously and had always intended to send him.

Garson was employed by Yamaha to record pieces for its Disklavier player pianos using sensors that sit on each of the eighty-eight keys 'like miniature typewriters.' He recorded 2,800 pieces for them over fifteen years, including about a hundred of his own, which were then processed for selling on floppy disks that could be inserted into their Disklavier models. This meant that people could have his performance re-created in their homes, with the keys moving up and down exactly as he had played them, and real hammers hitting real strings, rather than just an electronic re-creation of that sound.

He has also been a brand ambassador for the Ivory computerized sample piano produced by Synthogy. Each file of sample piano sounds weighs in at nearly 20 giga-bytes, many times greater than earlier generations. There have been times when he needed to record something to a deadline and had problems using microphones on his real piano, if the children were playing outside the studio, for example. By using this extraordinarily high-quality digital piano as his direct recording input, he was able to achieve results indistinguishable from the real thing. Even the company itself was fooled on one occasion, thinking that some examples he sent had been recorded on his real Yamaha grand rather than generated by the computer.

For some years, Garson was an M-Audio artist and brand ambassador, and was instrumental in testing and giving feedback on the keyboards the company made, including being involved in the subtle process of attempting to improve and refine the action of lighter key beds that could mimic the real action of a piano keyboard. M-Audio was founded by Tim Ryan, whose mother was an aspiring concert pianist but who became a prodigious talent himself in the field of music-making technology. He has played a key role in modern musical, social, and cultural history, through initiating the situation we now take for granted whereby music can be produced and recorded in small and affordable studio setups based around a computer.

At college in the 1970s, Ryan and two fellow students found that many of the synthesizer products that sold at that time for many hundreds of dollars were costing only tens of dollars to make, so decided to create their own equivalents and sell them for half the price. He became a pioneer in spearheading the introduction of digital sound processing and the computerization of the recording process, which has ultimately democratized music production and opened up access to this process for all.

Ryan first met Garson in about 2000, and they proved to be kindred spirits, becoming and remaining close friends in addition to enjoying various work projects together, both through M-Audio and since. In recent years, Ryan has organized and promoted jazz concerts in France and Spain at which Garson has been a special guest artist, playing alongside local talents who are delighted to have the bar raised by playing with an international virtuoso of his stature. Garson also acts as mentor to Ryan's son Theo, who plays fretless bass.[1]

When I spoke to Tim Ryan, he added further insights on Garson's approach to music and life in general:

> Mike Garson is a consummate professional . . . he's always playing, he's always improving . . . this is a guy who when he was younger would go to the Lincoln Center Library in New York every two weeks for another stack of classical sheet music, would practice sight-reading them all, then come back for the next batch. There's definitely a neo-classical edge to the flavors he adds to Bowie and other rock music. He keeps his body completely drug free. He's in better shape than all these younger guys in the bands, when he shows up with his energy and his drive . . . his consciousness is beautiful, he's aware of things at a high philosophical and spiritual level, and that comes out in his playing. When he plays, you can be transported. He's in great communication with his audience, so if they want to be taken someplace amazing, and are ready for the ride, then Mike will take them there!

Garson indeed recalls how, in his early twenties, he would struggle from the library to the trunk of his car each time with armfuls of that sheet music. He would sight-read each piece just once then move on to the next. He was reading music the same way that other people read books: it was a hobby for him. This trained his sight-reading abilities, which were already pronounced, but also allowed him to absorb a huge amount of music, from the sixteenth century onward: Palestrina, Buxtehude,

Bach, Mozart, Beethoven, Ravel, Debussy, Gershwin, Rachmaninoff, Hindemith, Stravinsky, Pärt, Messiaen, Ligeti. This vast grounding became a rich source of inputs in his improvisation and composition, and informs his playing to this day.

Ryan describes Garson as being happy to make use of keyboard technology where it is needed, but on the spectrum from technical keyboardist or programmer to pure pianist, he leans toward the latter. When M-Audio developed the key bed of its keyboards to a point that brought it much closer (though not quite) to that of a real piano, Garson interestingly reported that he would rather play a keyboard that was very different from the real thing, as he would more easily compensate accordingly, whereas if something initially seemed close to the real thing he may ignore or miss the subtle differences, and as a result his playing might suffer.

Ryan describes Garson as 'not just one of the greatest keyboardists on the planet but also one of the greatest *jazz* keyboardists on the planet,' and he believes that there has been a 'miscarriage of justice' in which Garson has been widely dismissed by the jazz community, simply because of his association and success with other genres of music and specifically because of his success in rock. Garson is almost certainly one of the top ten jazz pianists in the world today. He has played with legends like Elvin Jones, Freddie Hubbard, and Stan Getz. 'He went the Bowie route,' Ryan adds, 'and was making ten times more money than all the jazzers—and he could also play jazz better than them, as well as classical or rock. All they could do is say, he's not one of us, he's not in the club . . . When I hear who's being invited to play out on the road, they don't jump to ask Mike, they ask these other usual jazz suspects, they're just missing the boat!'

Ryan recalls a *Keyboard* magazine event at NAMM that corralled the best keyboard players in various fields—including Joe Zawinul, Bruce Hornsby, Patrick Moraz, and others—and reflects how, in his view, Garson could 'play circles around' just about all of these in their respective styles, great as they were.

The advances in music technology since Garson first played professionally in the 1960s have clearly transformed the possibilities for all of us, and he in particular has made full and extensive use of what has become possible, from automatically notating and scoring his 'Now' compositions to sending the output from his recording sessions to clients across the world. But the advent of processes like sampling and sequencing has not been without its mishaps or ironies.

Garson once played the Monterey Jazz Festival. At the time, he was a Yamaha artist and was using a lot of equipment, so the company had sent up various DX7 and other keyboards. Rather than bring in a trio, he was asked to program the drums and an acoustic jazz bass, using one of Yamaha's samplers, for his forty-minute set, which was to be performed in front of thousands. When the heavy velvet stage curtains parted to reveal his setup, they knocked all of his keyboards off the very high stage. The piano was intact, but all of the keyboards had gone, and had to be quickly salvaged. Despite the metal of the units being bent, everything functioned okay. As for his performance, Garson had done a good job with all of the advance programming. He had played with so many excellent jazz musicians over the years that he knew instinctively what a good bass line and a good ride beat for the drums should sound like, and had programmed it realistically—so much so that a review in the following day's newspaper complained that he had failed to acknowledge his rhythm section and had kept them hidden behind the curtains.

In 1990, Garson made a jazz album called *The Mystery Man* that hardly sold (making it quite aptly named). It includes an original piece of his called 'Illumination' featuring a great drummer called Billy Mintz, with whom he had played many times. He had trouble, however, finding the right bass player, so he programmed it instead using a sample sound from the 16W Yamaha sampler, and added some quantization (which regularizes the beat). As a little joke he credited the bass playing on the album cover to a certain 'Sam Pull.' One of the magazine reviews published a few months later stated, without any intended irony, that 'Sam' was a great bass player—not much of a soloist, but very steady and dependable.

Garson played a show with the Smashing Pumpkins in 1998 in Atlanta, Georgia, where Elton John has a home. John sat through the first set slightly offstage, watching Garson play, virtually looking over his shoulder. Garson reminded him that they had met once before in a 'crazy' clothes store in Hollywood in 1972. Having seen the wild outfits worn by Bowie and the Spiders even at his audition, Garson had decided that he had better get something, too. Elton asked if Garson was okay with him watching him play and Garson said it was fine. It was obviously a case of one pianist being keen and interested to watch another's technique.

Garson plays me a beautifully simple piano arrangement he has recorded of the Beatles' 'Blackbird' using the Ivory piano sampler. It is part of a collection of MP3s that he has made available for download together with the scores of his musical arrangements for them. He has also made forays into writing for string and wind instruments. He talks me through the modulations of Paganini's *Variations*, which he has rearranged for jazz cello, viola, violin, and flute, to striking effect.

In July 2011, Garson released an album of piano arrangements of David Bowie songs called *The Bowie Variations for Piano*, produced by 'Prof' Johnson and featuring

Garson's own computer-generated artwork on the cover. Jérôme Soligny explains that he had been urging Garson for years to embark on such a project, but that there had always been the feeling that to interpret these much-loved songs without vocals would be a tricky challenge, especially in terms of instrumentation and production. Soligny advised Garson simply to go ahead and do it himself, just with piano. This is how the album proceeded, though in some cases the simplicity ended there, as the reinterpretation Garson chose to create for songs like 'Let's Dance' was quite complex and layered, so that the song arrives incognito, to be rediscovered. It was fitting that the pianist most associated with David Bowie's canon of works should finally be heard exploring and experimenting with those themes himself, alone, in a way that comes across also at times as both relaxed and playful. Interestingly, only one of the tracks—a medley of three songs—features material for which Garson played on the original recorded version. Above all, he remains respectful of Bowie and his work, and the only track that is not a Bowie cover is entitled 'Tribute to David.'

Perhaps surprisingly, two albums hardly covered by these instrumental re-workings are 1977's *Low* and *"Heroes"*, from Bowie's 'Berlin trilogy,' despite their featuring several instrumental pieces combining Eno's beautiful textures with Visconti's impeccable production, both of which frame some of Bowie's most enduring masterpieces of contemplation and foreboding. On his *Variations*, Garson creates a richly textured and rhythmic solo piano version of the title track of *"Heroes"*, but otherwise he focuses his instrumental renditions on other Bowie vocals, rather than the 'Berlin' instrumentals.

The first reworking of the Berlin instrumental pieces fell initially to Philip Glass, with his Symphony No. 1 'Low' in 1992, and his Symphony No. 4 'Heroes' in 1996. In 2014, Dylan Howe's *Subterranean* album breathed a new kind of life into these remarkably resilient themes from those Bowie albums, with a jazz sensibility propelled by Howe's own superb drumming and production skills of great finesse. Meanwhile, Jérôme Soligny has since been encouraging Garson to proceed with a further project of recording solo piano interpretations of songs by the Beatles, for which Garson has already sent him several tracks.

In November 2014, David Bowie released a major retrospective, *Nothing Has Changed: The Very Best of Bowie*, featuring two new songs alongside over fifty earlier recordings. Inevitably, Garson's piano features on several tracks, including one of his personal favorites, 'Shadow Man,' as re-recorded in 2001 with a beautiful piano part. This had previously only been available on the limited-edition bonus disc for *Heathen*, and as the B-side to the 2002 single release of 'Everyone Says Hi.'

For inspiration, like many in that part of the world, Garson sometimes chooses to drive up the coast and contemplate the peace and beauty of the sea in a particular quiet corner of Malibu amongst the rocks and huge seabirds. Indeed, some of our interviews were conducted there. Toward the end of my work on this book, however, he explained that he has gradually become aware that although he is happy to have a lot of apparent 'downtime' in the balance of his life, even then he always finds himself cogitating, contemplating, or meditating on the goals he is pursuing the rest of the time.

Sometimes he spends time developing his graphic art, which he has been producing for several years now to some acclaim, in the form of computer-generated images, recast and processed in a way that strongly bears the stamp of his personality. In 2004, he enjoyed a well-received first showing of his artworks at Portland's Brian Marki gallery. Garson was there on a piano, and anyone who bought a piece of his artwork had a piece of music composed for them on the spot to accompany the artwork. There is the possibility in future of exploring further the interface between musical and visual creation, with perhaps digital canvases inspired by or even generated by some of the sound compositions, too.

Meanwhile, Garson continues to be sought out by rock bands across the world that want him to adorn and embellish their recordings with some of his unique pianistic sparkle. One such band contacted him around the time of my first visit and was very excited with the results, as he fulfilled their brief with ease in one take and emailed the finished product to them without even being sure which continent they were in, only that it must be another time zone, as their messages tended to come at three o'clock in the morning to Los Angeles. The piano part he recorded was completed during my week with him, and the results were astounding—proof, if any more were needed, that the genius of Garson's work on *Aladdin Sane* was far from a one-off. This particular work, being for a band of much lesser profile than Bowie, may not get to be heard as much, and yet it shows just the same powerful combination of deep emotional feeling and technical virtuosity, leaving the listener breathless, inspired, and uplifted.

Garson joined Free Flight, with flautist Jim Walker, in 1982, and they still perform together today. The Free Flight sound is beautiful and very much in contrast, once again, with all of Garson's other projects. In 1989, Garson recorded an instrumental cover version (produced by Stanley Clarke and remixed by Gene Leone) of Michael Jackson's 'Man in the Mirror,' having always greatly admired Jackson's mastery of the pop music genre in his work with Quincy Jones. More recent years have also seen him recording and performing live with artists and groups as diverse as the

Polyphonic Spree, New Jersey 'mathcore' band the Dillinger Escape Plan (on the 2010 album *Option Paralysis*), Aviv Geffen, St. Vincent, and Adam Lambert.

For the Polyphonic Spree's 2007 album *The Fragile Army*, the recording of his piano parts was done in the opposite way from the approach used on most of the David Bowie and other albums. He tends to be asked to play after most of the song has been put together, meaning that the piano track is added to the vocals and other instruments. With the Polyphonic Spree, however, the piano, bass, and drums were recorded during the first week, after which everything else was added to this foundation.

Also in 2007, Garson played in Paris with French singer Raphaël Haroche for his live acoustic album *Une nuit au Châtelet*, which was partly a tribute to French singers like Serge Gainsbourg and Gérard Manset. Haroche had occasionally played support for Bowie in the past and had various hit albums in France from 2003, some featuring Garson on piano, as well as others from Bowie's bands such as Carlos Alomar, Gail Ann Dorsey, and Zachary Alford, and some production and string arrangements by Tony Visconti.

Annie Clark, also known by her stage name of St. Vincent, was in the Polyphonic Spree when Garson played with them, and later called on him for some input on her subsequent solo material. He recorded two songs with her, 'Your Lips Are Red' and 'All My Stars Aligned,' for her debut solo album of 2007, *Marry Me*. The latter song has beautiful, high piano cascades that seem to just spill out of her voice, and the combined effect is intensely moving. The album also has an instrumental written and played by Garson called 'We Put a Pearl in the Ground.'

Clark shares Garson's view about the need to unlearn in order to create. Having attended the Berklee College of Music for three years before dropping out, she has since said, 'I think that with music school and art school, or school in any form, there has to be some system of grading and measurement. The things they can teach you are quantifiable. While all that is good and has its place, at some point you have to learn all you can and then forget everything that you learned in order to actually start making music.'[2]

When Adam Lambert came second on *American Idol* in 2009, Garson noted the power and quality of his voice and even recalls commenting to his wife, Susan, 'I could see myself playing for this guy!' In another strange piece of synchronicity, within a few weeks Garson had a call from a producer asking him to play on Lambert's performance of his hit, 'For Your Entertainment,' at the American Music Awards of 2009. Lambert's spectacular appearance on the show was later included in *Billboard*'s list of 'Top Ten American Music Awards Moments' through its forty-year history in November 2012; Garson's distinctive piano could be heard opening and closing the song.

Immediately after his appearance on *American Idol*, Lambert signed to RCA and enjoyed huge and rapid success. His debut album, *For Your Entertainment*, was released in November 2009 and sold 198,000 copies in the USA in its first week. Simon Fuller (creator of the *Idol* franchise) described Lambert as 'like Marc Bolan meets Bowie, with a touch of Freddie Mercury and the sexiness of Prince.'[3] To prepare for the American Music Awards appearance, Lambert came to Garson's studio in Bell Canyon. He wanted Garson to appear on the show with him, but Garson was unable to do so as he had a jazz concert to perform that night, so they recorded his playing in advance, for use on the night. Garson says that Lambert loved what he recorded for him that day, and he was interested to find that Lambert 'turned out to be a big Bowie fan.' In 2012, Lambert started performing with Queen, first in Russia and Ukraine and then London, and in the USA the following year. His second album, *Trespassing*, went straight to no. 1 on the *Billboard* albums chart on its release in May 2012. He has also collaborated with Nile Rodgers, with whom David Bowie had worked in the past, so Garson's work with him on that key show of 2009 holds some significant resonances.

In 2011, Garson performed a joint recital with Romanian virtuoso jazz pianist Marian Petruscu in Los Angeles, including a dazzling duet on a Disney medley of familiar melodies. In 2016, he released an album in the style of, and in homage to, the piano of Thelonious Monk. These multiple creative projects continue in profusion for Garson, who maintains a remarkably full work schedule.

During 2014, he recorded with singer Jilann O'Neill for an album, including some avant-garde torch song adaptations in French and some covers from the 1970s (including some Bowie songs), as well as original material. She says that he became a mentor to her over the period of their recordings together, adding, 'I have probably spent more time with Mike discussing the creative process and its connection to the spiritual journey than we've spent actually recording or playing. It is an exercise in listening when I work with him, in which the intuitive voice plays a big role.' They worked an intense schedule of recording over a period of months, with production from Michael Farrell, who has also worked with Macy Gray, Morrissey, and Alanis Morissette. O'Neill says of working with Garson that 'he is not caught in the past, in what was, in re-creating or even in the future of what should be created. He is in the moment, listening carefully for the whisper of the music that wants his attention now.'

When I asked him to look back on his life so far, Garson said that he sees his first six decades as 'just an apprenticeship,' and that 'now the real work begins.' He has been on a mission for some years to show, by example, three things: that being a musician can be combined with living healthily and respectfully, without the dependencies with which it has so often been associated; that music can itself be a healing force in all kinds of ways; and that true education simply means helping one another to find our true voice and vocation (musical or otherwise), even if that proves to lie in unexpected directions. Whilst hoping that the story of his life might bring some pleasure and insight to readers, his overriding wish is to encourage people more actively to 'take a few things from this book that ring true for them, and use that in their lives to bring joy to themselves and others.'

Back in London after completing my first visits to Garson's home in Ventura County, California, and returning to my own home in London's Fitzrovia, I experienced an odd coincidence—another example of the synchronicity with which this story began, and which seemed to complete this part of my journey. On the original 1971 recording of the song 'Life on Mars?' for David Bowie's *Hunky Dory* album, the piano was played by Rick Wakeman. The following year, Mike Garson joined Bowie's *Ziggy Stardust* Tour of the USA and started to play the piano part for that song, which he would then play with Bowie so many times right up to 2005. In 2013, the ringtone on my mobile phone consisted of the opening bars of 'Life on Mars?' with its unmistakable piano introduction being played by Wakeman over forty years before. As I walked past the Charlotte Street Hotel near my home a few days after my return, I happened to notice Rick Wakeman sitting on the terrace outside the hotel. As I walked past, my phone played its 'Life on Mars?' ringtone. Wakeman looked up. I answered the phone. It was Garson.

# 16

## Scandinavian Sessions

*'Mike is a magician, a true wizard of notes . . . he lets the universe flow through his fingertips.'*

—Jussi K. Niemelä

SUCH IS THE EXTENT of Mike Garson's work over the years that on this book's first appearance in 2015, we were contacted by a number of bands from around the world who had piano parts played by Garson in their back catalogues that had not been detailed in the first edition of this biography. The large number of recordings he has played on makes it very difficult to be comprehensive. Some more of these are discussed below, which also provides the opportunity to delve deeper into his creative process.

Garson's work on a project in Finland in recent years throws further light on his methods and on the nature of artistic endeavor generally. Jussi K. Niemelä is a prolific Finnish poet, writer, and lyricist who collaborated with Garson from 2008. He has explained to me in detail how this came about. He had long been a fan of both Bowie and Garson, particularly of *Aladdin Sane* and *1. Outside*. In 2005, Niemelä had worked with the classical composer Harri Kerko on an album by Kuusumun Profeetta (Moon Fog Prophet), one of two indie bands featuring Mika Rätto (the other being Circle) that combine input from the worlds of classical and rock music. In 2007, he was astonished to find Mike Garson on the then-popular music-based social media platform MySpace, and at how accessible and open Garson was. In 2008, Niemelä, Kerko, and Rätto formed Omfalos Renaissance and recorded the album *Miekka ja kirsikankukka (The Sword and the Chrysanthemum)*, featuring piano by Garson, which was released that year by Helmi-levyt.

Before creating his piano parts, Garson asked to be sent photographs of Niemelä's home area, the places in which he most liked to walk and think, which were the seaside haunts of the small island of Lauttasaari to the west of Helsinki. He also engaged in lengthy and deep philosophical conversations in order to 'tune in' better to the needs of the project. Unsurprisingly, the results were astounding. This demonstrates how seriously Garson takes the process of crafting his work for others. His improvised piano solo, finally executed in one take, on 'Sielunmessu' ('Requiem') was sent by him electronically from California, yet transports the listener instantly to the awe-inspiring landscape of Lauttasaari, wherever we may be whilst listening. Garson also created another track, 'Nocturno,' for the album. Further collaborations between him and Niemelä have included a series of piano improvisations called the 'Bird Suite,' each of which is a response to a poem from Niemelä about a certain species of sea bird in Finland. That this has all been done at long distance between two artists in such absolutely different terrains and climatic environments as California and the coast of Finland is also a wonderful example of inspired and passionate art harnessing modern technology to make it even stronger. The depth of feeling embodied in this work is best captured in the words of the poet, Niemelä, himself, who wrote at the time:

> Mike just created a piano bridge across infinite beauty, an astonishing piece of artistic brilliance, in between two composed sections. When you get the instinct of the art into your spine, sending electric shivers all over your body, you're connected to the wellspring of pure creation and creativity. You're actually intertwined with the slow and calm breathing of the universe. You are star-stuff, as the late Carl Sagan said . . . As Mike just told me on the phone, when he first heard the track a couple of days ago, he immediately knew what he wanted to play. The song played Mike's heart, and Mike played the song's heart.[1]

There was also a nice twist that followed from their musical collaboration. Niemelä happened to edit a humanist magazine in Finland and was so enthralled by Garson's frequent written musings on art, creativity, God, and philosophy, which were appearing on MySpace, that he obtained his permission to translate and publish them. This makes Garson almost certainly the only Los Angeles–based musician to have had a regular column in the Finnish press, which continued for over two years.

Niemelä's brother, Teemu, used Garson's arrangement of the Beatles' 'Blackbird' for the first dance at his wedding, and the birth of their first child was marked by another specially improvised piece from Garson. These little personal details fill in the canvas otherwise stretched between stadium tours, jazz trios, and thousands of hours of solitary hard work and practice by Garson. Niemelä adds, 'It is amazing to connect with a musician on a spiritual level this deep, across the ocean. Mike is a magician, a true wizard of notes . . . he lets the universe flow through his fingertips.'

A very different project, though also Scandinavian, is the Norwegian experimental and psychedelic music of Oliver Kersbergen's band Sleepyard, formed with his brother, Svein, in 1994. Kersbergen is a remarkable creative force himself, a fantastic musician with a very wide frame of reference in his work and an encyclopedic knowledge of all genres. Wanting to move away from his previous pop direction when he enlisted Garson in 2006, he provided him with a very rich range of suggested inspirations: 'Everything from Martin Denny exotica (I think Mike hearing "Quiet Village" brought back some fond memories) to Vince Guaraldi to experimental composers Béla Bartók and Charles Ives, plus the original ambient pioneers, Erik Satie and Claude Debussy. I guess my rule was not to ask him to play anything Bowie-like, as I thought he would like to do something else.'

That decision to steer away from the obvious request for him to play in the way he had for Bowie definitely paid off. The album was released on Norwegian label CCAP in 2009, as *Future Lines*. Garson's distinctive playing can be heard on several tracks. The instrumental 'Tangerine Road,' written for Kersbergen's mother, who was very ill at the time, was subsequently re-released with vocals on an EP with Jim Shepherd called *Down Tangerine Road*.

A further album, *Black Sails*, was released by GRA in 2014, and was dedicated to Kersbergen's mother, who had passed away during work on it. Once again, Garson features on several tracks, such as 'Rainy Day Vibration,' which features vocals from Judy Dyble (formerly of Fairport Convention). The album opens with a great song with vocalist Dawn Smithson and some wonderful romantic piano from Garson called '1000 Year Vacation.' The lyrics are by Smithson, but the title came from Kersbergen, who mentions that he was inspired by 'Frederick Barbarossa, who drowned on June 10, 1190, but is supposed to be sleeping in the Kyffhäuser hills.'

*Black Sails* also features Nik Turner of Hawkwind and Geoff Leigh of Henry Cow. Many of these songs by Sleepyard are atmospheric and emotionally evocative in a very intense way, and Garson's piano lines are often sparse and dreamlike in keeping with this, making them a perfect fit, as well as reflecting and extending the vocal lines, often in ways that are very minimalistic and subtle.

In addition, some superb short films have been made to accompany these songs. The first track they ever worked on together, 'Afternoon Suntrap,' and '1000 Year Vacation' are featured in beautiful films currently viewable on YouTube, and both are songs of great delicacy and power combined. Kersbergen modestly tells me that, in working with Garson, he hoped to 'bring his piano playing somewhere else. I was so glad when he liked my production. Such a thrill. I thought working with Mike was such fun as he is such a strong musical force. We can go anywhere, with imagination.' This was a great example of a relationship where both Garson and Kersbergen brought out something different in each other, together creating something new and beautiful.

Yet another Scandinavian recording project to which Garson has contributed in recent years is with the Swedish band Berlin Bar, whose recent releases feature Garson's piano on three songs, 'Lonesome Trail,' 'Wall of Fear,' and 'Hardly the Thing to Do' (with some funky chord chops not often heard elsewhere from Garson), all written by Anders Magnusson. He told me that his brief to Garson included reference to the live 1973 version of 'The Wild Eyed Boy from Freecloud,' which Garson said he had not even heard since playing it over forty years earlier.

Dutch artist René van Commenée is a man of generous spirit and expansive creativity. In 2006, he introduced Garson to Willem Tanke, which led to a most fruitful and ongoing collaboration.[2] More recently, I was fortunate to have the opportunity to interview van Commenée himself at length. He reveals that he introduced Garson and Tanke in 2006, specifically because he knew they 'would love one another,' as he had known them each for some years previously, and knew that they had a strikingly similar approach to musical composition and performance.

In the 1990s, the classical and jazz pianist, writer, and lecturer Dennis Thurmond (who has also written extensively on improvisation in music) was at the faculty of the Utrecht School of the Arts (HKU) in the Netherlands, at which van Commenée worked in the groundbreaking music technology department. Thurmond invited Garson over as a guest lecturer. From their first meeting, van Commenée and Garson formed a bond of work and friendship that still flourishes today, with Garson often sending his latest improvisations to van Commenée for his appreciation. Van Commenée also went on, himself, to invite Garson over on several subsequent occasions to deliver master classes and private lessons in the Netherlands. On one occasion, he, Tanke, and Henri Bok organized a weeklong improvisation seminar featuring Garson at the Rotterdam Conservatoire. He found that Garson could speak and perform to a packed lecture theater for several hours, so interestingly and entertainingly that all present remained rapt in attention throughout, silent apart from sporadic laughter and questions. 'It is quite amazing how flexible he is with students. He seems to understand what he can add to their vocabulary right on the spot, even having them around for just twenty minutes, regardless of whether they are pop, jazz, or classical students. Believe me: every student was extremely enthusiastic afterward!'

Van Commenée is a true renaissance man himself whose experimental art spans all media, from 'visual sound art installations' to his musical project under the name 'Mr. Averell,' which has generated two albums. On *Gridlock*, Garson plays piano on two tracks, 'Deliberately' and 'Sightseeings.' Van Commenée spoke to me of his experience of working with his long-term friend on this, and he summarizes very clearly what makes Garson distinctive: 'He is open-minded. He has no borders. Also he puts himself into your world, to meet the musical needs of your project, whilst at the same time retaining his own distinct individual sound within that, and playing what pleases him as well as you. On top of all this, his technical skills are amazing.'

The repeated piano notes with echo and delay effects on 'Sightseeings' were all spontaneously played live by Garson in real time. The track also features saxophone from David Jackson of Van der Graaf Generator. Van Commenée, unlike many with whom Garson has worked, insists on being in the same studio rather than sending files across long distances, and although it takes longer to organize this way, the results bear witness to the fact that this is what they did. After much long anticipation, they simply went into a room with a grand piano and wrote 'Sightseeings' together in a moment of natural spontaneity.

In recent years, Garson has also featured on several tracks by the New York band Lostdog in Loveland, with his unmistakable flourishes in evidence on five songs on their superb 2014 album *sadanthem*, released by Hedfonik Records. One song on which his distinctive piano work stands out especially is 'You're Lucky You're Beautiful.' Another is a powerful cover of 'Mother of Pearl' from Roxy Music's 1973 album *Stranded*. The original had featured saxophone from Andy Mackay, who also played, as did Garson, on Jérôme Soligny's 1991 soundtrack to the film *Gawin*.[3] Lead singer Robert Mag tells me the band is currently recording new material, and hopes to work further with Garson in the future.

In addition, Garson can be heard on the 2011 album by Spanish guitarist J21, *Beyond the Holographic Veil*, on which the tracks 'Calm' and 'Perpetuum' are beautiful classical solo piano pieces by Garson. Alongside recording work for other artists, Garson has engaged in a variety of projects of his own. He continues to compose a large number of classical pieces but also to record his own variations or arrangements of a variety of material, from Beethoven to songs like 'Yellow' by Coldplay. He is keen to reinterpret some Radiohead songs, too, and has arranged the Beatles' 'Yesterday' as a jazz waltz.

Despite the tendency for jazz to see itself as something apart, jazz has long taken pop songs as the starting point for creative interpretations. For example, Jamie Cullum has played distinctive variations on 'The Wind Cries Mary' by Jimi Hendrix and Elton John's 'Rocket Man.' It is a novel way of further breaking down the barriers between musical genres, but it also makes use of the audience's familiarity with these chord progressions and anthemic melodies. In this way the audience is successfully transported across genres, with a strong awareness of just how far the jazz is departing from the main theme before leaning back toward it again, as these pop melodies and chord progressions are so well known and part of the cultural consciousness of the era.

Regarding Coldplay, they happened in 2008 to be recording *Viva La Vida* in London with Brian Eno when they met Garson, who was working nearby with Israeli artist Aviv Geffen. He was happy to find that they recognized him and knew his work. With Coldplay, Brian Eno was still as eccentrically experimental as he had been in 1995 in the sessions for Bowie's *1. Outside*: it was reported, for example, that he had organized for the whole band to be hypnotized, to see how it affected their playing.

*David Live*, the 1974 double album recorded at the Tower Theatre in Philadelphia, is a great demonstration of the fusion of jazz and rock through Garson's contribution. His piano work on this album is amongst his best, and was given enough level in the mix to make this album an ideal starting point for an appreciation of his virtuosity in that period, and of the ways in which his jazz ability was marshaled by Bowie to enhance the richness and range of his own live stage impact. Take, for example, the mixture of jazz and pop piano on the backing of a rock anthem like 'All the Young Dudes,' and the way it lifts the song into something much bigger. Then, by contrast, Garson's R&B chops on the cover of the Eddie Floyd song 'Knock on Wood' (which Bowie released as a single).

However, it is important to place Garson's innovation in breaking down these boundaries within a cultural context, which is not without its antecedents. Composers like George Gershwin and Leonard Bernstein did not hesitate to fuse popular and classical music. Before meeting Garson, Becker KB was already developing his own concept of 'nu-classical,' which blends classical structures with more modern and popular musical languages. He says that, like Garson, he does not wish to live in 'historical re-enactment mode' or to fulfill traditional expectations, and is 'energized by pushing boundaries, aiming for innovation, seeking to express new ideas, and smashing barriers.' He finds that Garson's degree of technical competence and integrity distinguishes him from many of those rock keyboardists who make token gestures toward incorporating jazz elements or who turn in later years to composing pseudo-classical music as a way of extending their pop careers.

The path to this integrity of incorporating genres such as rock, jazz, and classical within a new cohesive fabric, as opposed to mere token gestures or references to one genre by another, necessitates rigorous classical and technical training and a deep knowledge and understanding of all of those threads. This is what Garson means by working hard for years to 'do the homework' or the preparation, then being ready to cast that aside and create something new.

One paradox that emerges from Garson's story is that when hard work is combined with creative flow, it ceases to seem like work. We lose the distinction between work and play, losing track of time as we become more and more at one with our making of something new. Garson's philosophy on this stands in the tradition of the great nineteenth-century English artist and thinker William Morris (see page 163).[4] From this point of view, the title of the Sleepyard song '1000 Year Vacation' might well describe the joy epitomized by this ongoing pleasure of working to produce something spontaneous and in the moment, without alienation from the task or the product.

# 17

# Seventy Years of Serendipity

*'The sun is always shining . . . you just have to remove the clouds. You don't have to do anything about the sun. So, if there are some clouds in my way, I will work on removing them. One time, I was really depressed, so I just practiced for twelve hours, and twelve hours later, I wasn't depressed. I forgot what I was depressed about, I overcame the negative or the destructive aspect of what was happening with positive energy and it dissolved after twelve hours. It was very upsetting, whatever this person had said to me, but I actually pushed through it just by playing all day.'*

—Mike Garson

A CURRENT STUDENT of Garson's, Laura Bedford, had this to tell me about his teaching methods:

My first lesson with Mike was unlike any I'd ever had. He talked about pulse and how music lives, demonstrating how melodies and rhythms are placed on top of a flow. He explained the importance of remaining relaxed, not getting stiff, letting the music flow through you, surrendering and connecting to it, and not giving yourself a hard time. It was a master class, yet geared to my level. Mike assessed my skills and something of my personality just from my playing. He agreed to take me on because of my desire to play and promise to practice for two hours a night. He insisted that I be ruthless with the timing. During this period I was also introduced to basic composing and improvising techniques. Prior to Mike, I couldn't simply sit at the piano and play what I felt without sheet music. Now I can. I finally feel comfortable calling myself a piano player.

To understand his working methods better, I also returned to my study of classical piano playing, with Garson as my guide and mentor. Within a very few sessions, he succeeded in encouraging me into the discipline of regular sustained practice with dramatic results, not just in my playing but even in my sense of satisfaction and engagement with life, because of the focus and discipline cultivated by this.

He still uses exercises of almost meditative precision, playing scales with a metronome in order to focus himself, in a way that is reminiscent of the extreme concentration, strength, and grace attained by practitioners of certain martial arts. There is even some overlap between this repetitive approach to learning or practicing a piece, and the therapeutic power of meditation, as typified by the use of mantras.

Garson tells a story of an early teacher of his, Mario Fenninger, having lost in a piano competition long before to a Russian concert pianist. That night, over dinner, Fenninger had asked his rival what had given him the edge. It transpired that whilst Fenninger had done three prior public performances of the concerto in question, the Russian government had ensured that the Russian pianist had toured throughout Russia playing that same piece hundreds of times in concerts. This repetition—not just in private practice sessions but also in public performance—is the only way reliably to move through confidence and familiarity with a piece, into intimate exploration of it, and finally mastery.

Garson is passionate about the idea that music education should be universally provided to young people. 'We're spiritual beings. What do spiritual beings do? They interchange, they exchange, they interact, they communicate, and they create. That's what they should be doing. Everything else is harmful to them, such as wars, drugs, overeating, decadences, lying, cheating, and everything that's going on on the planet . . . and yet, look what they've done, they've taken the music out of the schools! The countries that have the most war have the least music.'

Garson recalls a student of his who graduated with a perfect rendition of McCoy Tyner's 'Autumn Leaves' from a precisely transcribed copy of the solo. After graduation, as an afterthought, Garson asked him to play his own version, and it sounded awful. Garson felt that he had failed as a teacher at this point, and insisted that this student take away 'Autumn Leaves' and practice it, for two hours a day, for sixty days. When he came back, it sounded great. Paradoxically, it is with hard work, self-discipline, and the right guidance, that mere imitation can sometimes give way to originality and creativeness.

People perform better when they are trusted and expected to perform well. This is not the same as false praise or flattery. Good teaching and encouragement involves telling someone that you believe they can do it, not necessarily that they have done it yet. Garson says that he wants to break the paradigm, common in musical circles, of putting others down for not fitting a mold: 'We can practice compassion like we practice our scales.' He also regards it as important to help people to find a way to explore what they really want to be doing and then to excel at that. He has had music students come to him and, in the course of their sessions, it has transpired that their true calling was not music but medicine or psychology: for him, this is a real success. My own situation was indeed an example of this, since I first visited him for some piano lessons, but through those discussions arose the idea of my writing his biography. Life evolves in unexpected ways—or, as he aptly puts it, 'life is an improvisation.'

As a teacher of piano, I have always started young learners playing by ear before they are introduced to sheet music, whereas, like most people of my generation, I was introduced first to the mediating obstacle of the printed score, which stands between player and instrument, and discourages the confidence and sense of freedom that is so vital to later improvisation and creativity.

In the course of my discussions with Garson, there were many areas in common between us as pianists, and this gave rise to a further instance of his appealingly adaptable approach:

> When you start talking and going off into something that's connected with your playing or similar experience to me, or something we are learning, it gives you a relief that 'Wow! He felt the same way as I did!' These are common to piano players; this is common to working in those clubs. I'm leaving space to also switch roles, as if I was doing the biography of you. Because that's what two-way communication is. So, I'm equally as interested in your story, except that you happen to be doing my story! Which is what history is: his story!

Garson's connection with David Bowie is impossible to escape from for long, and interest in it cuts across genres. Even some of the jazz musicians with whom he collaborates turn out to have a fascination for Bowie's music. For example, during the 1990s, while Garson was playing with Free Flight, the drummer was Ralph Humphrey, who had played with Frank Zappa and Al Jarreau (and in more recent years has been the drummer for TV's *Dancing with the Stars*). He was more comfortable playing in odd meters like 9/8 or 13/8 than in 4/4. On one occasion he could not make a gig and was replaced by Whitney Houston's drummer at the time, Mike Baker. When Garson mentioned after the gig that he had played with Bowie, Baker 'freaked' and spoke about how he had a 'Bowie room' at home that was like a shrine. Despite his playing jazz, here was someone else who was deeply fascinated by Bowie, and his 1970s period especially.

Garson enjoys these examples of felicitous chance. He named one of his albums *Serendipity* with a knowing nod to Jung's 'synchronicity.' He again gives the example of how this book came about through an unexpected bond between two people, which for him again has something to do with synchronicity, serendipity, and spirituality. 'There are these things that are "in between the notes," that are happening in this book, and will happen between the lines.' He cites how, as a child, I had connected not only with Bowie's music but in particular with Garson's piano playing, and that years later our paths finally crossed:

> But the real thing is to show—it's pretty perceptive of you, let's face it, to have discovered me at such a young age. You were getting more than just David Bowie. And the other people around the planet—hundreds of pianists, not thousands or tens of thousands—I've affected. And, then, within those hundreds there's a few tens or dozens that really got me. For you to come this distance, take those lessons, come over to visit me, talk about getting intrigued in these subjects—that, to me, implies it's deeper than just the brain, or just that I played a nice piano part. Do you know how many people have good rhythm, good melody, good harmony, who can improvise, they can create, they can play classical jazz, that wouldn't do a thing for you, in moving you? Do you know how much music you've heard that bored the hell out of you? It's obvious, and me too, right? So, to me, it's a spiritual connection.

The idea of serendipity is central to Garson's outlook. It is not simply a question of happy chances, but rather of being open to make the most of opportunities, and even of being able to recognize them when they arise. The term was coined in 1754 by Horace Walpole, in a letter in which he refers to a Persian fairy tale, *The Three Princes of Serendip*.[1] The princes 'were always making discoveries, by accidents and sagacity, of things they were not in quest of.' Whereas a lucky chance describes a random event, a serendipity is the capacity or ability to 'see bridges where others see holes,' and it is significant that Walpole referred to sagacity as well as accident.

Recent years have seen the work of David Bowie increasingly assimilated into historical and popular consciousness, whilst continuing to arouse fascination from new generations. Garson is part of this process, having made such a significant contribution to that body of work. A new series of boxed sets that will cover Bowie's whole back catalogue is helping to cement his gravitas as an artist of enormous significance. The first of these sets, *David Bowie: Five Years (1969–1973)* was released by Parlophone in September 2015 and contains ten albums, six of which Garson played on. The second, *David Bowie: Who Can I Be Now? (1974–1976)*, released in 2016, again includes various albums from the 1970s featuring Garson's playing, such as *Diamond Dogs*, *Young Americans*, and *David Live*.

For the Bowie album of new material released in January 2016, ★ (*Blackstar*), he assembled a band of young, New York–based jazz musicians. Interviewed about the album in *MOJO* magazine, producer Tony Visconti commented that 'if we'd used David's former musicians, they would be rock people playing jazz. Having jazz guys play rock music turns it upside down.'[2] One of Bowie's longest-serving former musicians at that point was Garson, with his strong jazz background. Perhaps it might be said that the experimental integration of Garson's jazz piano into Bowie's rock music in the 1970s, 1990s, and 2000s was so successful that it formed a foundation on which further cross-fertilization using a new generation of jazz musicians could be explored. In the summer of 2017, Garson worked with Tony Visconti again for the first time since the mid-1970s and *Young Americans*, as Visconti was producing a new album by Perry Farrell, for which Garson played on four of the songs.

I was fortunate to have the opportunity to speak with Donny McCaslin, the virtuoso jazz saxophonist and bandleader who features, with his band, on *Blackstar*. There are some interesting parallels between his experience of working with Bowie and that of Garson.

McCaslin says that the first playing of Garson's he had heard was when his own keyboard player, Jason Lindner, played him 'Battle for Britain (The Letter).' He was struck immediately with curiosity about the pianist who had created that 'very interesting piano solo which combines angular rhythmic language with blues and avant-garde' against the drum and bass thrust of the song. I myself also played him a selection of Garson's work with Bowie, and he responded that he could hear for sure that Bowie must have allowed Garson great freedom to play what he heard in each moment, as he had done with McCaslin and the band on *Blackstar*.

McCaslin is skeptical about the perceived boundaries between jazz and rock or other genres. He sees the work he did with Bowie as having evolved organically and been driven by a combination of Bowie's song demos and the band's interpretation of them, without any preconceived plan to use a 'jazz' band, or make a 'jazz' album. McCaslin and the rest of the band all have diverse musical backgrounds and influences, including electronica alongside jazz, though with improvisation and experimentation as a common thread.

They had been given the demos of a number of songs. During the first day of the sessions, McCaslin asked Bowie if he could overdub some ideas he had orchestrated for woodwind on the songs. This was quickly approved by Bowie, which set the positive tone for the rest of the project. McCaslin says that he improvised in the spirit of each song 'by reacting and interacting with David as he was singing, because he did track with us when we did *Blackstar*.' Bowie sang while the four band members played together (five when joined by Ben Monder on guitar for the later sessions).

McCaslin says of Bowie that 'he encouraged us to go for what we were hearing.' This reflects almost verbatim what Garson has said about all of his own work with Bowie. This had not been the case with all of Bowie's band musicians or backup singers over the years. It may well be his lifelong love of jazz and respect for its improvisational idiom that drove Bowie's parallel approach to working with the first (Garson in 1972) and last (2015's *Blackstar* band) jazz musicians in his career. McCaslin had his first taste of this in 2014, when he played on the original recording of Bowie's 'Sue (Or in a Season of Crime)' with the Maria Schneider Orchestra, and was surprised to find that all of the sax solo he recorded remained on the final mix.

McCaslin emphasizes that the songs were so strong ('even the ones that didn't make the record') that their essence withstood this process of evolution and embellishment. I asked him whether the third note of the saxophone intro to 'Lazarus' (which is the ninth note of the F chord it plays over) came from him, and he replies that this detail was actually on Bowie's demo, whereas McCaslin did add the harmonies and octaves to it as the song progressed. Tim Lefebvre's bass vamp on the intro to 'Lazarus' arose from him spontaneously riffing and Bowie picking up on it and wanting to run with it. It was created in the moment. McCaslin points out that he felt 'Bowie was not trying to write songs within a specific genre, he was just writing what he was hearing.'

It was clear, though, that Bowie had listened to some of McCaslin's earlier material with typical diligence, which may have influenced the aesthetic of the new material. He made a reference during their correspondence, for example, to McCaslin's recording of 'Alpha and Omega' on his 2012 album *Casting for Gravity* (a cover of a song by the Scottish band Boards of Canada). He also referenced the song 'Praria Grande' from the same album, which was composed by David Binney, who has produced most of McCaslin's albums.

Bowie also spoke of his love for Gil Evans, Charlie Parker, Mingus (McCaslin himself played in the Mingus Big Band), Stan Kenton, and Maria Schneider, and it is once again apparent that the influence of jazz on his work may have been more explicit at certain times, but it was always present. Aside from Garson and McCaslin, he had of course also worked with others such as Pat Metheny and Lester Bowie.

In September 2005, interviewed by Courtney Pine for BBC Radio 2, Bowie showed a quite encyclopedic knowledge of even the more arcane nooks and crannies of the jazz world. He also mentioned the excellent jazz skills of Mike Garson, as well as Gail Ann Dorsey. He seemed to feel totally happy and at home in that environment, audibly blooming as he chatted expansively and warmly with Pine about jazz.

Completing the circle, I asked Donny McCaslin for his reflections on Mike Garson's playing. He observes that on songs like 'Bring Me the Disco King,' the block voicings are strongly in the modern jazz idiom. He hears 'a wonderful sense of freedom' in Garson's input, and sees this as Bowie having had the genius to bring in Garson as 'a wild card' encompassing rich inputs of blues, modern jazz, sophisticated rhythmic expression, avant-garde, and classical influences. 'He's just a wonderful player, and obviously added so much to David's career.'

At times, Garson may have been a victim of his own distinctiveness. Never one to melt into the background as an anonymous session player, he was told by Trent Reznor, for example, that some additional tracks he had played on for *The Fragile* were not included as it would have given the album too much of a 'Bowie' flavor.

In a feature in UK newspaper the *Guardian* to mark the release of Bowie's *The Next Day* album early in 2013, a number of people who had worked with him or otherwise known Bowie were invited to give their impressions and recollections. Mike Garson was described correctly as Bowie's longest-serving musician, and was quoted at length.[3] He says that he saw Bowie joyful when having created something new, but also sometimes nervous, fearful, and vulnerable before going onstage—which was why he sent Garson out first at Glastonbury to test the waters with the 100,000-strong crowd. Bowie's first performance in 2005 after recovering from a heart attack the year before was with Garson alone, and afterward he thanked his pianist, adding that if he had not pushed himself to get over the fear of returning to performance, he may never have been able to sing again.

Garson emphasized in the *Guardian* feature that despite Bowie's extraordinary gift, he was fundamentally a good, normal guy. They were friends, though Bowie was isolated by his status. There were people he had left behind along the way—in ways that Garson feels caused an undercurrent of regret—but he observes that Bowie tended to fix and repair these things with people in the end, in his own way.

Someone who is in a position to know Garson better than most is his sister, Barbara Breitbart. A psychologist who has specialized in mediation and conflict resolution and has received a World Health Organization award for her lectures on stress and the diseases of civilization, she is ten years his senior (although he always signs off his messages to her as from 'Your Big Brother'). She and her husband Sheldon live in Sedona, in Arizona's Red Rock country. She took piano lessons for many years herself and still plays, saying, 'It's still close to my heart, but Michael took to it more than anybody in the family.'

She confirms his early single-minded devotion to his music and lack of interest in inebriation—'Mike was the good boy. He wasn't into any of the lifestyles of the

1970s'—and emphasizes the bond Garson had with their father, who was himself artistic and liked to draw and paint as well as play the piano, whilst in turn giving unconditional support for his son's playing. Their mother was more disciplinarian, wanting him to obtain a teaching certificate in case the playing did not work out, whereas their father simply conveyed unalloyed confidence in his son's future success as a musical artist. This combination of approaches proved highly effective.

Barbara saw the early spiritual orientation of her brother evolve into a wisdom that in recent years he has deployed in mentoring many young people: 'The good boy became the good man. He is just a very, very fine person. Everybody seems to love him. That is a lasting legacy. He has done so much good work with young people, who wouldn't be where they are if it wasn't for Mike.'

In terms of his ongoing quest for the deeper meanings in life, she observes, 'He's always been an experimenter—except in drugs!' recalling how committed he was at one point to macrobiotics, subsisting on brown rice and losing a lot of weight, at which point she took him to the doctor to check his health and tried to get him back on to a more balanced diet.

Garson performed on several occasions in the Sedona area with the jazz clarinetist and saxophonist Eddie Daniels, and with Jim Walker of Free Flight, for Chamber Music Sedona. 'We've grown a little bit culturally here in Sedona since then,' Barbara reflects, 'but at that time those concerts were about the only thing here besides yogurt that had culture!' She has great pride in her brother's achievements, which she explains perceptively and with eloquence:

> I'm so proud of him. I think that he is a fabulous artist. The way he evolved from classical to jazz, to rock . . . he can do anything. Now, with the technology available, he can do even more. Michael was never a 'techy' person, but it's amazing what he does now with the technology available to him. The improvisation impresses me the most: it is such a talent to be so spontaneous in the moment, to listen to other players and to be able to jump in and do exactly the right thing to make it work as a unit. Also, his playfulness and mischievousness comes out in his playing. You can hear his humor in his playing.

She explains that whatever emotion he experiences is expressed through his music, as a direct manifestation of how he is feeling at that moment. This applies across the full spectrum, from humor to deep grief. For their parents' fiftieth wedding anniversary celebration in New York, brother and sister wrote a song together, with Barbara contributing the lyrics. When Barbara and Sheldon tragically lost their son Kevin to a heart-related illness, Garson composed a beautiful requiem for him, which somehow helped them to cope by expressing their loss. As Barbara puts it, he is 'always one with the music . . . he has the empathy and ability to portray the emotion he feels and transmit it to the listener.'

In February 2015, following a family member's research into their genealogy, a Garson extended family reunion was held at Sedona, at which Garson again performed. One cousin he met there for the first time, Karen Reinsch, told me:

> I have a neurological condition from a car accident. Mike's music has had a significant impact on helping me control and minimize my pain levels. What inspires him most is his compassion and empathy. He cares deeply about the world, peace and healing—spiritually, mentally, and physically. To channel the composition and playing of his healing music to help with autism, for example, is a primary motivator. He genuinely cares about humanity and people. He lights up a room without being aware of how his presence warms the hearts of the people surrounded by him. He is an awesome cousin, friend, and spiritual mentor.

Perhaps her reference to people being 'surrounded by him' rather than vice versa was not entirely an accidental slip of the tongue: he does have great presence.

Garson continues to expand further the range of his work, and to inspire more recent generations of artists. On September 7, 2013, Lady Gaga tweeted to her thirty-nine million followers at that time: 'Listen to *Aladdin Sane*. Listen to piano parts. Changed my life.' The 2014 production of *Hamlet* at Manchester's Royal Exchange with Maxine Peake in the lead role, released as a film in 2015, made heavy use of 'Lady Grinning Soul,' both performed live within the piece and heard in its original recorded form, featuring Garson's distinctive original piano part.

Late 2015 also saw the production of a new series of online video master classes given by Garson on the 'My Music Masterclass' platform. They provide a comprehensive overview of many of his techniques and approaches to music and to creativity generally. He identifies performance as a two-way, subjective process that is affected by who is listening as well as by who is performing. He also demonstrates his trademark challenge of improvising around four notes given to him by an audience. He is not the only improviser to use this method—he mentions having seen it done on *The Tonight Show* on American television many years earlier, and at a London show in October 2015 I saw another pianist, Steve Nieve, do likewise. But he does show, within these master class films, an astonishing example of this, in which he is off on a creative curve almost before the person has finished enunciating which notes to work from. It is as if he hears the whole improvised piece, at once, and then has to get it out, note-by-note, for the listeners and for himself.

The spring of 2016 saw Garson release *Monk Fell on Me*, an album of Thelonious Monk variations, on which he says he sought respectfully to capture some of Monk's distinctive styles but also, at points, to supplant some of Monk's quirkiness with touches of his own quirkiness. It is a heartfelt tribute, as Monk has been a constant influence and inspiration to him throughout his work.[4]

Concert performances are planned for his *Symphonic Suite for Healing* by the Nashville symphony and others, and work continues on developing the Music-Heals project in conjunction with Vanderbilt University (which happens to be where David Bowie's son, film director Duncan Jones, studied). The Vanderbilt Brain Institute is partnering with Dr. Christopher Duma, Mike Garson, and Music-Heals on a series of research studies evaluating the effects of music on autistic patients, to examine which specific musical elements might encourage the greatest improvements. The outline for the first of these studies has been announced, and 'A link between music and autism has been proposed. Preliminary observations suggest positive changes in a small cohort of autistic patients who displayed improvements in behaviors commonly associated with autism, including social impairment, communication deficits, and repetitive behavior, in response to music listening and playing. Our pilot study is designed to examine the effects of specific elements of music composed and performed by Mike Garson on piano, tailored to autistic patients who learned to play, and/or listened to the composition, on brain activity and behavior.'[5]

There are two documentary films in production about Garson's life and work. One is by the English cult horror-film producer Harry Bromley-Davenport, with the working title *Mike Garson and His 88 Friends*, referring to the keys of the piano. The other film is directed and produced by Jill and Gary Bandfield.

At several of Garson's recent performances, two of his grandchildren have performed with him onstage. Meeting Jacob (thirteen), and Max (eleven), one senses a palpable influence immediately. Max is already a keen and accomplished drummer, and Jacob, with a voracious appetite for learning, is becoming an adept pianist and has already composed some highly accomplished pieces. When I spoke to Jacob and Max it was clear that Garson's musical legacy is already in safe hands. We played a 'long-distance duet' across Skype, and Jacob played a beautiful rendition of Garson's 'Lullaby for Our Daughters.'

On July 29, 2015, Garson celebrated his seventieth birthday, and tributes poured in from around the world. Jacob wrote a touching song called 'Seventy Everything'

('Seventy things to love / Seventy things to hate . . . Seventy bombs of loving / That don't explode . . .'). All of his grandchildren also wrote and performed a song for him to the melody of 'My Favorite Things,' from *The Sound of Music*:

> Playful and gleeful, he really is ageless,
> Reading this book we love turning the pages,
> Seventy years old—no he's seventy young,
> Life is a song that remains to be sung

Garson has been asked to perform in the house where Beethoven was born, which is now a museum, in Bonn, Germany. This is part of a project organized by classical pianist Susanne Kessel, in which 250 composers from around the world will create pieces inspired by Beethoven for 2020's 250th anniversary of Beethoven's birth, all of which she will also learn and play. These will also be published as sheet music in ten collections of twenty-five pieces each. Garson used the Second Movement of the Sonata Pathétique as his starting point, and is premiering at the concert. It transpired that the museum curator was a great David Bowie fan, and has now asked Garson to do additional solo concerts there and to give a master class on Bowie, with reference to Beethoven and the history of musical invention.

There is one vivid though surreal image that lingers from one of the many amusing anecdotes Garson tells of his earlier years as a gigging pianist. A private party was once being held on a Malibu beach and his services were booked, as was a white grand piano. On arrival on the sand, the guests were milling around a lavish beach barbecue. Garson approached the host but could see no piano. Had they forgotten to hire the piano? When asked, the host said no, it was all in place, and gestured into the distance, down by the sea and along the beach. There, in splendid isolation by the ocean, 'about half a mile away,' was a white grand piano. One could view this as a symbol of the ignorant and insensitive notion of the pianist as 'background music' taken to the extreme. Garson had to play from so far away from the party that he might as well have been a distant songbird on the ocean. On the other hand, it is also an image of great beauty, as the piano and the pianist took their place in nature away from the smells and sounds of the burning flesh and the chattering guests at the smoking barbecue.

# 18

# From Outsider Art to Outsider Music

*'Within the context of several of the songs there is a certain amount of improvisation . . . it's a*
*real challenge, how far could one go onstage? I guess if I wanted to lose the audience entirely,*
*the idea of making each and every show totally improvisational is . . . terribly enticing!'*
—David Bowie at a press conference for the *Outside* Tour, London, 1995

MIKE GARSON'S COMMITMENT to his concept of 'Now' music means that improvisation, playing what you feel in the moment, and not being inhibited by boundaries of
genre are at the heart of his music and life. Placing sincere emotion and expression
above technical virtuosity, and regarding technique as merely the vocabulary or tool-
box for expressing how one feels in the moment, are also central to his work.

Though arrived at independently, all of this places him in some ways within the
thread of outsider art, which has its origins in the early twentieth century amongst
those on the margins of the mainstream who evade the limitations of conventional
social conditioning. By looking into the history of the idea of music that is truly
'outside,' we can understand Garson's music, and his work with Bowie, more deeply.

A key point both in Bowie's evolution and in the story of Garson's work with him
came with the release in 1995 of the album *1. Outside*. It marked a reconfirmation
and a cementing of Bowie's use of music as his chosen vehicle for a wider project of
artistic endeavor. His own painting and involvement in the art world also stepped
up during the 1990s. The album released was merely a fragment of the recordings
made, and was intended as a chapter of a longer, experimental cycle encompassing
conceptual and graphic art, as well as music. Much of the unreleased material now
circulates on the Internet, which is ironic since the arrival and likely future expansion of the Internet was one of Bowie's main themes at the time, with its 'information superhighway' spoken about by some of the fictional characters he voiced on the
recordings. The volume of creative inspiration, much of it led by Garson's piano at
its best, is vast. It is uncategorizable and unmanageable. The best way to appreciate
*1. Outside* may be to dive in and out with the same reckless abandon shown by the
musicians who performed it with such intense improvisational creativity.

The idea of outsider art, which was a key inspiration for the *1. Outside* album, was developed by Jean Dubuffet, who took his mission very seriously. 'For me, insanity is super sanity,' he wrote. 'The normal is psychotic. Normal means lack of imagination, lack of creativity.' He was also intent on exploring musical as well as visual communication.[1] As early as 1945, he criticized the quest for virtuosity, or 'generating streams of notes, and on hearing them we feel no emotion whatsoever.'[2] He emphasized instead the importance of emotion actually felt in the moment. He loved the simple, expressive accordion playing of Émile Vacher, developed an interest in improvisational jazz, and was keen to explore parallels between music and painting.

That quest was realized in a practical way in 1961 when, working with painter Asger Jorn,[3] he made a series of sound recordings seeking to establish a correlation between the two forms. Significantly, these were actually released that year (Time Records 3008) under the title 'Musique Brut,' thus establishing a connection with the *art brut* movement. Applying the paradigm of outsider art to the field of music makes equal sense but has remained less explored. Dubuffet had an intensely naturalistic conception of what this music would be: the expressing of emotions by vocalists singing lyrics would be replaced by 'cosmic rumors giving up their wild noise,' and 'an unpredictable expansion, without axis or centre, without any structure which might suggest notions of beginning, logical development, or ending, but which would rather give the impression of a slice randomly cut from an endless fabric.'[4]

Mike Garson has made his own innovation in moving between outsider art and outsider music, but in the opposite direction. Having developed his concept of 'Now' music during the late 1980s and early 1990s, for spontaneous musical composition, he started experimenting with improvised computer art, which he labeled Now art, whilst on the road in 1998 with the Smashing Pumpkins. Knowing that his musical creativity was founded on thousands of hours of practice and detailed knowledge of theory and structure, he wanted to experiment in a field of creation in which he had almost zero technical knowledge, having only taken a single one-hour lesson. His conclusion was that 'creativity had almost nothing to do with technique, and in fact some people liked my artwork better than my music!' The study of technique and of great pianists whose styles he can accurately imitate certainly adds hugely to his palette and vocabulary, but is not ultimately essential to creativity. This echoes Dubuffet's emphasis on emoting beyond virtuosity.

Indeed, the same point has also been made by David Bowie. Sean Mayes, who played piano for Bowie briefly in the late 1970s, kept a journal of his months on tour with him in 1978, which was published posthumously (Mayes died in 1995) with the assistance of Kevin Cann, in 1999, as *We Can Be Heroes: Life on Tour with David*

*Bowie.* The book focuses on the social aspects of touring more than the musical, but one point that he does touch on is this question of creativity versus technical knowledge, and the pointlessness of technical mastery unless it expresses emotion felt in the moment. Mayes recalls comments he says Bowie made whilst on tour in 1978: "'I'm suspicious of virtuosity,' he said, "it doesn't usually go with originality. I like people who have a style of their own.'"[5]

The spirit of experimentation present on 1995's *1. Outside* was consistent with Bowie's first explorations within rock music. Even as early as *The Man Who Sold the World* in 1970, he had been happy to trust his musicians to explore and experiment, and if something was seen to be working well then to let it stand.

Sometimes, the essence of avant-garde or 'outside' approaches—and Garson's playing as an instance of that—has been sorely misunderstood. As we have seen, even at its most dissonant, it is actually anything but random. One of the many guest artists with whom Garson played at the marathon final Nine Inch Nails show in 2009 was Gary Numan, who had long been a fan, not just of Bowie but also specifically of Garson's playing, which he had admired and even on one occasion tried to emulate, evidently on the basis of just such a misunderstanding. 'I can't play like Mike Garson, so what I used to do was just shut my eyes and hit any notes that my hands touched,' Numan recalled. 'On "Sleep by Windows," there's like a synth-y thing toward the end of it, and I swear to you, I'm sitting in front of it and have my eyes closed and I'm just hitting whatever notes come to hand!'[6]

Musicologist Howard Goodall describes David Bowie as 'one of the most significant musicians of the twentieth century.'[7] In his superb study of Bowie's music in the book published to accompany the vast exhibition *David Bowie Is*, which opened in London in 2013 and has since been touring the world, he sees Bowie as a channel for the cross-fertilization of artistic movements. Discussing minimalist modern-classical composers such as Steve Reich, for example, he writes that 'David Bowie is the conduit through which this relatively private, art-music idea made the leap across genres into modern pop.' In synthesizing the 'pioneer developments' he absorbs, Bowie performs a 'distortion of the template . . . rather than a homage' to create a sea change that can then, in turn, inspire further innovation from others. Goodall mentions 'Trent Reznor's industrial metal soundscapes' and 'early drum 'n' bass grooves' as two of the separate musical strands absorbed and resituated in this way on the *1. Outside* album.[8]

Mike Garson's improvisational approach to creating music dovetails nicely into this kind of artistic process, which helps to explain the strong creative bond over many years between him and Bowie. Just as Garson has made it his mission to transcend musical genres throughout his life, so one of Bowie's profound contributions has been to catalyze such fusions in cultural evolution. A key example of this, also given by Goodall, was the way in which the influence of composers like Philip Glass on Bowie's 1977 albums *Low* and *"Heroes"* came full circle when Glass himself composed his *Low* symphony in 1992 and his *"Heroes"* symphony in 1996, which was then in turn adapted into a contemporary dance work choreographed by Twyla Tharp. Goodall argues that this interaction, for which Bowie was the catalyst, 'represents a milestone in the convergence of musical genres that has been the story of recent musical history.'[9]

The *1. Outside* album was originally planned to be the first in a series of albums marking the closing years of the twentieth century, hence its title being printed with the number '1.' However, Garson explains, one of the engineers on the sessions took the tapes of initial work on the material intended for the subsequent albums, and some time later released them, unedited and without permission, online. These were just improvisations that were only a work in progress. This took the life out of the continuation of the project by preempting it. Bowie understandably declined to proceed with the rest of the series.

Many of Garson's live dates with Bowie in the early 1970s were not appreciated as much by him at the time as they are now in retrospect. There were long sections where he was not required to play, and then, when he did play, the piano parts often lacked the challenging complexity of the jazz he had been used to playing. It was only in later years that he came to realize how those shorter or simpler sections could embody deep, latent emotion, especially in the songs of Bowie. Conversely, in his jazz gigs now, he sometimes feels that he does not have enough to express to fill the advertised concert of, say, two hours, and feels that he would like to just play the one or two songs he feels most intensely, and then end. He jokes that the audience could get a refund and just pay sixty cents for the few minutes they would be there. 'If you tell your girlfriend or boyfriend that you love them, that's nice, but once that is expressed you do not necessarily want to hear it repeated forty-three times!'

Garson feels that in the past he took the simple, therapeutic process of musical communication for granted and, like so many musicians, was distracted by the sense of power that comes from being able to move people so much. But getting 'caught up in the bullshit,' as he puts it, 'ultimately makes any decent human being feel nauseous.' Complimenting one another is fine in itself; being kind to one another is the simplest and most compelling guide for human behavior and survival, and operates above and beyond any concepts of religion, spirituality, philosophy, intellectualism, morality, or law. But the music business, especially at its successful edge, is beset with distorted notions of importance and status that are light years away from that. In this respect, the greatest contribution that can be made by any creative or expressive artist involves building emotional bonds and connections, and this is something that Garson has exemplified increasingly over the years. 'Somehow society's got itself into the levels of purgatory and hell, that it's so dark and dirty that we've lost the knowingness of the most simple things. Music is coming out of me because . . . we're creating it, rather than creating a bomb . . . I'm at this stage where I'm trying to not "edge God out," and just let it flow. I don't even know what "God" is, and I don't think we're capable of knowing what it is, but I think we're capable of sensing something bigger than our stupid selves!'

Dr. Wayne W. Dyer (1940–2015) coined the acronym E.G.O. as representing the egotistical tendency to 'edge God out.' He quoted Sogyal Rinpoche from *The Tibetan Book of Living and Dying*: 'Two people have been living in you all of your life. One is the ego, garrulous, demanding, hysterical, calculating; the other is the hidden spiritual being, whose still voice of wisdom you have only rarely heard or attended to.'[10]

The ruthless division of people into makers and consumers of music is a feature of market society. This ascribing of 'performer' and 'audience' status as anything other than fleeting and interchangeable roles is merely a product of the ruthless division of labor and commodification of every aspect of present-day society. Within this there is also often an ambivalent attitude on the part of those consuming the product, easily switching from adulation to contempt, depending on context as much as on content.

The cult of celebrity, with its concomitant lack of self-worth in its fans, is also something Garson keenly and critically observes. 'They lose their identity and what they should be doing. And they're becoming you, because you get all the accolades and success, so they want to live through you, vicariously. And it works like a drug, but eventually it leaves a void.'

More and more, celebrities are being elevated for who they are rather than what they can do, and are lauded for their connection with money or sexual intrigue, in a process that has already started to spiral inward on itself. Meanwhile, working musicians continue to be taken for granted, and their joy in playing is often taken advantage of, as they are manipulated into playing for little or nothing. I have lost count of the number of party or event 'invitations' I have been pleasantly surprised to receive, only to have the penny drop when minutes later the host casually mentions, 'Of course, there will be a piano there, and should you feel like playing . . .' It is assumed that those providing live music somehow do not need, expect, or deserve to be paid in the way that all other service providers would automatically be remunerated without question. As Garson's wife Susan puts it, they are playing music, and so they are assumed to be just 'playing.' Garson reports having had exactly the same kinds of experiences himself, too—mainly, though not exclusively, in his early years. It is both amusing and depressing to discover that even a performer of his stature can relate readily to such frustrations firsthand, and we have exchanged many amusing tales of instances of this.

He observes that 'this world is set up for people to lose, not to win,' and explains that, for example, when he attended events like the huge annual NAMM (National Association of Music Merchants) convention and show, which happens every January in California, with thousands of people showing their music technology products, he would often feel completely disorientated and 'spinny,' somehow out of his comfort zone, in contrast to how confident he feels speaking to me, as a fellow musician. He says, tellingly, that 'when you're one individual, it's so easy to get overwhelmed by the masses.' For this reason he resolved to take a booking to perform there every year, for three or four separate one-hour sessions each day, and somehow that way it became more navigable. This sense of alienation, self-consciousness, or shyness, salved by focusing on the role of providing a creative performance, is something I can relate to strongly, as a thread in the evolution of my own personal identity as a musician.

Garson recalls playing in Long Island once, toward the end of his club gig years. It was a party outside in the sun. He plugged in his electric piano; it was 95 degrees out, and he was sweating in his tuxedo.

> There was a terrible drummer, a terrible sax player, people were dancing on the lawn—it's all just one nightmare—and I see this couple dancing, and they keep pointing at me, but very surreptitiously, and moving their eyes to the side so I wouldn't see them. They are pointing at me, though, and laughing at me. And I just was freaking out with rage, and everything, and what's going on here? So, on the break, I went out to them and actually confronted them and said, 'What's so funny?' and they totally lied and said, 'Oh, we were laughing at nothing to do with you.' So, I go back and play the next set, and they're doing it again. I was really upset. I came home. I set the piano up in front of my mirror, pictured the gig, and played what I was playing. And I looked at myself in the mirror—and I laughed! I saw how miserable I was, and they were probably thinking, 'How can this guy play so well, be so detached from what he's playing, and be so miserable?' You said you saw me laughing the other night with

total joy at my jazz concert? I couldn't help that, though when I was playing this horrible gig, I couldn't help but be this depressed—what am I doing with my life?—these people couldn't care less!

In seeking to understand Mike Garson's contribution to modern musical evolution, that 1995 album of Bowie's to which he contributed so dramatically is a key moment. Pieces like 'The Motel,' 'A Small Plot of Land,' and 'The Hearts Filthy Lesson' contain an interplay between the vocals and piano lines that celebrates the joy of spontaneous creation, and contains all of those elements that lay at the heart of Garson's contribution: improvisation, playing what you feel in the moment, and not being inhibited by boundaries of genre. In Switzerland in 1994, at the improvisation sessions from which *1. Outside* grew, the exciting and ecstatic evolution of outsider music had taken a bold step forward, and, with Bowie, Eno, and the rest of the musicians, Mike Garson played an instrumental part in that process.

In 1998, two years after the *Outside* Tour had culminated in a series of summer festivals in 1996, Garson found himself on the *Adore* tour with the Smashing Pumpkins. How did he adapt to this change of band, material, and style? In December of 2015, I interviewed Billy Corgan of the Smashing Pumpkins at length on his work and friendship with Mike Garson, which had begun in 1997. This grew into a long conversation exploring the nature of musical expression.[11]

Corgan started by telling me that Bowie was an 'auteur' with the artistry to incorporate others' contributions as part of his own sound, such as when Robert Fripp played the EBow on *"Heroes"*, and that this had meant that when Corgan first met Garson he had not been specifically very aware of him as an individual. His sound had been part of Bowie's sound. So it was fascinating for him to encounter the down-to-earth Brooklyn man who had modestly created all of those amazing piano parts. Garson proved very willing to explain his processes, with a generous openness, and Corgan says, 'One of the reasons I wanted to play with Mike was just to spend time with him!'

Prior to Garson joining the *Adore* tour in 1998, Corgan tells me, it was more a question of keyboard players simply playing the parts from the albums. With Garson's arrival, however, 'it was more a case of, now, how do we take advantage of this incredible talent, how do we make space for him, so that we're also reacting off of what he's playing?' Because Garson did not grow up as a lover of rock music, his aesthetic points of reference remained so 'off-base' to a rock band that it would sometimes seem that he was playing 'from a different page.' He lacked the context that other players might be picking up on, in terms of what they were accessing from rock history.

Especially during the *Adore* tour, however, Corgan made a point of giving Garson enough space and freedom within the fabric of the sound for this to work. Rather than trying to specify reference points or parameters from rock history, which may not have worked, he gave him emotional goalposts instead. The songs were melodically prettier than on some later material they worked on together, and this was a good fit. Corgan says he has great memories of that time.

Stepping subsequently into the studio to record with Garson on the *Machina/The Machines of God* sessions was not without its frustrations, however, as Corgan came to see just how far Garson had taken his *modus operandi* of both living and creating 'in the moment': 'He's impossible in the studio! He's incapable—and I mean this humbly—of playing the same thing twice. He will play the most incredible thing, and you'll be, like, "Wow, that was so fucking great. When it gets to this one chord, if you could only do this a little differently because it kind of fucks up this other thing?" And then you'll press record, and it won't be anything like what he just did. It won't even be in the same cosmos!'

If Corgan were to record with Garson again, which he says he would not hesitate to do, he would know just how to work with this. Beyond a few broad references ('a little bit more Duke Ellington,' 'a touch of Tchaikovsky'), he did not feel that Garson's playing could be 'tempered into a form' or particularly directed as to genre or detail, nor could it be edited, so that the best option would be to have him do a couple of takes on each song and then to choose one more or less as it stood: 'You get what you get.'

Corgan stresses that this characteristic of Garson's is not a limitation; that 'he's truly a free spirit' in his use of the languages of music. He has tried in vain to edit the incongruities in Garson's improvisations. 'It's a language, it is what it is, and there is a brilliance to it.' Surprisingly, this point has not been specifically put this way by any other of my interviewees, but Corgan comes close here to calling Garson a poet, which is very apt. Whether any individual finds the sounds pleasing is subjective, but the most important quality is that there is always more honest intent than there is artifice in Garson's spontaneous musical expression.

I asked Corgan about Garson's never drinking alcohol or taking drugs, and the interesting fact that so many of the people I have spoken to were unaware of this, despite working with him. He responds that through being gracious and nonjudgmental, Garson has been able to relate to others with different lifestyles. Unlike those who grew up steeped in rock 'n' roll mythology, Garson married young, and his life is dedicated to his family and his music. Although he came to inhabit the world of rock music, it would never define him. As Corgan puts it, Garson did not 'buy into that whole mythology or culture, even though he worked within it, and he was more interested in being an observer of the whole circus around him,' in which artificially altering consciousness had been *de rigeur* for so many.

With the Smashing Pumpkins, Garson could be critical of the musicianship of some band members and then perfectly affable moments later, discussing something else like food, since for him these creative judgments did not involve any ego or personal animus toward others. 'He treats people the same, with as much warmth for the second conga player as for the front man. He's not blind to the pecking order, but it's just not on his radar.'

For the second half of the *Machina* tour, and especially for the final show in Chicago at the end of 2000, Corgan knew the band was breaking up and wanted to end things with a special impact, for which Garson fitted perfectly. He joined the tour from the end of August, covering several European countries and South Africa, before returning to the United States toward the end of the year. Besides Garson, at this point the Smashing Pumpkins consisted of Billy Corgan, James Iha, Jimmy Chamberlin, and Melissa Auf der Maur. Corgan explains that he felt in those final months of 2000 he could use the darker elements in Garson's music as a weapon, powered by the tensions around the tour, 'almost as if to say to fans, "You're in an even scarier castle now than the one that I was already inhabiting!" It was very conceptually driven, in ways that not everyone realized at the time. Mike filled out the edges of this kind of musical statement that I was trying to make. He was certainly aware of what was going on personally in the band, because he's a good guy, and if I was going to sit there and talk to anybody it would be him, more than anybody else, so he probably got plenty of earfuls!'

Corgan amusingly sums up that last marathon concert as 'Four-plus hours, thirty-eight songs, and a weaponized Mike Garson!'

Corgan was playing a character in a way that he says 'was very influenced by Bowie.' His stage persona was something of a cartoon caricature at times, but when the press and others insisted on taking it crudely at face value, he stirred things up further by laying it on even more thickly. For him, it was all part of his art, and still the press largely failed to grasp it. Corgan felt that against this perverse background, Garson's extraordinary presence was a great addition to the ironic drama he was amusing himself creating: 'The weirder he played, the more he could help me create the spectral edges around this atmosphere, the better!' He says that James Iha and Jimmy Chamberlin had signed up with him to play out these characters but that they shied away from it, leaving Corgan to play that role alone, with just the moral support of Mike Garson (even though he may not have been fully cognizant of this situation).

There is a large archive of unreleased live work by the Smashing Pumpkins, much of it featuring Garson, and it is only the issue of economic viability that is holding up the release of more of it. That final 2000 show in Chicago is certainly a candidate for release before too long, and it featured a substantial input from Garson. Corgan recalls how improvisational and therefore unpredictable Garson's playing was during the *Machina* tour dates. 'There would be nights where Mike was so dead-on it could make you cry, in terms of what I wanted him to do, to support emotionally what I was doing out front, whatever was the mood of the evening. Yet on some nights he would be so emotionally off-key that I felt like he was playing to a 1950s country record, Floyd Cramer or something, and I'm like, "What the fuck is going on?" But there's nothing you could do about it!'

Corgan says that at this point, some of the hard-core or more purist Pumpkins fans were not enamored of Garson's contribution. It was clearly a bold step to incorporate the unpredictability of Garson's emotive piano within the sometimes brutally rapid and heavy thrust of the Pumpkins' sound. By contrast, when they worked together on occasions such as an acoustic show at the Shrine Auditorium, Los Angeles, on December 12, 1998, just the two of them, the intimacy of their two-way musical conversation generated some great results, and the audience was enraptured.

We moved on to discuss Garson's classical compositions, in which Corgan has taken a keen interest:

> There is a brilliance there that needs to be chased after. I would compare it with Bach. Like Bach, it must be channeling from some kind of spirit. I don't see how else you can put pen to paper and write like Bach wrote, there's too much fluidity. Mike helped me unlock the idea that Bach was an improviser. In turn, I heard the same ability in Mike. I told him, 'You're onto something here.' Then it's a question of someone of a higher mind, whether through distance or time, looking at it from a compositional point of view and seeing something that Mike couldn't see at that moment, to be able to decide whether it reaches the upper echelons of 'classical composition,' for this to be acknowledged as up there with the greats. It's certainly in the zip code. Because Mike moves so seamlessly through Aaron Copeland to Gershwin, to Liberace, to Mike Garson—it's got such a rogue, punk thing to it, because he's not really stuck in any genre, which really is groundbreaking, to have mastered that many different types of language. The closest analogy I would make in that regard would be

Jimi Hendrix, who could flip from blues to ragga to whatever, with the flick of a dime.

Corgan observes that, for example, George Gershwin's compositions were appreciated fairly soon, though not without attracting criticism for attempting to merge the classical tradition with Tin Pan Alley. Garson, on the other hand, is merging a much vaster range of sources in his compositional work, including strands of modern culture of which he has been a part or even a progenitor. But it is very hard 'to ascertain whether a distant culture down the road will see a higher mind in it, because the aesthetic judgment of anything creative really needs to be removed from the culture it was created in.' It is tantalizingly difficult to predict what currency any creative expression might retain hundreds of years from now. How many of the older paintings that we love and value today were known at the time of their creation to possess such longevity?

Perhaps the most likely assurance of the durability of Garson's music is that his immediacy of expression, always in the moment, always what he feels, improvisational, sincere, and true, comes close to a pure expression of emotion that is independent of cultural codes or constraints. It may be that in a hundred years, listeners will perceive the emotional content of these compositions as something far greater than they might today. Corgan enthuses:

> People then might say, 'Wow, this guy is like a time capsule!' There is no context you can point to in comparison with Garson—outside of Cecil Taylor, I don't even know who I would remotely point to. And it's still a stone's throw even to get there, to Taylor. We are now in a self-reflexive society, like the hall of mirrors which goes to infinity, a culture which is living that, because of technology. Kim Kardashian dressing up like Marilyn Monroe, shot by Kanye West on a camera that was used by a famous photographer? We are in a self-reflecting culture, and maybe Mike's early unconscious decision-making presaged that, such as his referencing 'Tequila' in his 1973 avant-garde piano solo; and on the Annette Peacock record he played on the year before, that's already there, it didn't just come out because he encountered David Bowie or was asked to play the Chinese-sounding notes at the end of the piano!

The naming of the English 1980s band Pop Will Eat Itself has proved prescient, with the twenty-first-century arrival of a kind of cultural cannibalism. Garson's goal of absorbing as many styles as he could devour as a young pianist, making weekly visits to the New York Public Library to collect reams of classical scores to sight-read, could well prove to have been a prototype of the way that culture is surging forward. Unlike the cannibalistic cultural vultures who then simply spew forth all that they have consumed, undigested, Garson realized already in his early twenties the importance of then unlearning, of ostensibly forgetting all of those inputs in order to become oneself, to create something relatively new out of all of those threads. In his study of David Bowie's time in Berlin, German writer Tobias Rüther identifies this same trend, estimating that it was in the 1970s that 'pop music starts to become self-reflexive.'[12]

Corgan wonders whether Garson will come to be seen as a great pioneer of such eclecticism in musical creativity, pondering that perhaps with even greater technological ease of access to absorbing and mastering diverse musical or other inputs in years to come, there will be others who will take that accomplishment much further. If so, might he still come to be respected even more then for having trodden this path so early? He describes Garson's 'ignorance of "cool" or of aesthetic "rules"' as being 'a blessing as much as a curse':

> When it does line up, it's shocking, and you're like, 'What the fuck did I just hear?'—it's organized, it has intent, it's not a 'cat running across the piano,' there's something happening, it's an organized mind at the speed of light, spitting out phrases! There were nights on that *Machina* tour, I wouldn't have changed one note he played, and you know how many notes he plays. If he played ten thousand notes, I wouldn't have changed *one* note, it was so fucking perfect to what I was feeling, thinking, seeing, reacting to, I mean, totally in tune! And the next night I would walk onstage and have the exact opposite experience, as if he was playing to another band. I think Mike might tell you it was because he was picking up on some dissonance in the air . . .

As a bandleader, Corgan would tell Garson, 'That's not working,' and Garson would reply, 'Well, I'm playing to the environment that I'm in. Maybe I'm picking up on the argument that I heard at 2 p.m., or maybe the frowning face in the front row . . . but I can only tell you that I'm playing what I feel.'

In this, he seems to carry some of the intense sensitivity of perception and expression that is often seen in those who are on the autistic spectrum, as is Garson's grandson Jacob, who is rapidly growing into an accomplished musician himself. Corgan sees this as a kind of obsession or compulsion found in many creative types of people, who follow their need to express artistically what they feel.

Recent years saw Corgan covering a couple of Bowie songs himself live, 'Space Oddity' on tour in 2012 and a very dark and heavy arrangement of 'Fame' in 2014. More recently, he and Garson were back onstage together in March 2016 in Los Angeles, playing 'Space Oddity' in tribute to Bowie, as well as 'Angie' by the Rolling Stones.[13]

Corgan would be happy to work with Garson again, but he says that maturity has taught him to 'put people in positions that succeed. Mike is an artist who needs the right space and the right challenge, which has not always happened on some of the rock shows he has played on.' He would like to place Garson in a context that would be more about the interaction or musical conversation involving him. He concludes:

> Who he is as a man is who he is as a musician, and you can't really say that about a lot of musicians. Maybe because he spent so much time on his craft— it's not been about him *per se*—there's a humility there which balances out the immense personality of his talent. His desire for total integration is almost unprecedented. It would be like saying you spoke eight languages and wanted to find a way to put them all together. I can't think of anybody else who's even trying to do that. You wouldn't necessarily know for a couple of hundred years whether it's been worth it, because as a project it's unprecedented, but it is really worth it to him!

I suggest that from this maximum integration, of all forms of music and of music and life, you may get maximum unity, to which Corgan aptly adds, 'Or dissonance!'

# 19

## We Spoke of Was and When
### Mike Garson in a Post-Bowie World

*'It feels like we lost something elemental, as if an entire color is gone.'*
—Musician and writer Carrie Brownstein on the death of David Bowie[1]

ON THURSDAY, JANUARY 7, 2016, I was at the Dolby headquarters on London's Soho Square for a special listening party at which David Bowie's latest album, ★ (*Blackstar*) was premiered. It was astounding, and the atmosphere was gently celebratory. The following morning, on Bowie's sixty-ninth birthday, it was released. On the Monday evening, January 11, 2017, I had to walk past the Dolby building on my way home. It was a different world by then, for Bowie had died on the 10th. I glanced across at the bolted door and darkened windows where we had celebrated just a few days earlier, still hearing the echoes of our voices, and wished I could go back and replay the intervening days differently.

The global outpouring of grief and mourning for his loss was almost unprecedented in modern times. Millions of people were reminded of just how much his songs, style, and artistry had been a backdrop and a soundtrack to their own lives. It was a precious memory and a privilege for me to have worked even briefly with David Bowie a few years before he left us.[2] I found him intelligent, charismatic, professional, perfectionist, instinctual, sensitive, kind, and very funny.

When Mike Garson heard that David Bowie had died, his profound shock threw him into a long mental process of free-falling, vivid recollection, from which he emerged with a series of deep insights. Asked during an interview on KABC Radio on January 14, 2016, about his friendship with Bowie, Garson broke down. When he had collected himself, he replied that there had been a spiritual camaraderie between them; that they had been creatively on the same page. Most significantly, he stated that despite being very different people, they had thought in the same way about art.

Through the grief of losing a friend and collaborator of almost half a century's standing, Garson started to understand, in a way he had not previously, the sheer depth of the connection he felt to Bowie and the significance of the work they had done together. A few days after Bowie's death, he reflected back on how my original research in 2014 for this book had included getting feedback from him on all of the songs they had worked on together, and how this had made him first realize how special a connection it was. 'After you had me listen to those fifty songs, I was really blown away, because it was like a compressed version of my history with David. I just loved what I heard, and realized that I had put my heart into every note that I played on those recordings. They were not taken lightly. Granted, I try to do that for every artist, but it was exceptionally easy for David, because I loved how he sang, and his music.'

Garson was besieged by media from around the world in the wake of Bowie's death, and he completed over fifty interviews in just the first few weeks, including a BBC television special broadcast the day after Bowie died, and a major piece in *Rolling Stone* magazine, in which he said, 'What I think it was, is that I listened to a lot of music when I was in New York through the 1960s . . . I could deliver any kind of piano playing he wanted . . . He loved my palette and wideness . . . We would talk about Vaughan Williams or Stan Kenton, Charles Mingus, Stravinsky.'[3]

A feature in UK newspaper the *Guardian* was also published in which Garson mentions that although Bowie often sang about mortality, he did not ever discuss it. He describes Bowie as unusually sensitive to life's pain and suffering, and his expression of this through his music. For Bowie, Garson contends, life and death *was* art.[4]

After initially being contracted for just eight weeks of touring with Bowie in the United States in September 1972, Garson's work with Bowie was extended throughout the early 1970s, resuming again in the 1990s, and he was still playing live with Bowie as recently as 2006. In more recent years, he and Bowie kept in touch by email, with Garson sending updates on his music, which were received by Bowie with enthusiastic interest, and he has kindly shown me all of this correspondence, in order to throw further light on their connection.

For New Year's Eve at the end of 2011, he sent a flute quartet arrangement of 'Auld Lang Syne,' with his love, to which Bowie responded positively. The following year he sent his 'Variations on Pictures of an Exhibition,' which reinterpreted the original by Mussorgsky. Bowie praised the arrangement and added that he was a fan of Mussorgsky, whom he described as a sad figure. He sent Garson a photo of a portrait of Mussorgsky in his last drunken months painted by Repin, one of the finest painters of the time. With his close knowledge of such things, Bowie must surely have noticed that the name of the original piece had been referred to mistakenly by Garson as 'Pictures of an Exhibition' rather than 'Pictures at an Exhibition.' It is perhaps an example of Bowie's courtesy that he declined to correct this detail.

In June 2014, Garson sent Bowie a clip[5] from his *Symphonic Suite for Healing* concert in California from March of that year. In September, Bowie replied that it was very good. Also that summer, the experience of being asked to listen back to all of the songs he had recorded with Bowie over the years, and comment on them for this book, moved Garson to write to Bowie on August 24, 2014, 'I have had a wild month as there is a biography being written by Cliff Slapper . . . I had to go through all the songs I played with you through the years as well as live concerts etc. It's been quite overwhelming, as I had to comment on many of them from as early as 1972, until 2006. I just wanted to thank you for that opportunity, as it's truly the best stuff I have recorded for any singer!'

Within minutes, Bowie had written back, saying that he would always treasure the times they had spent together, that the music was always the thing, and that they had made some great sounds together.

At the time when he received this, Garson was not aware of Bowie being unwell, but he noticed a certain finality in its use of the past tense. He asked me whether I thought that this meant that Bowie was not planning to work with him again. We discussed this for some time, together with Garson's wife, Susan. Of course, when the news arrived about sixteen months later that Bowie had been suffering from pancreatic and then liver cancer from about eighteen months prior to his passing on January 10, 2016, it became apparent that this email to Garson was in all likelihood a valedictory acknowledgment of all they had done together; a parting, tender, and very special message of gratitude and appreciation.

At the end of 2014, on December 29, Garson received another email from his friend, in which he called his pianist a good fellow and wished him and his family all the best, with love, for the new year to come.

The following year, in August 2015, Garson wrote to ask whether Bowie had seen the Nina Simone documentary on Netflix (*What Happened, Miss Simone?*) to which Bowie replied that he had not known there was one. Garson says it is 'pretty deep and sad,' to which Bowie replied with thanks to say that he would watch it. Garson then also sent him a link[6] to Nina Simone's extraordinary performance of 'Feelings' at the Montreux Jazz Festival in 1976, commenting to Bowie that 'this link of Nina singing Feelings if you haven't seen is quite potent.'

In this performance of the Morris Albert song, Simone speaks and sings purposely in a robotic way, without expression, in order to emphasize the song's story of someone in such pain that they try to extinguish all their feelings. She interrupts the song to say, 'I mean, God damn, what a shame, to have to write a song like that. I'm not making fun of the man. I do not *believe* the conditions that produced a situation that demanded a song like that!' Paradoxically, as her ten-minute arrangement of this song about trying to stop feeling unfolds, she exhibits and expresses such explosive and uncontainable emotion that it becomes simultaneously completely compelling and almost impossible to watch. Strangely enough, at another point in that same show at Montreux, she had stood up from the piano and demanded to know if her friend David Bowie was in the audience. He had recently moved to Blonay, very near Montreux. Having walked along the stage, looking into the audience for him, she said that he 'is my dear friend,' and that, were he there, he would announce himself to her. Nina Simone later recalled that, in 1974, Bowie had befriended her and had given a much-needed boost to her morale. She remembered being told by him that he was not a gifted singer, was not a genius, but that he planned. He had wanted to be a rock 'n' roll singer and had got the right formula. He had said that she, on the other hand, did possess genius, was gifted, and was compelled to perform.[7]

Bowie watched the clip Garson had sent him and replied, on August 16, 2015, that it had been quite a performance. This was the last email Garson ever got from him, forty-three years, almost to the day, after they first met at the studio in Manhattan where Garson was auditioned for the *Ziggy Stardust* Tour. Those three words from Bowie could almost have been an epitaph for his own dazzling and hypnotic spell on earth, were he to have stepped back and appraised his own life in the wittily pithy way he had of admiring the achievements of others.

In addition to the apparent 'farewell' email he had received in August 2014, another overwhelming memory hit Garson on hearing the shocking news that came two days after Bowie's sixty-ninth birthday in January of 2016. When they were on tour in the mid-1990s, there was a night when the others had gone to their bunks and Bowie and Garson were still talking at about 1 a.m. He mentioned to Garson that in the late 1970s a psychic had told him that he would live only to sixty-nine or seventy. He seemed totally convinced, without fear or doubt, that this was a clear certainty. Garson never breathed a word of this to anyone else but his wife in the years since. On hearing the news of his death, Garson went into shock, but moments later, this recollection came straight back to him. For Garson, this accentuates the degree to which Bowie was aware of his own life as a conscious work of art itself (as well as demonstrating their bond, to have shared this with him).

On hearing the news, he went without sleep or food for days. He had not realized until Bowie's passing just how large a part of his life Bowie had occupied. He was plunged into emotional turmoil. The memories started flowing in an uncontrollable tide. At the same time, the world's media, having spent years often ignoring the key role Garson had played in Bowie's music, was galvanized into doing its research and, as a result, started to beat a path to his door. This meant that, at the same time as trying to cope with his own personal grief, he was called on to conduct an extraordinary number of interviews for newspapers, magazines, podcasts, radio, and television.

Garson's old friend, the Hollywood producer Brooks Arthur, understands well the nature of the bond that Garson would have lost. When Bowie played Radio City Music Hall in 1973, Arthur was invited to go by Mott the Hoople manager Fred Heller. He clearly recalls the magical moment when he felt himself in a kind of cross-fade of applause and emotions, as Bowie descended from the Radio City rafters on a trapeze: 'It stopped me cold, and I got it—instantly!' He sympathizes with Garson's grief at losing Bowie, since band members on the road and in the studio 'are like blood brothers and sisters, regardless of who is the leader or the sideman.' Garson tells me that 'David really got me, appreciated me, more than I knew, which makes me miss him even more.'

He started, almost at once, to cope with his grief through musical creation, improvising a series of 'Tribute to David' pieces, which he performed at several concerts. He says that within the first day of Bowie's passing, he felt his presence come to him in a very real and positive way, guiding him with the music and communicating to him that he was in a good place, free from physical pain, from where he would look out for Garson's welfare.

Garson's own quest for spiritual understanding began with the Jewish belief system he grew up with as a child and his Bar Mitzvah at thirteen, in 1958, which he took seriously enough to study Hebrew more deeply than most Jewish boys in Brooklyn. This was followed by his methodical studying of a great range of other belief systems from his later teens onward. He says that Bowie did not have the same route into spirituality but was equally ravenous for insight and connection. Bowie was deeply influenced by Buddhism throughout his life, but above all else he conveyed his spirituality through his music.

In an unaired interview with the American television show *60 Minutes* in 2003, Bowie compared searching for music with searching for God. In both cases we try to say the unsayable or see the unseeable, to reclaim something ineffable. He explained how writing music involves seeking sounds or musical information that does not yet exist. He also revealed that when he thought about the content of his songs, the recurrent themes were always loneliness, isolation, a spiritual quest, and the attempt to communicate or connect with other people.

Mary Finnigan, with whom Bowie lived during 1969, and whose memoir of that time has been published,[8] has related his interest in spirituality to his subsequent

ability to adopt a series of theatrical personas. She believes that his early contemplation of such matters inspired his continuous shape-shifting in his subsequent artistic career, because meditation can help a person to lose their separate identity and
become more holistic, with the idea of the separate self vanishing.

Bowie's connection with Buddhism began when he was just nineteen. He visited
the Tibetan refugee and lama Chime Rinpoche at a Buddhist center in London to
inquire about becoming a monk. Chime asked him what his talent was, and Bowie
said music. Chime responded that in that case Bowie should not become a monk: he
should do his music.[9]

Even in 1995, Bowie still described himself as 'a mid-art populist and postmod-
ernist Buddhist surfing his way through the chaos of the late twentieth century,'[10]
and although he only studied with Chime for a year, they remained life-long friends.
Bowie never gave up his connection to Buddhism (or his support for Tibetan indepen-
dence). Chime saw Bowie as ultimately agnostic, but closer to Buddhism than to any
other belief system. What attracted him to it was the idea of transience, of having at
some point to let go of what is dearest to us in order to return to the eternal.[11]

Just one month after Bowie's death, Garson told me, 'In the past four or five
weeks my life has been completely topsy-turvy.' All of the many interviews and concerts he had been doing were based around Bowie and his passing, whereas in recent
years his main preoccupation had been his own work and in particular his *Symphonic
Suite for Healing*, as documented elsewhere in this book. This was forcing him to
focus on reappraising his long history of collaboration with Bowie, even though one
of many similarities between Garson and Bowie was their reluctance to look back.
'Prior to David's death I just wanted to keep moving forward and not dwell in the
past, and while that is still true, it's imperative to dig up all these [live recordings]
and share and love the amazing body of work. It's astounding how much we forget,
but once we see it, it all comes back.'

He now says that this has entirely changed how he expects to spend his working
time through the rest of his life. Previously, he was set on devoting most of his time
to developing further his own composing within a therapeutic and healing context,
but now he proposes to split his time evenly between doing his own music and performing the music of Bowie, in tribute to his lost friend and fellow artist. He can
foresee this being executed in various formats and instrumentations. In recent years
he had already created arrangements of 'Space Oddity' for full orchestra and choir.

Garson's shock at just how great a loss he felt was reflected in the loss many
others, myself included, also experienced. In a multitude of different ways, David
Bowie had played a significant role in the lives of millions of people. Not only had

his songs punctuated our growth through the decades, but he had also acted for many as a remote mentor, a distant life-coach and guide through modern culture, with his almost teacherly or donnish ability to reveal cultural connections and references to the rest of us, even whilst creating new trends and ideas out of the sources he navigated. For us teens of the 1970s, he had been our unofficial English teacher, as well as our artistic mentor. He once said that, had he not possessed the tools to be an expressive artist himself, he would quite happily have devoted himself to studying and teaching, and despite his voracious appetite for books, he expressed frustration at not having the time to read even more. Subsequent generations of teenagers have continued to delight in his appeal to the exploratory and questioning instincts of youth.

During my own brief experience of working with David Bowie, I sat with him during a filming break and he started examining a tea-light, looking underneath and saying he had always wondered about what was on their undersides. I felt like he was still exploring the ways of the world, a perennial outsider with the same alien delight shown by his character Thomas Jerome Newton in *The Man Who Fell to Earth* in discovering this planet and its culture. It was his alienation and 'alienism' that gave him strength and relevance, a translucent sponge able to absorb culture, reshape it, and hand it back to us.

In addition, Bowie played a part in validating those who were marginalized by their sexuality, style, or otherness. Those alienated from mainstream conventions found an ally in him from the onset of the 1970s onward. He made the connections between being lost in space, being lost in our own space, and being lost from ourselves.

Bowie's death coincided quite closely with the deaths of a number of other major cultural figures. Natalie Cole had died a week earlier, on New Year's Eve, and then during the following months there were many others, including Prince, Muhammad Ali, Eagles co-founder Glenn Frey, actor Alan Rickman, Harper Lee, Frank Sinatra Jr., Gene Wilder, Leonard Cohen, Carrie Fisher, George Michael, Debbie Reynolds, Billy Paul, and Zsa Zsa Gabor. Early in 2017 we lost a giant of rock 'n' roll, Chuck Berry, whose 'Around and Around' had been covered by Bowie as 'Round and Round' in 1971.

One musician who was lost to cancer during this period, on April 6, 2016, had played many times with Mike Garson and had played a key role himself in Bowie's work. Drummer Dennis Davis had, with his friend Carlos Alomar, been recruited to join the *Diamond Dogs*/Philly Dogs tour for its second half, and then to play on 'Across the Universe' and 'Fame' for the *Young Americans* album (the two tracks were recorded with John Lennon in New York in January 1975). Like Garson, he was a New Yorker, and had studied with the great jazz drummers Max Roach and Elvin Jones (with whom Garson had played). He went on to appear on six more Bowie albums, including *Low*, *"Heroes"*, and *Lodger*, and played on two more Bowie tours. His young friend and protégé, Sterling Campbell, went on to drum himself for Bowie from the 1990s onward. Davis returned as percussionist for a guest appearance at the Roseland Ballroom in 2000. He also played with Iggy Pop, Roy Ayers, George Benson, and Stevie Wonder. Again, like Garson, he had a jazz background yet happily threw himself into rock, funk, soul, or fusion without hesitation. His playing was imaginative and innovative. On the *Low* album, especially, he forged some truly unique sounds and rhythmic effects. 'In some ways, he would be the best of all the drummers,' Garson tells me. 'Always smiling, and had an amazing groove. He was fun to have on tour, and we had some amazing jazz jam sessions at sound checks, me, him, Carlos, Emir the bass player. With the Garson band, which did support for Bowie in 1974, we did some more jazzy material, and Dennis was really at home on the songs from *Young Americans*, too. Dennis brought a lot of joy.'

The BBC's obituary editor, Nick Serpell, theorized that there was a reason for this heavy toll, in that people who started to become famous in the 1960s were now passing into their seventies, and that this generation had more celebrated individuals than earlier generations due to the rise of television (and, one might add, globalization).

Still, amongst this pantheon of lost heroes, the reaction to Bowie's death stands out. Even alongside the huge public reaction to the deaths of Princess Diana or Elvis Presley, the public mourning for Bowie and the sheer number of tributes to him, worldwide, many of them quite spontaneous, was fairly unprecedented, certainly for a pop or rock star. I had a local taste of this when London's landmark British Telecom Tower near where I live mounted a lighting display spinning around the top of the tower, in huge letters, 'RIP David Bowie' on the day after he died, which could be seen across large parts of London. I took a photo of that from my front door and posted it on Facebook: within hours it had accumulated 3,500 'likes.' I was also asked to play at five Bowie tribute events within two weeks, all raising money for cancer charities. Spontaneous gatherings paying tribute to him and mourning his loss emerged in numerous major world cities, notably at his former homes in Brixton, Berlin, and New York, but also in New Orleans, where a street party celebrating his music drew large and enthusiastic crowds and a parade was led by one of his favorite bands, Arcade Fire. Even the German government Foreign Office issued a statement: 'Goodbye, David Bowie. You are now among Heroes. Thank you for helping to bring down the wall.' (In 1987, Bowie had performed a concert in West Berlin with the stage up against the wall, so that thousands of East Berliners gathered and, when Bowie spoke in German, could be heard cheering from the other side. That night saw the first of many riots on the eastern side of the wall. Two years later, the wall came down.)

Soon after Bowie's death, Mike Garson made a series of short, spontaneous, live broadcasts on Periscope in which he improvised loving piano tributes to Bowie and spoke about their work together. One of these was watched by ninety thousand people, and we could see a flood of warm and emotional comments coming through in real time as it progressed, from countries all around the world. These and his online posting of numerous performance clips, from YouTube and elsewhere, of concert footage from over the years, were a therapeutic release for grieving fans in the months following Bowie's death, as well as for Garson himself. The response was effusive, with thousands of respondents from around the world thanking him online for sharing these gems and making it easier for them to process what had happened.

He tells me that he was grateful that YouTube existed and that he found these performances 'breathtaking':

It softened me up to realize how much he loved the music, and that he was so sincere about everything he did. Perhaps when somebody leaves us you get what their basic core purpose and intention was, their essence. He left us an amazing body of work. I am just very humbled that I had the opportunity to work so much with him, especially the huge number of live appearances; and because I don't play a song the same way each time, I must have played 'Life on Mars?' a hundred different ways with him, likewise 'My Death,' 'Wild Is the Wind,' 'Changes,' 'Strangers When We Meet,' 'The Motel,' 'The Voyeur of Utter Destruction.' I was always searching for something new I could do with the songs . . . the memories are coming back more and more of these shows which I took for granted, you're on the road and you get into the stream of things. I wish I could go tour with him now, and I think I would appreciate every morsel. I think over the years I was in and out of recognizing just how wonderful it was.

During his life, Bowie's songs were noted for being only rarely covered by other artists. Indeed, he once commented that this was one of the things that had encouraged him to keep singing them, whereas initially he had seen himself as more of a songwriter (some of his earliest songs having been released by other artists). Perhaps other singers felt inhibited from tackling material that was so bound up with the unique persona of its author. In any case, it seems likely that this may change now.

Within days of David Bowie's death, the tribute concerts (or previously arranged shows that were then adapted into tributes) at which Garson was asked to play came in thick and fast. January 15, 2016, found him at the Cicada Club in Los Angeles. There was a special radio feature broadcast on January 20, 2016, entitled *Dear Mr. Bowie*, comprising an interview and solo piano performance by Garson on Californian radio station KPFK, across two hours. For this, he played on a nine-foot concert grand piano in the radio studio, performing two separate, remarkably emotional improvisations dedicated to Bowie, and also a hauntingly beautiful piano interpretation of 'Space Oddity.' The following evening, he was at the Baked Potato Club in Studio City, having spent the day performing for music-technology company Synthogy, at the NAMM Show in Anaheim. Three days later, there was a concert at Newport Beach for his Music-Heals-Project.

Garson has played in numerous concerts and tribute events since then. On February 8, 2016, there was a major event at legendary rock venue, the Roxy Theater in Hollywood. Under the title 'Celebrating David Bowie,' a diverse range of artists—both musicians and well-known friends and fans of Bowie—performed a long and heartfelt tribute through his music. The show was organized by local musician Angelo Bundini as a charity fundraiser and ran to over four hours. Ewan McGregor sang '"Heroes"' and fellow actor Gary Oldman, who had been a friend of Bowie's, sang 'The Man Who Sold the World.' Garson made a moving speech about his friendship and work with Bowie. He then performed yet another original improvised piece as a tribute to Bowie, followed by a rendition of 'Aladdin Sane (1913–1938–197?)' complete with solo, live for the first time since Loreley in 1996 (and before that not since 1974 on the *Diamond Dogs*/Philly Dogs tour, as captured on the album *David Live*). Seal then joined him for a superbly sung rendition of 'Bring Me the Disco King.'

*Billboard* magazine reported, 'The emotional core of the evening, though, came from longtime Bowie keyboardist Mike Garson, who nearly broke into tears explaining his long kinship with the late legend . . . who he said slept directly across from him on the tour bus. After delivering what amounted to a eulogy, Garson played on "Aladdin Sane" . . . Garson seemed like he was having a going-away party for his friend, complete with costumes and cheer. Whether or not the audience was on board for the whole thing was irrelevant to the catharsis that was obvious onstage.'[12]

This event would later be expanded into a much more ambitious and extensive 'Celebrating David Bowie' tour, featuring Garson and other Bowie musicians playing with local guest singers in London, New York, Los Angeles, Sydney, and Tokyo, in 2017. This was followed by an even more extensive world tour in 2018, with Garson playing alongside Gerry Leonard and Adrian Belew (who played guitar for Bowie in the late 1970s and in 1990), and with guest musicians in each country visited.

About a week later, Garson flew to London for several days of rehearsals for a performance at the BRIT Awards on February 24, 2016, at London's O2 Arena. This featured a reunion of Bowie's 2003–2004 band from the *Reality* Tour, comprising Earl Slick, Gerry Leonard, Gail Ann Dorsey, Sterling Campbell, and Catherine Russell, as well as Garson himself. The band members all seemed to be simultaneously delighted to be seeing each other again and devastated by both the reason for the reunion, and the absence of the one charismatic, witty, and inspirational individual who had brought them together in the first place. They threw themselves into the work and rehearsed hard all week to perfect their meticulously planned short set.

They played an instrumental set of sections from various Bowie songs, expertly crafted and edited together by musical director Gerry Leonard. I spent that day backstage with this remarkable group and watched as they made their final preparations after an intense few days of rehearsal. Drummer Sterling Campbell had worked with Leonard on a complex click track with tempo-change curves to fit together the very different beats of these songs as they moved from one to the next.

This then culminated with an unassuming figure elegantly strolling onto the stage in white shirt, black waistcoat, and baggy black trousers. Lorde sang a stunning rendition of 'Life on Mars?' She had met and received high praise from Bowie and did a perfect job of somehow making the song her own, and yet channeling him at the same time. It was a tender, passionate, heartfelt tribute, and she had the audience transfixed. Even at the soundcheck, there was hardly a dry eye in the building. This remarkable performance was also broadcast internationally.

Garson returned to Britain in November 2017 for a UK tour performing the whole *Aladdin Sane* album, with vocals from Gaby Moreno backed by Kevin Armstrong and the rest of Iggy Pop's touring band, plus Terry Edwards on sax. These stunning shows were a spectacular success and very well received, with more planned.

Immediately after performing at the BRIT Awards in London, Garson flew straight on to Tel Aviv to perform with Israeli rock star Aviv Geffen at a show again styled as a tribute to Bowie. The following month he was asked to appear as a guest at the Smashing Pumpkins reunion show at the Ace Hotel, Los Angeles, on March 26. He was delighted to be back onstage with Billy Corgan for the first time in sixteen years and found it an emotional meeting with a great artist for whom he has a lot of respect and love.[13] Garson's piano was featured on an arrangement of 'Space Oddity.' He contrasts the way he played it then with how he had played it in the past with Bowie, explaining:

When Billy plays, he takes up a lot of space and a lot of air. It's not like when I back up Bowie. When I play for Bowie, there's a give and take, he'll leave space, and I play these beautiful piano fills. When Billy Corgan's playing the acoustic guitar, it's nonstop, so I have to play on the sparse side so as not to step on him. But at the very end, when he's not singing anymore, and there's just one chord and it's fading, that's when I went to town. So, consequently, it's not as enjoyable as when I do it—when I did it—with David.

Aside from the deep sadness in that self-correction at the end of Garson's comment, this also confirms how, contrary to the easy assumption that an artist of Bowie's stature might have more ego and desire for control than others, the truth was that he was self-assured enough to do the opposite, and that he often gave considerable leeway to some of his handpicked master musicians.

The way in which Garson used that freedom is revealing of the connection and similarities between the two of them. He often played as he felt Bowie would have been playing, had he been a pianist. Watching extensive footage of live shows, it is noticeable how Bowie shows delight in some of Garson's solos, often name-checking and sometimes even applauding his accompanist, especially when it was just the two of them playing. Garson provided not just the piano but also the instrumental 'jazz' that Bowie would have expressed, had he possessed those tools. From listening as a young teenager in the 1950s to the jazz records of Charlie Mingus or Stan Kenton, picked up from his brother, Terry, through to the New York jazz band he employed on his last-ever album in 2016, jazz was Bowie's 'missing link,' and Mike Garson always kept it there for him through the years.

They were both magpies, absorbing a great wealth of diverse inputs and then making them their own, evolving a distinctive individual voice, something new that flows from all of those tributaries. They shared a similar musical intelligence and a passion for crossing boundaries artistically. This disregard for the borders between genres of music, together with his versatility and adaptability, is a key factor in explaining why Garson was Bowie's longest-serving and most frequent band member from 1972 onward.[14]

Even between mid-1972 and late 1974, Bowie changed his lineup of musicians several times, leaving Garson as the only one left from 1972. He recalls joking with Bowie at the time, asking, 'So, David, when is my time coming?!' He adds that, to Bowie's credit, several people with whom he broke off contact for long periods were eventually re-contacted by him years later, and would even in some cases return to working with him. It is also worth noting that when Bowie made the most famous of his culls by announcing his disbanding of the Spiders from Mars live from the stage of Hammersmith Odeon on July 3, 1973, the only band members who had been warned of this beforehand were the late Mick Ronson and Garson himself.

This book is already replete with instances of Garson defying compartmentalization, but Bowie also went on record in a similar way. Here he is in 1980, taking the point a step further, to decry not just the barriers between jazz and rock, but between music and other art forms, at a time when his stage acting in *The Elephant Man* was receiving rave reviews: 'The chauvinism between various art forms—theatre, film and music—it's all so silly because the creative force is operative in all these things. I think it might be evident that I never completely leave one for the other—there's no barrier.'[15]

By 1996, Bowie appeared more confident that those artificial boundaries were coming down—perhaps even, in part, due to his own efforts (Howard Goodall suggests that Bowie was especially instrumental in accelerating this fusion of all modern artistic expressions).[16] He observed a growing closeness and interaction between practitioners of music, literature, and the visual arts at that time, and declared his determination to write, paint, design costumes, or create installations if he felt inclined, regardless of his identification as a singer.[17]

Indeed, Bowie had been fascinated by the group of early-twentieth-century German artists known as Die Brücke (The Bridge) during his time in Berlin in the 1970s, who took their name specifically from the idea of forming a bridge between the different genres of creative art. He became a collector of their work, even adapting one piece by Erich Heckel, first as the cover for Iggy Pop's *The Idiot*, and then for the cover of his own *"Heroes"* album. One Berlin gallerist of the time, Artur Vogdt, said, 'David Bowie knows more about Expressionist art than 90 percent of the young people here.'[18]

Bowie did act on that determination to do whatever form of art or writing he wanted to, and his work was all the richer for it. He even collaborated with Damien Hirst on some action paintings, and with Tony Oursler on installation art. His lyrics for the *1. Outside* album contain a wide range of literary references, including to *Waiting for Godot* by Samuel Beckett. He could well have focused his energy in other directions than that of pop music, and he probably would have made a success of channeling his creativity primarily through one of the other areas he worked in, such as acting, mime, directing, sculpture, painting, or others. But the pop song is such an apt vehicle for the combination of many different artistic inputs, with costume, movement, and narrative alongside melody, symbolism, and film: 'Pop music is the only form of art uniting all three dimensions of the creative arts in one. Using the stage as a theatrical space, your own body as a launch pad and the album cover as a caption, with the help of sound and vision, pop music goes symbolically over the top.'[19]

Mike Garson's own bridge between jazz, rock, and other musical genres can be heard throughout Bowie's work. One example of this was at a show at New York's Roseland Ballroom in Manhattan on June 19, 2000.[20] This was a private show, exclusively for members of Bowie's online community, BowieNet, and a warm-up for his performance at Glastonbury a few days later. Garson played the band on with a solo piano rendition of the appropriately chosen jazz standards 'How About You?' of which the first line is, 'I like New York in June, how about you?' and 'I'll Take Manhattan,' in the stride style of Fats Waller. But once 'China Girl' gets under way, his power-octaves in the bass show him following the musical flow wherever it took him as a pianist.

Garson's role in Bowie's music, and his ability to play rock, pop, or soul styles so expressively, is all the more remarkable when we consider that he continued to make major achievements within the world of classical music. Between touring with Bowie and other work, he taught and performed at the 2002 World Piano Pedagogy Conference and received a standing ovation for his Paganini Variations, which was just the first of ten pieces he played.

One person who remained firm friends with Bowie throughout his life (from when they were both nine years old in the local Cub Scouts group) is the very genial and personable artist George Underwood, who has kindly given me his personal insights into Garson's work with Bowie. Underwood and Bowie played in bands together as teenagers, notably the King Bees. He was invited by Bowie to join him during the United States tour in 1972, and he told me his recollection of first meeting Garson:

> I first met Mike at the Beverly Hills Hotel during the *Ziggy Stardust* Tour. David had told me that he was excited to have a great jazz pianist joining the band on this tour, who had played on Annette Peacock's 'I'm the One,' which I loved. It was Annette who had introduced them. I remember seeing her by the hotel pool, she was there teaching her young daughter Apache to swim. She was telling Apache that she would never be a rock 'n' roll star if she didn't learn to swim! Mike was sensitive, softly spoken, and thoughtful. I liked him and found him easy to get on with. He was a gentleman, and easygoing.

With Gwen Stefani in Belgium, 2002. *Garson Family Archive*

David Bowie, Gail Ann Dorsey, and Mike Garson at the filming of a TV show in Paris, France, 2003. © *totalblamblam@davidbowie.com*

The *Reality* Tour band at the end of a show in Dublin, 2003. *From left*: Mike Garson, Earl Slick, Catherine Russell, David Bowie, Sterling Campbell, Gail Ann Dorsey, Gerry Leonard. © *totalblamblam@davidbowie.com*

Author and pianist Clifford Slapper with David Bowie at the filming of *Extras*, 2006. *Ray Burmiston*

Mike Garson rehearsing with Trent Reznor and Nine Inch Nails, 2009. *Tourbuslive.com*

Author
and pianist
Clifford
Slapper at
the piano
with David
Bowie on the
set of *Extras*,
2006. *Ray
Burmiston*

Onstage with Trent Reznor and Nine Inch Nails during the *Wave Goodbye* Tour's final farewell show, at the Wiltern Theatre, Los Angeles, September 10, 2009. *Tourbuslive.com*

'Focus,' 2009. *Fernando Aceves*

Mike Garson, Joe LaBarbera (drums), and Jim Walker (flute) at Segerstrom Center for the Arts, Orange County, California, March 1, 2014. *Barry Bittman*

Orchestra and choir, *Symphonic Suite for Healing*, Orange County, March 1, 2014. *Barry Bittman*

With grandson Max, playing congas, at the world premiere of *Symphonic Suite for Healing*, Segerstrom Center for the Arts, Orange County, California, March 1, 2014. *Barry Bittman*

A tear of joy at the performance of *Symphonic Suite for Healing*, 2014. *Barry Bittman*

Performing with Lorde at the BRIT Awards, London, England, February 2016. *Garson Family Archive*

Onstage with Seal at the Roxy, Los Angeles, February 2016. *Garson Family Archive*

The Garson family, summer 2016. *Back row, from left*: Jeremy, Mike, Susan, Jennifer, Heather, Mark, Zach, Peter. *Front row, from left*: Hannah, Maya, Max, Jacob, Maegan. *Garson Family Archive*

On set for the filming of *Sandy Wexler*, August 2016. *From left*: Brooks Arthur, Mike Garson, Adam Sandler. *Adam Sandler*

Mike Garson's grandson, Jacob Gilbert, in concert, 2016.
*Garson Family Archive*

Mike Garson and Gail Ann Dorsey perform 'Space Oddity' at the 'Celebrating David Bowie' show at the Wiltern Theatre, Los Angeles, January 2017.
© *Gerard Gibbons*

At the NAMM Show, Anaheim, California, January 2017.
© *Gerard Gibbons*

Underwood describes Garson's entrance into the band as 'seamless,' despite the many contrasts between him and the three 'Spiders' from the North of England. He recalls Bowie feeling the need to add an unpredictable ingredient, which Garson fulfilled perfectly, with his tendency to depart from the script in a way that is not common in rock music. This thrust the *Aladdin Sane* album into a new hybrid of rock and avant-garde, which was hard to categorize.

When Garson rejoined Bowie in the 1990s, the freedom Bowie afforded him to develop material improvisationally onstage, and even in the studio, secured the further evolution of their creative bond. George Underwood explains:

> David loved jazz, he loved Mingus, he loved the element of surprise and was delighted to have Mike provide that. Even in his teens he read Kerouac and related to the beat generation. He did live and breathe the jazz world—when he wasn't playing rock! He was great at discovering music which might be a bit off the wall for other people, but then he'd utilize it within his own records, by thinking, how would they have done this? And he did direct what other band members should play, even to some degree with Mick Ronson, but with Mike, he allowed him to play things differently each night.

Underwood recalls how, at school together, they had to see the careers advisor shortly before leaving, and Bowie (or Jones, as he was then) went up first and was asked what job he wanted to do on leaving school. Underwood laughs, even now, as he recalls his friend replying that he wanted to be the saxophonist in a modern jazz quartet. They both found it even more amusing that the advisor then looked under music in her encyclopedia of jobs and recommended he apply for work in a local harp-making factory in Bromley. 'David wanted to be Gerry Mulligan at the time,' Underwood says, 'and even looked like him, with his crew-cut!'

Underwood has also been badly hit by Bowie's death. The lifelong friends were almost like brothers: 'David wasn't flesh and blood, but it felt like it.' He ends by summing up beautifully the reason behind the special bond between Bowie and Garson. 'What I hear coming out of his piano says a lot about him as a person. Mike speaks through his playing; it's like a voice. You can almost tell someone's character by the way they play their instrument. And he and David spoke that language together, it was like conversations they were having, they were talking to one another onstage, in a shared language.'

There were several ideas for projects involving Garson that Bowie mentioned over the years, but that had not yet happened. One example was an acoustic tour by just the two of them, an idea that had been encouraged by Bowie's business manager, Bill Zysblat. A Broadway show was also mooted, as was an album involving Philip Glass, who had written the score for a Japanese film. Bowie gave Garson the score and spoke about producing an adaptation, with Garson doing an arrangement. He had also spoken to Garson about the idea of recreating the music from *Ziggy Stardust* as an instrumental piece, but then decided against it. In the 1990s, Bowie spoke to Garson about wanting to do a jazz big-band album with him. In a way, this idea did take shape, finally, in his recordings with Maria Schneider in 2014, whom Garson had recommended to Bowie in 2003.

Like the sequence of albums planned for 1995 to 2000, of which *1. Outside* was to be just the first, these plans were all well conceived and fully intended. Bowie's output even without them was vast. Garson is wistful, though, that these must now remain untried. Likewise, the day after Bowie died, Brian Eno said that the two of them had been discussing the possibility of revisiting the *Outside* project.

Bowie's hyperactive imagination generated endless ideas. Even when he died, it appears he was hoping to have time to produce yet another album. In the very witty song-by-song cover notes he penned for 2008's *iSelect* album release (how many other pop stars would have been able—with irony—to use the terms 'anomic,' 'cognomen,' 'palimpsest,' 'cavil,' and 'recidivism' in one set of self-penned album cover notes?), Bowie wrote of his earlier plan to have produced a musical show based around George Orwell's *Nineteen Eighty-Four*: 'Though I've never had the patience or discipline to get down to finishing a musical theatre idea other than the rock shows I'm known for, I know what I'd try to produce if I did.'[21] Sure enough, seven years later, the musical theater piece he created and co-wrote with Enda Walsh, *Lazarus*, had its debut in New York, and was an intense and emotive distillation of many of the recurring themes of his work, in both content and form.

After much careful thought and discussion about his emotional response to losing Bowie, Garson summarizes:

> When David was alive, he was both a genius and sometimes very aberrated, whether through the early excess, the drugs, sex, power trips, fame, vanity, money, whatever—but he did come through, fortunately for him, because he could have died several times. . . . Whatever that dark stuff was, was not something that was charming to me, you've got to understand, it was fucked up, and I didn't want any part of it, at those parties of the 1970s, and when I heard the stories from when he was living in Los Angeles. . . . But once he passed, those things disappear for me, and maybe a lot of people, and all we remember is

the beauty, the love, the words, the voice, the music, the tunes, the hooks, the impact.

David Bowie did once characterize his life's journey in terms that rather match Garson's description of this journey through bacchanalian excess to enlightenment. Interviewed by Mick Brown in 1996, he said that he had come to recognize how his early hedonistic experiences with drugs and promiscuity had been part of his own search for what was spiritual inside himself. Carefully distinguishing organized religion from a spiritual quest, he revealed that for him, fulfillment came from spiritual investigation, from studying the inner life of things that fascinated him—such as what makes a certain painting meaningful, or why he loved sailing, despite being a poor swimmer.[22]

On April 29, 2016, Garson posted online a video message in which he said that he felt the most important thing he had learned from David Bowie's passing and from his own emotional response to it, was 'never to take anything for granted':

> It's easy to get into a rut and take things for granted, and then you lose someone you love, and all the regrets come in. I've had my share of regrets regarding David's passing, because I don't think I appreciated the great music that we made and the humor that he had, and the joy. You're on the stage maybe for four nights a week for two hours a night, but what about all the other hours out of twenty-four, on a bus or an airplane, talking and laughing, having meals together. That's not to be any more with him. So, I think we need to re-evaluate where we want to go: being in the now, enjoying every moment, and being grateful for what we do have. I think that's the best way we can pay respects to him.

In these comments, Garson returns to the key cornerstone of all he does and makes the lesson from his loss a resolution to try even harder to live in the moment. His 'Now' music, his commitment to improvisation, his need to be constantly moving on to the next instance or opportunity for creativity are all manifestations of this love of immediacy rather than dwelling in the past.

After an exhausting few months of interviews, new compositions, and live tributes to Bowie, Garson told me in June 2016 that he felt the need to start moving forward in his own creative mission. 'It feels like there's a part of my life—and David would encourage this—that I just move on as Mike Garson. Whilst I have many fans of my work with Bowie, and I'll always stay connected and loyal to them, I just can't get stuck in the past, I have to do the same thing David would do, keep creating and making new music and doing my thing. But I'm forever grateful for that wonderful relationship.'

# 20

# Life on the Road with David Bowie
## Part I: 1972–1974

*'When I think now about all the years I spent on the road with David, I just miss that we won't perform again together. I feel I still have more to give him.'*

—Mike Garson, February 2016

MIKE GARSON PLAYED on nine of David Bowie's world tours between 1972 and 2004, a total of 961 concerts.[1] If we then factor in all of the additional television and radio appearances, weeks of rehearsals for each tour, studio sessions for albums, and several special charity event or private appearances for which just the two of them performed together in the 1990s and 2000s, it becomes clear that these two musicians played live together on well over a thousand occasions.

We can go even further. Analysis of the set lists performed across the entire set of nine tours shows an average per show of about twenty-two songs, including encores. This means that Garson completed about 22,000 individual song performances with Bowie on stages across the world since the autumn of 1972. And all of this started with his brief audition in Manhattan that summer, with Mick Ronson telling him after a few bars that he had the job, and his being contracted for just eight weeks.

There were also often numerous separate recording sessions for each album. In the case of *Earthling*, in particular, Garson recalls sitting in for some weeks of daily sessions but only playing for a few hours. Subsequently, Bowie responded to how fast Garson was at mastering the parts and was able to economize on payments by having him come in specifically as required. On the *Reality* album, he only attended for two or three days, within which time they completed the piano parts for gems such as 'The Loneliest Guy' and 'Bring Me the Disco King.'

Garson recalls his first few American shows with Bowie from the autumn of 1972: 'It was all done very high class. We had nice hotels everywhere. We were treated very well. Everything was hush-hush; David was not doing any interviews. I have great memories of New Orleans, because I sat in and played some jazz in a club there on a day off.'

Recently, some high-quality sound recordings have become available of some of those first *Ziggy Stardust* shows in the United States. The tour began at the Music Hall in Cleveland on September 22, 1972, but also returned to Cleveland on November 25 and 26 for shows at the Public Auditorium, from which a sound-desk recording reveals Garson having quickly found his place, just two months after joining the band. His piano stylings on 'Changes' were already every bit as jazzy as they would be on the more commonly heard *Diamond Dogs* Tour, as recorded for the *David Live* album nearly two years later. Even more strikingly, even at this very early stage, Bowie and Garson can be heard performing most of 'Life on Mars?' alone together (with the band only coming in on the choruses), just as they would in 2005 and 2006.

For what sounds like an exhausting schedule, covering a huge sweep across the United States before arriving in the UK just before Christmas 1972 to play the Rainbow in London and then on to Manchester, Garson says he believes the adrenaline carried him forward, and he does not recall feeling tired at all. In February and March they were back in the States, followed by shows in Japan in April and then back to Britain in May. He was struck by the way that on first arriving in Tokyo, a red carpet was laid on the platform for them as they got off the train. The reception was ecstatic, despite Bowie not having toured there before, so clearly the ground had been prepared. He also recalls the excitement of experiencing the speed of the Japanese 'bullet train' at that time (now overtaken by the Shanghai Maglev, which can reach about 270 miles per hour).

Garson had already done some touring of the United States with the band Brethren a couple of years earlier, and he says that Bowie seemed keen to tap into the experience Garson had as a native New Yorker to provide him with insight into this vast country, which so intrigued and fascinated him. Of special interest to him was the fact that Garson had not only lived in New York during the jazz days of the 1960s but had played extensively within that scene.

Bowie was also interested in hearing stories from Garson about his childhood piano lessons in New York from the eccentric, blind jazz pianist Lennie Tristano, from whom Garson picked up a commitment to improvisation without ever repeating licks or playing the same thing the same way twice. Bowie wanted to hear about how Garson had mastered the elusive jazz styles of all the greats through sheer determination, and was enthralled to hear about Garson's lessons from Hall Overton, who was the first to transcribe Thelonious Monk's big-band albums of 1959 and 1963, long before the prevalence of 'real books' or more modern methods of automated scoring.

They also spoke about their shared love of John Coltrane and Miles Davis. Garson observes now the close similarity between Miles Davis and David Bowie, both of whom were always moving forward and changing direction with their music, never standing still. He recalls one after-show dinner to which Bowie had invited the whole band during the late 1990s, at which all of this was discussed, and at which Garson also told the story of his lessons with the great Bill Evans and with Herbie Hancock (who had been working with Miles Davis at the time).

Garson and Bowie also discussed the philosopher Alan Watts, who did so much to bring elements of Eastern philosophy and Buddhism to a Western and secular audience. There is of course an affinity between the emphasis placed by him on being in the now, and the same principle applied in musical improvisation—and specifically in Garson's compositional approach as formalized in his 'Now' music. Likewise, Bowie was committed to integrity and immediacy in his creative work. They spoke about Bowie's childhood saxophone teacher, Ronnie Ross of the Modern Jazz Quartet, who later played the sax solo on Lou Reed's 'Walk on the Wild Side,' without realizing until after the session that the young co-producer in the control room had been a student of his as a child. Bowie told Garson how much he loved playing the sax but that he knew it was not his true calling. He even played some sax on the *Outside* Tour, and Garson believes that with more application he could have been recognized as a respected avant-garde saxophonist, in the style of someone like Albert Ayler.

The eclecticism of Bowie's musical passions seemed to know no limits, and this reinforced his respect for Garson's own extraordinarily broad musical awareness and repertoire. In 1999, Bowie addressed the music students at Berklee College of Music in Boston on the subject of creativity. He told them of his crusade to change 'the kind of information that rock music contained,' and said that he adored Coltrane, Harry Partch, Eric Dolphy, the Velvet Underground, and John Cage, as well as, 'unfortunately,' Anthony Newley, Florence Foster Jenkins, Johnnie Ray, Julie London, the Legendary Stardust Cowboy, Édith Piaf, and Shirley Bassey.

Who could foresee that Bowie would end up later living for many years in Manhattan? At this point, though, it was clear to Garson that Bowie

> wanted to be part of that, so he was asking me lots of questions. Little things—my jazz teachers, which jazz clubs I played, the artists I loved. I was quite naïve. At that time my world just revolved around being a guy from New York, I wasn't worldly, I hadn't been around the world, although I had been to Israel on a Hebrew scholarship at fourteen, and got to see Greece and a few other places, but basically I was from Brooklyn. But I did not see what I am still realizing

now, that I was in the training ground for jazz as well as classical music. There was no better place to study, jam, hang out as a jazz musician than in New York, and that's still the case, although there's also tremendous energy in Los Angeles or London.

In New York in the mid-1960s, everything was conveniently close, and he could sometimes move from club to club in one evening, playing at each, though some of his jazz gigs in those days could be as long as six hours. He says now that Bowie wanted to absorb all of this as part of his preparation for generating the *Aladdin Sane* album in 1973, which has been referred to as his 'postcard' from Ziggy Stardust in America. Bowie's interest in American culture was far from satisfied, however, and whilst touring the *Diamond Dogs* songs and previewing the *Young Americans* material live across the States in 1974, this pattern of questioning Garson on such matters continued unabated. Garson was still, as he puts it, 'the new kid on the block,' and he recalls vividly 'traveling in the limo with David as he listened to Aretha Franklin or Ray Charles' as part of his desire now to also soak up some of the black American musical treasures, too.

Bowie would watch old Frank Sinatra and Elvis Presley films in his room with Garson, and would look for stage moves to adapt from these past masters. It is whilst telling me about this that Garson casually mentions that he almost played for Sinatra himself. He was playing in a band in Caesar's Casino's jazz lounge at Lake Tahoe, around 1980, accompanying the jazz singer Kenny Colman, whom Sinatra was very keen on. Frank Sinatra walked in with some Italian-American restaurant owners from New York and approached Garson, shook his hand, and said he liked the way he accompanied Colman.

Around this time, Barry Manilow was due to perform in the main auditorium, but he was sick, so the hotel's musical director, Joe Parnello, asked Garson to play a lead piano part for *Rhapsody in Blue* with an orchestra instead. Garson was doing sets in the jazz lounge at midnight, 3 a.m., and 6 a.m., and he had to practice in between these for his stint standing in for Manilow. A few weeks later, when Sinatra's pianist was no longer available, Garson was offered the gig by Parnello, who was Sinatra's musical director and conductor. Garson passed it up, as he was keen to play jazz-fusion with Stanley Clarke instead. He says now that it was a mistake to miss out on being Sinatra's pianist, though he felt at the time that he might be both under- and overqualified in different respects, and also may have been nervous at how Sinatra might treat his musicians.

Similarly, he passed up opportunities to work with Sarah Vaughan and Buddy

Rich. His friend Carl Schroeder had played piano for Vaughan for seven years; when he resigned, he offered the job to Garson but said that he was quitting as it had been a nightmare, and that Vaughan had made his life a misery. Understandably, with this warning attached, Garson declined the offer, but he has since felt it was a mistake as others have said that she was fine to work with, so presumably it depended on her rapport with individual pianists.

When Garson was about to graduate, he heard that Buddy Rich was auditioning for a pianist. He drove two hours from Brooklyn to Philadelphia, but on arrival, from outside the ballroom where the auditions were taking place, he heard Rich screaming at the saxophonist so abusively that he turned the car around and drove home again.

Perhaps the most remarkable of Garson's near misses was when he was commissioned by Yamaha to do some work for President Bill Clinton. As Clinton played the saxophone, it was decided to install a Yamaha Disklavier in the White House.[2] Garson was commissioned and well paid to record the disc with which Clinton could play along. He worked for months, recording the piano parts for songs Clinton loved, such as 'Songbird' by Kenny G, and prepared notes for Clinton about the timing and so on, anticipating that they would eventually be playing along together, virtually, through this technology. Then suddenly the message came through that the project had to be abandoned, since it had been decided that the White House should obtain an American rather than Japanese piano.

During David Bowie's first American tour of 1972–1973, Bowie was so determined to soak up the culture that he took up residence in New York at the Sherry-Netherland hotel. He was highly skilled at being a sponge, absorbing what was around him and filtering it into his art. Garson does the same when he tours outside of the States and says that this absorption of the local culture is 'more emotional than verbal,' though when he was first touring in the UK he also needed to ask a lot of questions at times, to fill in the gaps. He recalls that for the European dates of the *Outside* Tour in 1996, he brought a keyboard and a sequencer to set up backstage at every show, and wrote a piece for every country they went to, simply naming each piece after that country.

He says that he was 'not as smart or as well-read as David by a long way,' but that he could totally relate to Bowie's compulsion to absorb every cultural influence around him and that, being totally and exclusively specialized in the piano, he was perfectly suited to deliver Bowie's needs in that area. Through his playing, he provided a multiplicity of musical inputs from all of the composers he had studied so thoroughly, whether Chopin, Liszt, Bach, Stravinsky, Bill Evans, Oscar Peterson, or

Art Tatum. Meanwhile, Bowie would rely on the specialized inputs of other experts to feed his insatiable hunger for knowledge of art, sculpture, history, and so on, as well as for the other instrumental components of his sound.

It was during the *Ziggy Stardust* Tour of 1972–1973 that the album *Aladdin Sane* was recorded, the first Bowie album on which Garson played. How appropriate that the first Bowie album on which the young American jazz pianist would appear was summed up by Bowie as 'Ziggy goes to America.' In April 2016, I went to Leeds in the northern English county of Yorkshire, to interview the co-producer of that album, Ken Scott. Aside from working with Bowie, Ken Scott has also engineered and produced a staggering range of historically significant music by the Beatles, Elton John, Pink Floyd, Jeff Beck, Lou Reed, Supertramp, the Tubes, and Level 42, amongst others.

Scott had been the engineer on the earlier David Bowie albums *Space Oddity* and *The Man Who Sold the World* and then co-producer on *Hunky Dory*, *The Rise and Fall of Ziggy Stardust and the Spiders from Mars*, *Aladdin Sane*, and *Pin Ups*, working closely with Garson on the latter two. He recalls his first encounter with the young American avant-garde jazz pianist who was to become such a recurring feature of Bowie's music over the years:

> I first met Mike when we started to record *Aladdin Sane* at RCA Studios in New York. David had this ability to pick amazing guitarists or pianists for what he was into. Whether they fitted in with David, or David fitted in with them, I've no idea. David allowed everyone their freedom, and Garson was allowed to go his own way. Musically, I didn't quite know where Mike was coming from. They were into Annette Peacock, some of which I just didn't get. There were a couple of occasions Mike tried to fit in with David, to move more toward David, whereas I think David wanted to move more toward him. David just allowed all of us the freedom that we needed to do the best that we could, and that's what he wanted out of Mike. I've been thinking about what *Aladdin Sane* would have been like if the pianist from *Hunky Dory* [Rick Wakeman] had still been in the band. The title track would not have been anything like what it is!

Scott says that it was not so much a case of Bowie knowing that the avant-garde element could make his music even more successful commercially, but rather

> He did not care; he was determined to make the music he wanted to make, and if he took other people along with it, that was the icing on the cake. That's

how amazing David was. The New York sessions were very easy. Then we went back to Trident [in London] and, once again, the sessions were remarkably easy. Of course, the amazing one was 'Aladdin Sane.' If I remember correctly, Mike passed a comment that he wasn't completely happy with it because he made two errors in the solo. One of us—either David, Ronno [Mick Ronson], or myself—asked which mistakes. Apparently there were certain rules to the way he plays avant-garde, there are certain notes that aren't supposed to follow other notes, if you play this, that, or the other. There was something like that, he played two notes in the wrong place. But we all said, 'You're nuts, it's great, it works perfectly!'

Scott is modest about the way he made the piano sound on *Aladdin Sane*, explaining that the Trident studio piano, a very old Bechstein built in the nineteenth century, was itself quite bright in tone—though he did also adjust the EQ for different songs. It had been used on 'Hey Jude' and on most of the early Elton John recordings, as well as by Supertramp, Harry Nilsson, and Queen. A few years later, when the piano was sent out to be restrung, it was dropped down the stairs. The soundboard got completely broken. Another one was put in, but it was never quite the same after that.

For 'Time,' Scott does recall making the effort to create a very different piano sound. He wanted to 'bring it down very small, lots of reverb, to start off with; then, once everything comes in, it opens out fully.' He says that through this period there was a strong understanding between Bowie, the band, and himself as to what was needed. On the sessions in France for the follow-up *Pin Ups* album, Scott recalls some misunderstandings between Ronson and Garson arising from the different terminology used in the United States and the UK for musical notes. What Garson called a 'half note,' Ronson called a 'minim'; Ronson's 'crotchet' was Garson's 'quarter note' (so-called because it formed a quarter of a typical four-beat measure—or a four-beat *bar*, in England). Regardless of this, however, 'It was just great working with Mike. At that point, he was still a bit of an outsider, so maybe he didn't want to stir it too much,' whereas later he may have felt more freedom to influence the sound more.

With an improviser like Garson, it is important to record everything that is played in the studio, Scott adds,

but then with David you tended to do that anyway, because he got so impatient in the studio. He hated being in the studio, and so he just wanted out as quickly as possible. Woody and Trevor were always on the edge of their seats. They'd learn a number, we'd do two takes, and they kind of knew it by then. We'd get to the third take and they'd be thinking, 'We've got to get through this and get it right, otherwise David will say it was shit and move on to something else!' There was always that tension for them, trying to finish their take correctly.

Scott says that in 90 percent of cases, Bowie's vocal would be nailed perfectly on the first take, from beginning to end, and describes Bowie as 'the best vocalist I've ever worked with.' His lasting impression of Mike Garson from that period is similarly emphatic:

A true professional, and so easy to work with. It was great—as long as one understood the difference between eighth notes and quavers! He was incredible. He wouldn't have been with Bowie if he wasn't. It's that simple. If he hadn't have been able to cut it, then he wouldn't have been with David, but he could, and it was great . . . That's been my life, working with talents like that, which makes it so easy. I can just set the mics, put my feet up on the desk and have this incredible music just pumping over my head.

In order to have a full picture of Garson's experience of touring with Bowie in the early 1970s, we need to consider his own beliefs at the time. He was at this point a member of the Church of Scientology. In 1970, he had been very friendly with the great jazz pianist Chick Corea, who later became godfather to his two daughters, and Dave Holland, the English bassist who worked with Miles Davis. He respected them very much as musicians, and when they introduced him to Scientology, it was suggested that it might help him with his musicianship, his communication ability, and his relationships with his friends and family. When he read the Scientology book *Dianetics*, he related to the idea that moments of past pain can continue to affect a person in the present (this is referred to as an engram in neuropsychology).

Because of its emphasis on communication, he feels that Scientology may have helped him for a time to be more confident and expressive both in his music and in other ways. However, for Garson, the benefits of the focus on strong communication methods started to become a problem when it 'reached the point where I was losing touch with what it is that I wanted to say, because there is a tendency to give one's power over . . . and when you do that with any person or thing, you lose your own inner strength.'

He says that the courses in communication he took helped him to be 'in the moment,' to listen respectfully, to answer properly, and to keep coming back to a question you want an answer to, even if someone is avoiding it. He studied Scientology's beliefs diligently, and he still recalls a lot of the ideas and theories, which he says he found and finds useful. Communication was defined as duplicating someone and giving them your full attention.

Garson threw himself into Scientology with enthusiasm, and he became very committed to it, which included making efforts to convince others to join. But as a musician and a 'natural rebel,' he knew that no group would ultimately suit his temperament. As an avant-garde composer, he works primarily alone. The mentality of groups or churches of any kind has never suited him (he had found the same when getting interested in theosophy around 1963), and as the 1970s progressed he started to feel less comfortable with being a part of the organization.

He has never cast aspersions, however, as he feels strongly that the decision to join Scientology was his alone, and he takes responsibility for that. Likewise, when he no longer found the organization amenable to his needs, in 1982, he left. He did not throw the baby out with the bathwater, however, continuing to hold onto the parts he found useful and disregarding the rest, which were mainly organizational aspects. He says that all such groups ultimately work against the unity of humanity, as they have their own identity and agenda, which in many cases will move toward being a cult or doctrinal clique. He now acknowledges that during those years, his enthusiasm to recruit others into Scientology was somewhat 'aggressive' and 'over the top.' He wanted to help, but now sees that the best way to help is by example, whereas his approach at the time must have annoyed and upset a lot of the people around him who were not involved in Scientology. 'Of course, it did create a problem in the band, with Woody and Trevor and Mick—let's face it, they all came into the [Church of Scientology] Celebrity Centre, which was the place for celebrities, in Hollywood at the time and, I brought them in. I have to be responsible for that, but I felt I was doing what I could to help them. We all do the best we can do with what we know, and when we know more, we do more.'

As long as he was convinced of the validity of Scientology, Garson was as energetic as possible in propagating what he believed at that time to be right. Ironically, on leaving, he then had to deal with hostility both from Scientologists and from others who assumed that he was still a Scientologist.

The symmetry and confidence of his assertion that he was right, at the time he joined, to do so, and equally right to leave when he did, reflects not diplomacy but rather his integrity. The fascinating part of this is that Garson seems to have proved immune to even the most overwhelming peer pressure. He not only had the courage to leave when he was ready to, but has since confounded expectations by continuing to insist that he took what he found helpful from what he found there, in the spirit of a true ingénue, and desisting from voicing anything negative, even now.

To help assess further what effect Garson's Scientology may have had on his fellow musicians on tour in the early 1970s, I interviewed Tony Zanetta, who was the road manager for the *Ziggy Stardust* Tour and was very close to the day-to-day relations between all involved at that time. Zanetta was a young New York actor in the London production of the Andy Warhol play *Pork* at the Roundhouse in August 1971 when he first met Bowie. He ended up assisting with arrangements in the States for Bowie's first tour there. Once the Ziggy tour began, his role evolved into that of road manager, and he recalls how Bowie's inspired inclusion of Garson on piano was finalized only days before the tour was due to begin.

Garson was different from the rest of the band and crew in several respects. A few years older, married, and settled in New York as a jazz musician and teacher, he got through the uncharted territory of being on a rock tour by focusing on his own professionalism: this was a specific job for him, rather than part of a broader vocation or personal exploration. He did, however, start to bond quickly with the rest of the band on a musical level.

Zanetta explains how Garson's Scientology won over bodyguard Tony Frost in particular, as well as drummer Woody Woodmansey and to a lesser extent bassist Trevor Bolder. Zanetta says that this area of discussion introduced by Garson was more a case of youthful open-mindedness than any sinister attempt to sway people, and that such enthusiasm was a part of the exuberance and naïveté of the whole period, in which Defries was catapulting Bowie and the entire entourage into a heady world of hyped star status, without any financial foundation.

The English band members were allowed to order anything, almost without limit, via hotel accounts, but there was very little cash allowance. Their rent back home was paid, and about £75 per month was supposed to be put into their English bank accounts. Garson, on the other hand, had been recruited into the tour in a completely different way and came from a very different background situation. He was giving up a stable income as a teacher back home, where he had a wife and child to support, and had not previously been any part of this band or project. As a result, Defries more or less asked him what he would need, and they agreed on $800 per week, which was not at all unreasonable, given his situation. When news of this slipped out, however, it understandably caused discontent amongst the others, who were shocked by this. On the other hand, Garson was not on expenses in the way that the others were.

In the words of Zanetta, who was helping to manage all of this, 'It was like a bomb going off . . . here's this guy who just steps into this and is suddenly making this enormous amount of money. When of course, the other side of it was, if you really looked at it, it wasn't so extreme, because everything was paid for, for them, if they needed a car it was bought, if they needed a coat it was bought, all their needs were being supplied, nothing for Mike was being paid for, he just got his eight hundred bucks a week.'

Garson, as an American musician who had been brought on board, had not been part of the organic structure of the band. For that matter, even the Spiders from Mars themselves were not an ordinary band: they were playing an assigned stage role as the backing band for Ziggy Stardust, who was himself a fictional character. But they had been playing together for some time before Garson was brought in.

Garson got on with the task of performing excellently at the gigs and otherwise tended to keep himself to himself, other than attending the occasional party. His marriage was, and remains, of central importance to him. His wife Susan joined him in Los Angeles and was there to welcome him when the tour reached their home-town of New York. The other band members shared rooms, whereas Garson had his own. He always got on cordially with everyone.

The band toured the States from September to December 1972, then everyone went home for Christmas. The second leg of the tour, arranged for the new year, was much more tightly planned, in conjunction with RCA. Although Garson's financial position was a catalyst for some subsequent tensions, and although his keenness to spread the word of Scientology also caused some ripples that would have their ramifications in due course, Zanetta recalls quite emphatically that Garson was 'not looked at in a negative light or ostracized at all' by anyone, on any of these issues, throughout this time.

Zanetta was appointed president of MainMan by Defries ('probably just so I could sign things he didn't want to sign!') and was again involved in arrangements for the *Diamond Dogs*/Philly Dogs tour schedule. He says that at this point he saw more of a development in Garson. After Michael Kamen left as musical director, the role fell to Garson for the second leg of the tour, in which the elaborate staging of the *Diamond Dogs* show was replaced by the Soul/Philly Dogs Tour, previewing the *Young Americans* material. Garson really started to come into his own as being instrumental to the evolution of the live material at this point.

His playing styles, though broad and extremely versatile, may not be thought of as immediately pertinent to Bowie's soul period. Yet when we listen to, for example, his gospel arrangement on the song 'It's Gonna Be Me' (an outtake from the 1974 Sigma Sound sessions in Philadelphia for the *Young Americans* album, which later appeared on various reissues), his soul credentials are hardly in doubt. Zanetta, having been in a position to closely observe Garson on both the *Ziggy Stardust* and Soul/ Philly Dogs tours, feels that he became more relaxed as the 1974 shows unfolded, in that the more tightly arranged ensemble this time placed him more in his element, working now with jazz saxophonist Dave Sanborn, for example, or the funky guitar of Carlos Alomar, to create a fusion in which he could thrive even more than a couple of years earlier.

He felt more at home and more secure. In addition, he now had more experience of being on the road and had already become one of Bowie's more established group members. Certainly, his piano stylings on the *Aladdin Sane* album were both striking and somewhat central to the sound, and yet this was still an exciting splash of unnerving color brilliantly thrown into the mix by Bowie and executed with sparkling assurance by Garson, bringing something shockingly alien to the rock genre of the music as a whole. On a song like 'Sweet Thing,' on the other hand, the interplay had evolved to the point where Garson's piano parts were no longer a separate interlude or visitor from outside but had become integral to the structure itself. This is even more obviously the case on, for example, the piano-led 'Rock 'n' Roll with Me.' At this stage in his career, Garson was truly starting to mature into an extremely rounded and versatile musician with great powers of expression at his fingertips, and all without any recourse to the transient consolations of drink or drugs.

Bowie's decision to invite Garson back to record and tour with him from 1992 onward, after a hiatus of about eighteen years, did owe something to the fact that he had by then long since left the Church of Scientology. Garson had informed Bowie's personal assistant, Corinne 'Coco' Schwab, of that fact in the late 1980s, and she would certainly have passed the information along. Then, in 1991, Tin Machine played at the Roxy in Los Angeles, and a work colleague of Garson's wife, Susan, by the name of Yolanda, went to the show and told them that she had gone backstage by using Susan's name. Susan wrote and apologized to Bowie for this. He replied that Yolanda had not in fact come backstage, but this incident would have been another factor in bringing Garson's name to mind again. Reeves Gabrels was also pushing for Garson to be brought back on board. It was against this background that Jérôme Soligny gave Bowie yet another reminder of Garson, when he interviewed Tin Machine in Paris in October 1991, and surprised Bowie by saying 'Mike says hi,' and that he had been working with Garson in his capacity as a singer/songwriter.[3]

All of these circumstances, combined with David Bowie's own artistic evolution in the early 1990s, created the propitious moment for Mike Garson to begin the second chapter of his work with Bowie in 1992.

# 21

# Life on the Road with David Bowie
## Part 2: 1995–2006

*'He's still as eccentric and as quirky as ever, in his playing . . . I still enjoy the experience of working with Mike, a lot.'*

—David Bowie on Mike Garson, 1995[1]

AT THE TIME OF the *Outside* Tour in 1995, an international press conference was held in London, at which Bowie spoke about working with Garson and gave great insight into the position he was in at this pivotal and central stage of his evolution as an artist. Asked about his use of computerized, random generation of lyrical material, he said, 'I'm not actually a very good writer, but my choices are very good. That's my strength. I can intuitively feel when there's an interesting poignancy or extremism or passion.' (This might also be applied to his choice of musicians.) He then spoke of the coming millennium as being a challenge in terms of 'the ritual of looking for a spiritual foundation, which I think is the shakiest part about living at the end of the twentieth century. Spiritual, not religious, I might add.' He told the press how visiting the artists at Gugging psychiatric clinic prior to recording *1. Outside* had reminded him of Dubuffet's *Collection de l'Art Brut* at Lausanne and of outsider art, which 'became one of the atmospheres for the album.'[2] He commented too on a possible art project he had been discussing with Damien Hirst, and spoke about the central role of improvisation in his work at that time.

Of his band of 1995, Bowie said that he had at that point 'a dream band, just the best musicians I've ever worked with,' and that he wanted 'to keep them together as long as possible.' On working again with Mike Garson, he added:

I actually started working with him again on an album called *The Buddha of Suburbia*, which started out as the soundtrack to a BBC play a couple of years ago.[3] Mike did some work with me on that, and it was just astonishing, that he still had the zest for 'playing around at the edge of the pool' again. I mean, he's still as eccentric and as quirky as ever, in his playing. He's been playing with some interesting people in California, he's been playing jazz for the past fifteen years or so. Stanley Clarke, in fact, he's been working with an awful lot. So, I still enjoy the experience of working with Mike, a lot.

It was not just fans of jazz or fusion who would have heard Garson's work with Stanley Clarke: his keyboards can also be heard on Clarke's soundtrack for 1991's popular film *Boyz n the Hood*, which won the BMI Film Music Award.

In some ways, Bowie's recruiting of a younger New York jazz band to record his final album in 2015 was his completing of the circle and a return to his early passion for New York and for jazz, which had never really left him. Garson's recurrence on so many of the albums is testimony to this. Bowie himself had started out by learning jazz saxophone in his youth from a teacher, Ronnie Ross, who based his style on Stan Getz.

Garson regards his own jazz training as having been invaluable, even though he did not adhere to its prescriptions as closely as the purists might have. He felt at liberty to fuse it with the full range of other genres of music, as the feel and the needs of the moment might determine. Of the 1974 live album *David Live*, for example, he says that his playing was very jazz-based as well as being very prominent, that he played more than at other times, even to the point of it being 'borderline too much,' but that Bowie appeared very happy with it. The musical director at the time, Michael Kamen, was also on a keyboard, and Garson recalls perhaps some youthful brinkmanship on his own part. His proximity onstage to the great Latin percussionist Pablo Rosario also led to him playing more loudly in order to hear himself.

Perhaps for the same reason, his live solo on 'Aladdin Sane (1913–1938–197?)' is even more Latin in style than on the studio version from the year before. Rosario was fascinated to hear of the friendship between Garson and the great Latin pianist Eddie Palmieri. Palmieri had given Garson some Latin piano lessons during the 1960s, and Garson had given him some jazz lessons in return. On the live solo there is a kind of interplay between the piano and percussion that drives each further into their shared expressiveness—the kind of interplay that can more commonly be heard between piano and guitar, for example between Garson's piano and Mick Ronson's beautiful Spanish guitar on 'Lady Grinning Soul.'

There were many moments of tenderness, humor, and creative passion onstage and backstage over the years, through the one thousand shows that Garson played with Bowie. As the years went by, the accumulation of shared experiences between Bowie and his longest-serving band member created a noticeable bond. By late 2003, Garson was firmly in the role of elder statesman; no one else onstage with Bowie had also been there when he was performing the role of Ziggy Stardust and first provoking Bowiemania across the United States, Japan, and Europe.

At West London's Riverside Studios on September 8, 2003, at a concert that was beamed live to cinemas around the world, Bowie introduced 'Hang on to Yourself' by turning to Garson and saying, 'Mike, you played on this one didn't you? Onstage, this next one, 1972?' Garson smiles and says, 'Watching!' at which point Bowie recalls and turns back to the audience, 'Oh, this is so funny! Mike told me earlier today that this is the one song—because, he worked with me and the Spiders—in '72!—the one song he never actually played on, so he used to go into the audience to see what we looked like.' He turns to Garson. 'Right?' Garson nods to confirm this, to which Bowie responds 'You too, mate!' to hearty laughter from both Garson and the audience. Bowie continues, as if vouching with affection for his friend, to the audience, 'Actually, he wouldn't, you know, he looks like he's [making aggressive face] "grrrr," but he's not, he's not.' Garson makes a face of stern, mock indignation, and Bowie adds, 'Yes he is!' as they launch into the song.

After a stirring rendition of '5.15 The Angels Have Gone,' in France, he listened in awe to the open jazz dialogue between Garson and drummer Sterling Campbell at the end, proudly commenting on their performance after the applause, 'Mike Garson and Sterling Campbell firing canons at each other over there,' confirming the joy he experienced from listening to the master musicians he had assembled.

Often, onstage, Bowie would show particular delight at Garson's playing—even punching the air with unbridled pride at Garson's stunning piano solo on 'Life on Mars?' at a Paris show in 1999 and saying, 'Thank you, Michael. Mike Garson, ladies and gentlemen.' Bowie was always very gracious about introducing band members, and especially so with Garson.

Whilst touring during the 1990s and 2000s, Garson's bed was generally just across from Bowie's on the tour bus, so there was plenty of conversation. On the *Reality* Tour, all of the other musicians were on a second bus, whereas the first bus carried just Bowie, personal assistant Coco Schwab, tour manager Frankie Enfield, bodyguard Erik Hausch, and, at Bowie's request, Mike Garson. There were eight beds arranged in pairs. Sometimes, Garson says, he and Bowie would each be in bed, reading, but then they might come out from their bunks and sit and chat, sharing stories. On other tours they would also have some great long conversations with Reeves Gabrels, too. Garson recalls one such three-way discussion exploring the special factors that distinguish great performing artists. Bowie continued to study such things with a keen eye throughout his life, and the movements and gestures of the film stars he sometimes watched with Garson in his hotel room were added to his stage vocabulary with ease.

These long and often philosophical conversations, shared late at night on tour with Bowie, sometimes together with other band members such as Zachary Alford or Reeves Gabrels, remain cherished memories of Garson's. He says that Gabrels had an encyclopedic knowledge of modern music but that Bowie was unrivaled in the extent of his overall knowledge. David Bowie was a true autodidact, and once he warmed to a subject, he could speak fluently, at length, and succeed in holding the enrapt attention of all those around him. Garson recalls, 'There were many times David would just pontificate, and he would be very excited to just talk to us endlessly, about almost anything! He was just so wide and brilliant in the self-learning that he had done throughout his life.'

The exceptional distinction and charisma that Bowie possessed did perhaps come at a price, in some ways. This implicitly emerges, in a thought-provoking way, from Garson's fond reminiscences of the physical fooling around that some of them engaged in. 'With Reeves, I'd jump on him and start tickling him, and he'd jump on me. This would be inches from where David was, backstage, after shows. David always looked at us like, "Wow, these guys are really close," as if he'd not ever had friendships like that, and that's the sad part, where he'd end up sort of being a little isolated. But he admired it from a distance, and laughed. But none of us did that to him.' One episode on the road that Bowie himself never got to hear of was a misadventure that occurred on the Mediterranean. They were touring in the South of France, and one day Zachary Alford and Garson went with a couple of the bodyguards at about 1 p.m. to hire a motorboat (one of Garson's favorite pastimes). Alford decided to go for a dive, searching for sea urchins—and did not resurface. Garson and the bodyguards, starting to fear the worst, called the police and requested a search party. Alford was Garson's best friend on the tour. Garson knew his wife and baby, and he was in a terrible state of panic. They finally gave up and returned to the hotel—only to find Alford walking into the lobby in his wet bathing suit. He had lost his way and could not find the boat, so another boat had picked him up and taken him safely to a port, where he had caught a train back to the hotel. Garson says he shouted angrily at Alford when he saw him, but there was an immense sense of relief. Alford even made it to the 4:30 p.m. soundcheck in time, and they decided to keep the incident to themselves, so as not to upset Bowie or risk the jobs of the bodyguards. The bodyguards, for their part, never again let them go on any such excursions on a show day.

Garson believes that the reasons for his being invited to travel in that front bus with Bowie may have included the fact that he had never had any interest in alcohol or taken drugs. Once Bowie had put those things behind him in later years, he never tried to control what others might choose to do, but he may well have preferred to share his closest space with someone who had not been part of that. There was also the shared history. They had grown older together. Mike Garson had been onstage with him when he retired the Ziggy Stardust character so dramatically in July 1973 in Hammersmith. He had been there with him at his fiftieth birthday celebration show at New York's Madison Square Garden in January 1997. They were onstage together at Wembley Stadium in 1999, playing to eighty thousand people for NetAid, where they opened with Garson's piano introduction to 'Life on Mars?'—just the two of them performing that song together without the rest of the band—and they were onstage together again at the Isle of Wight festival in June 2004, for Bowie's last full live set in Britain.

In more recent years, Bowie had been keen for Garson to move to New York, so that when he wanted to create, he would have access to him, and was disappointed that family reasons on Garson's part prevented this. Had he moved, it may have made it more likely for Garson to have played on Bowie's final two albums. He did propose staying in New York for a couple of weeks each month instead, and even located a possible place to stay, but he did not hear back from Bowie at that point. Garson, although a New Yorker, had long since established his home in Los Angeles and had only positive impressions of it in terms of the sunshine and the greater space for his family and his studio, whereas because his darkest days had been spent there in the mid-1970s, Bowie had a very negative impression of Los Angeles, and wrote to Garson on various occasions to that effect.

At one stage, Bowie's assistant, Coco Schwab, prompted Garson to call Bowie, suggesting that Bowie would be happy to hear from an old friend. He did call, and they spoke, but he felt that Bowie did not really respond. They had never socialized away from touring or working and the many conversations, dinners, and parties around that, which still somewhat saddens Garson, who got the impression that Bowie perhaps wanted to keep business and personal friendships separate. This is another example of the petty things that float away as we get close to death, he reflects. He does however recall Bowie saying during the *Reality* Tour to all of the band members, 'These here are my true friends!' A lot of this is conjecture, though, and, as with so much regarding David Bowie, the essence remains an enigma.

'But what was he trying to do with his life?' asks Garson now, before concluding, 'He was trying to change things for the better, he was trying to say some things that would help kids who were having a hard time in life, so they would know that they're "not alone" . . . I believe that his intentions were great, and I was just a little weak that way and I understand it now.'

Looking back over the decades, Garson can now distinguish his and Bowie's musical bond from their personal bond. Regarding their creative work together, he sees little change, since from day one they were on the same wavelength creatively, and that proved incredibly consistent. On the more personal level, there was inevitably more of an evolution. He says that there were many dinners and after-show parties on that first tour, and they started to share a lot of information. In England, Garson's oldest daughter, Jennifer, would go to play with Bowie's son Duncan (then Zowie, later Joe), who was just three months older than her, and they also got on well with Marion Skene, Duncan's nanny. Bowie got to know Garson's wife, Susan, and there was a lot of connection, right from the very start. His conversations on the road with Bowie in the early 1970s had more to do with Bowie's hunger for knowledge about American life or the New York jazz scene, whereas in the 1990s they started to have longer and deeper conversations, with the discussions often becoming more philosophical.

Whilst recording the (unreleased) album *Toy* in Manhattan in 2000, Bowie said to Garson, 'Mike, you would not want to be in my shoes, and you would not want to have the fame I have; my life is not my own.' Garson joked back, 'Well, I wouldn't mind a little of your money!'

Garson's wife, Susan, echoes Bowie's point by saying how much she has always loved the anonymity they enjoy by living in a remote gated community, and that Garson has come to appreciate this too. But Bowie was also aware of Garson's relative lack of acumen with handling money. Another time, on tour, Bowie said to Garson, 'You know what makes you different from people like me or Mick Jagger, Mike? Me and Mick are great businessmen, and you're not!'

It was around this time that Mike Garson was included in a book about Jewish rock musicians. The book, by Scott Benarde, was entitled *Stars of David*, though not in reference to Bowie. For the contents of that book, Bowie was asked if he would be willing to write a few lines about his work with Garson, and without delay he penned and sent straight back this fulsome tribute to their work together:

> Mike has been working with me, on and off, since 1972. I was looking for a pianist to flesh out the Spiders stage sound, as there were a number of songs that we wanted to do that required keyboard and as Ronno and myself didn't feel we could cut it on things like 'Life on Mars?,' we went searching. Annette Peacock, the avant-garde jazz writer/performer, recommended Mike to Ronno so we gave him a super fast audition at a recording studio in New York. Within ten or twenty notes we knew he was the guy. He was quite astounding.

Because of his varied background I will often throw a composer's name at him mid-recording and he'll pick up on it immediately and respond with something that touches that area. He is so fast to respond in that way. It is pointless to talk about his ability as a pianist. He is exceptional. However, there are very, very few musicians, let alone pianists, who naturally understand the movement and free thinking necessary to hurl themselves into experimental or traditional areas of music, sometimes, ironically, at the same time. Mike does this with such enthusiasm that it makes my heart glad just to be in the same room with him.[4]

Whilst touring Japan in June 1996, Garson recalls Bowie taking the band to a Buddhist monastery. A young monk whom Bowie knew there had been to see their show in Tokyo. The monk's teacher was ninety-eight and a Zen master, and they held a tea ceremony for the band, which Reeves Gabrels, Zachary Alford, and Gail Ann Dorsey all attended. They all sat at a long table, with the Zen master at the head of the table, and Bowie across from Garson. The Zen master turned and said to them, through an interpreter, that perhaps the rock music they were making would turn out to be the new religion.

In 2004, they were walking into a rehearsal and, knowing Garson's commitment to spirituality, Bowie turned and made a startling declaration, which Garson recalls and paraphrases as, 'Mike, I know how much you're into spirituality. I'm a rock star, I am who I am; this is going to play out in this way in this lifetime. I'll probably tend to that more in the next lifetime.'

The final world tour that Garson did with Bowie proved also to be Bowie's own last world tour, the *Reality* Tour of 2003–2004. During the tour, a lot of great footage was filmed backstage and on the road by Jimmy King and made available to BowieNet private subscribers. Anyone who bought a ticket for any of the shows also got an access code to view the footage as the tour went around the world. The footage provided a wonderful documentary record of the great atmosphere of bonhomie backstage, portraying a world-class group of musicians at the height of their powers who clearly got on especially well, were very fond of one another, and had endless good humor led by the sharp wit of Bowie himself. His happy, relaxed, and creative approach seemed to set the tone for everyone and everything else around that tour.

What is especially noticeable about the *A Reality Tour—Behind the Scenes* footage is the almost constant laughter. This was surely one of the happiest times for Bowie, and he was incredibly entertaining both onstage and off. It is also rather touching to see Garson's imposing frame standing reliably by his friend's side night after night as they prepare to step onto the various stages around the world, given that he was also there with him, night after night, during the *Ziggy Stardust* Tour, over thirty years earlier.

The tour's musical director, Gerry Leonard, has also given me a vivid picture of just what a wonderful atmosphere prevailed within that magical combination of band members who were all brilliant musicians but also warm, funny, caring, passionate people.[5] I had the privilege to spend the day with them all at the BRIT Awards in London in February 2016, and this is really no overstatement. Meeting them then, it was clear to me that the bond they forged through working together for Bowie was so strong that it remains special even now. Their collective sense of loss that day was palpable and deeply moving, but they approached the challenge of their performance with such grace and dignity, and executed it with a near-perfect artistic flair that would have hugely delighted the one person missing that day, who had brought them all together and had inspired so much love and such creativity.

Garson reminisces again about how warm and convivial Bowie could be. 'Maybe there were times in his life he was cold, the drugs might have been blocking it out, but through the years and everything he went through, in the end, he was a warm guy. I would see him talk to people and it was genuine. He could get into a conversation with anybody about anything, and there were many times we'd be sitting around, with Zach and Gail, and he would really get on a subject and we would be sitting there just taking it in.'

Garson was onstage with Bowie in Germany in 2004 when he had a heart attack, resulting in the last fifteen shows of the tour having to be canceled. He recalls how, a couple of years later, Bowie called him and asked whether he thought that they should resume touring again. 'Only if you're feeling it,' Garson replied. Bowie seems to have acted on that; a year later, he told drummer Sterling Campbell that he was not touring, as 'I'm not feeling it.' In addition, he had determined to be there more for his daughter, Lexi, in a way that he had not, years earlier, for his son, Duncan.

Garson also recalls Bowie telling him, a few years earlier, that he was frustrated to have been put on cholesterol-reducing medication by his doctor, despite his lifestyle having become dramatically healthier in later years. The band had a fitness trainer, and Garson would meet Bowie in the gym; the past had taken some toll, but Bowie remained a very keen boxer through most of his life, which helped to keep him strong and in shape.

On May 19, 2007, David Bowie performed a brief rendition, a cappella, of the song 'Pug Nosed Face' from *Extras* before introducing Ricky Gervais to the stage of the Theater at Madison Square Garden, as part of the High Line Festival, which he was curating. I myself had played piano for Bowie on that same song on his last-ever television appearance in the world, which was on *Extras* (HBO/BBC), filmed in June 2006 and first broadcast in the UK on September 21, 2006. However, his last full live performance in the United States was on November 9, 2006, at the Black Ball benefit concert for the Keep a Child Alive charity. The venue was New York's Hammerstein Ballroom and the event was hosted by Bowie's wife, Iman Abdulmajid, and by Alicia Keys.

Bowie sang 'Wild Is the Wind' accompanied only by Mike Garson on piano, then 'Fantastic Voyage' accompanied by Keys's band. For his final song, 'Changes,' he was joined onstage by Alicia Keys, who duetted with him. Her band was playing, but she asked Garson to play the piano for this. At the time, the Bowie website, www.davidbowie.com, published reviews of the event written by BowieNet members who had attended:

'His hands were folded in front as he acknowledged Mr. Garson, then turned to face the audience . . .'

'Opening with "Wild Is the Wind" in a simple and elegantly stripped down version, he was mesmerizing . . . Mike's gentle and masterful piano work was the perfect accompaniment.'[6]

There is a poignant symmetry in the fact that Mike Garson was onstage with David Bowie for both his first-ever concert in the United States—when the *Ziggy Stardust* Tour began its American leg at Cleveland on September 22, 1972—and his very last. In the intervening years, the virtuosity and versatility of Brooklyn's master improviser served as the perfect foil for Bowie's timeless voice of alienation and exploration. The phone call that Garson took that day in 1972 changed his life. He was ready and open for change. But it also added something to the tapestry of modern music that can inspire us all.

Spontaneity; breaking down barriers and erasing boundaries; cultivating profound knowledge of our musical heritage, and absorbing myriad cultural inputs, in order to transcend them and create something new; wild imagination combined with meticulous discipline; emotional honesty and immediacy: these were the connections cementing the collaboration between Bowie and Garson, and, as we have seen, they are also the linchpins of all of Garson's other work as pianist, improviser, composer, and educator.

# Appendix I: Watch That Man
## Garson's Playing on Twenty-One Bowie Albums—Selected Highlights

*'I always tell people that Bowie is the best producer I ever met, because he lets me do my thing . . . He would play me something and the music sort of told me what to do. He's never been one that micromanaged me, which is why I always thought he was my best producer.*

*'With Bowie I know exactly how far I can go with my jazz and my classical, my harmonies, my pop, and my avant-garde. I know what he doesn't like and what he likes, so I play within that window. He's wonderful to work for, just wonderful . . . it's his musicality, he's dead serious about his music . . .*

*'I sometimes play in the way I think David would play piano if he were the pianist.'*

—Mike Garson on playing for David Bowie

### *SANTA MONICA '72* (RECORDED 1972, RELEASED 1994, 2008)
Garson: 'I was new to the band. I remember Paul McCartney being in the audience. I remember playing "Changes" and "Life on Mars?" and that was kind of special.'

### *ALADDIN SANE* (1973)
#### 'Watch That Man'
Garson's playing on the opening track of his first Bowie album was a dynamic debut, combining Jerry Lee Lewis–style rock 'n' roll, bluesy boogie-woogie riffs, and percussive eighth-note octave chords. In the breakdown toward the end, the half-spoken lyrics 'watch that man!' are responded to with classic rock licks as crisp and striking as those of any rock pianist playing in the world in 1973.

Garson: 'I really hadn't had an opportunity to play something like that, except on that day. I certainly knew that this song wasn't really featuring me, but I still wanted to be a band member and feel included in the group. I don't really think I got any direction on that. I really think I just heard it and it seemed the appropriate thing to play: what would Nicky Hopkins, or a rock player who knew little about classical or jazz, play? A Rolling Stones type of vibe.'

### 'Aladdin Sane (1913–1938–197?)'

Much has been written about Garson's solo on this track. His performance on the whole song is remarkable, however, from the delicate arpeggios of the opening verses to the distinctive ending, slightly reminiscent of Schoenberg's *Six Little Piano Pieces*. With its quotations from *Rhapsody in Blue*, *Tequila*, and *On Broadway*, this was a spontaneous master performance that perfectly embodies many of the ideas we have explored in these pages: building on well-studied inputs to generate something new, composing by improvising; capturing the moment.

The solo was recorded in one take. Garson's timing throughout the song is superb, sometimes lingering behind the beat and responding to or even imitating the vocals, at other times matching the beat with bullet precision. His splintered-glass stylings were enhanced by Ken Scott's expert engineering of a condensed and brittle sound, with a sonorous reverb, from the Bechstein grand piano at Trident Studios on St. Anne's Court in London's Soho. Garson also uses a great range of dynamics, from the ghostly softness of touch in the opening bars to the much more strident percussive stabs in the solo. He recorded his part for this song as an overdub, whereas for most of the other tracks he played with the band. He says now that one of his wishes on the title track was to employ an avant-garde or 'outside' way of playing, whilst 'making it more spirited, less dark . . . I wanted audiences to sort of love it and be able to embrace it, and yet still have that chilling effect.'

### 'Time'

Garson: 'First of all, the tune is phenomenal. It was one or two takes, and I felt it required the old stride style of piano, but I took it left-field . . . it was just the sensibility David was looking for. The piano itself sounded great because Ken Scott made it sound like these old-fashioned rinky-dink bar-room pianos.'

This style combines those elements of stride with a taste of Weimar and the theatrical music written by Kurt Weill for Brecht. There are fantasy flourishes of faded grandeur and mid-twentieth-century, mid-European decadence, with a touch of the circus or fairground. This recording is also one of the best examples of the dazzling interaction between Garson's piano playing and the extremely expressive and wildly melodious, classically influenced guitar work of Mick Ronson. Some have heard strains of Beethoven's Ninth in the riffs Ronson launches into later in the song.

### 'Let's Spend the Night Together'

Garson: 'This was pure jovial . . . like, David was doing a Rolling Stones song—what can I do here that's going to be so outrageous, and just take it off the map, go left-field with it, and yet still keep that excitement? The intro had to not be too long, just a brief avant-garde moment then into the piece; it was a one-take thing for me, and a total joy, just a pleasure to play.'

### 'Lady Grinning Soul'

Garson: 'I just pulled out all the knowledge I had about Franz Liszt, Chopin, and this romantic way of playing, mixed with a tinge of something Spanish, which Mick Ronson picked up. I was using some Spanish little fills, scales that were a little Spanish in sound. Again, it was one of those one-take magic things, and it's one of my favorite tracks of all time of David's.'

Bowie wrote of this song, 'Mike Garson's piano opens with the most ridiculous and spot on recreation of a late nineteenth-century music hall "exotic" number. I can see now the "*poses plastiques*" as if through a smoke filled bar. Fans, castanets and lots of Spanish black lace and little else.'[1]

## ZIGGY STARDUST: THE MOTION PICTURE (RECORDED 1973, RELEASED 1983)
### 'Wild Eyed Boy from Freecloud'—live

Garson plays some beautiful piano work on this live version of a Bowie song from the *Space Oddity* album, which predated his arrival in the band.

## PIN UPS (1973)
### 'See Emily Play'
*See chapter 7 for some discussion of this recording.*
Garson: 'What a great track. The first time I heard our recording properly was after Syd Barrett passed away in 2006. I knew when to keep it simple and when to really get out there and stretch it, and I think that helped to inspire the strings and the Bach ending . . . it was just a very special track.'

### 'Where Have All the Good Times Gone'
Rapid repeated chords on the piano achieve a great percussive effect. Garson recalls that they ran the piano through a Leslie amp for some of the songs on the album.

### 'Sorrow'
The piano lines just 'go for a walk' without too much embellishment, prefiguring the gentle soul stylings of the *Young Americans* album, which would come later.

## *DIAMOND DOGS* (1974)
### 'Sweet Thing / Candidate / Sweet Thing (Reprise)'

Garson: 'I think I was in the zone for this . . . it was pretty magical. I don't recall the *Diamond Dogs* process, as much as David just played me songs and I figured out the chords and I did my thing. He truly trusted my instincts.'

The piano work on 'Sweet Thing' suggests a narrative subtext for the album, with its stylistic references to the theatrical form in which these songs had been conceived, the album's genesis having been as a stage show based on Orwell's *Nineteen Eighty-Four*. The D chords against the C bass and the classical motifs for the minor-key turnarounds hint at musical theater, but then the virtuoso rapid runs and the incongruous pure darkness of it all move it into less cozy territory.

Garson has rarely heard these recordings since contributing to them, but hearing this now he describes the material as 'deep, and with a maturity.' At the end there is an incredible dexterity with which Garson plays the flattened fifth on a B-flat chord with his right hand whilst rolling up and down some deep bass runs with what sounds like at least three further hands. This part of the song was prefigured in an outtake or rough demo from the *Pin Ups* sessions in France a few months earlier, on a piece that is sometimes referred to by fans as 'Zion.'

Garson only realized the quality he had achieved years later when guitarist Page Hamilton sang its praises during the 1999 *'hours . . .'* Tour and got him to listen to 'Sweet Thing' for the first time since recording it. He says, 'I tend to just play these things and not judge them. It's like throwing spaghetti on the wall—some sticks!'

### 'We Are the Dead'

This starts with an eight-note, syncopated, two-handed descending G minor scale, taking us quickly into somber and studied, steady chords on an electric piano. This gives way to beautifully poised gentle arpeggios in the verses, which contrast chillingly with the darkness of the lyrics. The four words of the chorus and title are a direct quotation from Orwell's *Nineteen Eighty-Four* (originally from the First World War poem 'In Flanders' by John McCrae), and the feel conveys that sinister atmosphere perfectly.

### 'Rock 'n' Roll with Me'

Garson: 'Just locked-in-the-pocket, real great steady feel, held the tune together, the piano part was very solid.' He can also be heard playing organ on this track.

## DAVID LIVE (1974)

As a live show from a period when Garson's piano was at its most prominent in Bowie's instrumentation, almost every track carries great examples of his playing, from the rapid scales and Latin fills on 'Rebel Rebel' and the syncopated chords of 'Moonage Daydream' to a sweet and sensitively poised jazz piano part on 'All the Young Dudes.' The opening track of '1984' begins with some oboe from Michael Kamen followed by Garson imitating the theme from *The Twilight Zone*, which also closes the song.

'Changes,' the song on which he had auditioned for Bowie a couple of years earlier, shows how elements from his jazz background found space to shine onstage. Listening back to it in 2014, Garson says that he feels perhaps the band slightly overplayed some of the embellishments, given their role as supporting Bowie's vocal. The introduction to 'Changes' leads as a segue from the end of 'Sweet Thing' and there is a sense of confidence and command of the instrument, that he could do anything with it. There are other segues led by piano, for example from 'Time' to 'The Width of a Circle,' that add to the theatricality of the show. This album was also an opportunity to hear what Garson was doing with the earlier songs from *Hunky Dory* and *Ziggy Stardust*, which had not featured his playing on the original studio recordings—indeed, many of them had originally had no piano parts at all.

### 'Aladdin Sane (1913–1938–197?)'—live
A much more Latin version, driven by Pablo Rosario's percussion.

### 'Space Oddity'—live (added as a bonus track on the 2005 EMI/Virgin CD release)
Atmosphere is created with some great improvised piano runs during the first part of this interpretation.

### 'Time'—live (added as a bonus track on the 1990 CD reissue by Rykodisc/EMI)
This arrangement includes a strangely playful and quirky solo, the apparent childishness of which is belied by the virtuoso run that follows.

### 'Rock 'n' Roll Suicide'—live
Some rapid virtuoso classical runs toward the end.

## YOUNG AMERICANS (1975)
### 'Young Americans'
Garson: 'For the title track I pulled out those *montunos*, the piano *ostinati* repeated

figure from Cuban music . . . it kind of generated a lot of the impetus for the song—though of course, the background vocals and the song itself was great, and David was singing beyond belief, but the piano had a nice vibe, and of course Sanborn was right there killing it, you know!'

### 'Right'
Clavinet is played by Garson.

### 'Somebody Up There Likes Me'
There are some chunky chords and chops in the verses, but it is the simple little runs of a few notes added into the groove, at 3:50, imitating and echoing the vocal, that is the stroke of genius. It is so spare and effortless yet genuinely spine-tingling, and it is the restraint in his playing that is beautiful. This ability to create simple piano lines that 'converse' with the vocals is a key feature of Garson's work on such albums.

Garson: 'So funky, it is all about Dave Sanborn's sax . . . simple studio funky piano playing, locked into a groove with an amazing rhythm section and spearheaded by our boss.'

### 'It's Gonna Be Me'
Recorded between August 11 and 18, 1974, and performed on some of the late 1974 Soul Tour shows, the studio take was not released until the Rykodisc CD reissue of *Young Americans* in 1991.

Garson: 'I never heard it since I recorded this, not once, maybe not even at the recording sessions. I didn't know I could play like that, but perhaps being with those amazing players brought it out of me.'

### 'Can You Hear Me?'
Effortless, laid-back soul chords and licks adorn this exquisitely beautiful song, and the piano is always supportive and never intrusive.

## BLACK TIE WHITE NOISE (1993)
### 'Looking for Lester'
A funky groove is the platform for various solos, including piano from 4:18.

Garson: 'A tinge of the avant-garde but not my favorite performance. It felt forced.'

## *THE BUDDHA OF SUBURBIA* (1993)
### 'South Horizon'
This piano part really is a work of art in itself. As often, the genius lies in the tangential or angular way in which Garson responds to the rest of the music, instantaneously absorbing it, reflecting it back, and elevating it into further dimensions. Garson rates the solo as being in the 'top three' that he has done on Bowie's albums.

### 'Bleed Like a Craze, Dad'
This starts with a complex flurry of wind-up music-box notes, which resolves into some single notes distantly playing mournful scales. There is a surprisingly sweet broken chord at the very end, as if from the same old music box.

## *I. OUTSIDE* (1995)
### 'The Hearts Filthy Lesson'
A few seconds in, we hear ominous rumbling runs, Lisztian octave surges, then insistent chord stabs of fourths and percussive high-pitch jazz riffs. The genesis of this song came within the studio improvisations from these repeated piano chords; when Garson started playing them, the music just grew around them.

### 'A Small Plot of Land'
Rapid jazz runs and trills in a fully 'outside' style on the piano, with only Sterling Campbell's drums as accompaniment for about the first forty-five seconds. Discordant piano juxtaposed with unnerving synth, with Stravinskian chord *ostinati*. 'As "outside" as I have ever played,' says Garson.

### 'The Motel'
Unlike the rest of the material on the album, which was improvised, Bowie brought this in as a complete song. Garson regards it as one of the best Bowie songs and certainly one of his own best performances. There is some dazzling virtuoso piano from 3:00 to 3:46. A Gm7 flat fifth chord at 4:49 gives it a lift, with emotive piano runs set against a frenetic electronic drumbeat.

### 'The Voyeur of Utter Destruction (as Beauty)'
Garson: 'There was a nice jazz vibe on this song, and another opportunity to improvise.'

## 'I'm Deranged'

Middle-Eastern style vocals make for a striking combination, with inventive piano solos and octaves from 2:09 and then at intervals to the end. Garson says that he loves both the song and piano part.

## 'Strangers When We Meet'

Garson says this was 'always good on tour . . . a simplistic piano part, but I fell in love with that piece. It's an underrated song.' He compares his style on this to the playing on 'Absolute Beginners' from *Bowie at the Beeb*. It first appeared on *The Buddha of Suburbia* in 1993, then was re-recorded in 1995 for *1. Outside* with delicate and very high piano lines adding more depth and dimension.

## *EARTHLING* (1997)

Garson: 'Through all these albums I needed to soul-search and bring something fresh to each recording, never to rest on my laurels. That sometimes was difficult as there were so many songs, and I was trying not to repeat myself, even though our styles are based on the vast array of licks we know, coupled with the magic of the moment. I gave much thought and practice prior to the recordings—quite a challenge, to balance the boundaries and the freedoms.'

## 'Battle for Britain (The Letter)'

Garson's favorite piano part of all: 'The solo starts a bit like "Time" on steroids, crazy! I feel I got a bit lucky on this piece, thanks to the inputs of Mark Plati, Reeves Gabrels, Zachary Alford, Gail Ann Dorsey, and of course David.'

Bowie asked him to listen to Stravinsky's Octet for Wind Instruments before recording this.

## 'Seven Years in Tibet'

The organ solo uses a Farfisa sound accessed via a Kurzweil. 'It had a very creepy, snaky kind of feel. Straight after I played it, David said it was the best solo I had played for him since *Aladdin Sane*.'

## 'Dead Man Walking'

Garson said this was the first time he played some fairly straight jazz on a Bowie track. He ended with a 'funny little Latin thing' in a bebop style over the long fadeout.

## *VH1 STORYTELLERS* (RECORDED 1999, RELEASED 2009)

Garson: 'That whole show was totally miraculous; everyone was in the moment. Something about the way we were playing in that period, we all loved it.'

### 'China Girl'—live

Garson: 'I took it in a whole different direction, played a very different kind of piano part, but everyone seemed to like it.'

### 'I Can't Read'

Garson played only strings from the Disklavier, using a soft-enough touch to bypass its real piano action, producing a subtle build in which the strings envelop the song and add dimension.

## *'HOURS . . .'* (1999)

Garson did not play on this album, but he can be heard on one bonus track on the 2004 reissue, 'Something in the Air (American Psycho Remix).' Piano was added to this song for its use on the soundtrack to *American Psycho* (2000). It was also performed live with piano on various occasions.

## *BOWIE AT THE BEEB* (2000)

The bonus (third) CD on early editions of this set carries a recording of the Bowie band's live show at the BBC Theatre, June 27, 2000. Garson says that everything felt right that night, that he was inspired by the intimate audience, which included his old friend Lulu (with whom he had toured twenty-five years earlier) and Russell Crowe, who went to various Bowie shows.

### 'Wild Is the Wind'—live

This recorded live performance is a perfect example of the full range of Garson's more tonal, less discordant playing with Bowie, with many of its greatest features distilled into one song. This had been one of Garson's favorite songs ever since he heard Johnny Mathis, aged just twenty-two, sing the original as the theme to the film of the same name in 1957. Bowie's cover on his 1976 album *Station to Station* has no piano. When they were going to start doing it live, he asked Garson to listen to Nina Simone's typically inspired version. He did so, but as always he went on to do it in his own distinctive way, albeit with some subtle influence from her interpretation, and Bowie appreciated that.

Garson says that his version has cleaner runs and steadier timing, though he also loved Simone's soulful, grittier feel: 'Ultimately Bowie is enough of an artist to want me to get a hit on what she did and then obviously do my own thing.' Some of his best memories are of playing this (and 'Life on Mars?') for Bowie. He starts the song delicately, with a very romantic 'less is more' approach, but then gets bigger with block chords, double descending chromatic scales in thirds, and a lot of cascading arpeggios, all the while still 'staying out of the way of Bowie's vocal, and leaving space for the guitar and everything.'

Garson: 'The perfect tune for me to open up on and support a singer like David, who just sings the hell out of that song! Every time we've done that song it's been very special. I remember this like it was yesterday. Sometimes one knows they are in the magical zone. I knew it that whole night, and this tune sums it all up.'

## 'Absolute Beginners'—live

The original 1985 recording of this song was produced by Clive Langer and Alan Winstanley, and has piano by Steve Nieve and additional keyboards by Rick Wakeman. This live version is another of the best showcases demonstrating the full range of Garson's playing with Bowie. It does not have as much of his 'outside' playing as some others, but is replete with Gershwin-like figures and motifs, fantastic poise, sweep, and embellishment, and pure lyrical musicality from the piano.

Garson: 'Every lick I know—well, every lick that's tonal! I loved playing this song live.'

## 'Ashes to Ashes'—live

This performance includes a great synth solo from Garson.

## *TOY* (2000)

This album was not released, but it was leaked onto the Internet in 2011, and also generated some of the material that appeared on *Heathen*.

## 'Uncle Floyd'

This song was re-recorded for *Heathen* as 'Slip Away.' Garson's piano is on the 'Uncle Floyd' version.

## 'Conversation Piece,' 'Shadow Man'

See below.

## HEATHEN (2002)
**'Conversation Piece'**
Extra track on the *Heathen* limited-edition bonus disc; written in 1969, recorded in 1970, this version was re-recorded in 2000 for the unreleased *Toy* album.

**'Shadow Man'**
Extra track on *Heathen* limited edition bonus disc; written and recorded c. 1970–1971, this version was re-recorded in 2001 for *Toy*. It also appeared as the B-side to the 'Everyone Says Hi' single from *Heathen* in September 2002, and on the 2014 retrospective *Nothing Has Changed—The Very Best of Bowie*.

This and 'Conversation Piece' are two of Garson's favorite Bowie songs and recordings, which he feels 'have beautiful piano parts because those tunes of David's were so gorgeous that I couldn't help but find the right notes in that particular space.' Tony Visconti told Garson that he built the string arrangement for 'Conversation Piece' around the piano parts.

## REALITY (2003)
**'The Loneliest Guy'**
Featuring ominous, low, hypnotic, accompaniment-style piano.

**'Bring Me the Disco King'**
Garson: 'Late-1950s jazz in the Brubeck tradition, but in my own style. There is a partly chordal solo toward the end. It is amazing how David, after the end of his vocal, had the meditative patience to allow me to play out my solo for nearly another two minutes.'

## iSELECT (2008)
This compilation of songs chosen by David Bowie himself includes two of Garson's finest performances with him, 'Sweet Thing / Candidate / Sweet Thing (Reprise)' (see page 270) and 'Lady Grinning Soul' (see page 269).

## A REALITY TOUR (RECORDED 2003, RELEASED 2010)
Live double album, recorded in Dublin in 2003.

**'Battle for Britain (The Letter)'—live**
An electrifyingly exciting live rendition of Garson's duet with drummer Sterling Campbell. A DVD version of the *Reality* Tour was released, and the visual impact

of this performance, with the interaction between Garson and Campbell, makes it even more compelling.

### 'Ashes to Ashes'—live

This version has an exciting jazz piano solo, rather than the synth solo that is heard on many of the other live versions of the song.

### 'The Motel'—live

This takes the studio version even further, with the majestic, baroque grandeur of Garson's piano lines on the original sounding even more exquisite in the rapid high runs performed here.

### 'Bring Me the Disco King'—live

Garson recalls that this was often an encore during the *Reality* Tour.

## NOTHING HAS CHANGED—THE VERY BEST OF BOWIE (2014)

This major retrospective featured two new songs alongside over fifty earlier recordings. Notable Garson contributions include 'Shadow Man,' 'The Hearts Filthy Lesson,' 'Strangers When We Meet,' and 'Young Americans' (2007 Tony Visconti mix single edit).

## FIVE YEARS (1969–1973) (2015)

A collection of ten albums, five of which include piano played by Garson.

## DAVID BOWIE—WHO CAN I BE NOW? (1974–1976) (2016)

A collection of nine albums, including those with piano played by Garson from this period, such as *Diamond Dogs*, *David Live*, and *Young Americans*, plus the earlier version of the latter album, entitled *The Gouster*, featuring, for example, some strongly authentic gospel piano playing from Garson on the song 'It's Gonna Be Me.'

# Appendix 2: Forensics

## Analysis of Mike Garson's Techniques in Playing, Improvising, and Composing

*'Strong, muddy, prolix, gritty, Garsonic, modern...'*
—Brian Eno, describing David Bowie's 1995 album *1. Outside*[1]

As a pianist in rock music, Garson has the perfect kind of timing, sometimes choosing to sit slightly behind the beat, at other times sitting squarely on it. He makes use of the full range of the keyboard, more than many pianists, with the top two octaves of keys cutting nicely through the forbiddingly amplified sounds of the rest of the band. His playing also shows strong contrasts: extreme complexity and embellishment, with cascading arpeggios, is often followed by a slow and simple sequence of single notes within the middle octave. These simpler lines with which he reflects and reinforces the melody of the vocals are not unlike string-section lines in their phrasing. A further contrast within his playing is of course that of genre: classical arpeggios are freely mingled with jazz chords and blues notes. All of these striking characteristics are found in the examples that follow.

### I. CREATING PIANO PARTS FOR SONGS: TWO EXAMPLES FROM WORK WITH MICK RONSON

The way in which Mike Garson's distinctive piano parts helped to shape the sound of numerous recordings by David Bowie is well established. Some of his most striking contributions to modern music can also be heard on the solo recordings of the great guitarist Mick Ronson (who played on several early Bowie albums). Here we take two examples of solo recordings by Ronson that feature prominent Garson piano parts, and use these to explore in more detail some of the ways in which Garson uses his instrument to add texture and musical substance to a song, lifting it into something more focused and expressive than it would otherwise be.

#### 'I'm the One' (*Slaughter on 10th Avenue*, 1974)

This cover by Mick Ronson of the Annette Peacock song displays many of Garson's defining techniques, as well as his hugely expressive musical personality. For this song he plays electric piano as well as piano. He comes in dramatically with a *glis-*

279

*sando*, followed soon afterward by some syncopated chords, and then staccato pairs of blues chords with grace notes at 0:20.

At 0:38 the vocal phrase 'I'm here to fight for you' is beautifully imitated and echoed by electric piano almost at the moment it is sung (as Ronson sings the word 'you,' Garson plays the melody of 'to fight for you'). This same melody is further echoed by Garson in the minor instrumental section, and at this point he starts to introduce some more 'outside' elements that reference the more avant-garde performance of the original by Peacock—on which he also played.

At 1:28 there is a rapid multiple repetition of a five-note phrase against the modulating bass. Each time, a different note of the five is emphasized. That, plus the fact that the bass is changing, gives a different effect to each repetition. He relates to the singer's phrasing by responding, imitating, harmonizing, playfully dancing around the voice and yet never getting in the way of it.

The song has a complete change of pace and mood at 2:20, reinventing itself as a plaintive gospel, and the piano adapts to this seamlessly with languorous, bluesy seventh chords and jazzy *acciaccatura* notes, with a folksy feel. This is strongly underpinned by true gospel style, with big chords and a bass declension that features some inversions with the third as the bass note. The long play-out from about 3:28 features wonderfully rich piano chord runs and syncopations weaving themselves around Ronson's powerful vocal, against a plaintive brass section crescendo.

### 'This Is for You' (*Play Don't Worry*, 1975)
This is another beautiful piano part, though with many contrasts to the above. This is more of a pop-romantic style, conveying deep emotion and using many classical touches. Garson starts with a trademark entrance halfway through the first verse, via an ascending scale that, crucially, is accelerating. This is followed by some strong, Spanish-style, simple figures in the middle octaves and arpeggiated chords in the upper octaves, which play their own sparse melody as if they were single notes.

From the second verse the piano part starts to fill out more with more classical arpeggiation and some elegant syncopated octaves with, at 2:14, the first of several of his signature rapid bravura runs building the drama until, from about 3:30 to the end, the virtuosity of the piano becomes almost harp-like in its fluency. From 3:59 he makes great use of repeating phrases in a 'circular' way to create greater rhythmic expression.

I asked Garson whether it might have been the case that when working with Mick Ronson he was given more free rein to bring in jazz elements whenever the urge took him, whereas perhaps Bowie had been more directing. 'Mick was more of a musician than David,' he responded, 'thus he had a higher tolerance and provided a wider net for me regarding jazz, but David had a more specific intention for me which included less jazz vocabulary, more avant-garde, classical, and romantic. Different songs and artists bring out different things in me.'

## 2. THE FELLOW PIANIST-COMPOSER

As a classically highly trained pianist-composer (who is also, like Garson, multi-genre, or beyond genre, in both his playing and writing), Becker KB makes many acute observations about Garson's 'Now' music compositions:

> The jazz influences of the likes of Art Tatum can be heard in the animated bass movement, and the presence of Bach or Rachmaninoff in the great motion and interaction of lines overall. There are natural limits to the complexity of counterpoint and strata created through improvisation rather than writing, and yet there exist many instances of multi-layered voices, explicit or suggested, even in the faster pieces. Garson often employs a big, sweeping and robust sound, unleashing the piano's soul in, for example, his *Ballade in G-sharp Minor* and a number of the *Nowtudes*, with the latter also in places exhibiting a surreal texture. Garson's recently premiered *Symphonic Suite for Healing* likewise displays imaginative, emotionally penetrating, and mesmerizing textures, with sheen and mystique.

> What other specific features can be isolated as hallmarks of Garson's improvisations? A lot of his work is through-composed, partly as a result of its improvisational origins, and this can make it a stimulating challenge to learn. At the same time the pieces possess solid coherence and elements of cyclical return, which makes memorizing them well manageable. Garson has a technique of quickly and subtly shifting the tonal center, as if a focal point of gravity were arrived at and then rapidly transcended. His harmonies span from standard triads and extensions to polytonal, jazz, and experimental combinations and voicings. Melodies range from beautiful and expressive to more aggressive and avant-garde, with both long lines and short spirals.

> In the midst of all this diversity and complexity, there is always a definite coherence which elevates these creations 'of the moment' into more permanently rewarding and bona fide compositions. Regarding rhythm, Garson's work occasionally features steady grooves that somehow evade the ready recognition of a regular meter, resulting in a modernist disjuncture, which at the same time still hangs together. Serene and poignantly lyrical passages and

pieces of melancholic or joyful contemplation abound in addition to Garson's trademark frenetic and often discordant flurries and wildly disturbed arpeggios and rapid runs, all of which make such utterly full use of the instrument in every sense.

## 3. THE ORCHESTRATOR

Bruce Donnelly is Mike Garson's orchestrator and copyist. He has transcribed 375 of his pieces; he has studied every note. He believes that even Garson's most dissonant pieces are genuinely musical and coherent, and uncontrived in a way that a lot of twentieth- and twenty-first-century 'progressive' music is not. He attributes this to their extended harmonic language.

I would guess most musicians and critics familiar with Mike's music would focus on his concept of improvisation as composition, and the incorporation of an encyclopedic variety of piano idioms and musical styles. There are two other aspects of his music, however, that stand out for me.

The first stems from several conversations we had about learning styles. For example, he often plays ballads in what most people would consider a Tatum-esque style. Interestingly, he told me he had only studied three or four Art Tatum arrangements, and from those worked out a set of principles regarding right and left hand figures and patterns, chord voicings, and so on. Similarly, although a number of his 'Now' pieces might be considered Chopin-esque, he only studied a handful of Chopin pieces in his lesson days. This approach has enabled him to avoid the trap many excellent pianists have fallen into of sounding derivative.

For example, one might consider his *Nowtude in F-sharp Major* as 'Prokofiev meets Eddie Palmieri,' but this breaks down quickly upon further scrutiny. It is not really possible to identify what is specifically from one artist or the other, or to figure out exactly where the styles meet or blend, or if those stylistic labels are actually valid as other elements begin to reveal themselves. This combining and sublimation of styles is a characteristic factor in much of his music.

The other aspect is in his harmonic language. Many of his pieces are obviously tonal, but others take what he himself considers an atonal approach. Having edited a number of such pieces, however, I believe there is generally always a functional harmonic underpinning which is a major factor in the unity in his 'Now' pieces, for example *Homage to Ligeti* or *Nowtude in A-flat Minor*. These have an extended system of chord substitution where, taken to its furthest limit, almost any chord or series of chords can be substituted without disrupting the underlying harmonic structure. To my ear, even the freest of his pieces are coherent in a way many other 'free' or atonal pieces from other artists are not.

## 4. MIKE GARSON ON HIS OWN PLAYING

Garson has done many thousands of hours of methodical practice—scales, sight-reading, and experimenting—leading to an almost complete technical, harmonic, and melodic fluency. He incorporates and fuses elements from the full range of classical music from the sixteenth century onward, plus the whole repertoire of twentieth-century jazz. He plays truly how he feels in any moment, and he says that his expression is helped by knowing 'who I am and how I fit into the scheme of things.'

He also stresses the importance, when improvising, of 'trusting that it will sound good.' He knows 'that we each have an individual voice and that if we keep searching, it will emerge. I also have a deep desire to interact and create with other musicians and singers, and know when to be supportive and when to stand out,' which he identifies as a test of real communication and connection. Finally, he gets 'out of my own way' and loves what he does. He adds that, with all this, there is a 'mystery element—and only God knows what that is!'

He elaborates very clearly on some of these points:

The thing is, I'm obsessed with the piano. Some people, they orchestrate, they conduct, they play drums, they play guitar, they play bass, they sing, they write harmony parts. I hardly do any of that. My whole life has been dedicated to the piano, and it's ongoing. So, I've looked at so much music and listened to so much music and sight-read so much music. I've composed over five thousand pieces for the piano, of which half are classical.

I play what I feel in the moment. That's really what I do with David Bowie on those albums, and I've had it on my mind for thirty or forty years. I learned it from Lennie Tristano. He told me he felt that true jazz was really playing what you hear on the spot, in the moment. A lot of guys play a lot of licks, and things they have memorized and worked out. There's nothing wrong with that, and I certainly do a bit of that, but I like the concept of trying to play what you feel in the present time, and that's what I've been developing for many years.

Whatever I hear is what I play, whether I'm playing solo piano, jazz with my trio, or playing rock 'n' roll with David. In other words, if I hear it, I play it. I don't feel, 'Oh, I'm slipping out of rock, I'm playing jazz.' If I hear it—inside, something more than just notes or rhythms—and it seems appropriate for that music, I'll play it. At first that takes a leap of courage but then you start to trust yourself. Once in a while, somebody will say that didn't sound right, but usually because I'm not in the moment. If I'm in the moment, I'll usually make the right calculation.

# Appendix 3: Discography

*Reflections*, Reference Recordings, 1985
*Walker and Garson Play Gershwin*, Walker/Garson, 1997
*Tranquility*, Walker/Garson, 2000
*Jim Walker Plays the Music of Mike Garson*, Walker/Garson, 2007
*Pied Piper*, Reference Recordings, 2010
*The Music of George Gershwin*, Walker/Garson, 2012

**BILLY CORGAN/MIKE GARSON**
*Stigmata (Original Soundtrack)*, Virgin Records, 1999

**AS A GUEST ARTIST, WITH:**
David Bowie
*Aladdin Sane*, RCA, 1973
*Pin Ups*, RCA, 1973
*Diamond Dogs*, RCA, 1974
*David Live*, RCA, 1974
*Young Americans*, RCA, 1975
*Ziggy Stardust—The Motion Picture*, RCA, 1983
*Black Tie White Noise*, Arista/BMG, 1993
*The Buddha of Suburbia*, Arista, 1993
*Santa Monica '72*, Trident/Golden Years, 1994
*1. Outside*, RCA, 1995
*Earthling*, RCA, 1997
*'hours . . .'* (2004 bonus track), Virgin, 1999
*Bowie at the Beeb*, EMI, 2000
*Heathen* (bonus tracks/B-sides), ISO/Columbia, 2002
*Reality*, ISO/Columbia, 2003
*iSelect*, EMI, 2008
*VH1 Storytellers*, EMI, 2009
*A Reality Tour*, ISO/Columbia/Legacy, 2010
*Nothing Has Changed—The Very Best of Bowie*, Parlophone/Columbia/Legacy, 2014
*David Bowie—Five Years (1969–1973)*, Parlophone, 2015
*David Bowie—Who Can I Be Now? (1974–1976)*, Parlophone, 2016

Mick Ronson
*Slaughter on 10th Avenue*, RCA/Victor, 1974
*Play Don't Worry*, RCA/Victor, 1975

**Nine Inch Nails**
*The Fragile*, Interscope Records, 1999

**Smashing Pumpkins**
*Machina/The Machines of God*, Virgin Records, 2000

**Stan Getz**
*Stan Getz Live at Midem '80*, Kingdom Jazz, 1989

**Stanley Clarke**
*Modern Man*, Nemperor/Epic, 1978
*I Wanna Play for You*, Nemperor/Epic, 1979

## MISCELLANEOUS ALBUMS
Brethren, *Moment of Truth*, 1971
Annette Peacock, *Bley/Peacock Synthesizer Show*, 1971
Annette Peacock, *I'm the One*, 1972
Open Sky, *Open Sky*, 1973
Bob Sargeant, *First Starring Role*, 1975
David Essex, *All the Fun of the Fair*, 1975
Lulu, *Heaven and Earth and the Stars*, 1976
Spiders from Mars, *Spiders from Mars*, 1976
Paul Horn, *Riviera Concert*, 1977
Robin Williamson, *Songs of Love and Parting*, 1981
Robin Williamson, *Five Bardic Mysteries*, 1985
Guy Pastor, *It's Magic*, 1988
Various Artists, *Reference Jazz: First Sampling*, 1990
Mike Garson and Los Gatos, *Admiration*, 1991
Brian Bromberg, *It's About Time: The Acoustic Project*, 1991
Jérôme Soligny, *Gawin* (original film score), 1991
Jérôme Soligny, *Thanks for the Wings*, 1992
Jazz at the Movies Band, *A Man and a Woman/Sax at the Movies*, 1993
The Michael Garson Ensemble, *Screen Themes '93*, 1993
The Michael Garson Ensemble, *Screen Themes '94*, 1994
Jazz at the Movies Band, *Reel Romance*, 1994
Ava Cherry and the Astronettes, *People from Bad Homes*, 1995
Jazz at the Movies Band, *Sax on Broadway*, 1997

Yamaha Flute, *Contemporary Virtuosos*, 1998
Seal, *Human Being*, 1998
Brooks Arthur, *Songs Are Like Prayers*, 1998
C. Gibbs, *Twenty Nine Over Me*, 1999
John Lucien, *Sweet Control: The Best Of*, 1999
Various Artists, *Great Horns*, 1999
No Doubt, *Return of Saturn*, 2000
Raphaël, *La Réalité*, 2003
Jimmy Chamberlin Complex, *Life Begins Again* (bonus tracks), 2005
Something for Kate, *Desert Lights*, 2006
Raphaël, *Résistance a la nuit*, 2006
Raphaël, *Une nuit au Châtelet*, 2007
St. Vincent, *Marry Me*, 2007
The Polyphonic Spree, *The Fragile Army*, 2007
Emma Burgess, *Swim*, 2007
Various Artists, *The Jewish Songbook: the Heart and Humor of a People*, 2008
Juno Reactor, *Gods and Monsters*, 2008
Aviv Geffen, *Live '08*, 2008
Sibyl Vane, *The Locked Suitcase*, 2008
Omfalos Renaissance, *Miekka ja kirsikankukka (The Sword and the Chrysanthemum)*, 2008
Sleepyard, *Future Lines*, 2009
The Dillinger Escape Plan, *Option Paralysis*, 2010
J21, *Beyond the Holographic Veil*, 2011
James Iha, *Look to the Sky*, 2012
Mr. Averell, *Gridlock*, 2013
Trent Reznor and Atticus Ross, *Gone Girl (Soundtrack from the Motion Picture)*, 2014
Sleepyard, *Black Sails*, 2014
Lostdog in Loveland, *sadanthem*, 2014

# Appendix 4: Milestones

*'Mike is one of the most incredible human beings that I've ever encountered . . . one of the deepest searchers or seekers, both philosophically and musically, I've ever met. He is an incredibly dedicated family man, absolutely dedicated to his family. His goal as an artist is to share his vision—I completely love his vision. He's got more tools than most people. As a colleague, as a performing colleague, he is a powerhouse.'*

—Jim Walker, flautist in Free Flight

**1945, JULY 29:** Born in Brooklyn, New York, United States.

**1952, SEPTEMBER:** First lessons with Mr. Scatura.

**1959:** Plays first gig, earns $5.

**1960:** Begins working with first band, the Impromptu Quartet, in the Catskill Mountains, Upstate New York (and continues to do so every summer for eight years).

**1962:** While working in the Catskill Mountains, meets future wife, Susan.

**1963:** Graduates Lafayette High School, Brooklyn, New York. Begins Brooklyn College as a premed student, then majors in music with a minor in education.

**1963–1966:** Receives piano lessons from Lennie Tristano.

**1964:** Three piano lessons with Herbie Hancock.

**1964–1967:** Piano lessons from Hall Overton.

**1966:** One extraordinary and life-changing six-hour piano lesson with Bill Evans.

**1967–1969:** Military service/playing in army band: stationed in Fort Dix, New Jersey, for basic training, and then at Fort Wadsworth, Staten Island, New York.

**1968, MARCH 24:** Marries Susan Ellen Taylor, in Great Neck, New York.

**1969:** Graduates Brooklyn College after completing army duties.

**1969:** Joins the group Brethren on piano and organ.

**1971, AUGUST 20:** Jennifer Anne Garson is born in New York City.

**1971–1972:** Various 'Mike Garson Trio' lineups play live in New York.

**1972–1975:** First period of work with David Bowie, including Bowie's 'retirement' announcement (as Ziggy Stardust) on July 3, 1973, at Hammersmith Odeon, London, England, and ending with release of *Young Americans* on March 7, 1975.

**1974, DECEMBER 11**: Heather Kim Garson is born, New York City.

**1982**: Joins flautist Jim Walker in Free Flight, starting a long and prodigiously fruitful collaboration, with regular touring and live work until 2004, after which they continue with occasional concert appearances together.

**1992–2006**: Second period of work with David Bowie, starting with recording for *Black Tie White Noise* up to the *Reality* Tour and some subsequent special appearances, including a performance by Bowie together with Alicia Keys in New York in 2006.

**1995**: 'Now' music launched as a compositional system.

**1995–2005**: Composes approximately 2,800 classical pieces (total original pieces composed by 2017 totals around 5,000).

**1998–2000**: Plays on the Smashing Pumpkins' *Adore* tour and on the album *Machina/ The Machines of God*; also plays on the final part of the *Machina* tour, including the band's Farewell Concert at the Metro, Chicago, December 2, 2000.

**1998**: Works with Billy Corgan on the film score for *Stigmata*.

**1998**: Records with Trent Reznor and Nine Inch Nails for the double album *The Fragile*, released in September 1999.

**2000**: Works with Gwen Stefani and No Doubt on the *Return of Saturn* album.

**2009**: Commissioned by the Kennedy Center in Washington, D.C., to create new arrangements of Duke Ellington, combining jazz and classical ensembles.

**2009, SEPTEMBER**: Appears at the Nine Inch Nails concerts at the Henry Fonda Theatre and the Wiltern Theatre, Los Angeles, September (at the end of the Wave Goodbye tour).

**2010–2011**: Private teaching in Los Angeles; master classes in various universities; records *The Bowie Variations*, an album of piano interpretations of David Bowie songs.

**2011–2013**: Gives a series of performances in the South of France with various French jazz musicians each January.

**2013**: Continues composing, including a special series of eighty-eight complex improvisations, each lasting fifteen minutes or more.

**2013**: Starts work on the newly commissioned *Symphonic Suite for Healing* for orchestra, keyboards, children's choir, jazz band, vocalists, dancing ensemble, and piano.

**2014, MARCH 1**: World premiere performance of *Symphonic Suite for Healing* at Segerstrom Center for the Arts, Orange County, California.

**2015**: Continues to perform *Symphonic Suite for Healing* with key orchestras globally while working on a new commission to compose a major work around theme of autism.

**2016, JANUARY 10:** Death of David Bowie.

**2016, FEBRUARY 24:** Performs at the BRIT Awards, London, UK, with the 2003–2004 *Reality* Tour band and vocals from Lorde.

**2017, JANUARY 8:** Performs at Brixton O2 Academy as part of the Celebrating David Bowie world tour with all of the David Bowie touring band from the *Reality* Tour and many other guest musicians.

**2017, NOVEMBER:** Tours Britain performing all of the songs from the *Aladdin Sane* album, with Gaby Moreno singing and with Kevin Armstrong and the rest of Iggy Pop's touring band, Terry Edwards, and guest appearances from Steve Harley and Steve Norman.

**2018:** Celebrating David Bowie world tour, with Gerry Leonard and Adrian Belew joining Garson and many different guest performers in each country visited.

# Select Bibliography

## SUMMARY OF BOOKS REFERRED TO

Ansdell, Gary. *How Music Helps in Music Therapy and Everyday Life*. Ashgate, 2014.

Benarde, Scott R. *Stars of David: Rock 'n' Roll's Jewish Stories*. Brandeis University Press, 2003.

Broackes, Victoria, and Geoffrey Marsh (eds.). *David Bowie Is Inside*. V&A Publishing, 2013.

Buckley, David. *Strange Fascination: David Bowie, The Definitive Story*. Virgin, 2005.

Cann, Kevin. *David Bowie: Any Day Now, The London Years, 1947–1974*. Adelita, 2010.

Congreve, William. *The Mourning Bride*. 1697.

Corinthians 1.

Dubuffet, Jean. 'L'art brut préféré aux arts culturels' in *L'homme du commun à l'ouvrage*. Paris: Gallimard, 1973.

Dubuffet, Jean. *L'Avant-projet d'une conference populaire sur la peinture*. 1945 (www.dubuffetfondation.com).

Eno, Brian. *A Year with Swollen Appendices: Brian Eno's Diary*. Faber and Faber, 1996.

Ericsson, K. Anders with Neil Charness, Paul J. Feltovich, and Robert R. Hoffman (eds.). *Cambridge Handbook of Expertise and Expert Performance*. Cambridge University Press, 2006.

Ferand, Ernst. *Die Improvisation in der Musik*. Rhein-Verl., 1938.

Ferand, Ernst (ed.). *Improvisation in Nine Centuries of Western Music: An Anthology*. Arno Volk Verlag, 1961.

Finnigan, Mary. *Psychedelic Suburbia: David Bowie and the Beckenham Arts Lab*. Jorvik Press, 2016.

Forster, E. M. *Howards End*. Penguin, 2012 (first published 1910).

Gladwell, Malcolm. *Outliers: The Story of Success*. Little, Brown and Company, 2008.

Hooker, Lynn M. *Redefining Hungarian Music from Liszt to Bartók*. Oxford University Press, 2013.

Jones, Dylan. *When Ziggy Played Guitar: David Bowie and Four Minutes That Shook the World*. Preface Publishing, 2012.

Kandinsky, Wassily. *Concerning the Spiritual in Art*. Dover Publications, 2000 (first published 1911).

Kureishi, Hanif. *The Buddha of Suburbia*. Faber and Faber, 1990.

Landesman, Jay. *Tales of a Cultural Conduit*. Tiger of the Stripe, 2006.

Light, Alan. *What Happened, Miss Simone? A Biography*. Canongate, 2016.

MacDonald, Raymond, with Gunter Kreutz and Laura Mitchell (eds.). *Music, Health, and Wellbeing*. Oxford University Press, 2012.

Morris, William. *Useful Work Versus Useless Toil*. Penguin, 2008 (first published 1885).

Mayes, Sean. *We Can Be Heroes: Life on Tour with David Bowie*. Independent Music Press, 1999.

Niemelä, Jussi K. *The Heart and Soul of Art*. 2008

O'Leary, Chris. *Rebel Rebel*. Zero Books, 2015.

Orwell, George. *Nineteen Eighty-Four*. Secker and Warburg, 1949.

Pegg, Nicholas. *The Complete David Bowie*. Titan Books, 2016.

Rinpoche, Sogyal. *The Tibetan Book of Living and Dying*. HarperCollins, 1992.

Rock, Mick, with David Bowie. *Moonage Daydream: The Life and Times of Ziggy Stardust*. Genesis Publications, 2002.

Rubinstein, Arthur. *My Young Years*. Jonathan Cape, 1973.

Rubinstein, Arthur. *My Many Years*. Alfred A. Knopf, 1980.

Rüther, Tobias. *Heroes: David Bowie and Berlin*. Reaktion Books, 2014.

Schuller, Gunther. *Musings: The Musical Words of Gunther Schuller*. Oxford University Press, 1986.

Shakespeare, William. *The Comedy of Errors* (c. 1594).

Shakespeare, William. *Hamlet* (c. 1599–1602).

Soligny, Jérôme. *David Bowie*. 10/18, 2002.

Trynka, Paul. *Starman: David Bowie, The Definitive Biography*. Sphere, 2011.

Walpole, Horace. *Horace Walpole's Correspondence*. Yale University Press, 1983.

Yoshihara, Mari. *Musicians from a Different Shore: Asians and Asian Americans in Classical Music*. Temple University Press, 2007.

## SOME RECOMMENDED ONLINE RESOURCES

Mike Garson website: www.mikegarson.com

David Bowie official site: www.davidbowie.com

Bowie Songs Project, recording arrangements of the songs of David Bowie for piano and voice: www.bowiesongs.com

Becker KB plays Mike Garson's 'Now' Music: www.soundcloud.com/beckerkbmikegarson

Pushing Ahead of the Dame: bowiesongs.wordpress.com/bowiesongs.tumblr.com

Hans Morgenstern's *Independent Ethos* blog has an archived series of interviews with Mike Garson: www.indieethos.wordpress.com

# Notes

### From Wembley to Bell Canyon, the Long Way

1. For a more detailed account, see Chris O'Leary's excellent blog: bowiesongs.wordpress. com/tag/extras/.
2. We are indebted to Julian Vein, who was responsible for the difficult task of transcribing these many hours of rapid dialogue between us, despite the difficulties posed by the fact that our enthusiasm often led to us both speaking at once.

### 1. Hammersmith, 1973

1. Benarde, *Stars of David: Rock 'n' Roll's Jewish Stories.*
2. See chapter 5, 'Abstinence Amongst Excess,' page 51.
3. Rock, Bowie, *Moonage Daydream: The Life and Times of Ziggy Stardust.*

### 2. GI Garson

1. *Alternative Press*, San Francisco, October 1999.
2. See, for example: Ericsson, Charness, Feltovich, and Hoffman (eds.), *Cambridge Handbook of Expertise and Expert Performance.*
3. 'Only connect the prose and the passion, and both will be exalted, and human love will be seen at its highest. Live in fragments no longer.' Forster, *Howards End.*
4. See chapter 5 for a fuller description of that show.

### 3. Ziggy's Support Act

1. *New Musical Express*, July 6, 1973, quoted in Cann, *David Bowie, Any Day Now: The London Years, 1947–1974*, which provides a superbly detailed diary of this whole period for Bowie.
2. Shakespeare, *The Comedy of Errors.*
3. 'Living the Dream: Robin Clark and Carlos Alomar Remember David Bowie and Luther Vandross,' *PopMatters*, June 20, 2016.
4. See Appendix 2, 'Forensics,' for analysis of Garson's playing on this Mick Ronson recording.
5. Garson used a Yamaha Disklavier, a modern version of the 'player-piano,' to generate and record (with microphones) a performance on a real piano action, which was identical to his own playing on the keyboard back in New York.
6. Garson describes this same incident from his own angle on page 129.

## 4. BROOKLYN, 1945–1969

1. See also page 160 for details of Hall Overton and other teachers Garson studied under.

## 5. ABSTINENCE AMONGST EXCESS

1. *Melody Maker*, October 27, 1973.
2. 'At the Marquee,' *Music Scene*, January 27, 1974.
3. Shown, for example, in *David Bowie—Five Years*, BBC TV, first broadcast May 25, 2013.

## 6. SUPPORTING THEIR EATING

1. Introducing Garson to the stage at the Henry Fonda Theatre, Los Angeles, September 8, 2009.
2. See chapter 14, 'Music Has Charms to Sooth a Savage Breast . . . ,' for discussion of music as therapy.
3. Landesman, *Tales of a Cultural Conduit*.
4. See Yoshihara, *Musicians from a Different Shore: Asians and Asian Americans in Classical Music*.
5. Rubinstein, *My Young Years* and *My Many Years*.
6. *New York Times*, November 21, 1937.

## 7. BREAKING DOWN BARRIERS

1. Schuller, *Musings: The Musical Words of Gunther Schuller*.
2. Brethren was an odd hybrid product of the later 1960s. It was *pre* art-rock. More like folk-rock or country-rock or blues-rock. They combined rock, blues, jazz, country, and funk. This is significant, as so much of Garson's later work was marked by combining many genres and even removing the boundaries between them.

## 8. FROM LULU TO LIBERACE

1. *Liberace*, ABC, 1988 (not to be confused with another TV movie of the same year, *Liberace: Behind the Music*).
2. This idea is further explored in Gladwell, *Outliers: The Story of Success*.
3. See also pages 15–16.
4. For a full examination of improvisation as a valid compositional method, see chapter 11, 'Music in the Moment.'
5. 1 Corinthians 13:4–8.

## 9. INSIDE *OUTSIDE* AND THE 1990s

1. David Bowie, liner notes to *The Buddha of Suburbia*, 1993.
2. Soligny, *David Bowie*.
3. See *Q* magazine, February 1997.
4. www.indieethos.wordpress.com/2011/07/21/from-the-archives-mike-garson-on-working-with-david-bowie-the-later-years-part-2/. (These online interviews include some good links to Garson playing and demonstrating points.)
5. See *Q* magazine, February 1997.

6. See page 238.
7. David Bowie, liner notes to *The Buddha of Suburbia*, 1993. (These appear only on the UK release, not the US version issued in 1995.)
8. As above. See quotations from Dubuffet on page 214 on creating a new form of music.
9. An adaptation of the website has been published as *Rebel Rebel* (Zero Books, 2015), with a further volume in preparation.
10. www.bowiesongs.wordpress.com.
11. See chapter 18 for further discussion of outsider art and *1. Outside*.
12. For the most detailed and reliable account of David Bowie's production history, see Pegg, *The Complete David Bowie*.
13. www.bowiesongs.tumblr.com.
14. Eno, *A Year with Swollen Appendices: Brian Eno's Diary*, page 383.
15. Paul Gorman, 'Journalism: Interviewing David Bowie on Working with Eno + Engaging with Visual Arts, 1995' at www.paulgormanis.com.
16. Eno, *A Year with Swollen Appendices: Brian Eno's Diary*, entry for June 18.
17. See *Q* magazine, February 1997.

### 10. Reality, 2003

1. Beats per minute, as indicator of tempo, especially in dance music.
2. *Reality* was recorded at Looking Glass Studios, New York and released September 15, 2003.
3. This same incident is recounted by Tony Visconti on page 33.

### 11. Music in the Moment

1. *Addicted to Noise*, September 5, 1999.
2. *Music & Letters* Vol. 43, No. 2 (April 1962), pages 174–176 (review by 'T.D.').
3. *The Musical Quarterly* LX, No. 1, January 1974.
4. See page 166.
5. Hooker, *Redefining Hungarian Music from Liszt to Bartók*.
6. www.soundcloud.com/beckerkbmikegarson. See also www.BeckerKB.com.
7. www.kbfrozenheat.com.
8. See chapter 13, 'Teaching People to Find Their Voice.'

### 12. Nine Inch Pumpkins

1. See chapter 18, 'From Outsider Art to Outsider Music,' for a detailed interview with Billy Corgan about his work with Garson.
2. However, see page 225. Audio from the show is archived at www.archive.org/details/tsp2000-12-02.baker.

### 13. Teaching People to Find Their Voices

1. See pages 48–49.
2. Kandinsky, *Concerning the Spiritual in Art*.
3. See page 135.
4. See page 63.

### 14. 'Music Has Charms to Sooth a Savage Breast . . .'

1. www.music-heals.com/video.
2. www.musicandmemory.org.
3. In *Trends in Cognitive Sciences*, April 2013, Vol. 17, No. 4.
4. MacDonald, Kreutz and Mitchell, eds., *Music, Health, and Wellbeing*
5. www.nordoff-robbins.org.uk.
6. Ansdell, *How Music Helps in Music Therapy and Everyday Life.*

### 15. From Ventura to Fitzrovia, a Pilgrimage Complete

1. See pages 49–50.
2. Tom Murphy, 'Q&A with Annie Clark of St. Vincent,' *Denver Westword*, February 12, 2010.
3. *Rolling Stone*, June 25, 2009.

### 16. Scandinavian Sessions

1. Niemelä, *The Heart and Soul of Art.*
2. See page 164.
3. See page 101. In 2016, I started work myself as pianist with Andy Mackay on an experimental project for piano and saxophone.
4. Morris, *Useful Work Versus Useless Toil.*

### 17. Seventy Years of Serendipity

1. Walpole, *Horace Walpole's Correspondence.*
2. *MOJO* 266, January 2016.
3. See the *Guardian* (UK), February 23, 2013.
4. See also pages 45 and 85.
5. www.music-heals.com.

### 18. From Outsider Art to Outsider Music

1. See page 108 for further discussion of how *1. Outside* was directly inspired by outsider art and of David Bowie and Brian Eno's visit to Gugging at that time.
2. Dubuffet, *L'Avant-projet d'une conference populaire sur la peinture.*
3. Asger Jorn, together with Guy Debord, was a founder in 1957 of the Situationist International, which opposed capitalist alienation through the construction of subversive situations, using play and artistic freedom. Jorn also applied these political principles to his painting.
4. Jean Dubuffet, cited on www.dubuffetfondation.com, my translation. Compare with Bowie's experimental ambitions quoted on page 106.
5. Mayes, *We Can Be Heroes: Life on Tour with David Bowie.*
6. Quoted in Buckley, *Strange Fascination: David Bowie, The Definitive Story*, page 311.
7. Broackes and Marsh, eds., *David Bowie Is Inside*, page 163.
8. ibid., pages 177, 179.
9. ibid., page 180.
10. Rinpoche, *The Tibetan Book of Living and Dying.*
11. See also chapter 9, 'Inside Outside and the 1990s,' for Garson's work with Billy Corgan and the Smashing Pumpkins. The extensive, exclusive interview with Corgan

in this chapter was not available at the time of publication of this book's first edition (of fifteen chapters) in 2014, but is added now as part of this expanded new second edition.

12. Rüther, *Heroes: David Bowie and Berlin*, page 91.
13. See page 237.

### 19. WE SPOKE OF WAS AND WHEN: MIKE GARSON IN A POST-BOWIE WORLD

1. Posted on Twitter on January 10, 2016.
2. See pages xix and xx.
3. *Rolling Stone* magazine (USA), January 29, 2016.
4. See the *Guardian* (UK), January 14, 2016.
5. www.youtube.com/watch?v=PjBRPaKFLAY&feature=youtu.be.
6. www.youtube.com/watch?v=mH5ZE3N8cxU.
7. See Light, *What Happened, Miss Simone? A Biography*.
8. Finnigan, *Psychedelic Suburbia: David Bowie and the Beckenham Arts Lab*.
9. See the *Telegraph* (UK), January 30, 2016 and May 22, 2016.
10. Jones, *When Ziggy Played Guitar: David Bowie and Four Minutes that Shook the World*, page 194.
11. See the *Telegraph Magazine*, December 14, 1996.
12. *Billboard*, February 9, 2016.
13. See chapter 18, 'From Outsider Art to Outsider Music,' for an extensive interview with Billy Corgan.
14. See page 106.
15. *New Musical Express*, September 13, 1980.
16. See chapter 18, 'From Outsider Art to Outsider Music.'
17. See, for example, the *Telegraph Magazine*, December 14, 1996, interview with Mick Brown.
18. Rüther, *Heroes: David Bowie and Berlin*, pages 109, 113.
19. ibid., page 115.
20. www.youtube.com/watch?v=3cDRpbVDS5c.
21. Notes on *iSelect* album, June 29, 2008.
22. See the *Telegraph Magazine* (London), December 14, 1996.

### 20. LIFE ON THE ROAD WITH DAVID BOWIE, PART 1: 1972–1974

1. This figure of 961 includes the 118 shows of the 1972–1973 *Ziggy Stardust* Tour at which Garson played, of a total of 182 shows on that tour. He joined the tour at Cleveland on September 22, 1972.
2. See page 184.
3. See pages 103–104.

### 21. LIFE ON THE ROAD WITH DAVID BOWIE, PART 2: 1995–2006

1. At press conference to announce the *Outside* Tour, 1995.
2. See page 108 and chapter 18, 'From Outsider Art to Outsider Music.'
3. Bowie appears to have forgotten here that in fact Garson's recording for the *Black Tie White Noise* album, though only for one song, did come before his work on *Buddha of Suburbia*.

4. Benarde, *Stars of David: Rock 'n' Roll's Jewish Stories.*
5. See pages 119–122.
6. Written under the online names 'youtoo' and 'MandN' (Mandy Dunham Smith), respectively.

APPENDIX 1: WATCH THAT MAN: GARSON'S PLAYING ON TWENTY-ONE
BOWIE ALBUMS—SELECTED HIGHLIGHTS

1. David Bowie, liner notes to *iSelect*, June 29, 2008. *Poses plastiques* are near-naked *tableaux vivants.*

APPENDIX 2: FORENSICS: ANALYSIS OF MIKE GARSON'S TECHNIQUES
IN PLAYING, IMPROVISING, AND COMPOSING

1. Eno, *A Year with Swollen Appendices: Brian Eno's Diary*, entry for June 18.

# Index